STUDENT WORKBOOK  **Capstone** Cur

MW00635467

Module
4

Urban Mission

Foundations
for Christian
Mission

This curriculum is the result of thousands of hours of work by The Urban Ministry Institute (TUMI) and should not be reproduced without their express permission. TUMI supports all who wish to use these materials for the advance of God's Kingdom, and affordable licensing to reproduce them is available. Please confirm with your instructor that this book is properly licensed. For more information on TUMI and our licensing program, visit *www.tumi.org* and *www.tumi.org/license*.

Capstone Module 4: Foundations for Christian Mission Student Workbook

ISBN: 978-1-62932-004-5

Contents

About the Instructor

Rev. Dr. Don L. Davis is the Executive Director of The Urban Ministry Institute and a Senior Vice President of World Impact. He attended Wheaton College and Wheaton Graduate School, and graduated summa cum laude in both his B.A. (1988) and M.A. (1989) degrees, in Biblical Studies and Systematic Theology, respectively. He earned his Ph.D. in Religion (Theology and Ethics) from the University of Iowa School of Religion.

As the Institute's Executive Director and World Impact's Senior Vice President, he oversees the training of urban missionaries, church planters, and city pastors, and facilitates training opportunities for urban Christian workers in evangelism, church growth, and pioneer missions. He also leads the Institute's extensive distance learning programs and facilitates leadership development efforts for organizations and denominations like Prison Fellowship, the Evangelical Free Church of America, and the Church of God in Christ.

A recipient of numerous teaching and academic awards, Dr. Davis has served as professor and faculty at a number of fine academic institutions, having lectured and taught courses in religion, theology, philosophy, and biblical studies at schools such as Wheaton College, St. Ambrose University, the Houston Graduate School of Theology, the University of Iowa School of Religion, the Robert E. Webber Institute of Worship Studies. He has authored a number of books, curricula, and study materials to equip urban leaders, including *The Capstone Curriculum*, TUMI's premiere sixteen-module distance education seminary instruction, *Sacred Roots: A Primer on Retrieving the Great Tradition*, which focuses on how urban churches can be renewed through a rediscovery of the historic orthodox faith, and *Black and Human: Rediscovering King as a Resource for Black Theology and Ethics*. Dr. Davis has participated in academic lectureships such as the Staley Lecture series, renewal conferences like the Promise Keepers rallies, and theological consortiums like the University of Virginia Lived Theology Project Series. He received the Distinguished Alumni Fellow Award from the University of Iowa College of Liberal Arts and Sciences in 2009. Dr. Davis is also a member of the Society of Biblical Literature, and the American Academy of Religion.

Introduction to the Module

Greetings, in the strong name of Jesus Christ!

The theme of mission has not received the kind of focus and attention in our urban churches that it should. Having been seen largely as a work across the ocean in far flung corners of the world, we have failed to give it the kind of critical analysis that it deserves. From one vantage point, the entirety of the Christian faith could be seen as a response of mission, the call to go to the nations and proclaim Jesus of Nazareth as Lord and King of the reign of God. The NT is a collection of missionary documents given to churches that were founded by the apostles, the original missionaries of the Christian faith. God himself is the original missionary, coming to the world in Christ and reconciling it to himself (2 Cor. 5.18-21). Indeed, Christianity is mission.

This module, therefore, deals with this key subject with the intent to help you, God's emerging leader in the city, to understand both the theology and ramifications of mission from a biblical point of view. In a real sense, we cannot understand what God is doing in the world through mission without an overview of the vision of God's purpose and working. So, in our first two lessons we will look at mission through four distinctive lenses: mission as drama and promise, and mission as romance and warfare respectively.

In our first lesson, *The Vision and Biblical Foundation for Christian Mission (1)*, we deal with the perspective of Mission as the Drama of All Time. Our intent here is to provide a framework for understanding the work of mission from the Scriptures themselves. We will begin by giving a general definition of mission, and then outline a quick summary of the critical elements of a biblical understanding of mission. We will look at mission through the lens of story and drama, showing from Scripture that mission is God's sovereign working through history through the various epochs or sections of time to bring about redemption in Christ. We also explore Mission as the Fulfillment of the Divine Promise, envisioning mission as God fulfilling his promise as the covenant God of faithfulness. We will describe the role of biblical covenants in the Scriptures, and trace God's action as response to his covenant promise to Abraham, confirmed in his sons and the patriarchs, identified with the tribe of Judah and clarified in the promise to David to have a perpetual heir on his throne. In the person of Jesus of Nazareth, the promise of Abraham and David has been fulfilled, and now, through mission proclamation of the Gospel, the promise of new life is offered to the nations through the preaching of the cross.

In lesson two, *The Vision and Biblical Foundation for Christian Mission (2)*, we will explore Mission as the Romance of the Ages and as the War of the Spheres. These images in Scripture allow us to see just how critical mission is to our theological framework as believers. As the romance of God, we see God's determination to draw out of the world a people for his own possession. We will review this grand theme, beginning with the history of Israel as the wife of God, and her unfaithfulness through idolatry and disobedience. We will trace this theme in the person of Jesus, and see how the new covenant expanded the people of God to include the Gentiles. As the warfare of the ages, we see the proclamation of God's kingdom rule in the person of Jesus of Nazareth. Beginning with the clear affirmation of God's sovereignty, we see God has determined to reestablish his rule over his creation, which fell from his grace through the rebellion of the devil and humankind at the Fall. Since this time, God has taken the position of warrior to bring the universe back under his rulership. In the person of Jesus of Nazareth, God is reasserting his right to rule over the universe, and mission is the proclamation of that Kingdom come in Christ.

In lesson three, *Christian Mission and the City*, we turn our attention to the object of mission and God's intent for the city and the poor. We begin by looking at the ancient city, its organization and characteristics, especially its symbolic feature as a sign of rebellion against the Lord. We will consider the spiritual significance of the city, looking at God's interaction with a number of cities in Scripture, and exploring their meanings. We will see how God has adopted the city concept for his own purposes, overruling its association with rebellion and idolatry, and redeeming its meaning for mission, and for the future glory of the Kingdom. In this lesson, then, we will also provide a rationale for our involvement in urban mission. As the seat of influence, power, and spiritual activity as well as the magnet for the oppressed, the broken, and the poor, we as 21st century disciples must strive to speak and live prophetically to the city. As the picture and symbol of our spiritual destiny and inheritance, we must do all we can to evangelize, disciple, and plant churches in our cities, both at home and abroad.

Finally, in lesson four we explore another critical component of Christian mission. In *Christian Mission and the Poor*, we will examine the concept of the poor and mission through the lens of the rich biblical concept of *shalom*, or wholeness. As the covenant community of Yahweh, the people of Israel were called to live in such faithfulness to the Lord's covenant that poverty would be replaced with justice and righteousness. Building on the fact of God's deliverance of his people from Egypt at the Exodus, God gave his people in his covenant a blueprint for justice that would address the issue of poverty and oppression. Armed with this biblical vision, we will then consider how Jesus as Messiah and Head of the Church fulfills the Messianic prophecy regarding the One who would bring justice and peace to the poor. Jesus as Lord and Head of the Church continues to express God's mandate for *shalom* among the people of God, and through his people, to the world. The Church, God's new covenant community by faith in Jesus, is called to live in *shalom* and demonstrate both to its own members and to the world the justice of God for the broken. This is possible now because of the Holy Spirit who empowers and strengthens the people of God today.

As believers in Jesus Christ, each of us, every congregation has been redeemed in order that we might be redemptive, proclaiming and living out the truth of God where he has placed us. Truly, to be Christian is to be mission-oriented and mission-formed; we were born from above to become co-laborers with God in his mission to win the world for his Son (Acts 9.15).

May God use this course of study to challenge you to play your part in the remarkable story of God's glory, and his mission to win the world to himself through his Son and our Savior, Jesus Christ!

- Rev. Dr. Don L. Davis

Course Requirements

Required Books and Materials

- Bible (for the purposes of this course, your Bible should be a translation [ex. NIV, NASB, RSV, KJV, NKJV, etc.], and not a paraphrase [ex. The Living Bible, The Message]).

- Each Capstone module has assigned textbooks which are read and discussed throughout the course. We encourage you to read, reflect upon, and respond to these with your professors, mentors, and fellow learners. Because of the fluid availability of the texts (e.g., books going out of print), we maintain our *official* Capstone Required Textbook list on our website. Please visit *www.tumi.org/books* to obtain the current listing of this module's texts.

- Paper and pen for taking notes and completing in-class assignments.

Suggested Readings

- Erickson, Millard J. *Introducing Christian Doctrine*. 2nd. ed. Grand Rapids: Baker Book House, 2001.

- Phillips, Keith. *Out of Ashes*. Los Angeles: World Impact Press, 1996.

- Winter, Ralph D, and Steven C. Hawthorne, eds. *Perspectives on the World Christian Movement: A Reader*. 3rd. ed. Pasadena: William Carey Library, 1992.

- Yohannan, K. P. *Revolution in World Mission*. Carrollton, TX: GFA Books (a division of Gospel for Asia), 2004.

Summary of Grade Categories and Weights

Attendance & Class Participation . . . . 30% 90 pts

Quizzes . . . . 10% 30 pts

Memory Verses . . . . 15% 45 pts

Exegetical Project . . . . 15% 45 pts

Ministry Project. . . . . 10% 30 pts

Readings and Homework Assignments. . . . . 10% 30 pts

Final Exam . . . . <u>10%</u> <u>30 pts</u>

Total: 100% 300 pts

Grade Requirements

Attendance at each class session is a course requirement. Absences will affect your grade. If an absence cannot be avoided, please let the Mentor know in advance. If you miss a class it is your responsibility to find out the assignments you missed, and to talk with the Mentor about turning in late work. Much of the learning associated with this course takes place through discussion. Therefore, your active involvement will be sought and expected in every class session.

Every class will begin with a short quiz over the basic ideas from the last lesson. The best way to prepare for the quiz is to review the Student Workbook material and class notes taken during the last lesson.

The memorized Word is a central priority for your life and ministry as a believer and leader in the Church of Jesus Christ. There are relatively few verses, but they are significant in their content. Each class session you will be expected to recite (orally or in writing) the assigned verses to your Mentor.

The Scriptures are God's potent instrument to equip the man or woman of God for every work of ministry he calls them to (2 Tim. 3.16-17). In order to complete the requirements for this course you must select a passage and do an inductive Bible study (i.e., an exegetical study) upon it. The study will have to be five pages in length (double-spaced, typed or neatly hand written) and deal with one of the foundational theologies and principles of Christian mission which are highlighted in this course. Our desire and hope is that you will be deeply convinced of Scripture's ability to change and practically affect your life, and the lives of those to whom you minister.

As you go through the course, be open to finding an extended passage (roughly 4-9 verses) on a subject you would like to study more intensely. The details of the project are covered on pages 10-11, and will be discussed in the introductory session of this course.

Ministry Project

Our expectation is that all students will apply their learning practically in their lives and in their ministry responsibilities. The student will be responsible for developing a ministry project that combines principles learned with practical ministry. The details of this project are covered on page 12, and will be discussed in the introductory session of the course.

Class and Homework Assignments

Classwork and homework of various types may be given during class by your Mentor or be written in your Student Workbook. If you have any question about what is required by these or when they are due, please ask your Mentor.

Readings

It is important that the student read the assigned readings from the text and from the Scriptures in order to be prepared for class discussion. Please turn in the "Reading Completion Sheet" from your Student Workbook on a weekly basis. There will be an option to receive extra credit for extended readings.

Take-Home Final Exam

At the end of the course, your Mentor will give you a final exam (closed book) to be completed at home. You will be asked a question that helps you reflect on what you have learned in the course and how it affects the way you think about or practice ministry. Your Mentor will give you due dates and other information when the Final Exam is handed out.

Grading

The following grades will be given in this class at the end of the session, and placed on each student's record:

A - Superior work	D - Passing work
B - Excellent work	F - Unsatisfactory work
C - Satisfactory work	I - Incomplete

Letter grades with appropriate pluses and minuses will be given for each final grade, and grade points for your grade will be factored into your overall grade point average. Unexcused late work or failure to turn in assignments will affect your grade, so please plan ahead, and communicate conflicts with your instructor.

Exegetical Project

As a part of your participation in the Capstone *Foundations for Christian Mission* module of study, you will be required to do an exegesis (inductive study) on one of the following passages on the nature of Christian mission and urban ministry:

❏ Matthew 28.18-20

❏ 2 Corinthians 6.1-10

❏ Luke 4.16-22

❏ 2 Timothy 4.1-5

❏ Matthew 5.13-16

❏ Colossians 1.24-29

The purpose of this exegetical project is to give you an opportunity to do a detailed study of a major passage on the nature and practice of Christian mission. To see that God is a God of missions is fundamental to every phase of urban ministry; missions is neither a seasonal emphasis nor the work of a handful of oddball people willing to go overseas for a time. Mission, rather, is the lifeblood of the Judeo-Christian worldview, the very heart and soul of God's working in the world. In one sense, the entire Christian story could be described as God's intent to draw out of the earth a people that would belong to him; missions is God's business as much as it is our work.

The aim of this study is for you to select one of the above texts and use it as a lens by which you may think critically about mission–its foundation, its practice, and its importance for urban Christian leadership. As you study one of these texts (or one which you and your Mentor agree upon) our hope is that you will highlight a key aspect of the foundation for Christian mission. We also desire that the Spirit will give you insight as to how you can relate its meaning directly to your own personal walk of discipleship, as well as to the leadership role God has given to you currently in your Church and ministry.

This is a Bible study project, and, in order to do *exegesis*, you must be committed to understand the meaning of the passage in its own setting. Once you know what it meant, you can then draw out principles that apply to all of us, and then relate those principles to life. A simple three step process can guide you in your personal study of the Bible passage:

1. What was *God saying to the people in the text's original situation*?

2. What principle(s) does *the text teach that is true for all people everywhere*, including today?

3. What is *the Holy Spirit asking me to do with this principle here, today*, in my life and ministry?

Once you have answered these questions in your personal study, you are then ready to write out your insights for your *paper assignment*.

Here is a *sample outline* for your paper:

1. List out what you believe is *the main theme or idea* of the text you selected.

2. *Summarize the meaning* of the passage (you may do this in two or three paragraphs, or, if you prefer, by writing a short verse-by-verse commentary on the passage).

3. *Outline one to three key principles or insights* this text provides on the foundations for Christian mission.

4. Tell how one, some, or all of the principles may relate to *one or more* of the following:

   a. Your personal spirituality and walk with Christ

   b. Your life and ministry in your local church

   c. Situations or challenges in your community and general society

As an aid or guide, please feel free to read the course texts and/or commentaries, and integrate insights from them into your work. Make sure that you give credit to whom credit is due if you borrow or build upon someone else's insights. Use in-the-text references, footnotes, or endnotes. Any way you choose to cite your references will be acceptable, as long as you 1) use only one way consistently throughout your paper, and 2) indicate where you are using someone else's ideas, and are giving them credit for it. (For more information, see *Documenting Your Work: A Guide to Help You Give Credit Where Credit Is Due* in the Appendix.)

Make certain that your exegetical project, when turned in meets the following standards:

- It is legibly written or typed.

- It is a study of one of the passages above.

- It is turned in on time (not late).

- It is 5 pages in length.

- It follows the outline given above, clearly laid out for the reader to follow.

- It shows how the passage relates to life and ministry today.

Do not let these instructions intimidate you; this is a Bible study project! All you need to show in this paper is that you *studied* the passage, *summarized* its meaning, *drew out* a few key principles from it, and *related* them to your own life and ministry.

Grading

The exegetical project is worth 45 points, and represents 15% of your overall grade, so make certain that you make your project an excellent and informative study of the Word.

Ministry Project

The Word of God is living and active, and penetrates to the very heart of our lives and innermost thoughts (Heb. 4.12). James the Apostle emphasizes the need to be doers of the Word of God, not hearers only, deceiving ourselves. We are exhorted to apply the Word, to obey it. Neglecting this discipline, he suggests, is analogous to a person viewing our natural face in a mirror and then forgetting who we are, and are meant to be. In every case, the doer of the Word of God will be blessed in what he or she does (James 1.22-25).

Purpose

Our sincere desire is that you will apply your learning practically, correlating your learning with real experiences and needs in your personal life, and in your ministry in and through your church. Therefore, a key part of completing this module will be for you to design a ministry project to help you share some of the insights you have learned from this course with others.

There are many ways that you can fulfill this requirement of your study. You may choose to conduct a brief study of your insights with an individual, or a Sunday School class, youth or adult group or Bible study, or even at some ministry opportunity. What you must do is discuss some of the insights you have learned from class with your audience. (Of course, you may choose to share insights from your Exegetical Project in this module with them.)

Planning and Summary

Feel free to be flexible in your project. Make it creative and open-ended. At the beginning of the course, you should decide on a context in which you will share your insights, and share that with your instructor. Plan ahead and avoid the last minute rush in selecting and carrying out your project.

After you have carried out your plan, write and turn in to your Mentor a one-page summary or evaluation of your time of sharing. A sample outline of your Ministry Project summary is as follows:

1. Your name

2. The place where you shared, and the audience with whom you shared

3. A brief summary of how your time went, how you felt, and how they responded

4. What you learned from the time

The Ministry Project is worth 30 points and represents 10% of your overall grade, so make certain to share your insights with confidence and make your summary clear.

Grading

The Vision and Biblical Foundation for Christian Mission: Part 1

Lesson Objectives

Welcome in the strong name of Jesus Christ! After your reading, study, discussion, and application of the materials in this lesson, you will be able to:

- Outline a "prolegomena" ("first word") or "big picture" overview to mission.

- Define mission as "the proclamation of God's offer of salvation and redemption in the person and work of Jesus Christ in the power of the Holy Spirit to all people groups."

- Reproduce the elements of a biblical understanding of mission, including its need for a clear understanding of God and his purposes for the universe, to relate all the details of history to a single unified whole, to be rooted in the Scriptures themselves, to be anchored in the person and work of Jesus Christ, and to take seriously the biblical way of discussing mission through image, pictures, and stories.

- Lay out the four theological frameworks/pictures of mission in Scripture, i.e., Mission as the Drama of all time (God as the major character in the greatest plot motif of all time), as the Fulfillment of the Divine Promise (God fulfilling his covenant promise in Jesus Christ), as the Romance of the Ages (God as the bridegroom of his redeemed humanity), and as the War of the Spheres (God as the warrior reestablishing his rule over the universe).

- Give an overview of the major elements in the *Drama of All Time* in terms of the major phases of God's unfolding purpose, including *Before Time* (which highlights God's pre-existence and purpose, the mystery of iniquity and the rebellion of the powers), *Beginning of Time* (which includes the creation of the universe and humankind, the fall and the curse, the *protoevangelium*, the end of Eden, the reign of death, and the first signs of grace), and the *Unfolding of Time* (which includes the Abrahamic promise, the Exodus, the Conquest of the Land, the City-Temple-Throne, the Captivity and Exile, and the Return of the Remnant).

- Complete the phases of God's unfolding purpose with *the Fullness of Time* (which includes the incarnation, the Kingdom revealed in Jesus, the passion, death, resurrection, and ascension of Christ), *the Last Times* (including the descent of the Holy Spirit, the formation of the Church, the inclusion of the Gentiles, and age of world mission), *the Fulfillment of Time* (which includes the end of world evangelization, the apostasy of the Church, the Great Tribulation, the *Parousia*, the reign of Christ on earth, the Great White Throne, the Lake of Fire, and turning the Kingdom over to God the Father), and finally *Beyond Time* (which includes the new heavens and new earth, the descent of the New Jerusalem, the times of refreshing, and the ushering in of the Age to Come).

- Summarize the implications of Mission as the *Drama of All Time*: how God's sovereign purpose underwrites all human history, God as the central character in the unfolding phases of the divine drama, mission as the recovery of that which was lost at the *beginning of time*, and the making of disciples among all nations as our part in *fulfilling our role in the script of Almighty God*.

- Give an overview of the major elements of Mission as the *Fulfillment of the Divine Promise* beginning with a definition of covenant as a contract between two parties, whether individuals, tribes, or nations, with both having obligations to fulfill, and benefits and advantages as a result of the fulfillment of those conditions.

- Outline key characteristics of covenant making in Scripture including how they were invoked by a witness, were sober (i.e., breaking them was seen as a great moral evil), were given witness by giving gifts, eating meals, and setting up stones of remembrance, confirmed with an oath and with sacrifice.

- Provide several examples of covenants in the Bible, including marriage, the covenant with Noah, the covenant of Sinai with the children of Israel, all of which speak to the solemn contract between individuals, or God and individuals.

- Trace the framework as Mission as *Fulfillment of the Divine Promise* from covenant made with Abraham, with its condition that he leave his country and kindred to go to a land of God's own choosing, with the corresponding blessing that God would make him a great nation, bless him and make his name great, bless and curse those who did the same to him, and bless all the families of the earth in him.

- Highlight how this Abrahamic covenant was renewed, confirmed in both Isaac and Jacob, and related to Judah as the tribe out of which the divine Messiah would come, and show how the royal Seed of Abraham's blessing would come through God's covenant with David and his house, whose heir would reign forever over the house of Israel and be a blessing to the nations.

- Show how this promise was fulfilled in the person of Jesus of Nazareth, who represents the embodiment both of the Abrahamic and Davidic promises. Through his life, death, resurrection, and ascension, the covenant promise of God is fulfilled.

- Explain how mission is the proclamation of the Good News regarding God's covenant faithfulness, with the Great Commission as a responsibility to proclaim the promise fulfilled for the salvation of all humanity, beginning at Jerusalem, to the very ends of the earth.

- Show the linkage between the role of mission in this age and the declaration that in the person of Jesus of Nazareth, the promise of Abraham and David has been fulfilled, and now, through mission's proclamation of the Gospel, the promise of new life is offered to the nations through the preaching of the cross.

Devotion

"It's Always Story Time"
The Story of God's Glory and the Call to Mission

Rom. 16.25-27 - Now to him who is able to strengthen you according to my gospel and the preaching of Jesus Christ, according to the revelation of the mystery that was kept secret for long ages [26] but has now been disclosed and through the prophetic writings has been made known to all nations, according to the command of the eternal God, to bring about the obedience of faith- [27] to the only wise God be glory forevermore through Jesus Christ! Amen.

1

Perhaps nothing is as intriguing or attention getting as the phrases, "Once upon a time," and its close companion, "And they lived happily ever after." We have heard them before–they are the beginning and end notes of fairy tales or stories, tales that most of us have heard while growing up. Just to hear this can stop us in our tracks, turn our heads, and get us interested in how the story will go, and how it turns out.

In a real sense, we are not just rational beings, as Socrates suggested, but rather (and more fundamentally) story-telling beings; we understand ourselves in terms of the stories we cherish, tell, and identify with. The stories that we speak of our nation, our family, and our person determines our self-understandings and allegiances. The characters, themes, plots, and settings of the stories we tell make up our own sense of reality, morality, and values that we embrace and live by. Truly, it is hard to find a person, a family, a clan, a culture, or a nation that does understand itself in terms of their key stories that underlie their philosophies, determine their view of history, and shape their social, cultural, and national commitments. In a sense, we live true to the stories that we tell, believe, and base our lives upon.

This ordinary social and interpersonal focus on the role of stories (whether we view them to be fictional or historical) seems to be lost in many ways among many church men and women today. In many of our churches we place the focus on propositional truth, on creeds and statements of faith, on the nice, tight summaries of the stories of the Gospel boiled down to a few ready sentences easily covered and even more easily memorized. While this kind of approach to Christian theology and truth may be useful in some preaching and teaching, especially to the young in the faith, the heart and foundation of the Gospel is rooted in the story of Jesus which is not summarized in a neat outline. Rather, it is best told with passion, joy, and wonder as we highlight the amazing tale of God's perfect love displayed in his Son's remarkable humility in the incarnation, deep love demonstrated on the cross of Calvary, and mighty victory shown in his resurrection and ascension to the Father's right hand.

Indeed, the power and grace of Jesus Christ cannot be experienced in creed and statement alone; it must be told and reenacted in Word and sacrament. It is the nature of Christian faith to tell and retell the story. We are saved by our clinging to and shaping our lives on the "Good News" which has become "glad tidings of great joy," at least for those who believe.

It should be little wonder, then, that we define the nature of Christian mission as telling the story of Jesus to those who need to hear it. Mission has always been about going to those who have not heard the word of God's great love in Jesus of Nazareth and telling the story in a way that is both clear and compelling to them. Taking into account their language, culture, and norms of communication, we seek to make the Gospel of God's grace plain in the context of their culture and society. Mission has always been about telling the story of God's glory in Christ again and again and again. The goal is that we take this story to the ends of the earth in order that every people may hear, and that those who repent and believe the truth of the story may inherit eternal life. In direct and clear terms, this represents one of the great foundations of Christian mission: telling the old, old story of Jesus and his love.

Unfortunately in a number of Christian circles today, many have abandoned the story-ordered world of the Bible, the Gospel of Jesus, and the story-oriented methodology of mission for more scientifically inclined ways. Many Christians have abandoned the power of story for more rationalistic methods. As a matter of fact, in some of our churches we have lost the wonder and compelling nature that story-telling provides. Story lays out the concrete, bare bones quality of the truth in a way that a philosophical text or a scientific essay never could or can. With an emphasis on expository sermons based on scientifically credible exegetical methods that pass the bar of historical criticism, many Bible believers have simply abandoned their native language for a more dry, rationalistic, and less gritty apology of the Gospel. Although these have chosen the method of the world to communicate to it, the results have been less than convincing. By refusing to tell the story, and to tell it well, we are neither convincing to the world nor true to the "native tongue" of the Gospel, which is to lay out the historical facts of the truth in the story of Jesus of Nazareth.

Leland Ryken, like a handful of evangelical scholars today, notices the Bible's habit of speaking in terms of images and story over against technical language. He talks of our proneness to error, to slip into seeing the message of Jesus as merely a theological outline with proofs attached:

Because of the predominantly theological and devotional purposes to which Christians put the Bible, it is almost impossible not to slip into the error of looking upon the Bible as a theological outline with proof texts attached. Yet the Bible is much more a book of images and motifs than of abstractions and propositions. This is obscured by the way in which preachers and theologians gravitate so naturally to the epistles. A biblical scholar has correctly said that the Bible speaks largely in images. . . . The stories, the parables, the sermons of the prophets, the reflections of the wise men, the pictures of the age to come, the interpretations of past events all tend to be expressed in images which arise out of experience. They do not often arise out of abstract technical language.

~ Leland Ryken. **Dictionary of Biblical Imagery**. (electronic ed.).
Downers Grove, IL: InterVarsity Press, 2000.

In the story of the Gospel the images of the story of God loom large and clear: the Lamb of God is placed upon the tree as a substitutionary sacrifice for the sins of the world. Everyone who believes that this one who died is the Christ, that he died and rose again the third day, will be delivered from their sins, forgiven of all penalty before God, and granted the Holy Spirit who will indwell them throughout this life, and raise them up at the last day. This story has been repeated in the lives of millions of men and women, boys and girls, for over 2,000 years who cling to the story of Jesus as the Good News of salvation and life for all people. Mission is telling this story to the peoples of the world, in their own language, in a way that they can both understand and appreciate the love and grace of the One who is its main actor and protagonist. God is the hero of his own story, and the history of salvation is nothing more than "His Story". The story of God's glory by faith can actually become our very own story as we embrace it for ourselves.

The rediscovery of the heart of the Christian message as story is long overdue, and the signs of the new theologies of "story theology" and "narrative theology" need to come back in order for us to understand the foundation for Christian discipleship and mission. At the root of our faith is a story about an itinerant Jewish preacher who claimed God as his Father. Those of us who believe that Jesus of Nazareth was in fact the Messiah and Lord of all cling to this story as our lives, our hope, and our ministry depend on it.

Let us never forget that our "Once upon a time" certainly has a "And they lived happily ever after." To be engaged in local and world mission is to proclaim this story, the story of God's glory, living each day right here and right now in the presence of the Lord who writes it through us, before those who have yet to hear and understand it.

In the world of world mission, it's always story time.

Nicene Creed and Prayer

After reciting and/or singing the Nicene Creed (located in the Appendix), pray the following prayer:

Give us grace, O Lord, to answer readily the call of our Savior Jesus Christ and proclaim to all people the Good News of his salvation, that we and the whole world may perceive the glory of his marvelous works; who lives and reigns with you and the Holy Spirit, one God, for ever and ever. Amen.

~ Episcopal Church.
The Book of Common Prayer and Administrations of the Sacraments and Other Rites and Ceremonies of the Church, Together with the Psalter or Psalms of David.
New York: The Church Hymnal Corporation, 1979. p 215

Quiz

No quiz this lesson

Scripture Memorization Review

No Scripture memorization this lesson

Assignments Due

No assignments due this lesson

The God of History and the Drama of God

 In a world which sees Christian faith as a mere personal and existential choice (not truth based on historical fact), many Christians have abandoned their defense of Christianity as a historical faith. Large sections of the liberal wing of the mainline denominations have all but renounced the essential "historicity" of the Christian claims about Jesus. For instance, the Jesus Seminar (i.e., that highly advertised scholarly research committee assigned the task of discerning which of Jesus' sayings in our Gospels were actually spoken by him) can find only a handful of scattered sayings they are willing to say for certain are probably historically accurate tellings of Christ. Many seminaries have opted for the "scientific study of religion" which focuses not on what Christians have held and believed throughout the centuries, but rather on what science now allows by virtue of its ability to verify the claims of Christianity. These and other assaults have made it hard for many to embrace Christianity as a historically air-tight argument, and the resurrection as the confession of the truth. Why do you think it is critical for mission to always begin with a historical understanding of the Christian faith before it begins to speak of its sharing that faith with others. Why does Paul's view of the resurrection as the ground of all true preaching and teaching about Christ disallow any view of Christianity that refuses to embrace the historical truth value of our story and Gospel?

Are We Completely Misreading the Signs of Culture?

At a time when Hollywood is exploding with grand, epic tales of myth and fairy tale (*Gladiator, The Lord of the Rings, The Chronicles of Narnia*, etc.) many Christian pulpits remain bound to the "three-points, a poem, and a prayer" format of homiletics and sermon giving. This kind of preaching and presentation appears to be ignoring the power of story in our general society. More concerned with offering "proofs" of Christianity and apologetic defenses with "evidences that demand a verdict," many Christian expositors and preachers have all but abandoned the telling of the Story as the heart and soul of Christian ministry and mission. In an effort to reach the hearts and minds of those accustomed to speaking of truth in a digital age, many have abandoned the native language of the Bible in terms of imagery, prophecy, poetry, and story for more teaching that deals with "contemporary" issues of concern, issues of morality and social change than with the kinds of stories that both Hollywood and the Bible seem to be interested in. Do you think the current focus on moralistic teaching and straightforward theological outlines is a misread of culture? What do you believe—is the culture looking for a story that can command their attention and vision or an explanation that can resolve their problems? Explain.

Nobody Keeps Their Promises These Days

With fewer and fewer instances in general society where promises are taken seriously, how do we make the story of the promise of God clear and convincing? Promises are made and broken with dramatic ease in our society today: promises of marriage are ending up as horrible divisive divorces, politicians take vows to protect their constituencies only to be caught in corruption and abuse, preachers weep crocodile tears while they confess their remorse for (getting caught?) their shameful escapades now the subject of late night comic monologues. It seems today that very few people tend to keep or value the power of a kept promise. Yet, the entire story of Christian faith is rooted in the ability to recognize how significant the promise of

God for a Savior really was, and how this promise was fulfilled in the person of Jesus of Nazareth. How does the erosion of promise making and promise keeping in our society affect our ability to understand the nature of the Christian faith, as well as to do ministry and mission in a society like ours? Do you think that the lack of integrity in our society affects our ability to understand and appreciate the integrity of God in the Gospel, the salvation that he has provided to us in Christ? Explain.

CONTENT ▶ **The Vision and Biblical Foundation for Christian Mission: Part 1**

Segment 1: Mission as the Drama of All Time

Rev. Dr. Don L. Davis

1

Summary of Segment 1

Mission is *the proclamation of God's offer of salvation and redemption in the person and work of Jesus Christ in the power of the Holy Spirit to all people groups.* Viewed as the drama and story of God, from *Before to Beyond Time*, we can begin to see how in the story of mission the Triune God is at work as the *Sovereign God,* working all things together for his own glory and our good.

Our objective for this segment, *Mission as the Drama of All Time,* is to enable you to see that:

- The term "prolegomena" means "first word," and the prolegomena to mission must begin with a biblical worldview of God and his work in the world in the person of Jesus of Nazareth.

- Mission can be defined as "the proclamation of God's offer of salvation and redemption in the person and work of Jesus Christ in the power of the Holy Spirit to all people groups."

- A biblical understanding of mission contains certain elements which can be deduced from a reading of the Scriptures themselves. Mission must be grounded upon a clear understanding of God and his purposes for the universe, and relate all the details of history to a single unified whole. A biblical view of mission, too, must be rooted in the Scriptures themselves, anchored in the person and work of Jesus Christ, and take seriously the biblical way of discussing mission through image, picture, and story.

- Four major theological frameworks/pictures of mission can be found in Scripture, i.e., Mission as the *Drama of All Time* (God as the major character in the greatest plot motif of all time), as the *Fulfillment of the Divine Promise* (God fulfilling his covenant promise in Jesus Christ), as the *Romance of the Ages* (God as the bridegroom of his redeemed humanity), and as the *War of the Spheres* (God as the warrior reestablishing his rule over the universe).

- The elements of the *Drama of All Time* framework can be understood in terms of the major phases of God's unfolding purpose, from Before to Beyond Time. *Before Time* highlights God's pre-existence and purpose, the mystery of iniquity and the rebellion of the powers, and the *Beginning of Time* includes the creation of the universe and humankind, the fall and the curse, the *protoevangelium*, the end of Eden, the reign of death, and the first signs of grace. The *Unfolding of Time* includes the Abrahamic promise, the Exodus, the Conquest of the Land, the City-Temple-Throne, the Captivity and Exile, and the Return of the Remnant.

- God's unfolding purpose in the *Fullness of Time* phase includes the incarnation, the Kingdom revealed in Jesus, the Passion, death, resurrection, and ascension of Christ. The *Last Times* include the descent of the Holy Spirit, the formation of the Church, the inclusion of the Gentiles, and the age of world mission.

- The *Fulfillment of Time* phase includes the end of world evangelization, the apostasy of the Church, the Great Tribulation, the *Parousia*, the reign of Christ on earth, the Great White Throne, the Lake of Fire, and turning the Kingdom over to God the Father. Finally, the *Beyond Time* phase includes the new heavens and new earth, the descent of the New Jerusalem, the times of refreshing, and the ushering in of the Age to Come.

- The framework of Mission as the *Drama of All Time* explains how God's sovereign purpose underwrites all human history, and how he himself is the central character in the unfolding phases of the divine drama. Furthermore, it enables us to see mission as the recovery of that which was lost at the *beginning of time*, and the making of disciples among all nations as our part in *fulfilling our role in the script of Almighty God*.

**Video Segment 1
Outline**

I. Prolegomena to Mission: The Big Picture

- -

The Mission of God Is about the Body of Christ, a Worldwide Body

The crucified body of Jesus and the ecclesial body, the church, therefore cannot be separated. Several consequences for the meaning of the image flow from this. First, though, we must note that in the earlier epistles, particularly Corinthians and Romans, the emphasis is on the local church as expressing in its unity the crucified and living Christ. But in the later epistles, Colossians and Ephesians, the image has moved outward to embrace the universal church (Col. 1.18; 2.19; Eph. 1.22–23; 4.16). Christ is the "head" of a body which is more than the local community of faith, and this change in the image is of the greatest importance, because it marks through its shift a vision of a church "producing fruit and growing ... all over the world" (Col. 1.6 NIV), a calling to mission which is at least as imperative as the call to build up the life of the local faith community.

~ Leland Ryken. **Dictionary of Biblical Imagery.** (electronic ed.)
Downers Grove, IL: InterVarsity Press, 2000, p. 109.

- -

A. Definition: *Mission is the proclamation of God's offer of salvation and redemption in the person and work of Jesus Christ in the power of the Holy Spirit to all people groups.*

1. The proclamation of God's offer of salvation and redemption: *mission concerns the purposes of God and his offer of grace and forgiveness.*

   a. 2 Tim. 1.8-10

   b. Rom. 5.8

   c. Eph. 1.6-8

    d. Eph. 2.7

2. Through the person and work of Jesus Christ: *Jesus of Nazareth is the center of God's salvific and redemptive work in the world.*

    a. Acts 10.42-43

    b. 1 Cor. 3.11

    c. 1 Tim. 2.5-6

    d. 1 John 5.11-12

3. In the power of the Holy Spirit: *the person of the Holy Spirit is the operating power of mission work.*

    a. Zech. 4.6

    b. John 16.13-15

    c. Luke 24.49

    d. Acts 1.8

    e. Acts 2.1-4

4. To all people groups: *the Gospel of God's redemption in Christ is to be proclaimed to all nations (people groups), beginning at Jerusalem and continuing to the ends of the earth.*

    a. Acts 1.8

    b. Mark 16.15

    c. Luke 24.46-47

B. Elements of a biblical understanding of mission

1. It must be rooted in a clear understanding of God and his purposes for the universe, 2 Tim. 1.8-10.

2. It must relate all the details of history to a single unified whole, Rom. 8.29-30.

3. It must be rooted in the Scriptures themselves, John 5.39-40; Luke 24.44-48.

4. It must be anchored in the person and work of Jesus Christ, Acts 4.12; 1 John 5.11-13.

5. It must take seriously the Bible's own way of discussing mission: through image, picture, and story.

C. Four pictures of mission in Scripture

1. Mission is the *Drama of All Time*: God is the major character in the greatest plot motif of all time.

2. Mission is the *Fulfillment of the Divine Promise*: God fulfilling his promise as the covenant God of faithfulness.

3. Mission is the *Romance of the Ages*: God as the bridegroom of his redeemed humanity.

4. Mission is the *War of the Spheres*: God as the warrior reestablishing his rule over the universe.

II. Mission as the *Drama of All Time*

From Before to Beyond Time. Adapted from Suzanne de Dietrich, *God's Unfolding Purpose* (Philadelphia: Westminster Press, 1976).

A. Before Time (Eternity Past), Ps. 90.1-2, "Lord, you have been our dwelling place in all generations. [2] Before the mountains were brought forth, or ever you had formed the earth and the world, from everlasting to everlasting you are God."

1. The eternal Triune God, Ps. 102.24-27

2. God's eternal purpose, 2 Tim. 1.9; Isa. 14.26-27

a. To glorify his name in creation, Prov. 16.4; Ps. 135.6; Isa. 48.11

Theology is first the activity of thinking and speaking about God (theologizing), and second the product of that activity (Luther's theology, or Wesley's, or Finney's, or Wimber's, or Packer's, or whoever's). As an activity, theology is a cat's cradle of interrelated though distinct disciplines: elucidating texts (exegesis), synthesizing what they say on the things they deal with (biblical theology), seeing how the faith was stated in the past (historical theology), formulating it for today (systematic theology), finding its implications for conduct (ethics), commending and defending it as truth and wisdom (apologetics), defining the Christian task in the world (missiology), stockpiling resources for life in Christ (spirituality) and corporate worship (liturgy), and exploring ministry (practical theology).
~ J. I. Packer, Concise Theology: A Guide to Historic Christian Beliefs. (electronic ed.). Wheaton, IL: Tyndale House Publishers, 1995.

b. To display his perfections in the universe, Ps. 19.1

  c. To draw out a people for himself, Isa. 43.7, 21

 3. The Mystery of Iniquity: the rebellion of the "Dawn of the Morning" (*Lucifer*), Isa. 14.12-20; Ezek. 28.13-17

 4. The principalities and powers, Col. 2.15

B. Beginning of Time (the Creation), Gen. 1-2

 1. The creative Word of the Triune God, Gen. 1.3; Ps. 33.6,9; Ps. 148.1-5

 2. The creation of humanity: the Imago Dei, Gen. 1.26-27

C. The Beginning of Time (the Fall and the Curse), Gen. 3

 1. The Fall and the Curse, Gen. 3.1-9

 2. The *protoevangelium*: the promised Seed; Gen. 3.15

 3. The end of Eden and the reign of death, Gen. 3.22-24

 4. First signs of grace; Gen. 3.15, 21

D. The Unfolding of Time (God's plan revealed thru Israel)

1. The Abrahamic Promise and the covenant of Yahweh (Patriarchs); Gen. 12.1-3; 15; 17; 18.18; 28.4

2. The Exodus and the covenant at Sinai, Exodus

3. The Conquest of the inhabitants and the Promised Land, Joshua-2 Chronicles

4. The City, the Temple, and the Throne, Ps. 48.1-3; 2 Chron. 7.14; 2 Sam. 7.8ff.

    a. The role of the prophet, *to declare the word of the Lord*, Deut. 18.15

    b. The role of the priest, *to represent God and the people*, Heb. 5.1 - "For every high priest chosen from among men is appointed to act on behalf of men in relation to God, to offer gifts and sacrifices for sins."

    c. The role of the king, *to rule with righteousness and justice in God's stead*, Ps. 72

5. The Captivity and the Exile, Daniel, Ezekiel, Lamentations

6. The return of the Remnant, Ezra, Nehemiah

E. The Fullness of Time (Incarnation of the Messiah), Gal. 4.4-6

   1. The Word becomes flesh, John 1.14-18; 1 John 1.1-4

   2. The testimony of John the Baptist, Matt. 3.1-3

   3. The Kingdom has come in the person of Jesus of Nazareth, Mark 1.14-15; Luke 10.9-11; 10.11; 17.20-21; Matt. 12.28-29.

      a. Revealed in his person, John 1.18

      b. Exhibited in his works, John 5.36; 3.2; 9.30-33; 10.37-38; Acts 2.22; 10.38-39

      c. Interpreted in his testimony, Matt. 5-7

   4. The secret of the Kingdom revealed, Mark 1.14-15

      a. The Kingdom is already present, Matt. 12.25-29.

      b. The Kingdom is not yet consummated, Matt. 25.31-46.

   5. The Passion and death of the crucified King, Matt. 26.36-46; Mark 14.32-42; Luke 22.39-46; John 18.1ff.

a.   To destroy the devil's work: *Christus Victor*, 1 John 3.8; Gen. 3.15; Col. 2.15; Rom. 16.20; Heb. 2.14-15

b.   To make atonement for sin: *Christus Victum*, 1 John 2.1-2; Rom. 5.8-9; 1 John 4.9-10; 1 John 3.16

c.   To reveal the Father's heart, John 3.16; Titus 2.11-15

6.   *Christus Victor*: the resurrection of the glorious Lord of life, Matt. 28.1-15; Mark 16.1-11; Luke 24.1-12; John 20.1-18; cf. 1 Cor. 15

F.   The Last Times (the Descent and Age of the Holy Spirit)

1.   The *arrabon* of God: the Spirit as Pledge and Sign of the Kingdom's presence, Eph. 1.13-14; 4.30; Acts 2.1-47; 2 Cor. 1.22; Rom. 8.14-16

2.   "This is that": Peter, Pentecost, and the Presence of the Future

a.   The Church as foretaste and agent of the Kingdom of God, Phil. 2.14-16; 2 Cor. 5.20

b.   The present reign of Messiah Jesus, 1 Cor 15.24-28; Acts 2.34; Eph. 1.20-23; Heb. 1.13

c.   The ushering in of God's kingdom community "in-between the times;" Rom. 14.7

3. The Church of Messiah Jesus: sojourners in the Already and the Not Yet

    a. The Great Confession: Jesus is Lord, Phil. 2.9-11.

    b. The Great Commission: go and make disciples among all nations, Matt. 28.18-20; Acts 1.8.

    c. The Great Commandment: love God and love people, Matt. 22.37-39.

4. The announcement of the mystery: Gentiles as fellow-heirs of the promise, Rom. 16.25-27; Col. 1.26-28; Eph. 3.3-11

    a. Jesus as the Last Adam, 1 Cor. 15.45-49

    b. God drawing out of the world a New Humanity, Eph. 2.12-22

5. In-between the times: tokens of the Age of Sabbath and of Jubilee, Acts 2.17ff. Cf. Joel 2; Amos 9; Ezek. 36.25-27; Ps. 110.1ff.

G. The Fulfillment of Time (the *Parousia* of Christ), 1 Thess. 4.13-17

1. Completion of world mission: the evangelization of the world's *ethnoi*, Matt. 24.14; Mark 16.15-16; Rom. 10.18; 15.18-21; Col. 1.23

2. The apostasy of the Church, 1 Tim. 4.1-3; 2 Tim. 4.3; 2 Thess. 2.3-12

3. The Great Tribulation, Matt. 24.21ff; Luke 21.24

4. The *Parousia*: the Second Coming of Jesus, 1 Thess. 4.13-17; 1 Cor. 15.50-58; Luke 21.25-27; Dan. 7.13; Matt. 26.64; Mark 13.26; Acts 1.9-11

5. The Reign of Jesus Christ on earth, Rev. 20.1-4

6. The Great White Throne and Lake of Fire, Rev. 20.11-15

7. "For He Must Reign": the final placement of all enemy's under Christ's feet, 1 Cor. 15.24-28

H. Beyond Time (Eternity Future)

1. The Creation of the new heavens and earth, Rev. 21.1; Isa. 65.17-19; 66.22; 2 Pet. 3.13

2. The Descent of the New Jerusalem: the abode of God comes to earth, Rev. 21.2-4

3. The times of refreshing: the Glorious Freedom of the Children of God, Rom. 8.18-23

4. The Lord Christ gives over the Kingdom to God the Father, 1 Cor. 15.24-28

5. The Age to Come: the Triune God as all-in-all

    a. Zech. 14.9

    b. Jer. 23.6

    c. Matt. 1.23

    d. Ps. 72.8-11

    e. Mic. 4.1-3

    f. Zech. 2.10

III. Implications of Mission as the *Drama of All Time*

A. God's sovereign purpose underwrites all human history

    1. Whatever he pleases, he does, Ps. 135.6.

    2. God's counsels and plans stand forever, to all generations.

        a. Ps. 33.11

        b. Ps. 115.3

3. God declares the end of all things from the beginning, Isa. 46.10.

4. Nothing and no one can withstand the plan of God for salvation and redemption, Dan. 4.35.

B. God is the central character in the unfolding of the divine drama, Eph. 1.9-11.

C. Mission is the *recovery of that which was lost* at the beginning of time.

1. God's sovereign rule, Mark 1.14-15

2. Satan's infernal rebellion, Gen. 3.15 with Col. 2.15; 1 John 3.8

3. Humankind's tragic fall, Gen. 3.1-8 cf. Rom. 5.5-8

D. Making disciples among all nations is *fulfilling our role in the script of Almighty God!*

Conclusion

» Mission is *the proclamation of God's offer of salvation and redemption in the person and work of Jesus Christ in the power of the Holy Spirit to all people groups.*

» Viewed as the drama and story of God, the story of mission is simultaneously God at work as the Sovereign God, working all things together for his own glory and our good.

Segue 1

**Student Questions
and Response**

Please take as much time as you have available to answer these and other questions that the video brought out. In this section we gave a "prolegomena" or "first word" regarding the framework of biblical mission, including its definition as *the proclamation of God's offer of salvation and redemption in the person and work of Jesus Christ in the power of the Holy Spirit to all people groups.* Viewed as the drama and story of God, from *Before to Beyond Time*, we can begin to see how in the story of mission the Triune God is at work as the *Sovereign God*, working all things together for his own glory and our good. What we will seek to accomplish in this module is the "big picture" underwriting the nature of mission in Scripture, and the first step is to understand the motifs covered in this segment. Review the key ideas of this material by answering carefully the questions below, and support your answers with the Scriptures.

1. What is the meaning of the term "prolegomena," and why do we need a "prolegomena to mission" that begins with a biblical worldview of God and his work in the world in the person of Jesus of Nazareth?

2. Define "mission," and list the key elements that go into a biblical understanding of mission? Why is it so necessary that our view of mission *begins with the Scriptures themselves*, and not with the experience of missionaries and mission organizations throughout history?

3. Why must a biblical view of mission, too, be anchored in the person and work of Jesus Christ, and take seriously the way the Bible discusses mission in the form of images, pictures, and stories?

4. What are the four major theological frameworks/pictures of mission that can be found in Scripture, and what are the definitions of each?

5. List out the major elements of the *Drama of All Time* framework, and in particular the phase of *Before Time*, the *Beginning of Time*, and the *Unfolding of Time*. Highlight the central elements of each, and explain the implications of each for understanding mission.

6. Explain God's unfolding purpose in the *Fullness of Time*, the *Last Times*, the *Fulfillment of Time*, and the *Beyond Time* phases of the *Mission as the Drama of All Time* framework. Again, highlight the central elements of each, and explain their role and relationship to the concept of world mission.

7. How does the framework of *Mission as the Drama of All Time* explain God's sovereign purpose and role in the unfolding phases of the divine drama? How does this framework enable us to see mission as the recovery of that which was lost at the *beginning of time*, and disciple making as fulfilling our specific role in God's divine drama?

....

Missiology is the formal study of the mission of the Church. Missiology is the ordered study of the Christian church's mission. As such it is a discipline within theology, incorporating a number of strands. Biblical study investigates the basis of the church's mission in the missio Dei, the calling of Israel to be a light to all nations (Isa. 49.6) and Jesus' commission to his disciples to be his witnesses to the ends of the earth and the end of time (Matt. 28.18–20; Acts 1.8). Historical study surveys the growth and expansion of the church at various periods and assesses its impact on different societies and cultures. Systematic theology studies the interaction of Christian faith both with secular philosophies and ideologies and with other systems of belief. Ethical studies, are incorporated into missiology where the church has a responsibility to declare God's will for the whole of life. . . . Pastoral theology seeks ways to instruct new converts and integrate them into the church. Because of the wide scope of missiology it has an important role to play in the integration of other areas of theology. Put another way, every aspect of theology has an inescapably missiological dimension, for each one exists for the sake of the church's mission.

~ J. A. Kirk. "Missiology." **The New Dictionary of Theology.** S. B. Ferguson, ed. (electronic ed.). Downers Grove, IL: InterVarsity Press, 2000. p. 434.

....

The Vision and Biblical Foundation for Christian Mission: Part 1

Segment 2: Mission as Fulfillment of the Divine Promise

Rev. Dr. Don L. Davis

Summary of Segment 2

The *Mission as Fulfillment of the Divine Promise* framework describes the work of God as fulfilling his promise as the covenant God of faithfulness to Abraham and David. Built upon the role of biblical covenant in the Scriptures, this motif begins with God's covenant promise to Abraham, confirmed in his sons and the patriarchs, and later identified with the tribe of Judah. This covenant promise for a Seed who would bless the nations was amplified and clarified in the promise to David to have a perpetual heir on his throne. Now in this age and in the person of Jesus of Nazareth, the promise of Abraham and David has been fulfilled. Likewise, in this age through the proclamation of the Gospel in mission, the promise of new life is offered to the nations through the preaching of the cross.

Our objective for this segment, *Mission as Fulfillment of the Divine Promise*, is to enable you to see that:

- One of the four major motifs (themes) that explains mission in Scripture is the *Mission as the Fulfillment of the Divine Promise* motif. In the biblical sense, a covenant is an agreement or contract between two parties, whether individuals, tribes, or nations, with both having obligations to fulfill and benefits and advantages as a result of the fulfillment of the conditions.

- Biblical covenants abound, and share common characteristics, including how the agreements and/or contracts were invoked by a witness and carried severe consequences for breaking (i.e., breaking them was considered a great moral evil). Covenants were sealed and given witness by giving gifts, eating meals, and often included the setting up stones of remembrance. They were confirmed with an oath and with sacrifice.

- Perhaps the most common form of biblical covenant was the marriage ceremony, and other prominent covenants can be seen throughout the history of Israel, e.g., God's covenant with Noah, and his covenant of Sinai with the children of Israel. God's covenants, whether conditional or unconditional, all speak to the solemn contract between God and individuals or with his people.

1

- The *Mission as Fulfillment of the Divine Promise* framework can be traced from God's covenant made with Abraham, with its *condition* that he leave his country and kindred to go to a land of God's own choosing, and *the corresponding blessings* that God would make him a great nation, bless him and make his name great, bless and curse those who did the same to him, and bless all the families of the earth in him.

- God's covenant with Abraham to provide a Seed who would bless the nations was renewed and confirmed in Abraham's descendants, Isaac and Jacob, and later clarified for Judah, the tribe out of which the divine Messiah would come. Among the families of Judah, the house of David was selected by God to be the house from which the royal Seed of Abraham's blessing would come. David's heir would reign forever over the house of Israel and be a blessing to the nations.

- The promise of God in Abraham and David was fulfilled in the person of Jesus of Nazareth, who represents the Seed of Abraham and the son of David through whom God's reign would be established. Through the life, death, resurrection, and ascension of Jesus, the covenant promise of God is fulfilled.

- Mission is the affirmation and proclamation of this Good News regarding God's covenant faithfulness in Jesus, and the Great Commission is an charge to proclaim and teach this fulfilled promise for the sake of all humanity, beginning at Jerusalem, to the very ends of the earth.

- The heart of the missionary enterprise is that in the person of Jesus of Nazareth, the promise of Abraham and David has been fulfilled, and now, through the proclamation of the Gospel, the promise of eternal life is offered freely to the nations through the preaching of the cross.

Promise in the Bible

*There is in the Hebrew OT no special term for the concept or act of promising. Where our English translations say that someone promised something, the Hebrew simply states that someone said or spoke (**'amar, dabar**) some word with future reference. In the NT the technical term, **epangelia**, appears chiefly in Acts, Galatians, Romans and Hebrews. A promise is a word that goes forth into unfilled time. It reaches ahead of its speaker and its recipient, to mark an appointment between them in the future. A promise may be an assurance of continuing or future action on behalf of someone: "I will be with you", "They that mourn shall be comforted", "If we confess our sins, God will forgive us our sins." It may be a solemn agreement of lasting, mutual (if unequal) relationship: as in the covenants. It may be the announcement of a future event: "When you have brought the people from Egypt, you will serve God on this mountain."*

~ J. W. L Hoad. "Promise." **The New Bible Dictionary.**
D. R. W. Wood, ed. (3rd ed., electronic ed.). Downers Grove: InterVarsity Press, 1996. p. 963.

Video Segment 2
Outline

I. Mission Is the *Fulfillment of the Divine Promise*: God Fulfilling His Promise as the Covenant God of Faithfulness

A. The meaning of covenant

1. Hebrew, "*b'rit*," "cutting." A term applied to different contracts and transactions between God and humankind, and among people.

   a. Rendered "allies," Obad. 1.7

   b. Our word for Old and New "Testament" has the same meaning as "covenant."

2. May indicate a contract between two parties, whether individuals, tribes, or nations

a.   Between nations, Josh. 9.6; Josh. 9.15

b.   Between cities, 1 Sam. 11.1

c.   Between individuals, Gen. 21.27

3. Covenants made involved both *obligations to fulfill and benefits and advantages as a result of the fulfillment of the conditions.*

4. Nature of covenant making

a.   God was invoked as a witness, Gen. 31.52-53, see also 1 Sam. 20.8; Jer. 34.18-19; Ezek. 17.19.

b.   Breach of a contract was viewed as a serious moral evil, even a sin, Ezek.17.12-20; cf. Ezek. 17.16.

c.   Covenants were given witness by the giving of gifts or setting up stones as a remembrance, with a meal or grains of salt (cf. Gen. 26.30; 31; 54; 2 Sam. 3.12, 20).

(1) Gen. 21.30-31

(2) Gen. 31.52

5. Marriage in the Bible was a common covenant made, Prov. 2.17.

6. Covenants were confirmed with an oath (Gen. 26.28; 31.53; Josh. 9.15, etc.) and the slaughtering and cutting of a victim into halves, with the parties passing between them (Gen. 15.9-10, 17-18; Jer. 34.18-20).

a. Seals the contract between the two parties

b. Visually shows what would happen if the parties reneged on their word of promise

B. Examples of biblical covenants between God and others

1. The covenant with Noah (*that no judgment by rain would occur again, and that the seasons and cycle of day and night should not cease*), Gen. 9.8-13

2. The Sinai covenant with the children of Israel (*the giving of the Ten Commandments and the Law through Moses, to be rewarded with prosperity for keeping and judgment for disobeying*)

a. Exod. 24.3

b. Exod. 34.28

c. Deut. 4.13

d. Deut. 29.1

II. Mission Is the *Fulfillment of the Divine Promise*: God Fulfilling His Promise as the Covenant God of Faithfulness

A. The Promise Made – the Abrahamic Covenant: the hope of a Seed

1. The condition of the covenant and the fourfold blessing, Gen. 12.1-3,

   a. Condition: *leave your country, kindred, and father's house, and go to the land that I show you*, Gen. 12.1

   b. Blessing

      (1) I will make of you a great nation.

      (2) I will bless you and make your name great.

      (3) I will bless those who bless you and curse those who curse you.

      (4) In you all the families of the earth will be blessed.

2. Promise was renewed with Abraham, along with the promise of a son and with a legacy of people too numerous to count, Gen. 15.4-6.

3. Fourteen years after the covenant was made it was affirmed again, confirmed by a change of Abraham's name and the establishment of circumcision as a sign of accepting the covenant, Gen. 17.1-10.

4. Affirmed after the test of Abraham's willingness to sacrifice Isaac at God's command, Gen. 22.16-18

B. The Promise Confirmed in the Patriarchs

   1. Confirmed with Isaac, Gen. 26.24-25

   2. Confirmed with Jacob, Gen. 28.13-14

3. God acts in conformity with the keeping of his covenant with Abraham, Isaac, and Jacob.

    a. Ps. 105.8-11

    b. Mic. 7.20

C. The Promise Identified–the tribe of Judah: the Seed of Abraham will come out of the tribe of Judah, Gen. 49.8-10.

    1. Scene of the prophetic word: Jacob's blessing upon his sons before his death, Gen. 49

    2. Judah's tribe and lineage identified as the one from which the One who will reign will come (i.e., "the scepter shall not depart from Judah")

    3. The blessing: the scepter (right to rule) shall be his, and to him shall be the obedience of the peoples (universal salvation)

D. The Promise Clarified: the Davidic Covenant

2 Sam. 7.8-16 - "Now, therefore, thus you shall say to my servant David, 'Thus says the LORD of hosts, I took you from the pasture, from following the sheep, that you should be prince over my people Israel. [9] And I have been with you wherever you went and have cut off all your enemies from before you. And I will make for you a great name, like the name of the great ones of the earth. [10] And I will appoint a place for my people Israel and will plant them, so that they may dwell in their own place and be disturbed no more. And violent men shall afflict them no more, as formerly, [11] from the time that I appointed judges over my people Israel. And I will give you rest from all your enemies. Moreover, the LORD declares to you that the

LORD will make you a house. [12] When your days are fulfilled and you lie down with your fathers, I will raise up your offspring after you, who shall come from your body, and I will establish his kingdom. [13] He shall build a house for my name, and I will establish the throne of his kingdom forever. [14] I will be to him a father, and he shall be to me a son. When he commits iniquity, I will discipline him with the rod of men, with the stripes of the sons of men, [15] but my steadfast love will not depart from him, as I took it from Saul, whom I put away from before you. [16] And your house and your kingdom shall be made sure forever before me. Your throne shall be established forever.'"

1. Marks with precision and exact clarity the line through which the blessing of Abraham would occur

2. The royal Seed of Abraham's blessing would come through the house of David.

    a. 2 Sam. 7.12

    b. 2 Sam. 22.51

3. Through this promised One, God would restore his reign over the house of Israel and bless all the nations through his kingship.

    a. Isa. 9.6-7

    b. Ps. 72.8-11

    c. Ps. 89.35-37

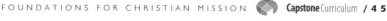

Jesus as the Centerpiece of the Promise Between the OT and the NT

The point of convergence of the OT promises (to Abraham, Moses, David and the Fathers through the prophets) is Jesus Christ. All the promises of God are confirmed in him, and through him affirmed by the church in the 'Amen' of its worship (2 Cor. 1.20). The OT quotations and allusions in the Gospel narratives indicate this fulfilment. The Magnificat and the Benedictus rejoice that God has kept his word. The promised Word has become flesh. The new covenant has been inaugurated—upon the 'better promises' prophesied by Jeremiah (Jer. 31; Heb. 8.6–13). Jesus is its guarantee (Heb. 7.22), and the Holy Spirit of promise its first instalment (Eph. 1.13–14).
~ J. W. L Hoad. "Promise." *The New Bible Dictionary*. D. R. W. Wood, ed. (3rd ed., electronic ed.). Downers Grove: InterVarsity Press, 1996. p. 963.

d. Jer. 33.15-18

e. Dan. 7.13-14

4. The Gentiles would participate in God's fulfillment of his promise to David, Acts 15.15-18 (cf. Amos 9.11-12).

E. The Promise Fulfilled: *in the person of Jesus of Nazareth, the promise of God to Abraham and David has been fulfilled.*

1. Before his birth, the promise regarding Jesus' connection to David as the promised royal Seed was clarified, Luke 1.32-33.

2. The covenant to Abraham is in fact the Gospel message given to Abraham; Jesus is the Seed referred to in the covenant of God to Abraham, Gal. 3.16.

3. The promises of rulership over the Kingdom have been given to Messiah Jesus.

a. Heb. 1.8 (cf. Ps. 45.4-6)

b. Rom. 14.8-9

4. Jesus' broken body and shed blood upon the cross establish a new covenant with those who believe, for both Jews and Gentiles, resulting in forgiveness and eternal life.

1

a. Jer. 32.40 (cf. Heb. 8.6-12)

b. Matt. 26.28

c. Luke 22.20

d. 2 Cor. 3.6

5. Jesus of Nazareth, because of his death on the cross, has been glorified by God to an exalted rank, and is ruling by God's leave.

a. Acts 2.22-23

b. Acts 2.32-36

6. The promise to Abraham was proclaimed to Israel as fulfilled in the person of Jesus of Nazareth.

a. Luke 1.72-74

b. Acts 3.25-26

7. God has exalted Jesus to be Leader and Savior of Israel to give repentance and forgiveness, Acts 5.30-31.

8. Salvation is in no one else but Jesus of Nazareth; mission is rooted in the promise of God in him, Acts 4.11-12.

F. Implications for understanding mission today: *Mission is the Promise Proclaimed to the Nations.*

1. God commanded the apostles to proclaim to the world that Jesus of Nazareth is the fulfillment of the promise, Acts 10.37-42.

2. Jesus gave a commission to his disciples to proclaim the promise fulfilled in himself beginning at Jerusalem, to the very ends of the earth.

    a. Acts 1.8

    b. Acts 2.32

    c. Acts 3.15

    d. Acts 4.33

3. The Scriptures, both OT and NT, give clear witness that Jesus of Nazareth is the fulfillment of the promise of God to Abraham and David, and that salvation according to the promise should be preached to all nations, beginning at Jerusalem.

    a. Luke 24.26-27

    b. Luke 24.46-48

    c. Acts 17.2-3

d. Acts 28.23

e. John 20.30-31

4. In Jesus Christ, the promise of Abraham has been fulfilled, with the Gentiles having access to redemption and salvation by faith.

a. Gal. 3.7-9

b. Acts 15.13-18

c. Rom. 15.8-12

III. Implications of Mission as the *Fulfillment of the Divine Promise*

A. God's covenant faithfulness is the ground of his covenant with Abraham and David.

1. To Abraham, Gen. 17.7

2. To David, Ps. 89.20-24

B. God as the Divine Partner underwrites mission activity: God is the source both of the message and the meaning of all mission activity through the covenant.

C. Mission is the fulfillment of God's intent to draw out of the earth a people that will be his forever and ever.

1. God's covenant promise is sure and certain, Heb. 6.13-18.

2. His faithfulness in spite of his covenant partners, cf. Jer. 31.31-33.

D. Making disciples among all nations is *the proclamation of the covenant faithfulness of a God who cannot lie and who fulfills his promise for a Savior to the world!*

Conclusion

» Mission is the work of the God and Father of our Lord Jesus Christ through his promise to Abraham and David as the covenant God of faithfulness.

» Our God has sworn by his own mighty nature and name to fulfill his promise to his servants Abraham and David, and now, all the world, including Gentiles, can participate in that promise by faith in Jesus of Nazareth.

» Our Lord Jesus Christ is the One who fulfilled the promise of Abraham through his death and resurrection.

The following questions were designed to help you review the material in the second video segment. In this section we discovered the elements of the *Mission as the Fulfillment of the Divine Promise* framework which sees God's working as the fulfillment of the divine promise to Abraham and David. God's covenant promise to Abraham for a Seed that would bless his descendants, and through them all the families of the earth, was confirmed in Isaac and Jacob, and with the tribe of Judah. This covenant promise for a Seed who would bless the nations was also connected with the mercies God gave to David in the promise to possess a perpetual heir on his throne. Now, in the person of Jesus of Nazareth, God's covenant promise to Abraham and David has been fulfilled. Mission declares this new life through God's covenant faithfulness. It is critical that you are able to reproduce this brief outline in your preaching and teaching, so review the key points here through the questions below.

Segue 2

Student Questions
and Response

1. Briefly define the *Mission as the Fulfillment of the Divine Promise* motif. In what way does this theme depend on a biblical understanding of covenant? What is a covenant?

2. How often are covenants found in the Scriptures, and what are some of the common characteristics true of all covenants in the Bible? How did the Israelite culture view the covenant-breaker? Explain the conditions and benefits connected with covenants in the Bible, and how were they sealed, borne witness to, and confirmed?

3. What is perhaps the most common form of a biblical covenant? List two of the more prominent covenants God made that can be seen throughout the history of Israel.

4. Lay out the specifics of the Abrahamic covenant–what were its conditions and promised benefits? How was the promise specified to the tribe of Judah, and when was this realization given?

5. How does God's promise to David recorded in 2 Samuel 7 relate to the promise to Abraham that was clarified through Judah? What were the specific promises that God made to David regarding the royal Seed–what would he do, and what would God do for him?

6. How do the promises of God to both Abraham and David find their fulfillment in the person of Jesus of Nazareth? How does his life, death, resurrection, and ascension give clear evidence that God's promise to Abraham and David are now fulfilled?

7. In what sense can we say that mission affirms and proclaims God's covenant faithfulness in Jesus as the present day fulfillment of his promise to Abraham and David? How does making disciples of all nations in obedience to the Great Commission represent the expression of the fulfilled promise to the nations (cf. Gal. 3 with Rom. 16.25-27, Col. 1.25-29, and Eph. 3.1-10)?

8. Why does this motif of promise and fulfillment lie at the heart of the missionary enterprise? Is it possible to clearly proclaim the Gospel in mission without reference to Jesus' fulfillment of the promise to Abraham and David? Why or why not?

Summary of Key Concepts

This lesson focuses upon two distinct motifs of mission that enable us to get the "big picture" of what God has been doing in the world, and how it relates to our task of advancing his kingdom reign. The following statements represent the central concepts covered in the lesson, and ought to be reviewed again for emphasis and understanding. (Always remember, to have the same concepts repeated and reviewed is to ensure their mastery, cf. Josh. 1.8; Phil. 3.1.)

☞ The term "prolegomena" means "first word," and the prolegomena to mission must begin with a biblical worldview of God and his work in the world in the person of Jesus of Nazareth.

☞ Mission can be defined as "the proclamation of God's offer of salvation and redemption in the person and work of Jesus Christ in the power of the Holy Spirit to all people groups."

☞ A biblical understanding of mission contains certain elements which can be deduced from a reading of the Scriptures themselves. Mission must be grounded upon a clear understanding of God and his purposes for the universe, and relate all the details of history to a single unified whole. A biblical view of mission, too, must be rooted in the Scriptures themselves, anchored in the person and work of Jesus Christ, and take seriously the biblical way of discussing mission through image, picture, and story.

☞ Four major theological frameworks/pictures of mission can be found in Scripture, i.e., Mission as the *Drama of All Time* (God as the major character in the greatest plot motif of all time), as the *Fulfillment of the Divine Promise* (God fulfilling his covenant promise in Jesus Christ), as the *Romance of the*

Ages (God as the bridegroom of his redeemed humanity), and as the *War of the Spheres* (God as the warrior reestablishing his rule over the universe).

⌁ The elements of the *Drama of All Time* framework can be understood in terms of the major phases of God's unfolding purpose, from Before to Beyond Time. *Before Time* highlights God's pre-existence and purpose, the mystery of iniquity and the rebellion of the powers, and the *Beginning of Time* includes the creation of the universe and humankind, the fall and the curse, the *protoevangelium*, the end of Eden, the reign of death, and the first signs of grace. The *Unfolding of Time* includes the Abrahamic promise, the Exodus, the Conquest of the Land, the City-Temple-Throne, the Captivity and Exile, and the Return of the Remnant.

⌁ God's unfolding purpose in the *Fullness of Time* phase includes the incarnation, the Kingdom revealed in Jesus, the Passion, death, resurrection, and ascension of Christ. The *Last Times* include the descent of the Holy Spirit, the formation of the Church, the inclusion of the Gentiles, and the age of world mission.

⌁ The *Fulfillment of Time* phase includes the end of world evangelization, the apostasy of the Church, the Great Tribulation, the *Parousia*, the reign of Christ on earth, the Great White Throne, the Lake of Fire, and turning the Kingdom over to God the Father. Finally, the *Beyond Time* phase includes the new heavens and new earth, the descent of the New Jerusalem, the times of refreshing, and the ushering in of the Age to Come.

⌁ The framework of *Mission as the Drama of All Time* explains how God's sovereign purpose underwrites all human history, and how he himself is the central character in the unfolding phases of the divine drama. Furthermore, it enables us to see mission as the recovery of that which was lost at the *beginning of time*, and the making of disciples among all nations as our part in *fulfilling our role in the script of Almighty God*.

⌁ One of the four major motifs (themes) that explains mission in Scripture is *Mission as the Fulfillment of the Divine Promise* motif. In the biblical sense, a covenant is an agreement or contract between two parties, whether individuals, tribes, or nations, with both having obligations to fulfill and benefits and advantages as a result of the fulfillment of the conditions.

⌁ Biblical covenants abound and share common characteristics including how the agreements and/or contracts were invoked by a witness and carried severe consequences for breaking (i.e., breaking them was considered a great moral evil). Covenants were sealed and given witness by giving gifts, eating meals, and often included the setting up stones of remembrance. They were confirmed with an oath and with sacrifice.

☞ Perhaps the most common form of biblical covenant was the marriage ceremony, and other prominent covenants can be seen throughout the history of Israel, e.g., God's covenant with Noah, and his covenant of Sinai with the children of Israel. God's covenants, whether conditional or unconditional, all speak to the solemn contract between God and individuals or with his people.

☞ The *Mission as Fulfillment of the Divine Promise* framework can be traced from God's covenant made with Abraham, with its *condition* that he leave his country and kindred to go to a land of God's own choosing, and the *corresponding blessings* that God would make him a great nation, bless him and make his name great, bless and curse those who did the same to him, and bless all the families of the earth in him.

☞ God's covenant with Abraham to provide a Seed who would bless the nations was renewed and confirmed in Abraham's descendants, Isaac and Jacob, and later clarified for Judah, the tribe out of which the divine Messiah would come. Among the families of Judah, the house of David was selected by God to be the house from which the royal Seed of Abraham's blessing would come. David's heir would reign forever over the house of Israel and be a blessing to the nations.

☞ The promise of God in Abraham and David was fulfilled in the person of Jesus of Nazareth, who represents the Seed of Abraham and the son of David through whom God's reign would be established. Through the life, death, resurrection, and ascension of Jesus, the covenant promise of God is fulfilled.

☞ Mission is the affirmation and proclamation of this Good News regarding God's covenant faithfulness in Jesus, and the Great Commission is a charge to proclaim and teach this fulfilled promise for the sake of all humanity, beginning at Jerusalem, to the very ends of the earth.

☞ The heart of the missionary enterprise is that in the person of Jesus of Nazareth, the promise of Abraham and David has been fulfilled, and now, through the proclamation of the Gospel, the promise of eternal life is offered freely to the nations through the preaching of the cross.

Now is the time for you to discuss with your fellow students your questions about the motifs and frameworks covered in this lesson. What particular questions do you have in light of the material you have just studied? Maybe some of the questions below might help you form your own, more specific and critical questions.

Student Application and Implications

* What has been your experience in your church with the subject of "mission?" How has mission typically been portrayed in your experience?

* Have you ever met any missionaries? Where were they serving? What were the kinds of issues, themes, and concepts they emphasized while you spent time with them? In light of your experience, what observations did you make regarding the work that missionaries do and the motives that drive them?

* Why do you think it is important to begin discussions about mission with what the Scriptures teach, and not with the experiences and histories of various missionaries down through history? Explain.

* Have you ever considered full-time missionary service? What were the things that made you think about it as a possibility for your own life?

* How well can you reproduce from memory (without notes) the story of God as laid out in the outline of *From Before to Beyond Time*? Why is such an outline helpful to summarize mission as the current proclamation of God's story, i.e., his offer of salvation and redemption in the person and work of Jesus Christ?

* Complete the following sentence: "The one thing that moves me and challenges me most in discussing mission in terms of God's story in *From Before to Beyond Time* is . . ."

* Without the use of notes or a Bible, trace the covenant promise of God from the Seed of the woman in Genesis 3.15 to the fulfillment of the covenant in Jesus Christ. Include God's promise in the Garden, to Shem, to Abraham, Isaac, and Jacob, to Judah, to David, and finally to Christ. (How did you do? Were you able to include the verse references, too?)

* Do I tend to see the work of God in terms of the big picture, or do I get lost in the everyday details of my walk with God? Explain. Where did this habit of either *farsightedness* or *nearsightedness* begin in your Christian walk?

* Why would it be important always to see what is taking place in our lives *against the backdrop of what God has been doing across the centuries*? How can a mission vision and focus provide such a backdrop for us?

* Complete the following sentence: "The one thing that would help me broaden my perspective of what God is doing in the world today is to . . ."

CASE STUDIES

Mission as Storytelling–A Model for Ministry

Tom Steffen in his interesting book *Reconnecting God's Story to Ministry: Cross-cultural Storytelling At Home and Abroad* argues aggressively for a return to narrative and storytelling in evangelism and discipleship. He identifies what he calls "storylands" among various people groups, and argues that mission, that is, the task of the Church to tell the Good News to the lost among unchurched and unreached peoples, is to be faithful to the story of God while being open to the story of others and our own stories. "To reach those living within a specific storyland, the storyteller must be cognizant not only of the land contours of the Bible, but also those of the people group, and especially, his or her own." (Tom Steffen, *Reconnecting God's Story to Ministry*. La Habra, CA: Center for Organizational and Ministry Development, 1996, p. 15). He believes that each of these "storylands" are foundational and critical for doing mission in today's world. What do you think of his general view, that the core of mission and ministry is learning to tell and hear the stories of others and ourselves, while always being careful to reconnect both of these to the one, true foundational storyland, the story of God in Scripture regarding Jesus of Nazareth and salvation through him?

Personalizing the Promises of God Just a Little Too Far?

With a focus on the individual and the personal today, Christianity for many has become an entirely private affair. All the promises, claims, and affirmations of the Bible are understood in existential, overly personal ways, and many have gone so far as to see the entire Christian experience as a "relationship between me and God." This trend is shown in a number of different elements: the rash of worship music that is entirely focused on the emotional and psychological state of the worshiper, the mega-church phenomenon that emphasizes the resolution of the problems of the individual, the explosion of para-church ministries all tailored to helping individuals overcome their personal issues and problems, and the mass exodus of many from the Church, psychologically speaking. Many today ignore church membership, seeing church attendance as either unnecessary or only relevant if it addresses particular needs of the individual and/or family. Churches have responded to these trends, becoming more like religious department stores than living communities. What do you make of the "privatization" of Christian experience? Does the promise of God for a Savior for the world allow itself to be easily personalized, or do our current trends of hyper-individualized Christianity represent a departure from the "people of God" emphasis in both Old and New Testaments?

The Recovery of Christian Myth

What is the most effective language in which to communicate the Gospel to the lost culture today? Guilford Dudley III argues that the language of myth is the language we must recover. Dudley is not using this term to mean unhistorical tales of the gods, but the kind of total life and world story that dare to explain all of life and the world in its drama. "A leading figure in American Protestantism has frequently told the press: 'With the decline of Christianity, it is necessary to travel light. I want to get rid of as much theological baggage as I can.' That laconic remark typifies an attitude that is growing among Protestant churches in this country. In their zeal to arrest the so-called decline of Christianity, the churches are showing an alarming readiness to jettison all concepts and language that do not immediately conform to what they have judged to be the canons of modernity. The language they have abandoned most willingly and with least discrimination is symbol and myth. This decision has put them on a perilous course, leaving them adrift and even farther removed from genuine communication with our culture. They are misassessing the culture, and limiting both the meaning of modernity and the language of the Gospel. This book is a study of how much is at stake in the very mythic language which the churches are hastening to disown, and indeed how hard that language dies in the heart of our famished culture. For even though mythic language seems to have been banished from the official parlance of the church, it has reappeared in major works of literary art that give testimony to its vivifying power" (Guilford Dudley III, *The Recovery of Christian Myth*. Eugene, OR: Wipf and Stock Publishers, 2004, p. 13). Although written in the late 60s, Dudley's work prophetically argues that we have abandoned Christianity's "native language" of image, symbol, myth, and story for scientific explanations about the possibility of faith. What do you make of Dudley's claim, and if it is true, what do you think might be the effect on Christian mission to turn over the communication of our faith to the logical side of our brains and experience?

Restatement of the Lesson's Thesis

Mission is *the proclamation of God's offer of salvation and redemption in the person and work of Jesus Christ in the power of the Holy Spirit to all people groups*. Viewed as the drama and story of God, *From Before to Beyond Time*, we can begin to see how in the story of mission the Triune God is at work as the *Sovereign God*, working all things together for his own glory and our good.

The *Mission as the Fulfillment of the Divine Promise* framework describes the work of God as fulfilling his promise as the covenant God of faithfulness to Abraham and David. Built upon the role of biblical covenants in the Scriptures, this motif begins with God's covenant promise to Abraham, confirmed in his sons and the patriarchs, and later identified with the tribe of Judah. This covenant promise for a Seed who would bless the nations was amplified and clarified in the promise to David to have a perpetual heir on his throne. Now in this age and in the person of Jesus of Nazareth, the promise of Abraham and David has been fulfilled. Likewise, in this age through the proclamation of the Gospel in mission, the promise of new life is offered to the nations through the preaching of the cross.

Resources and Bibliographies

If you are interested in pursuing some of the ideas of *The Vision and Biblical Foundation for Christian Mission: Part 1*, you might want to give these books a try:

Bartholomew, Craig G., and Michael W. Goheen. *The Drama of Scripture: Finding Our Place in the Biblical Story*. Grand Rapids: Baker Academic Books, 2004.

Goldsworthy, Graeme. *According to Plan: The Unfolding Revelation of God in the Bible*. Downers Grove, IL: InterVarsity Press, 2002.

Roberts, Vaughan. *God's Big Picture: Tracing the Story-Line of the Bible*. Downers Grove, IL: InterVarsity Press, 2003.

------. *Life's Big Questions: Six Major Themes Traced Through the Bible*. Downers Grove, IL: InterVarsity Press, 2005.

1

Your ability to apply the motifs and perspectives of the Scriptures to your own life and ministry will condition your ability to make these motifs plain to others. The drama of Scripture, the vision of God's promise and its fulfillment in Christ, is for you first, before you think about expressing, declaring, or inviting others to experience its truth and life giving power. Meditate upon these truths, and ask the Holy Spirit to direct you to a real practical ministry connection—one which you will think about and pray for throughout this next week. God does not merely want you to think about the drama of God; rather, he wants you to *live it*. Correspondingly, God does not merely want you to read of the promise and its fulfillment in Jesus; he wants you to *claim it* with all your heart. Ask the Holy Spirit to apply these truths and perspectives to your life, and yield yourself to him to lead you as you meditate upon these truths this week.

Ministry Connections

Pray to the Lord for strength to understand and apply these truths to your own life, and in the lives of your fellow students. Remember, the goal is that we would be completely compelled by the story, and that we would see ourselves as a part of the promise fulfilled in Christ. Pray to the Lord that these truths will take on a new significance in your life and ministry, and that the Spirit would help you to see the Bible as a single unfolding story, the story of God's work in the world, and our place as characters in that story. Pray that the Lord might help you get a greater sense of the unity of the Bible, of the power of the OT as preparation for the work of Christ, and as mission as the expression of the unity between what God promised in the OT and what he fulfilled in the NT in Christ. Above all, ask the Lord to make these truths come alive in your life as you seek the mind of God through your ongoing study and application of the Scriptures.

Counseling and Prayer

ASSIGNMENTS

Hebrews 6.17-18

Scripture Memory

To prepare for class, please visit *www.tumi.org/books* to find next week's reading assignment, or ask your mentor.

Reading Assignment

Other Assignments

In order to ensure that your module study is successful, you will need to set aside time to spend on your upcoming assignments, including your review of this week's material in preparation for your reading assignment.

In the next class session, you will be quizzed on the content (the *video teaching* content and outline) of this week's material. Make sure that you spend time covering your notes, especially focusing on the main ideas of the lesson. Also, please complete your assigned reading, and summarize your reading with no more than a paragraph or two for each assignment. Your summary should be your reaction and best response to what you saw to be the main point in each of the readings. Do not be overly concerned about giving detail; simply write out what you consider to be the main point discussed in that section of the book. Please bring these summaries to class next week. (Please see the "Reading Completion Sheet" at the end of this lesson.)

Looking Forward to the Next Lesson

In this lesson we discovered a "prolegomena" for mission: a concise definition of mission is *the proclamation of God's offer of salvation and redemption in the person and work of Jesus Christ in the power of the Holy Spirit to all people groups.* We saw how two motifs, *Mission as the Drama of All Time* and *Mission as the Fulfillment of the Divine Promise* can enable us to see God's working in the world as a single unfolding story. God Almighty, the God of covenant faithfulness, has fulfilled his promise in the person of Jesus of Nazareth, who represents the fulfillment of God's plan and purpose to redeem his creation. Mission is the outworking of that sovereign purpose for his own glory and the salvation of the nations.

In our next lesson, we will continue to explore images of mission in Scripture, viewing God's work of rescue as both *The Romance of God* and *War of the Spheres.* In regard to the romance of God , the Lord has determined to draw out of the world a people for his own possession, and now through Jesus Christ and his Church, the romance motif finds its richest fulfillment. In regard to the warfare motif, God has determined to reestablish his kingdom rule in the person of Jesus of Nazareth. Since the Fall, God has taken the position of warrior to bring the universe back under his rulership. In the person of Jesus of Nazareth, God is reasserting his right to rule over his universe, and mission is the demonstration and proclamation of that kingdom authority, which has now come in Christ.

Capstone Curriculum

Name _____

Date _____

For each assigned reading, write a brief summary (one or two paragraphs) of the author's main point. (For additional readings, use the back of this sheet.)

Reading 1

Title and Author: _____ Pages _____

Reading 2

Title and Author: _____ Pages _____

The Vision and Biblical Foundation for Christian Mission: Part 2

Lesson Objectives

Welcome in the strong name of Jesus Christ! After your reading, study, discussion, and application of the materials in this lesson, you will be able to:

- Lay out the divine romance between God and his people as one of the major motifs of mission in Scripture, that is, God's determination to draw out of the world a people for his own possession, a possession fulfilled and completed in Jesus' love for his Church.

- Outline the notion of the bride and bridegroom in the OT, including its connection to the idea of mirth and gladness in Scripture, its use as a basic image of God's relationship to his people (as seen in the book of Song of Solomon), and the way in which God's relationship with his people matured, from the pitiful origins of Israel to its judgment and exile by God due to her unfaithfulness.

- Detail the remnant's return to the land, from Cyrus' decree for the remnant to return, its actual reentry into the land through Ezra, Zerubbabel, and Nehemiah, and God's promise for a new covenant, not based on their obedience and faithfulness but rather his writing his law on their hearts and giving them a new spirit. Ultimately, his people would be restored to God, who would dance and rejoice over his people like a bridegroom over a bride.

- Trace some of the major hints of the promise of a new covenant given in the OT, including the Abrahamic covenant and its prospect of Gentile inclusion, and show how with Jesus, the bride metaphor is extended and completed. Jesus becomes the source and life of the Church, his new bride, with John the Baptist being the friend of the bridegroom.

- Show how the idea of God's people was revealed through the disclosure of the mystery revealed through the apostles and prophets, that Gentiles are fellow heirs with the Jews in the new covenant promise of God, and through it, are welcomed as members of God's new humanity and Christ's bride.

- List the major doctrinal points associated with Gentile inclusion in the bride of Christ, including their welcome through faith, the resolution of the issue at the Jerusalem Council, the power of the blood of Christ to include them in the covenant, how the heart of apostolic ministry is preparing God's people as a bride, whom Christ will receive at his coming blameless in his sight.

• Detail how the divine romance will be consummated with the coming of the New Jerusalem from heaven, the dwelling place of God and his people, who will totally identify with Christ, the bridegroom, in being made like him, becoming joint-heirs with him, being in his presence forever as his co-regent.

• Draw out the main implications of the divine romance, including God's desire to draw from all nations a people for his own, a drawing that includes both Jews and Gentiles, and therefore mission is the testimony that God is drawing members of his kingdom community from both the Jews and Gentiles who will live with him forever.

• Outline the motif of *Mission as the War of the Spheres*, which is perhaps the most dynamic image of mission in Scripture, the proclamation of God's kingdom rule in the person of Jesus of Nazareth.

• Give an overview of the reign of God in Scripture, beginning with the Lord as creator and sustainer of all, and the mystery of iniquity (the satanic rebellion in the heavenlies), which resulted in the temptation and fall of humankind, and the curse, yet ended with God's promise to crush the head of the serpent through the Seed of the woman. As a result of the Fall, the universe is at war and God is a warrior.

• Lay out the major points of God as the divine warrior in the OT, including God as warrior defeating evil in its symbolism as a river and sea, defeating Pharaoh and his armies, who led his people into victory as the great Lord of armies, and who fought against his own people because of their disobedience and rebellion. Also, Israel's prophets pictured God as a divine warrior who through his Messiah would finally destroy all evil once and for all time.

• Show how the promise of the Messiah in David's heir represented God's intent to provide a king who would restore the reign to his people, rule the nations with justice and righteousness, and bring a knowledge of God to the entire earth as Lord and King.

- Argue from Scripture how God's promised rule has been inaugurated through the person and work of Jesus Christ, who is the one from the Davidic line who will restore the reign of God. In him and the various aspects of his birth, teaching, miracles, exorcisms, deeds, death, and resurrection, the Kingdom of God is now here, already present in the life of the Church.

- Explain the "already/not yet dimension" of the Kingdom of God; although the Kingdom of God has come in the fulfillment of the Messianic promise in the person of Jesus, the Kingdom will only be consummated at his Second Coming, when the full and final manifestation will occur. The Church is both sign and foretaste of the Kingdom present today, who is authorized to proclaim and demonstrate the victory of Christ over Satan and the curse as his agent and deputy.

- Draw out the main implications of the *Mission as the War of the Spheres* motif, including the reassertion of God's rule today over his universe in Jesus Christ, God as the warrior who through his anointed One has defeated the power of the devil and the effects of the curse, and how mission through this lens becomes the display and proclamation of the rule of God here and now. Making disciples among all nations is advancing the reign of God by testifying to its coming in the person of Jesus of Nazareth.

Devotion

The Divine Romance

Eph. 5.25-32 - Husbands, love your wives, as Christ loved the Church and gave himself up for her, [26] that he might sanctify her, having cleansed her by the washing of water with the word, [27] so that he might present the church to himself in splendor, without spot or wrinkle or any such thing, that she might be holy and without blemish. [28] In the same way husbands should love their wives as their own bodies. He who loves his wife loves himself. [29] For no one ever hated his own flesh, but nourishes and cherishes it, just as Christ does the church, [30] because we are members of his body. [31] "Therefore a man shall leave his father and mother and hold fast to his wife, and the two shall become one flesh." [32] This mystery is profound, and I am saying that it refers to Christ and the church.

One of the great wonders of Scripture is its deep and profound mysteries which are embedded in the lives and experiences of its great characters. In a real sense this quality of Scripture speaks to its inspiration; great lessons can be gleaned about the nature of God and his relationship with his people from the lessons learned in sync with its chief characters. The example of Adam and Eve, and their union together as man and wife is a symbolic representation of the great unity between Christ and his people, who, amazingly according to this text, is his bride.

What an amazing lesson for us today, one which reveals God's heart for humankind as it has been fulfilled in the Church. Almighty God has determined from the beginning of time to gather from among all peoples a peculiar possession for Jesus of Nazareth. Here this text reveals a profound mystery: at the heart of the universe lies a marvelous cosmic drama, a divine romance, a marvelous and epic true myth and legend of an undying love relationship between an Almighty God, and a people. We are living witnesses of it, and as those who believe in the truth of the Gospel regarding Jesus of Nazareth, we too have actually become a part of that people, called and chosen to live out that drama of the divine romance.

What is the nature of this divine romance? You see it in the Old Testament between God and his people Israel:

> Isa. 62.5 - For as a young man marries a young woman, so shall your sons marry you, and as the bridegroom rejoices over the bride, so shall your God rejoice over you.

Again, we read of the Lord's determination to delight in his people like a bridegroom:

> Isa. 62.4 - You shall no more be termed Forsaken, and your land shall no more be termed Desolate, but you shall be called My Delight Is in Her, and your land Married; for the Lord delights in you, and your land shall be married.

The righteous of the Lord will be adorned as a bride at a wedding–his wedding. (Cf. Isaiah 61.10 : "I will greatly rejoice in the Lord; my soul shall exult in my God, for he has clothed me with the garments of salvation; he has covered me with the robe of righteousness, as a bridegroom decks himself like a priest with a beautiful headdress, and as a bride adorns herself with her jewels.") The God of heaven sees his people as a bride, and himself as her bridegroom and lover.

This same dramatic image is seen most clearly in the drama of Christ and his Church, with our Lord as the bridegroom and the Church as his bride. The following texts give a sampling of the reference of Jesus as the bridegroom of his people:

Matt. 9.15 - And Jesus said to them, "Can the wedding guests mourn as long as the bridegroom is with them? The days will come when the bridegroom is taken away from them, and then they will fast."

John 3.29 - The one who has the bride is the bridegroom. The friend of the bridegroom, who stands and hears him, rejoices greatly at the bridegroom's voice. Therefore this joy of mine is now complete.

Rev. 21.2 - And I saw the holy city, new Jerusalem, coming down out of heaven from God, prepared as a bride adorned for her husband.

The clearest and most direct association occurs in our devotional text itself:

Eph. 5.25-27 - Husbands, love your wives, as Christ loved the church and gave himself up for her, [26] that he might sanctify her, having cleansed her by the washing of water with the word, [27] so that he might present the church to himself in splendor, without spot or wrinkle or any such thing, that she might be holy and without blemish.

According to this text, the love that a man has for his wife should be patterned upon the love that Jesus has for his people. Furthermore, the heart and goal of all apostolic ministry should be the preparation of the people of God for the ceremony and union ahead: "I feel a divine jealousy for you, for I betrothed you to one husband, to present you as a pure virgin to Christ" (2 Cor. 11.2). Christ is building his Church, his sacred company of disciples from all eras, places, and times, those whom he personally purchased for himself, and those who will serve him, with not even the gates of Hades being able to overcome their onslaught (Matt. 16.15-19).

Any of us who have gone to a wedding know the difference between the bride as she ordinarily appears over against how she is adorned for the wedding day! In the same way, God is preparing for his Son a bride, a people, a divine assembly who will forever be at his side and who will reign with him in the coming Kingdom.

This makes it simple and easy to understand the role of mission: the task of mission is to gather the remaining souls unto Christ, to fill up that number that has been given to him by his Father (John 6.44). Simply stated, there can be no salvation apart from the people of God in the body of Christ. If there is no Church, there can be no Christianity, no salvation, no hope for this world. An urbanized version of a saying by the great Latin father, Cyprian, makes this even more plain: *"If the Church ain't yo' mama, then God ain't yo' daddy!"* Yes, and amen!

As believers we have been apportioned to the great mystery, the prospect of sharing eternity and the Kingdom with our bridegroom, who also is our Savior and Lord, the Lord Jesus Christ. The means by which we come to acknowledge our connection to him is not apart from the Church, but rather, as a part of her, as a member of the Church of God in Jesus. Unfortunately, some people never come to church except for their baptism, their marriage, and their funeral, or, as some might say, when they're *hatched, matched, and dispatched*! In my mind, no informed and biblical Christian can claim intimacy with God and deny and ignore the Church; such a one is confused at best, and perhaps not a Christian, at worst.

To be a Christian is to be a member of the bride of Christ, and be a part of the divine romance. In a real sense, the "two becoming one" will occur at the consummation of all things at the Second Coming, but the Church knows this unity and intimacy now, today. Truly, the Church is utterly connected and integrated into and with the person of Jesus of Nazareth: we enjoy total identification and association with Christ. We are "made one in Christ" (1 Cor. 6.15-17), were baptized into him (1 Cor. 12.13), and died with him in his death on the cross (Rom. 6.3-4). Furthermore, we were buried with him by baptism into death (Rom. 6.3-4), and were raised with him in the resurrection (Eph. 2.4-7). We ascended with him (Eph. 2.6), we are seated with him in heavenly places (Eph. 2.6), and we suffer with him in this life as we serve him (Rom. 8.17-18). Soon, we will be glorified with him (Rom. 8.17), will be resurrected in him (1 Cor. 15.48-49), and will be made like him when we see him at his appearing (1 John 3.2). Then, we will inherit all things with him as joint-heirs with him (Rom. 8.17), and will reign forever with him as his co-regents in the new order (Rev. 3.21). What an extraordinary mystery, indeed, for the "two to become one flesh."

Take your place as a believer in Christ in the company of honored human beings who make up the one, holy, apostolic, Church, the bride of Christ, that sacred company that will rule with Christ in the Kingdom. What a blessing to be a part of the divine romance. The banquet is almost ready.

> Rev. 19.6-8 - Then I heard what seemed to be the voice of a great multitude, like the roar of many waters and like the sound of mighty peals of thunder, crying out, "Hallelujah! For the Lord our God the Almighty reigns. [7] Let us rejoice and exult and give him the glory, for the marriage of the Lamb has come, and his Bride has made herself ready; [8] it was granted her to clothe herself with fine linen, bright and pure"— for the fine linen is the righteous deeds of the saints.

Have you made yourself ready? Will you be there?

Nicene Creed and Prayer

After reciting and/or singing the Nicene Creed (located in the Appendix), pray the following prayer:

God, Almighty Father who chose your servant Abraham and made him faithful to obey your call and to rejoice in your promise that all families on earth would be blessed in him: Grant us so firm a faith that your promises may be fulfilled in us; through Jesus Christ our Lord.

~ The Church of the Province of South Africa.
Minister's Book for Use With the Holy Eucharist and Morning and Evening Prayer.
Braamfontein: Publishing Department of the Church of the Province of South Africa. p. 15

Quiz

Put away your notes, gather up your thoughts and reflections, and take the quiz for Lesson 1, *The Vision and Biblical Foundation for Christian Mission: Part 1.*

Scripture Memorization Review

Review with a partner, write out and/or recite the text for last class session's assigned memory verse: Hebrews 6.17-18.

Assignments Due

Turn in your summary of the reading assignment for last week, that is, your brief response and explanation of the main points that the authors were seeking to make in the assigned reading (Reading Completion Sheet).

The Resurgence of the Image of the Bride

In some quarters of the evangelical church today, there is a resurgence of the bride imagery in the life and worship of the church. However, this resurgence is not applying the symbolic imagery to the corporate body, but to the individual walk with Christ. In order to capture the sense of personal intimacy and connection that this imagery provides, some congregations are focusing nearly exclusively on the motif as a personal thing. For instance, teachers will teach the imagery to individuals about their individual walks with God. Songs of worship and praise are written in light of the believer's personal marriage to Christ, and spirituality is redrawn to discuss these great truths and images in purely private terms. Obviously, this has led to some confusion about the marriage of Christ, and how far (if at all) the symbolic can be connected to individuals. What is your opinion about the personal application of this motif to the walk and life of the individual believer? Is such an application misapplying the symbolism, one which ought to be limited to the people of God and not to us as being personally married to Christ?

The Mystery of Iniquity

Because of the heightened sense of the principalities and powers in some Christian circles, questions abound about the way in which we ought to speak and think about the dark powers mentioned in Scripture. The apostles were careful not to go into great detail regarding the inner workings of the demonic, or exorcisms, or providing instructions on these regions of the shadows; some ministries today, however, seem to specialize in this focus. Seeking to understand some of these highly developed demonologies and strategies to overcome the dark powers, many Christians become overwhelmed in their personal walks with a near preoccupation with the demonic, and its influence in their lives. Others, being afraid of this kind of over-emphasis, ignore altogether the frequent mention and reporting of the encounters of Christ and the apostles with the demonic. In light of our warfare with the rulers and principalities, what ought to be our perspective on the dark powers which Paul says we wrestle with in our Christian walk (cf. Eph. 6.11ff.)? How should we approach the description and appropriate Christian response to Satan, the demonic, and evil in general?

The Heart of Apostolic Ministry

The heart of apostolic ministry according to Paul is to prepare the people of God for the upcoming marriage to Christ (2 Cor. 11.2). The people of God are in fact the bride of Christ, being prepared by him to be a faultless and beautiful bride, a people without spot or wrinkle (Eph. 5), in every way outfitted for the great day of union and consummation when the people of God meet him and never leave his side (1 Thess. 4.13-17). In a real sense, all mission and ministry has a peculiar eschatological flavor: all evangelism adds to the number of the Lamb's bride who will inhabit the New Jerusalem, and all disciple making is preparing and readying the people of God for the great union and marriage of the Lamb (Rev. 19). How does or should it affect and influence our understanding of ministry to see it through the lens of feeling a divine jealousy for those whom we serve, of betrothing the people of God to one husband, to present them as a pure virgin to Christ (2 Cor. 11.2)? How might it impact our perspective and practice if we saw mission and ministry as the attempt to prepare God's people for the upcoming union with Christ? Is it too abstract, too symbolic, or is it dramatically empowering and clarifying?

The Vision and Biblical Foundation for Christian Mission: Part 2

Segment 1: Mission as the Romance of the Ages

Rev. Dr. Don L. Davis

Summary of Segment 1

The divine romance between God and his people is one of the major motifs of mission in Scripture, that is, God's determination to draw out of the world a people for his own possession, a possession fulfilled and completed in Jesus' love for his Church. The notion of the bride and bridegroom in the OT is prominent, related to idea of social union, mirth, and gladness in Scripture, as well as its use as a basic image of God's relationship to his people (as seen in the book of Song of Solomon). Ultimately, his people would be restored to God, who would dance and rejoice over his people like a bridegroom over a bride. Clues for the hope and promise of a new covenant are included in God's covenant with Abraham, and its prospect of Gentile inclusion. In the person of Jesus, the bride-bridegroom metaphor is extended and completed. Jesus has now become the source and life of the Church, his new bride, and John the Baptist, his forerunner, has become the friend of the bridegroom. The mystery of the body has now been revealed through the apostles and prophets, that Gentiles are fellow heirs with Jews in the new covenant promise of God, and through it, are welcomed as members of God's new humanity and Christ's bride. The divine romance will be consummated with the coming of the New Jerusalem from heaven, the dwelling place of God and his people, who will totally identify with Christ the bridegroom in being made like him, becoming joint-heirs with him, in his presence forever, as his co-regent. Mission, therefore, is the work of sharing this message of God's selecting a people from all nations who by faith in Jesus Christ form the members of his kingdom community who will live with him forever.

Our objective for this segment, *Mission as the Romance of the Ages*, is to enable you to see that:

- The divine romance between God and his people is one of the major motifs of mission in Scripture, that is, God's determination to draw out of the world a people for his own possession, a possession fulfilled and completed in Jesus' love for his Church.

- The notion of the bride and bridegroom in the OT is prominent, related to idea of social union, mirth, and gladness in Scripture, as well as its use as a basic image of God's relationship to his people (as seen in the book of Song of Solomon).

2

- The concept of Israel as the bride of God begins with God's relationship with Israel in its pitiful and neglected origins, to God's gracious selection, courtship, and marriage, Israel's adulterous faithlessness with idolatry and injustice, to God's judgment and exile upon both Israel (the Northern Kingdom), and Judah (the Southern Kingdom).

- The return of God's people to the land began with Cyrus' decree and permission to reenter the land, which was carried out through Ezra, Zerubbabel, and Nehemiah. God promised his people he would make a new covenant with them, not based on their obedience and faithfulness but rather his writing his law on their hearts and giving them a new spirit. Ultimately, his people would be restored to God, and he would one day dance and rejoice over his people like a bridegroom over a bride.

- Clues for the hope and promise of a new covenant are included in God's covenant with Abraham, and its prospect of Gentile inclusion. In the person of Jesus, the bride-bridegroom metaphor is extended and completed. Jesus has now become the source and life of the Church, his new bride, and John the Baptist, his forerunner, has become the friend of the bridegroom.

- The *make-up* of God's people was revealed through the disclosure of the mystery revealed through the apostles and prophets, that Gentiles are fellow heirs with the Jews in the new covenant promise of God, and through it, are welcomed as members of God's new humanity and Christ's bride.

- All Gentiles (like Jews) are welcomed into the body and bride of Christ by faith, washed in his blood and included in God's Church. Gentiles need not renounce their cultural identity as clarified at Jerusalem Council (cf. Acts 15), and now the heart of all apostolic ministry is preparing God's people as a bride, whom Christ will receive at his coming, blameless in his sight.

- The divine romance will be consummated with the coming of the New Jerusalem from heaven, the dwelling place of God and his people, who will totally identify with Christ, the bridegroom in being made like him, becoming joint-heirs with him, being in his presence forever as his co-regent.

• For mission, the main implications of the divine romance are these: God is drawing from all nations a people for his own, which includes both Jews and Gentiles. Mission, therefore, is the work of sharing this message of God's selecting a people from all nations who by faith in Jesus Christ form the members of his kingdom community who will live with him forever.

Video Segment 1
Outline

I. **Mission as the *Romance of the Ages*: God's Resolve and Desire to Draw Out from among the Nations a People Which Would Belong to and Serve Him Forever**

. . . .

The Covenantal Union between God and His People

The NT takes up the OT theme of the covenant between God and humanity as the framework within which the Christian's and the church's relationship with God through Christ is understood. Christians are united with him in a covenant relationship grounded on better promises and a surer foundation through Christ's work on our behalf. The marriage picture, used by some OT prophets to describe God's covenant with his people, is taken over in the NT and applied to Christ (the Bridegroom) and the church (his bride). This underlines the nature of the covenant union as one of committed mutual love, respect, trust and faithful allegiance. (Other family-relationship pictures are also used, as father/son, and the older brother and other children.) The Puritans, among others, especially loved this theme.

~ J. P. Baker. "Union With Christ." The New Dictionary of Theology. S. B. Ferguson, ed. (electronic ed.) Downers Grove, IL: InterVarsity Press, 2000. p. 698.

. . . .

A. The notion of the bride and the bridegroom in OT use

1. "Bride" and "bridegroom" are used together in a connected way in John 3.29.

2

2.   Occurrences of the words appear together in a number of texts, always connected to the idea of the "voice of mirth and gladness" associated with the idea of marital joy (cf. Isa. 62.5; Jer. 7.34; 16.9; 25.10; 33.11; Rev. 18.23).

3.   A basic image and picture of God's relationship to his people: the Lord is the husband of his people, Isa. 54.5.

4.   The Lord chose his people Israel, not because of their greatness or wealth, but because of his deep love for them, his desire for them to be his special people, Deut. 7.6-10.

   a.   Exod. 19.5-6

   b.   Deut. 14.2

   c.   Deut. 26.19

   d.   Deut. 28.9

   e.   Amos 3.2

B.   The call of love: the Lord's kindness to his people; Ezek. 16

   1.   The pitiful origins of Israel, Ezek. 16.1-5, cf. Ezek. 16.5

2. God's mercy and cherishing of Israel until she became beautiful and advanced to royalty, Ezek. 16.8-14, cf. Ezek. 16.13-14

3. Israel trusted in her beauty and played the whore with many suitors, whoever they were, Ezek. 16.15-22.

4. Israel's illicit relations with Egypt, the Assyrians, and the Chaldeans, Ezek. 16.23-34, cf. Ezek. 16.30-32

5. God's judgment on his adulterous people, Israel, Ezek. 16.35-43, Ezek. 16.42-43

C. The breakup: the faithlessness of God's people

1. Israel abandoned its love for God, although God never abandoned his love for her, Jer. 2.2.

2. The covenant promise of Israel to God was heartily agreed to, showing devotion and love to God as a husband.

   a. Exod. 24.3-8

   b. Hos. 3.1

3. Because of the lack of faithfulness of his people, God had to punish them (he sent his people into exile for punishment).

   a. Isa. 63.7-10

b. Lam. 1.1-8

4. God viewed Israel as a treacherous wife who leaves her husband without cause.

   a. Isa. 54.6

   b. Jer. 3.20

5. God pleaded with his people to return to him.

   a. Jer. 3.1

   b. Jer. 3.8

   c. Jer. 3.14

6. When God's people refused to return to him, he sent them into exile.

   a. The Northern Kingdom, Israel, sent into captivity and exile by the Assyrians, 720 B.C.E.

      (1) 2 Kings 15.29

      (2) Isa. 10.5-6

b. The Southern Kingdom, Judah, sent into captivity and exile by the Babylonians in 588 B.C.E.

    (1) 2 Kings 25.8-9

    (2) 2 Chron. 36.18

c. The seventy years of Judah's captivity lasts from the period when the temple was destroyed (2 Kings 25.9) to the complete restoration (Ezra 6.15).

D. The bride returns to the land

    1. Cyrus grants permission for the remnant of the Jews to return to their own land.

       a. Ezra 1.5

       b. Ezra 7.13

    2. Many belonging to the kingdom of Israel joined this remnant under Ezra, Zerubbabel, and Nehemiah to Jerusalem (Jer. 50.4-4, 17-20, 33-35).

E. The promise for a new covenant of love

    1. Hos. 2.19-20

2

2. God would satisfy his wrath and restore his people to their position of mercy and prominence.

    a. Isa. 40.1-2

    b. Ezek. 39.29

    c. Isa. 54.9-10

3. God promises to make a new covenant with his people, not based on their obedience and faithfulness to their vows, but he would write his law upon their hearts, Jer. 31.31-34.

4. Dancing and rejoicing over his people like a bridegroom over a bride, God and his people (cf. Song of Solomon), Isa. 62.5

II. Hints of a New Covenant: Messiah Jesus as the Bridegroom of the Lord

A. The Abrahamic Covenant and Gentile inclusion

1. God's covenant with Abraham includes the blessing of all the families of the earth, Gen. 12.1-3.

2. Gentiles will have the light of God shine on them, Isa. 9.1-2.

B. The entrance of Jesus: hail to the Jewish Messiah!

1. The calling of the Twelve as a kind of new 12 tribes, cf. Mark 3.14

2. Messiah Jesus, the source and life of the Church, Matt. 16.13-19, cf. Matt. 16.17-18

3. The Jews were expecting a Messiah which would deliver God's people Israel, cf. John 4.22, Isa. 12.6; 46.13; Zeph. 3.16; Zech. 9.9.

4. Definition of the Church

    a. *Ekklesia* - (Gk. "To call out from") 111 times in the NT

        (1) "Assembly," cf. Acts 19.39, 7.38

        (2) "Called out ones," cf. Rom. 8.30; 1 Cor. 1.2, 2 Cor. 6.17

    b. *Kuriakon* - (Gk. "That which belongs to the Lord")

        (1) "The supper of the Lord," 1 Cor. 11.20

        (2) "The Day of the Lord," Rev. 1.10

C. A Jewish romance novel?: Messiah Jesus as the bridegroom and now, the *Church as his bride*!

1. Messiah Jesus is the bridegroom (John the Baptist is the best man!), John 3.29.

2. The Kingdom of heaven is like a king who prepares a wedding feast for his son (but none invited determine to attend), Matt. 22.1-14.

    a. Many were invited but were filled with excuses.

    b. In order to fill up the banquet, they were sent to others who gladly came (the Gentiles?).

3. The Good News was given to the Jews (and they expected that Messiah Jesus had come for them, and them alone).

    a. Rom. 9.4-5

    b. Acts 1.6

4. The prophetic promise of Messiah was perceived by the apostles as a Jewish revelation for Jews alone.

    a. Jer. 23.5-6

    b. Jer. 33.15-16

    c. Ezek. 37.24

    d. Joel 3.16

D. The "mystery" revealed: Gentiles are fellow heirs with Jews in the new covenant promise of God! (three citations in the NT)

Through the revelation of God, he has now made known through the prophets and apostles that Gentiles are to be included into this New Bride of the new covenant by faith in Jesus Christ!

1. The Romans citation: *all nations now are invited to respond to the Good News of salvation given to the Jews*, Rom. 16.25-27.

2. The Ephesians citation: *Gentiles are fellow heirs and members of the same body*, Eph. 3.4-10.

3. The Colossians citation: *Christ among the Gentiles, the hope of glory*, Col. 1.24-29

E. The Gospel is now proclaimed to the Gentiles, who with the Jews, have become a part of God's new humanity and Christ's bride.

1. Those who believe are included in the promise of God to Abraham, Gal. 3.7-9.

2. The apostles at the Jerusalem council recognize that the prophets foresee that the Gentiles would also call upon the name of the Lord, Acts 15.13-18.

3. Gentiles who were foreigners to the promise of God are now included within God's covenant people by faith in the blood of Christ, Eph. 2.12-13, Rom. 9.24-26.

2

4. The very heart of apostolic ministry now is to prepare the people of God (including the Gentiles) as a bride for the Lord Jesus, 2 Cor. 11.2.

5. Christ is preparing his people, both Jews and Gentiles, to become his very own bride at his appearing, Eph. 5.25-27.

    a. He is sanctifying his bride with the Word of truth, John 17.17-19; Acts 26.18; 1 Cor. 6.11; Titus 2.14.

    b. We who believe, both Jews and Gentiles, will be presented blameless and holy in his sight, 2 Cor. 4.14; Col. 1.22; 2 Cor. 11.2; Jude 1.24.

F. The romance consummated: the New Jerusalem, the City of God, Rev. 21.1-4

- -

Imagination and Revelation Connected

A biblically Christian conception of imagination will distinguish imagining from perceptual error, from imaging and from being an oracle of truth. Imaginative human activity is quite distinct from sensing or thinking but is also a bona fide activity interrelated with all human functioning. Imagining is a gift of God with which humans make-believe things. With imagining ability one pretends and acts 'as if' this is that (e.g. God is a rock, Isa. 17.10; Christ is a bridegroom, Matt. 25.1–13). Human imagination is the source of metaphorical knowledge and the playfulness so important to anyone's style of life. Imagination is meant to be an elementary, important, residual moment in everything God's adopted children do. Imagination becomes a curse only if it becomes an exercise in vanity.

~ C. Seerveld. "Imagination." **The New Dictionary of Theology**. S. B. Ferguson, ed. (electronic ed.). Downers Grove: InterVarsity Press, 2000. p. 331.

- -

1. The image of the City of God as a bride is clear, Rev. 21.2.

2. Only those properly dressed will be invited to attend, Rev. 19.7-8.

3. We will share with Christ by being one with him in all things, Eph. 5.30-32.

4. Our joy will be complete, for the consummation will be our forever union with him (*our total identification with our bridegroom, Messiah Jesus*).

    a. We are made one in Christ, 1 Cor. 6.15-17.

    b. We were baptized into him, 1 Cor. 12.13.

    c. We died with him, Rom. 6.3-4.

    d. We were buried with him, Rom. 6.3-4.

    e. We were raised with him, Eph. 2.4-7.

    f. We are ascended with him, Eph. 2.6.

    g. We sit with him in heavenly places, Eph. 2.6.

    h. We suffer with him, Rom. 8.17-18.

2

i.   We will be glorified with him, Rom. 8.17.

j.   We will be resurrected in him, 1 Cor. 15.48-49.

k.   We will be made like him, 1 John 3.2.

l.   We are joint-heirs with him, Rom. 8.17.

m. We will forever be with him, 1 Thess. 4.17.

n.   We will reign forever with him, Rev. 3.

III. Implications of Mission as the *Romance of the Ages*

A. God's desire is to draw from all the nations, including Gentiles, a people who will belong to him forever.

1. This was in fulfillment of the Scriptures regarding Messiah, Luke 24.45-47.

2. This proclamation of Jew and Gentile salvation was to begin with the Jews, but be proclaimed to the ends of the earth, Acts 1.8; cf. Acts 2.32ff; 3.15-16; 4.33; Acts 8.5-35; Rom. 10.18; 15.19.

B. God has a heart for all human beings, not just his people Israel: this is the central vision of the divine romance of God.

   1. Ps. 22.27

   2. Isa. 52.10

   3. Rom. 10.18

C. *Mission is the testimony to all the nations that the God of the Jews is the God of the Gentiles also!*, Rom. 3.29-30.

   1. The Gentiles will be included within God's righteous bride and offer him praise, Rom. 15.9-13.

   2. The mystery is unsealed: Gentiles are fellow heirs and members of the same body: mission delivers the Good News to them, Eph. 3.6.

   3. In the bride of Christ, Jew or Gentile mean nothing for Christ is all, Col. 3.11.

Conclusion

» The kingdom proclamation to the Gentiles extends and expands God's desire to draw out of the earth a people of his own possession.

» By faith in Jesus Christ, now even the Gentiles can participate in God's wonderful design to create a people who will live with him forever.

» Mission is participating in this divine romance, preparing a people who will forever belong to God.

Please take as much time as you have available to answer these and other questions that the video brought out. In this segment we saw how in the motif of *Mission as the Romance of the Ages* God determined to draw from the earth a people that would belong to and serve him forever. Through the mystery revealed through the apostles and prophets, we now see how God has extended the kingdom proclamation to the Gentiles, who have been made fellow heirs and mutual members of the body and bride of Christ. By faith in Jesus Christ, now even the Gentiles can participate in God's wonderful design to create a people who will live with him forever. Mission is participating in this divine romance, preparing a people who will forever belong to God. Understanding the elements of this motif can greatly aid you in understanding what mission seeks to do through its various efforts, so please review the materials just covered using the questions below, and cite Scripture to support your conclusions.

Segue 1

Student Questions and Response

1. Briefly define the motif of *Mission as the Romance of the Ages*. How does the motif of divine romance between God and his people highlight God's determination for himself and his world? Explain.

2. Trace the notion of the bride and bridegroom in the OT. In what sense is this image a prominent idea as it relates to God's relationship to his people? How does the Song of Solomon relate to this theme?

3. Where does the "courtship" between Yahweh and his people begin? In what way was the relationship between God and his people Israel based upon God's gracious selection, courtship, and marriage to her?

4. According to the Scriptures, how did faithless Israel commit "adultery" against the Lord? What did God do as a result of her faithlessness, and how did it affect both the Northern and Southern Kingdoms?

5. Under what secular ruler did the return of God's people to the land begin, and who were the leaders of the people who actually brought the remnant back to Israel to rebuild its walls? What was the nature of God's promise for a new covenant, and upon what would it be based? After the new covenant was ratified, what would be the result for God and his people?

6. List some of the more obvious "clues" given in the OT that Gentiles would have a place in the coming salvation of the Lord. How does the bride-bridegroom metaphor get extended and completed in Jesus and his relationship with his people, the Church? What was John the Baptist's role in this relationship?

7. What is the mystery that was revealed through the apostles and prophets about the *make-up* of God's people, the bride? What then can we say about the believing Gentiles as members of the bride of Christ? How did the Jerusalem Council solidify the place of Gentiles as members of the body and bride of Christ, and what can be said now about the nature of all apostolic ministry?

8. When and where will the divine romance be consummated between God and his people? What is the hope that those who are members of the bridegroom have about their high rank and role in the upcoming Kingdom of God?

9. What are the main implications of this motif of *Mission as the Romance of the Ages* for mission? What does mission seek to do among the nations as related to this message of God's selecting a people for himself?

2

The Vision and Biblical Foundation for Christian Mission: Part 2

Segment 2: Mission as the War of the Spheres

Rev. Dr. Don L. Davis

Summary of Segment 2

The motif of *Mission as the War of the Spheres* is perhaps the most dynamic image of mission in Scripture, and begins with the sovereign rule of Yahweh God as creator and sustainer of all. God's reign was resisted in the rebellion of the mystery of iniquity (i.e., the satanic rebellion in the heavenlies), which resulted in the temptation and fall of humankind, and the curse of creation. God placed hostility between the Seed of the woman and the serpent, and sovereignly and graciously promised to end the rebellion through the Seed of the woman. As a result of the Fall, the universe is at war and God has declared himself at war with the serpent and those who side with him. God displayed himself as divine warrior in his conflict with evil symbolized as a river and the sea, his defeat of Pharaoh and his armies, and the nations of Canaan. Unfortunately, God also had to fight against his own people because of their disobedience and rebellion. In addition, Israel's prophets pictured God as a divine warrior who through his Messiah would finally destroy all evil once and for all time. This Messianic rule has been inaugurated in the person of Jesus, who in his birth, teaching, miracles, exorcisms, deeds, death, and resurrection has brought the Kingdom of God into being. The Kingdom is both "already" and "not yet;" it has already come in Jesus' fulfillment of the Messianic promise but will be consummated at his Second Coming. Today in this world and in our age, the Church of Jesus Christ is both the sign and foretaste of the Kingdom present, indwelt by the Holy Spirit, the pledge of the full inheritance. The Church is now authorized to proclaim and demonstrate the victory of Christ over Satan and the curse as his agent and deputy. Mission proclaims that God is presently reasserting his rule today over his universe in Jesus Christ, and through his agent, the Church.

Our objective for this segment, *Mission as the War of the Spheres*, is to enable you to see that:

- The motif of *Mission as the War of the Spheres* is perhaps the most dynamic image of mission in Scripture, and deals directly with the establishment and proclamation of God's kingdom rule in the person of Jesus of Nazareth.

- A brief overview of the warfare motif in Scripture begins with Yahweh as creator and sustainer of all. At some time in the ancient and distant past, the mystery of iniquity occurred (i.e., the satanic rebellion in the heavenlies), which resulted in the temptation and fall of humankind, and the curse. Still, God placed hostility between the Seed of the woman and the serpent, and sovereignly and graciously promised to crush the head of the serpent through the Seed of the woman. As a result of the Fall, the universe is at war and God has declared himself at war with the serpent and those who side with him.

- Some of the major points of God as divine warrior include the image of God defeating evil symbolized as a river and the sea, as well as God as man-of-war defeating Pharaoh and his armies, and leading his people into victory over the nations of land as the great Lord of armies. Unfortunately, the Lord also had to fight against his own people because of their disobedience and rebellion. Also, Israel's prophets pictured God as a divine warrior who through his Messiah would finally destroy all evil once and for all time.

- Through his promise of the Messiah as the son of David, God revealed his intent to provide a king who would restore the reign to his people, rule the nations with justice and righteousness, and bring a knowledge of God to the entire earth as Lord and King. This Messianic rule has been inaugurated in the person of Jesus, the heir from the Davidic line who is restoring God's reign.

- In the various aspects of Jesus' birth, teaching, miracles, exorcisms, deeds, death, and resurrection, the Kingdom of God is now here, already present in the life of the Church. The Kingdom has already come, and yet is not yet consummated; although the Kingdom has come in the fulfillment of the Messianic promise in the person of Jesus, it will only be consummated at his Second Coming, when the full and final manifestation will occur.

- Today in this world and age, the Church of Jesus Christ is both the sign and foretaste of the Kingdom present, indwelt by the Holy Spirit, the pledge of the full inheritance. The Church is now authorized to proclaim and demonstrate the victory of Christ over Satan and the curse as his agent and deputy.

- The main implications of the *Mission as the War of the Spheres* motif is that God is presently reasserting his rule today over his universe in Jesus Christ, and through his agent, the Church. God is the warrior who through his anointed One has defeated the power of the devil and the effects of the curse. Mission is the display and proclamation of the rule of God here and now, and making disciples among the nations advances the reign of God by testifying to its coming in the person of Jesus of Nazareth.

2

Video Segment 2
Outline

I. Mission as the *War of the Spheres*: God as the Warrior Reestablishing His Kingdom Rule over the Universe

Mission Announces God's War with Idolatry

The fundamental question of theology, 'What do we mean by "God,"' can be answered from a variety of angles by exploring God's various relations to the world and to ourselves. Ironically, the study of idolatry also gives us some insight into the nature of the true God. What constitutes a god? Martin Luther's answer, as he reflected on the first commandment in his larger catechism, was 'whatever your heart clings to and relies upon, that is your God; trust and faith of the heart alone make both God and idol'. We wish to confirm his view, but also to emphasize love and service: a god is that which one loves, trusts and serves above all else. This definition suggests both the possibility and the urgency of making clear the relevance of idolatry to the modern world. In one sense idolatry is the diagnosis of the human condition to which the gospel is the cure. The root problem with humans is not a horizontal 'social' problem (like sexual immorality or greed), but rebellion against and replacement of the true and living God with gods that fail (which lead to these destructive sins). If the story of the human race is a sorry tale of different forms of idolatry, the height of human folly, the Good News is that God reconciles his image-bearers back to himself in Christ. It is no coincidence that the prophets envisage a time when idols will finally be eradicated and replaced by true worship.

~ Brian S. Rosner. "Idolatry." **The New Dictionary of Biblical Theology**. T. D. Alexander, ed.(electronic ed.). Downers Grove, IL: InterVarsity Press, 2001.

A. The Triune God as Sovereign Lord over the heavens and the earth

1. The Lord is the creator and sustainer of all things, and rules all things according to his wisdom, Isa. 40.21-31, cf. Isa. 40.28.

    a. Ps. 33.6

    b. Ps. 104.5-6

    c. Ps. 136.6

    d. Jer. 10.16

2. As Sovereign Lord over all, God's will was supreme in all things among all beings in all places, Ps. 135.6.

a. Ps. 33.11

       b. Ps. 115.3

       c. Dan. 4.35

B. The mystery of iniquity: war in the heavenlies through satanic rebellion, Isa. 14.12-17

    1. At some point in time, after the creation of all things, there was rebellion in heaven fueled by God's creature, Lucifer, the son of the Dawn.

    2. The source of his rebellion was envy toward God as a result of pride, Isa. 14.12-15.

    3. His extraordinary beauty and glory caused him to rebel against the authority of God, Ezek. 28.12-18.

    4. This spiritual rebellion is the root and cause of all other forms of rebellion among human beings today, 1 John 5.19.

C. The Fall as humankind's participation in the rebellion of the spheres: pride, lust, and greed, Gen. 3.1-7

    1. Temptation and disobedience: Eve and the serpent, 2 Cor. 11. 2

2

2. The loss of freedom: the entrance of sin and satanic bondage

3. The absence of wholeness: the inauguration of sickness and reality of death

4. The end of justice: the brokenness and fragmentation of human relationships

D. The *protoevangelium*: the first telling of the Gospel, Gen. 3.15

1. God will place hostility between the serpent's seed and the Seed of the woman.

2. The Seed of the woman will crush the head of the serpent.

3. The serpent will bruise the heel of the Seed of the woman.

4. This is the first telling of the Gospel and the outline of the story: the universe is at war, and God is the warrior.

E. Senses of God's role as divine warrior in the OT

1. In the times before the monarchy, God is viewed as a warrior who defeats the sea or river (Exod. 15.4–10; Judg. 5.19–21; Ps. 68.22–23; Hab. 3.8–15).

a. The sea is a symbol of disorder and chaos, viewed with a kind of unstable, chaotic, even frightening sense.

  b. When God overcomes this enemy, nature returns to life and produces abundant crops, Deut. 23.28; Ps. 68.10–11.

2. God is a warrior, defeating Pharaoh and his armies as they sought to destroy his covenant people, Israel, Exod. 15.3-4.

3. The Psalms reveal the God of Israel to be a God who honors his rule, and will uphold his Davidic king with power and protection (e.g., Pss. 2; 18; 24; 46; 48; 76; 89; 97; 132; 144).

4. The prophets spoke of Yahweh God as a great Lord whose armies he led into battle on behalf of his people and his honor (Isa. 6; Mic. 1.2–4; Zeph. 1.14–18; Joel 2.1–11).

5. As a result of Israel's disobedience and rebellion against God, the Lord through his judgment and the captivity of Israel and Judah became a warrior who fought against his own people.

  a. Jer. 12.7

  b. Jer. 15.14

  c. Lam. 2.3-5

2

6. As Israel's prophets continued to receive revelation about the coming of Messiah, they pictured God as a divine warrior who would engage the powers to come as in Israel's earliest divine warrior poetry (e.g., Isa. 26.16–27.6; 59.15b–20; 63.1–6; Zech. 9.1–17; 14.1–21).

F. The promise of David's son: a King to reign in righteousness

1. God gave a solemn promise through the prophets that he would restore his reign among his people and in the earth, Isa. 9.6-7.

2. The nations would respond to his lordship of justice and peace, Ps. 72.8-11.

3. This King of Israel, who would restore God's righteous rule, would be of David's house, 2 Sam. 7.8ff.

4. The nations of the earth would bow to this exalted ruler whom God enthroned in his authority, Ps. 2; Ps. 110.

5. As an apocalyptic figure, this ruler would rule over the nations as Lord and King, Dan. 2.35-44; Dan. 7.14, 27.

II. God's Rule has been Inaugurated through God's Covenant Promise Culminating in the Person and Work of Jesus Christ.

A. The coming of Jesus of Nazareth is viewed as the Davidic King who would restore the reign of God for Israel.

1. He would rule over the house of Jacob forever, Luke 1.31-33.

2. Jesus came proclaiming the Kingdom of God fulfilled with his appearing, Mark 1.14-15.

3. *Jesus is the Messiah, the prophesied Lord of the Davidic lineage who would restore God's reign in the earth.*

   a. Ps. 132.11

   b. Isa. 16.5

   c. Amos 9.11-12

4. Jesus announced himself as the fulfillment of the Messianic texts heralding the Day of Lord, cf. Luke 4.18-19 with Isa. 61.1-3.

5. In his overcoming of the signs of the curse and the dominion of the devil over people's lives, Jesus demonstrated that in his person the Kingdom had come!, Matt. 12.25-30.

   a. Mark 1.15

   b. Mark 11.10

   c. Luke 10.11

2

    d. Luke 11.20

    e. Luke 16.16

    f. Luke 17.20-21

B. The Kingdom (rule of God) becomes present in Jesus of Nazareth: *the Presence of the Future*

1 John 3.8 - Whoever makes a practice of sinning is of the devil, for the devil has been sinning from the beginning. The reason the Son of God appeared was to destroy the works of the devil.

In every dimension, the life and ministry of Jesus of Nazareth represents the authentic presence of the prophesied Age to Come in the here-and-now, today!

1. His *mission*: to destroy the works of the devil, 1 John 3.8

2. His *birth*: the invasion of God into Satan's dominion, Luke 1.31-33

3. His *message*: the Kingdom's proclamation and inauguration, Mark 1.14-15

4. His *teaching*: kingdom ethics, Matt. 5-7

5. His *miracles*: his kingly authority and power, Mark 2.8-12

6. His *exorcisms*: his defeat of the devil and his angels, Luke 11.14-20

7.   His *life and deeds*: the majesty of the Kingdom, John 1.14-18

8.   His *resurrection*: the victory and vindication of the King, Rom. 1.1-4

9.   His *commission*: the call to proclaim his Kingdom worldwide, Matt. 28.18-20

10. His *ascension*: his coronation, Heb. 1.2-4

11. His *Spirit*: the *arrabon* (surety, pledge) of the Kingdom, 2 Cor. 1.20-22

12. His *Church*: the foretaste and agent of the Kingdom, 2 Cor. 5.18-21

13. His *present session in heaven*: the generalship of God's forces, 1 Cor. 15.24-28

14. His *Parousia* (coming): the final consummation of the Kingdom, Rev. 19.11-19

C. Mission is the proclamation of the Kingdom come in the Lord Jesus.

In Jesus Christ, the Kingdom is both already present, but not yet fulfilled.

1.   The apostles preached in their mission message that Jesus of Nazareth, who was crucified, was the Messiah, Acts 2.32-36.

2. Jesus understood himself as the fulfillment of the Messianic prophecies regarding the suffering Servant of God, Luke 24.26-27, 44-48.

3. The Jesus rejected by the leaders and the nation of Israel has been exalted to the position of the Cornerstone, Acts 4.11-12.

4. Jesus has been granted all authority by God, and is proclaimed as the exalted Lord of all, Matt. 28.18.

    a. Acts 5.30-31

    b. Acts 10.36 - As for the word that he sent to Israel, preaching good news of peace through Jesus Christ (he is Lord of all)

5. The heart of the apostles' message as they traveled and preached the Good News was the *Messianic fulfillment of Jesus Christ and the presence of his kingdom reign*, Acts 28.23, 31.

6. Jesus' rule acknowledged in Church history

    a. *Christus Victum*: Jesus as ultimate sacrifice for sin

    b. *Christus Victor*: Jesus as conquering Lord over God's enemies

    c. *Christus Vicar*: Jesus as exalted Head of his Church

God's Kingdom means the divine conquest over His enemies, a conquest which is to be accomplished in three stages; and the first victory has already occurred. The power of the Kingdom of God has invaded the realm of Satan–the present evil Age. The activity of this power to deliver men from satanic rule was evidenced in the exorcism of demons. Thereby, Satan was bound; he was cast down from his position of power; his power was "destroyed." The blessings of the Messianic Age are now available to those who embrace the Kingdom of God. We may already enjoy the blessings resulting from this initial defeat of Satan. This does not mean that we enjoy the fullness of God's blessings, or that all that is meant by the Kingdom of God has come to us. . . . The Second Coming of Christ is absolutely essential for the fulfillment and consummation of God's redemptive work. Yet God has already accomplished the first great stage in His work of redemption. Satan is the god of This Age, yet the power of Satan has been broken that men may know the rule of God in their lives.

~ George Ladd. **The Gospel of the Kingdom**. Grand Rapids: Wm. B. Eerdmans Publishing Company, 1999. p. 50.

2

. . . .

III. God's Rule Is Invading this Present Evil Age through the Church Militant

A. The empowering presence of the Holy Spirit of God

Eph. 5.18 - And do not get drunk with wine, for that is debauchery, but be filled with the Spirit.

1. The Spirit is the sign of the Kingdom's presence and certainty, 2 Cor. 1.21-22.

2. All believers in Christ have been sealed with the Spirit as a pledge of the future inheritance (i.e., a down payment of the full display of the Kingdom to come, Eph. 1.13; 4.30).

B. The Church as *Sign and Foretaste* of the Kingdom, Eph. 5.25-32

1. Commissioned as his witnesses to the ends of the earth, Acts 1.8

2. Ambassadors of Christ and his Kingdom, 2 Cor. 5.18-21

3. Showcase of God's eschatological glory, 1 Pet. 2.9-10

4. Deputies of Christ's authority, Matt. 28.18-20; 16.18-19

C. God's intent in this present age: to empower and authorize his Church to do battle against his foes, bearing witness to God's rule today

1. Jesus' authority now in heaven and earth is absolute: he has been raised to the position of Lord of all by the Father, cf. Matt. 28.18 with Phil. 2.9-11.

2. The strong man must be bound: Jesus' authority over Satan must be enforced (even though he is defeated), 1 Pet. 5.8 with James 4.7.

3. The Church is the deputy and agent of the Kingdom of God: she has been granted the right and authority to represent Christ's authority in the earth, to do violence against all powers and entities which defy God's knowledge and authority, 2 Cor. 10.3-5.

D. Mission is engagement in the *War of the Spheres*.

    1. Mission is nothing less than the announcement of the coming of God's rule to earth in the midst of the devil's own territory, 1 John 4.4.

    2. Mission proclaims Messiah Jesus as the fulfillment of Messianic prophecy in our day and time, who must reign until all his enemies are under his feet, 1 Cor. 15.24-28.

    3. The Church has been granted authority to use the weapons of God's warfare in their proclamation of the Good News of the Kingdom throughout the world.

E. The weapons of our warfare

2 Cor. 10.3-5 - For though we walk in the flesh, we are not waging war according to the flesh. [4] For the weapons of our warfare are not of the flesh but have divine power to destroy strongholds. We destroy arguments [5] and every lofty opinion raised against the knowledge of God, and take every thought captive to obey Christ.

    1. The whole armor of God, Eph. 6.11

    2. Authority (by identification and organic unity with Christ), Eph. 1.13

    3. The Word of God, Eph. 6.17

    4. The shield of faith, Eph. 6.16

2

5. The blood of Christ and the word of their testimony, Rev. 12.10-11

Mission is nothing less than the insertion of God's shock troops into the enemy territory of the devil. Satanic opposition to Christ's victory and authority will be strong and vicious; only those commissioned with his sovereign Word and kingdom authority can stand in the evil day, Eph. 6.10-18.

F. Soon, God's rule will consummate in the Age to Come at the Second Coming of Jesus Christ, Rom. 16.20.

IV. Implications of Mission as the *War of the Spheres*

A. God's rule over his universe is now being reasserted in the person of Jesus Christ.

1. Jesus of Nazareth is the prophesied Messiah, who has been charged with the responsibility to restore God's rule in the universe, John 1.41-45; Matt. 28.18.

2. As a result of his obedience and death, he has been exalted to the Father's right hand, as Lord over all, Phil. 2.9-11; Eph. 1.20-23; Phil. 3.20-21.

3. As Lord of all, he is the Lord of the harvest (of mission), and is leading his people to victory all over the world as they declare his glory to the nations, Acts 1.8; Matt. 9.35-38; Matt. 28.18-20.

B. God is the warrior whose authority in Messiah Jesus has defeated the powers of the devil and the effects of the curse.

   1. He has openly disarmed and shamed them through the cross, Col. 2.15.

   2. He has granted to his people authority over the evil one by transferring them from the kingdom of darkness to the Kingdom of Christ, Col. 1.13.

C. Mission is the *display and proclamation of the rule of God in operation in the here and now.*

   1. Mission is prophesying deliverance to the captives, Rom. 10.9-10.

   2. We are set free from the bondage of the enemy in Christ, Heb. 2.14-15; 1 John 3.8; 1 John 4.4.

   3. Satan's infernal rebellion has been put down, but he still has power to deceive and persecute, 1 Pet. 5.8; James 4.7.

   4. His doom is sure; nothing can prevent the full restoration of the will of God over all things, Rev. 11.15-18, cf. 15.

D. Making disciples among all nations is *advancing the reign of God by testifying to its coming in the person of Jesus of Nazareth!*

Conclusion

» One of the most intriguing and powerful images of mission in Scripture is the proclamation of God's kingdom rule in the person of Jesus of Nazareth.

» Through the death, burial, and resurrection of Jesus, God has defeated the powers of the devil and rescinded the effects of the curse. Now, in the very life of the Church, the rule of God is present and alive on planet earth.

» The Kingdom is not yet fully consummated, however, and will not be until Christ comes again.

The following questions were designed to help you review the material in the second video segment. In our last section we briefly reviewed what may arguably be considered one of the most integrating and dynamic motifs of mission in the entire Bible: the *Mission as the War of the Spheres* motif which is anchored in the reassertion of the rule of God in the person of Jesus of Nazareth. This motif traces the notion of divine warrior through the Bible, a theme which finds its zenith in the person of Jesus, the Messiah of God. Through the death, burial, and resurrection of Jesus, God has defeated the powers of the devil and rescinded the effects of the curse. Now, in the very life of the Church, the rule of God is present and alive on planet earth. This motif carries special significance for urban communities, which especially are attuned to this kind of ongoing spiritual warfare. Be thorough and complete in your answers to the questions below, and make certain you understand the basic concepts related to this important motif.

1. Why can it be said that the motif of *Mission as the War of the Spheres* may be the most integrating and dynamic image of mission as well as spirituality in the entire Scriptures? How does this motif relate to the idea of the establishment and proclamation of God's kingdom rule in the person of Jesus of Nazareth? Explain.

2. Provide a concise overview of God as the divine warrior motif in Scripture. What does this motif assert about the "mystery of iniquity?" What occurred as a result of the resistance to God's reign in the heavenlies, and what was its result for creation?

3. Why is the *protoevangelium* so important for understanding God's role and identity as a warrior (cf. Genesis 3.15)? How did the mystery of iniquity, the

Segue 2

Student Questions
and Response

2

Fall, and the curse change fundamentally God's relationship with his creation, especially with humankind?

4. How was God's conflict with evil symbolized in the OT? How did God's conflict with Pharaoh and the nations of Canaan help us understand God as divine warrior? Why did God also take up the position of warrior against his own people?

5. How did the prophets of Israel picture the coming of Messiah as an extension of God as a divine warrior, and how would this Messiah finally destroy all evil once and for all time?

6. Briefly lay out the ways in which the promise of the Messiah has been inaugurated in the person of Jesus, the heir from the Davidic line who is restoring God's reign. How do the various aspects of his birth, teaching, miracles, exorcisms, deeds, death, and resurrection show that the promised Kingdom of God is now here, already present in the life of the Church?

7. Explain the way in which the Kingdom of God can be said to be "already present" but "not yet consummated." Why is this distinction important to keep in mind when discussing the work of Jesus Christ in this present age?

8. In what sense can we say that the Church of Jesus Christ today in this age is both the sign and foretaste of the Kingdom present? In what sense is the Holy Spirit, who indwells the Church, providing evidence that the Kingdom of God has in fact arrived in Jesus? What is the Church now authorized to do on behalf of Christ for the sake of the Kingdom?

9. What are the main implications of the *Mission as the War of the Spheres* motif for mission? In light of God reasserting his rule today over his universe in Jesus Christ, what ought missionaries do and how ought they to represent their work and ministries among the lost?

10. Read the Ryken quote on the next page. Why is it important to see these various motifs of God as interrelated and connected, rather than isolated and separate? How does Ryken help us to connect these images as we use them to understand who God is and his actions in the world (which, in fact are the foundations for doing mission today)?

The God of the Promise Is also a God of War

When God appears as the divine warrior in the OT, he most often comes to save his people from their enemies. This happens from the time of the crossing of the Red Sea until late in the history of Israel. The divine warrior theme is closely connected to the idea of covenant in the OT. God reveals himself as king through covenant-treaty and then promises to protect his subject people from danger threatened by their enemies. We can see this in the blessings that flow if the law of the covenant is obeyed. In Deuteronomy 28.7 God the king promises that if Israel obeys him, "The Lord will grant that the enemies who rise up against you will be defeated before you. They will come at you from one direction but flee from you in seven" (NIV). He does this many times in the history of Israel, appearing in a variety of forms and using different means to win the battle. God often uses forces of nature, his own creation, as his weapons. At the crossing of the Red Sea when Israel is saved and Egypt judged, God uses the winds to push back the waters of the Sea to allow Israel safe access to the other side and then collapses the waters to kill the Egyptians (Exod. 14 and 15). Later when Joshua fights against a coalition of southern Canaanite kings, God uses large hailstones to kill the enemy and causes the sun to stop in the sky so there would be more daylight in which to finish the battle (Josh 10.1–15). On other occasions God uses his heavenly army to fight Israel's enemies.

~ Leland Ryken. *The Dictionary of Biblical Imagery.* (electronic ed.)
Downers Grove, IL: InterVarsity Press, 2000. p. 211.

CONNECTION

Summary of Key Concepts

This lesson deals with two of the single most important motifs in all of Scripture, and not merely in relationship to the issue of mission. The motif of *Mission as the Romance of the Ages* and *Mission as the War of the Spheres* touch upon truly significant themes that hold great significance for our understanding of the work of Messiah and of the Church. It could easily be argued that grasping these themes are the central notions for grasping the meaning of not only mission, but the very identity and work of the Church. Therefore, review these concepts carefully, and ensure that you can support them with an appeal to Scripture.

⌐ The divine romance between God and his people is one of the major motifs of mission in Scripture, that is, God's determination to draw out of the world a people for his own possession, a possession fulfilled and completed in Jesus' love for his Church.

- The notion of the bride and bridegroom in the OT is prominent, related to idea of social union, mirth, and gladness in Scripture, as well as its use as a basic image of God's relationship to his people (as seen in the book of Song of Solomon).

- The concept of Israel as the bride of God begins with God's relationship with Israel in its pitiful and neglected origins, to God's gracious selection, courtship, and marriage; Israel's adulterous faithlessness with idolatry and injustice, to God's judgment and exile upon both Israel (the Northern Kingdom), and Judah (the Southern Kingdom).

- The return of God's people to the land began with Cyrus' decree and permission to reenter the land, which was carried out through Ezra, Zerubbabel, and Nehemiah. God promised his people that he would make a new covenant with them, not based on their obedience and faithfulness but rather his writing his law on their hearts and giving them a new spirit. Ultimately, his people would be restored to God, and he would one day dance and rejoice over his people like a bridegroom over a bride.

- Clues for the hope and promise of a new covenant are included in God's covenant with Abraham, and its prospect of Gentile inclusion. In the person of Jesus, the bride-bridegroom metaphor is extended and completed. Jesus has now become the source and life of the Church, his new bride, and John the Baptist, his forerunner, has become the friend of the bridegroom.

- The *make-up* of God's people was revealed through the disclosure of the mystery revealed through the apostles and prophets, that Gentiles are fellow heirs with Jews in the new covenant promise of God, and through it, are welcomed as members of God's new humanity and Christ's bride.

- All Gentiles (like Jews) are welcomed into the body and bride of Christ by faith, washed in his blood and included in God's Church. Gentiles need not renounce their cultural identity as clarified at Jerusalem Council (cf. Acts 15), and now the heart of all apostolic ministry is preparing God's people as a bride, whom Christ will receive at his coming, blameless in his sight.

- The divine romance will be consummated with the coming of the New Jerusalem from heaven, the dwelling place of God and his people, who will totally identify with Christ the bridegroom in being made like him, becoming joint-heirs with him, in his presence forever, as his co-regent.

↪ For mission, the main implications of the divine romance are these: God is drawing from all nations a people for his own, which includes both Jews and Gentiles. Mission, therefore, is the work of sharing this message of God's selecting a people from all nations who by faith in Jesus Christ form the members of his kingdom community who will live with him forever.

↪ The motif of *Mission as the War of the Spheres* is perhaps the most dynamic image of mission in Scripture, and deals directly with the establishment and proclamation of God's kingdom rule in the person of Jesus of Nazareth.

↪ A brief overview of the warfare motif in Scripture begins with Yahweh as creator and sustainer of all. At some time in the ancient and distant past, the mystery of iniquity occurred (i.e., the satanic rebellion in the heavenlies), which resulted in the temptation and fall of humankind, and the curse. Still, God placed hostility between the Seed of the woman and the serpent, and sovereignly and graciously promised to crush the head of the serpent through the Seed of the woman. As a result of the Fall, the universe is at war and God has declared himself at war with the serpent and those who side with him.

↪ Some of the major points of God as divine warrior include the image of God defeating evil symbolized as a river and the sea, as well as God as man-of-war defeating Pharaoh and his armies, and leading his people into victory over the nations of land as the great Lord of armies. Unfortunately, the Lord also had to fight against his own people because of their disobedience and rebellion. Also, Israel's prophets pictured God as a divine warrior who through his Messiah would finally destroy all evil once and for all time.

↪ Through his promise of the Messiah as the son of David, God revealed his intent to provide a king who would restore the reign to his people, rule the nations with justice and righteousness, and bring a knowledge of God to the entire earth as Lord and King. This Messianic rule has been inaugurated in the person of Jesus, the heir from the Davidic line who is restoring God's reign.

↪ In the various aspects of Jesus' birth, teaching, miracles, exorcisms, deeds, death, and resurrection, the Kingdom of God is now here, already present in the life of the Church. The Kingdom has already come, and yet is not yet consummated; although the Kingdom has come in the fulfillment of the Messianic promise in the person of Jesus, it will only be consummated at his Second Coming, when the full and final manifestation will occur.

2

☛ Today in this world and age, the Church of Jesus Christ is both the sign and foretaste of the Kingdom present, indwelt by the Holy Spirit, the pledge of the full inheritance. The Church is now authorized to proclaim and demonstrate the victory of Christ over Satan and the curse as his agent and deputy.

☛ The main implications of the *Mission as the War of the Spheres* motif is that God is presently reasserting his rule over his universe in Jesus Christ, and through his agent, the Church. God is the warrior who through his anointed One has defeated the power of the devil and the effects of the curse. Mission is the display and proclamation of the rule of God here and now, and making disciples among the nations advances the reign of God by testifying to its coming in the person of Jesus of Nazareth.

Student Application and Implications

Now is the time for you to discuss with your fellow students your questions about these important motifs of mission in Scripture. The following questions are designed to help you grapple with the personal implications of this material, so strive to be as transparent as possible as you explore these and other questions related to the material.

* Have you ever studied thoroughly and clearly either the motif of *divine romance* or the *war of spheres* in Scripture, and if so, what were you major conclusions about them? Do either of these provide you with a clear grasp of "what the Bible is getting at," especially in terms of the unity between the Old and New Testaments?

* How important do you think either of these motifs are for the *urban experience*? Why would a breakdown of the family and fidelity in man/woman relationships actually impact whether or not people would find the *divine romance* motif more or less compelling?

* Ought we concentrate only on motifs that people resonate with or like, or should we teach all the major motifs of the Bible, no matter what? Explain thoroughly your answer.

* How does the relationship of Israel with the Lord parallel your own relationship with the Lord? Are you more *like* the Israelites than *unlike* them? Explain how so.

* In what way are we to teach the history of Israel as *our history* for the sake of instruction, learning, and edification? (Cf. 1 Cor. 10.6-11: "Now these things took place as examples for us, that we might not desire evil as they did. [7] Do not be idolaters as some of them were; as it is written, "The people sat down to eat and drink and rose up to play." [8] We must not indulge in sexual immorality as some of them did, and twenty-three thousand fell in a single day. [9] We must not put Christ to the test, as some of them did and were destroyed by serpents, [10] nor grumble, as some of them did and were destroyed by the Destroyer. [11] Now these things happened to them as an example, but they were written down for our instruction, on whom the end of the ages has come.")

* Does the language of the Bible about warfare, conflict, and struggle line up with your own experience as a believer? How ought we to apply this language and symbolism to our own life as disciples of Jesus?

* Are there people in particular that you have not wanted to respond to the Lord? What does it mean to you that God may draw whomever he will at any time an from any place to be a part of his body and bride (cf. John 6.44)?

* Do you think of yourself as a soldier of Jesus Christ, and if not, why not? If you feel comfortable with this imagery, why don't you think it is more prominent and acceptable in our circles today?

* Is it prudent to be using images, metaphors, and symbols of war today, with all of the conflict taking place in the world and the global concern about terrorism? Ought we to de-emphasize these symbols so as not to be misunderstood by others today?

* Do you live as if you believe that the Kingdom of God has been reasserted in the presence of Jesus in the Church? Do you see your own local church as a "sign and foretaste of the Kingdom of God" on earth today? Why or why not?

* Complete the following sentence: "If there was just one thing I could do to make these motifs come alive in my life right now, where I am, it would be . . ."

War Images Not Edifying for Faith

 Although the Bible is abundant with the metaphors, images, symbolism, and mythic outline of cosmic war, of Yahweh as a warrior, and Christ as the great Victor over Satan, death, the curse, and the powers, many modern Christians feel squeamish about them. In a world torn by terrorism, conflict, and war, many sincere Christians do not believe that such imagery and focus is helpful. Rather than pointing to the heart of the Gospel, the love of God expressed in the death of Jesus Christ for the world, such warfare imagery confuses people, imports ideas that are hard to understand in the world today, and even blur the overall vision of God's compassion for the poor and the oppressed. Others (equally sincere and biblical) feel that to ignore or overlook the biblical emphasis on spiritual warfare is to miss perhaps the most commanding and important motif for understanding the spiritual world given in Scripture. These who see the value of warfare images would affirm that we do not fight against human beings, but for them against those powers which would seek to destroy them: "For we do not wrestle against flesh and blood, but against the rulers, against the authorities, against the cosmic powers over this present darkness, against the spiritual forces of evil in the heavenly places" (Eph. 6.12). These images provide us with substantial insight into the world of Christian struggle for good against evil, and we ought to learn from them. Which of these groups are correct in communicating the nature of the Christian faith in today's world: ought we seek for other motifs to understand and communicate the faith in a world torn by war and conflict, or ought we to use them so others can better understand what the nature of the fight really is, and how much is at stake in them understanding and applying these images to their lives?

Over-personalizing the Marriage Motif?

 (Based on a true story). Two missionary sisters, both single, dedicated, and committed disciples of Christ, offered their opinion about the kinds of motifs and themes being emphasized today in the Church. Both are convinced that the emphasis on God as Judge, King, and Maker is far too generic and impersonal to communicate to today's modern urban environment. For them, the idea of the intimate, personal, and affectionate image of Jesus as bridegroom offered the best hope of communicating in the fullest and most contextualized way the heart of God for people today. Both expressed their understanding of the marriage symbolism in the most intimate way, even going so far as to be risque, on the verge of being a little too suggestive and even inappropriate. While they were aware of this possibility,

2

they rejected all claims that this symbolism ought not be appropriated personally for them as singles. After all, this motivation underlies much of the traditional Christian argument for celibacy for sisters who surrender themselves up to Christ and him alone. How would you answer these two dear missionary sisters in regard to this issue? Is the personalization of this symbol appropriate, or should we restrict its usage to the entire people of God as the bride of Christ, and not individuals seeing it as relevant for their personal lives?

Suburban vs. Urban Styles of Spirituality

In regard to the warfare motif of Christian discipleship and mission, one can notice a stark difference between urban and suburban styles of spirituality and battle. Speaking generally, for many suburbans who have attained a measure of affluence and convenience, a major emphasis in their spiritual journey is safety, protection, and security. Often the society is perceived as a evil counter force warring against the positive morals and decency of the nuclear family, and the goal is to conserve these values and belief systems to ensure that the family and neighborhood is kept secure from those forces which would seek to undermine that security. Urban styles of spirituality, on the other hand, tend to highlight the conflict and struggle with the world and its agents. Warfare is embraced as a necessary response to the ever-present evil all around that seeks to destroy and annihilate them. The predisposition of a mature Christian will be constant vigilance and engagement with powers, of struggling to overcome these powers on a daily basis. The assumptions are not rooted in conserving values, but liberating people from oppressive and dangerous structures that hold them in their grasp. With nothing to protect and no affluence to keep, they tend to embrace spiritual motifs which emphasize fighting, engagement, and struggle. What do you make of these different styles—are they simply the result of spiritual journeys based on different contexts, or is there something more fundamental in the different assumptions and their outworking in spiritual life?

Is Christianity a Western Religion?

Unfortunately, many wrongly have associated the entire Christian enterprise with a kind of controlling Euro-centrism that would see Christianity as Western, white, and middle class. Although the strongest and most intense Christian movements are currently third-world and involve people of color, the centers of power and finance for much of the Christian world are still white and western. Most of the seminaries, publishing houses, and church and parachurch organizations are run by those who are European or North American in background, usually white, and with connections of power and means. For many from the outside, then, Christianity does not appear to be a new people of God built on inclusion, equality, diversity, and unity—multi-national and multi-cultural, enjoying one bond in the Spirit. Rather, the body and bride of Christ appears to be Gentile in orientation, and western in domination. These perceptions are undermining our ability to enter into certain societies, which see Christianity as essentially a western, cultural religion; many nations are no longer open to receive Christian missionaries, seeing them as agents of western values and norms, not the representatives of the citizenry of heaven. With the ever increasing animosity towards Christianity and the West, how ought we as mission leaders think about the next generation of communicating Christ across cultures, especially those which are highly suspicious and skeptical of anything western and white?

Restatement of the Lesson's Thesis

The divine romance between God and his people is one of the major motifs of mission in Scripture, that is, God's determination to draw out of the world a people for his own possession, a possession fulfilled and completed in Jesus' love for his Church. The notion of the bride and bridegroom in the OT is prominent, related to idea of social union, mirth, and gladness in Scripture, as well as its use as a basic image of God's relationship to his people (as seen in the book of Song of Solomon). Ultimately, his people would be restored to God, who would dance and rejoice over his people like a bridegroom over a bride. Clues for the hope and promise of a new covenant are included in God's covenant with Abraham, and its prospect of Gentile inclusion. In the person of Jesus, the bride-bridegroom metaphor is extended and completed. Jesus has now become the source and life of the Church, his new bride, and John the Baptist, his forerunner, has become the friend of the bridegroom. The mystery of the body has now been revealed through the apostles and prophets, that Gentiles are fellow heirs with Jews in the new covenant promise of God, and through it, are welcomed as members of God's new humanity and Christ's bride. The divine romance will be consummated with the coming of the New Jerusalem from heaven, the dwelling place of God and his people, who will totally identify with Christ the bridegroom in being made like him, becoming joint-heirs with him, being in his presence forever as his co-regent. Mission, therefore, is the work of sharing this message of God's selecting a people from all nations who by faith in Jesus Christ form the members of his kingdom community who will live with him forever.

The motif of *Mission as the War of the Spheres* is perhaps the most dynamic image of mission in Scripture, and begins with the sovereign rule of Yahweh God as creator and sustainer of all. God's reign was resisted in the rebellion of the mystery of iniquity (i.e., the satanic rebellion in the heavenlies), which resulted in the temptation and fall of humankind, and the curse of creation. God placed hostility between the Seed of the woman and the serpent, and sovereignly and graciously promised to end the rebellion through the Seed of the woman. As a result of the Fall, the universe is at war and God has declared himself at war with the serpent and those who side with him. God displayed himself as divine warrior in his conflict with evil symbolized as a river and the sea, and in his defeat of Pharaoh and his armies and the nations of Canaan. Unfortunately, God also had to fight against his own people because of their disobedience and rebellion. In addition, Israel's prophets pictured God as a divine warrior who through his Messiah would finally destroy all evil once and for all time.

This Messianic rule has been inaugurated in the person of Jesus, who in his birth, teaching, miracles, exorcisms, deeds, death, and resurrection has brought the Kingdom of God into being. The Kingdom is both "already" and "not yet;" its has already come in Jesus' fulfillment of the Messianic promise but will be only be consummated at his Second Coming. Today in this world and age, the Church of Jesus Christ is both the sign and foretaste of the Kingdom present, indwelt by the Holy Spirit, the pledge of the full inheritance. The Church is now authorized to proclaim and demonstrate the victory of Christ over Satan and the curse as his agent and deputy. Mission proclaims that God is presently reasserting his rule over his universe in Jesus Christ, and through his agent, the Church.

Resources and Bibliographies

If you are interested in pursuing some of the ideas of *The Vision and Biblical Foundation for Christian Mission: Part 2*, you might want to give these books a try:

Costas, Orlando E. *Christ Outside the Gate: Mission Beyond Christendom.* Maryknoll, NY: Orbis Books, 1982.

Curtis, Brent, and John Eldredge. *The Sacred Romance: Drawing Closer to the Heart of God.* Nashville: Nelson Books, 1997.

Jones, E. Stanley. *Is the Kingdom of God Realism?* New York: Abingdon-Cokesbury, 1940.

Newbigin, Lesslie. *Sign of the Kingdom.* Grand Rapids: Eerdmans, 1980.

Yoder, John Howard. *The Politics of Jesus.* Grand Rapids: Eerdmans, 1972.

Ministry Connections

Ask God the Holy Spirit to help you so meditate on the motifs covered in this lesson that you may find real and practical ministry connections in your own life and ministry. Select one or more key themes and ideas to think about and pray for throughout this next week, and be open to the Spirit's leading about specific ways you can better understand and apply the meaning of these motifs to your teaching, preaching, and testimony.

Counseling and Prayer

Seek the Lord together with your classmates in prayer for one another and the things God has revealed in this material. Also, make a commitment to spend extended times of prayer with the Lord, both alone and if possible with others during the week. Extended time of prayer is key to the application of truth and the transformation of one's life before the Lord. E. M. Bounds makes this point plain:

> *While many private prayers, in the nature of things, must be short; while public prayers, as a rule, ought to be short and condensed; while there is ample room for and value put on ejaculatory prayer — yet in our private communions with God time is a feature essential to its value. Much time spent with God is the secret of all successful praying. Prayer which is felt as a mighty force is the mediate or immediate product of much time spent with God. Our short prayers owe their point and efficiency to the long ones that have preceded them. The short prevailing prayer cannot be prayed by one who has not prevailed with God in a mightier struggle of long continuance. Jacob's victory of faith could not have been gained without that all-night wrestling. God's acquaintance is not made by pop calls. God does not bestow his gifts on the casual or hasty comers and goers. Much with God alone is the secret of knowing him and of influence with him. He yields to the persistency of a faith that knows him. He bestows his richest gifts upon those who declare their desire for and appreciation of those gifts by the constancy as well as earnestness of their importunity. Christ, who in this as well as other things is our Example, spent many whole nights in prayer. His custom was to pray much. He had his habitual place to pray. Many long seasons of praying make up his history and character. Paul prayed day and night. It took time from very important interests for Daniel to pray three times a day. David's morning, noon, and night praying were doubtless on many occasions very protracted. While we have no specific account of the time these Bible saints spent in prayer, yet the indications are that they consumed much time in prayer, and on some occasions long seasons of praying was their custom.*

> ~ E. M. Bounds. **Power Through Prayer**. (electronic ed.). Oak Harbor, WA: Logos Research Systems, 1999.

Make a commitment throughout this module to pray long over your own heart, the requests of your fellow students, and open prayers to the Lord about his leading and these truths in your life.

2

Ephesians 5.25-27 and Ephesians 6.10-13

Scripture Memory

To prepare for class, please visit *www.tumi.org/books* to find next week's reading assignment, or ask your mentor.

Reading Assignment

Please read carefully the assignments above, and as last week, write a brief summary for them and bring these summaries to class next week (please see the "Reading Completion Sheet" at the end of this lesson). Also, now is the time to begin to think about the character of your ministry project, as well as decide what passage of Scripture you will select for your exegetical project. Do not delay in determining either your ministry or exegetical project. The sooner you select, the more time you will have to prepare!

Other Assignments

In this lesson we explored two motifs, the *divine romance* and the *war of the spheres*, and considered their implications for understanding the role of the Church's mission today. We saw how God's desire to draw out of the earth a people for his own possession included even the Gentiles, who now by faith can participate in God's wonderful design to create a people who will live with him forever. We also saw how God is reasserting his kingdom rule in the person of Jesus of Nazareth, whose death, burial, and resurrection defeated the powers of the devil and rescinded the effects of the curse. Now, in the very life of the Church, the rule of God is present and alive on planet earth.

Looking Forward to the Next Lesson

In our next lesson we will further look at aspects of the foundation of Christian mission, concentrating upon one of its more important objects of consideration: the city. In our next lesson we will consider the spiritual significance of the city, and God's adoption of its as symbol for his own purposes, transforming it from an image of rebellion and idolatry to his dwelling place above. Building on this understanding, we'll explore three critical reasons why urban mission is critical for us today. The city as the seat of influence, power, and spiritual activity in the world, is becoming a magnet for the oppressed, the broken, and the poor, and is seen as the picture of our spiritual destiny and inheritance. These three reasons offer a compelling biblical case for us to do all we can to evangelize, disciple, and plant churches in our cities, both at home and abroad.

2

Name _____

Date _____

For each assigned reading, write a brief summary (one or two paragraphs) of the author's main point. (For additional readings, use the back of this sheet.)

Reading 1

Title and Author: _____ Pages _____

Reading 2

Title and Author: _____ Pages _____

LESSON
3

Christian Mission and the City

Lesson Objectives

Welcome in the strong name of Jesus Christ! After your reading, study, discussion, and application of the materials in this lesson, you will be able to:

- Define the concept of the city from the Bible, including the fact that cities were a collection of houses and buildings surrounded by walls, were significant and impressive for their time, and that some were dependent for protection and supply upon others. Cities, common in the ancient world, were relatively small, typically unpaved, strengthened by thick walls and high towers, and seats of government and power.

- Lay out the spiritual meaning of the city, that is, the ways in which cities were associated with human rebellion and idolatry (*Enoch*, the city of Cain), with independence and arrogance (as in the case of the Tower of Babel), and with evil and godlessness (as with Babylon). Cities were judged by God for their sinfulness (e.g., Sodom and Gomorrah, Jericho, Nineveh), and denounced for their false sense of security and power (specifically, Jerusalem).

- Show how God adopted the city as symbol of his dwelling place and blessing, i.e., his selection of Jerusalem for himself, and his determination to make her a praise in the earth. Show further the divine irony of God transforming the image of rebellion into an image of refuge (i.e., the cities of Refuge), as well as the image of a place which can know and experience his forgiveness and blessing (i.e., Jonah and the experience of Nineveh).

- Detail how, because of God's own mercy and graciousness, there can be hope for any city which repents in the face of his judgment, yields in the face of his demands, and seeks his mercy in the face of his punishment.

- Give evidence of the three critical reasons why urban mission must be a priority for all mission activity today. These include the following: the city as the seat of influence, power, and spiritual activity in the world, is becoming a magnet for the oppressed, the broken, and the poor, and is seen as the picture of our spiritual destiny and inheritance.

3

- Show how Jesus' own ministry was rooted in city work, and his proclamation mandate included the preaching of the Kingdom in Jerusalem; also, how Christianity was birthed in a city, and spread through the Roman empire in the first century via the great urban centers of the time (in places such as Damascus, Antioch, Corinth, Philippi, Thessalonica, Athens, and Rome itself). The apostolic ministry (including the Pauline journeys) were urban in character, centers which proved to be the gateways to the larger Roman empire.

- Give an overview of the size, scope, and population of some of the major urban centers today. Further, show how these cities serve as centers of government, education, health-care, information, entertainment, trade, commerce, business, industry, jurisprudence, the military, and religion. Outline the cities in regard to their significance in terms of *cultural cities* (which lead the world in fashion, trends, and ideas), *political and administrative cities* (centers of worldwide decision making bodies, or those containing governments and their bureaucracies), *industrial cities* (noisy, blue-collar, factory centers host to central manufacturing industries) *commercial cities* (giant marketplaces or bazaars where goods and services are exchanged on worldwide basis), *symbolic cities* (cities where great historical struggles are fought, settled, and symbolized), and *primary cities* (those which combine all of the characteristics together).

- Lay out the ways in which cities today serve as magnets for the oppressed, the broken, and the poor, including the biblical focus on God's heart for the poor, the trend of urbanization (and its concentration on the poor) as the most powerful characteristic of modern times, and the logical argument that if God is concerned for the poor, he likewise is concerned about the American inner city because of its staggering number of underclass and poor families.

- Summarize the key biblical data on how the city is the picture and symbol of our spiritual destiny and inheritance, in the sense of the hope of the New Jerusalem; this will be the city not where God is absent and where arrogance rules, but where God is present, and Jesus is adored as Lord of all. Show how the explicit goal of mission is to rob the cities of the world in order to *fill up and populate* the New Jerusalem, the true mother of all believers (*God's final urban renewal project*).

3

- Restate the key implications for understanding the centrality of the city for urban mission, i.e., how in all our mission praying, giving and sending we must focus on the cities, we must recruit more spiritual laborers to serve in the city, strategize how to affect unreached cities with the Gospel, and pray for the city and seek its safety, finding our safety in its preservation.

Devotion

God Has Prepared for Us a City

Heb. 11.8-16 - By faith Abraham obeyed when he was called to go out to a place that he was to receive as an inheritance. And he went out, not knowing where he was going. [9] By faith he went to live in the land of promise, as in a foreign land, living in tents with Isaac and Jacob, heirs with him of the same promise. [10] For he was looking forward to the city that has foundations, whose designer and builder is God. [11] By faith Sarah herself received power to conceive, even when she was past the age, since she considered him faithful who had promised. [12] Therefore from one man, and him as good as dead, were born descendants as many as the stars of heaven and as many as the innumerable grains of sand by the seashore. [13] These all died in faith, not having received the things promised, but having seen them and greeted them from afar, and having acknowledged that they were strangers and exiles on the earth. [14] For people who speak thus make it clear that they are seeking a homeland. [15] If they had been thinking of that land from which they had gone out, they would have had opportunity to return. [16] But as it is, they desire a better country, that is, a heavenly one. Therefore God is not ashamed to be called their God, for he has prepared for them a city.

The great "hall of faith" spoken of here represents one of the mountain peaks of the NT, and speaks to the remarkable unity and connectedness that all believers have to one another through their faith in Christ. In a real sense, all believers of every age are connected in one seamless tapestry of hope and faith, of love for God and one another, of genuine expectation of the fulfillment of the promise of God for each one in particular and all together. Here, in this passage in Hebrews 11, we see that the hope is defined in terms of a better country, a heavenly country which involves a fellowship with God without shame, and the residence in a city whose maker and builder is God.

Does that strike you odd–that God would prepare for the saints of all the ages a city? For many Christians today, the city is an intimidating, frightening, and unappealing sight. A hulk of incredible complexity, overcrowding, pollution, and noise, they are associated with business, congestion and traffic, crime and violence, and

3

immorality. How (or even *why*) would God want to build a *city* for human beings to live in forever, and why would this be a significant element in the fundamental hope of all the saints, down through the ages? Great questions, but indeed, the Bible provides even better answers!

To begin with, the idea that God would prepare a place for his own is a common and much beloved theme in the Bible, one which is highlighted and mentioned often in the NT. At the judgment of the sheep and the goats, Jesus declares that the king will say to those on his right to come and inherit the Kingdom prepared by the Father for them since the foundation of the world (Matt. 25.34). Jesus comforted his disciples by commanding them not to fear, for it was the Father's good pleasure to give the Kingdom to them (Luke 12.32), and he promised that his Father's house possessed many dwelling-places, and he would prepare a place for them to be with him forever (John 14.1-4). Paul can say to the Philippians that the citizenship of the believing is in heaven, and it is from there that we await the Savior, the Lord Jesus Christ who would conform our feeble bodies to his glorious one by the power he possesses now to subdue all things to his will (Phil. 3.20-21). Truly, the vision of the Christian hope is the notion of God's preparation of a place for those who would inherit his salvation, and amazingly, it is described as a city.

Furthermore, no Christian can read the description of the New Jerusalem without wonder and expectation. A glistening city of pure gold, inhabited by the Father and the Son, without need of light since the splendor of the Lord himself illumines the city. Who can fathom a city whose inner workings were engineered by God himself, that has neither cemetery nor mortuary (because no dead are there), no hospital nor pharmacy (no sick are there), no court nor prison (no crime is there), and no psychiatrist nor counselor (no sorrow is there)? The dimensions of the city make it more of a moon than a mere place (1500 miles square, if we take John's measurements literally), fashioned all by the hand of the Cosmic Contractor, our Lord Jesus. As a theologian, the fact does not escape me that our Lord was a carpenter by trade, and there can be little doubt that a city designed and built by him will be spectacular beyond words, and wondrous beyond thought.

However, notwithstanding all of these amazing blessings of the city itself, its greatest wonder is that the abode of God now dwells with humankind:

> Rev. 21.1-4 - Then I saw a new heaven and a new earth, for the first heaven and the first earth had passed away, and the sea was no more. [2] And I saw the holy city, new Jerusalem, coming down out of heaven from God, prepared as a bride adorned for her husband. [3] And I heard a loud voice from the

throne saying, "Behold, the dwelling place of God is with man. He will dwell with them, and they will be his people, and God himself will be with them as their God. [4] He will wipe away every tear from their eyes, and death shall be no more, neither shall there be mourning nor crying nor pain anymore, for the former things have passed away."

What makes this city most desirable, most glorious, and most amazing is that God dwells with humankind in it, and he will be their God, and they his people. All tears are wiped away, death is done away with, as are crying and pain, and all the former cruelty of the ages of human rebellion are forever eliminated. Can anything truly be more amazing and desirable than this?

The fact that the city was originally a place of rebellion and idolatry makes the New Jerusalem an incredible reality and even more amazing irony. Who would have thought that the God of the heavens would embrace the notion of the wicked city and transform it into the very picture and image of paradise itself? Our God's wisdom and knowledge are inscrutable and past finding out (cf. Rom. 11.34ff.)!

Always take time to ponder the reality that the end of all things for humankind is a city—certainly a city of God's design and enriched infinitely by his very own presence, but still—a city. The hope of the saints of all the ages is to inhabit the city of God:

> Heb. 11.10 - For he was looking forward to the city that has foundations, whose designer and builder is God.

> Heb. 13.14 - For here we have no lasting city, but we seek the city that is to come.

The Divine Carpenter is finishing his grand task of building a city for his own to dwell in forever. Can anything sound or be more wonderful than that? Does anyone have a grander sense of symmetry, beauty, and excellence than he? The one who lavishes his genius on a rose or pine tree, shall we not trust him with the remarkable job of building a place for us, just for us?

Let us work in the city today as we seek the city that is to come, whose designer and builder is God. Yes, God has prepared for us *a city*.

3

Nicene Creed
and Prayer

After reciting and/or singing the Nicene Creed (located in the Appendix), pray the following prayer:

> *O Lord, our creator, by your holy prophet you taught your ancient people to seek the welfare of the cities in which they lived. We commend our neighborhood to your care, that it might be kept free from social strife and decay. Give us strength of purpose and concern for others, that we may create here a community of justice and peace where your will may be done; through your Son, Jesus Christ our Lord. Amen.*

~ Presbyterian Church (U.S.A.) and Cumberland Presbyterian Church.
The Theology and Worship Ministry Unit. **Book of Common Worship**.
Louisville, KY: Westminister/John Knox Press, 1993. p. 821.

Quiz

Put away your notes, gather up your thoughts and reflections, and take the quiz for Lesson 2, *The Vision and Biblical Foundation for Christian Mission: Part 2.*

Scripture
Memorization
Review

Review with a partner, write out and/or recite the text for last class session's assigned memory verses: Ephesians 5.25-27 and Ephesians 6.10-13.

Assignments Due

Turn in your summary of the reading assignment for last week, that is, your brief response and explanation of the main points that the authors were seeking to make in the assigned reading (Reading Completion Sheet).

CONTACT

1

Urban Renewal, Jesus Style

Any student of urban renewal in America knows that billions of dollars have gone into urban renewal projects in inner city communities across the country. Since the late 60s, an amazing amount of resources, monies, and efforts have gone into making the American inner city a safer, healthier, and more desirable place to live and raise a family. Despite this amazing amount of government and economic investment, our inner cities are still plagued by drugs, violence, broken families, and economic disenfranchisement. Various Christian groups have emerged with strategies to do urban renewal informed by more Christian principles of justice and peace. Some advocate a relocation of Christian individuals and families back into urban communities, calling for a more incarnational approach to the city. Others focus on strategies that emphasize more law-enforcement, holding heads of families more accountable, and rewarding the behavior of those who seek through education, hard work, and discipline to "join" the ranks of the others in society. In light of the call of Christians to do justice and discipleship in the city, what kind of strategies do you believe are most important for viable and successful urban ministry?

Families Must Flee the City, If They Intend to Thrive

▶**2** Many Christians today who believe deeply in the protection and health of the nuclear family are convinced that the environment of the inner city is both anti-family and anti-spiritual. In communities so spiritually dark and made vulnerable by gang violence, drugs, poor schools, substandard social systems, and economic deprivation, some Christians have advocated leaving the city as the only alternative for the Christian family. They have concluded that for these and other reasons, the city is toxic to the Christian family; those who *can* flee them *must* do so in order to protect their own from ongoing exposure to its immoral influences. Despite the appeal of some serious minded disciples to stay in the city to be salt and light within it, many sincere Christians and their churches have abandoned the city, leaving a moral and spiritual vacuum that is difficult to fill. Some have simply given up altogether, suggesting that the modern American inner city is too large and dangerous to be redeemed. They would argue that it is simply not a place to raise a family; if you are not there, do not go there. The best way to help the ghetto or the barrio it is not to add to the problem by being a part of it. These would advocate that Christian families find alternatives and relocate *out of the city* as a viable strategy of urban change. What is your answer to this kind of realistic (even *pessimistic*) vision of the city and its impact on the family today?

Crying against the Great City

▶**3** There is a rich biblical and contemporary tradition that suggests that the primary relationship of informed, dedicated Christians to the modern city is prophetic and dialectic, that is, to cry against the injustices, abuses, and idolatry of the modern city. Rightly these traditions would suggest and note the many biblical examples of prophets who were given burdens to cry against the sins of the cities of their time, Isaiah with Jerusalem, Hosea with Samaria, and Jonah with Nineveh (among others). The arrogance, power, and self-sufficiency of the modern city suggests (they would argue) that the only way to enable the city to see itself as it is is through

3

prophetic confrontation, the direct and unashamed proclamation of the truth to the seats of power regarding their need to repent and change in light of God's demand for justice and righteousness in the city. How effective do you think that such a strategy might be in confronting the numerous evils and injustices that occur in most of our cities today? How are we to understand our Christian role in relationship to the city today—has it changed from the times of the prophets, and if so, how so?

Christian Mission and the City

CONTENT

Segment 1: Defining and Discerning a Biblical Understanding of the City

Rev. Dr. Don L. Davis

The concept of the city is central within the Old and New Testaments, and provides us with a simple overview of their ancient characteristics. Cities in the ancient world were different than villages in that they were a collection of houses and buildings surrounded by walls, were significant and impressive for their time, and that some were dependent for protection and supply upon others. A common reality in the ancient world, cities of old were relatively small, typically unpaved, strengthened by thick walls and high towers, and seats of government and power. In terms of their spiritual meaning as outlined in Scripture, cities were associated with human rebellion and idolatry (e.g., Enoch, the city of Cain), with independence and arrogance (as in the case of the Tower of Babel), and with evil and godlessness (as with Babylon). Cities were judged by God for their sinfulness (e.g., Sodom and Gomorrah, Jericho, Nineveh), and denounced for their false sense of security and power (specifically, Jerusalem). Although associated with the rebellion of humankind, the Scriptures teach that God adopted the city as a symbol of his dwelling place and blessing. In spite of the fact that David won the city in battle, God selected Jerusalem for himself, and determined to make her a praise in the earth. Divine irony is present here; God transforms the secular image of self-dependence and rebellion into an image of *refuge* (i.e., the cities of Refuge), as well as the image of *reconciliation*, a place which can know and experience his forgiveness and blessing (i.e., Jonah and the experience of Nineveh). Because of the mercy and grace of Almighty God in Christ, hope exists for any city which repents in the face of his judgment, yields in the face of his demands, and seeks his mercy in the face of his punishment.

Summary of Segment 1

3

Our objective for this segment, *Defining and Discerning a Biblical Understanding of the City*, is to enable you to see that:

- The concept of the city is central within the Old and New Testaments, and provides us with a simple overview of their ancient characteristics. Cities in the ancient world were different than villages in that they were a collection of houses and buildings surrounded by walls, were significant and impressive for their time, and some were dependent for protection and supply upon others. A common reality in the ancient world, cities of old were relatively small, typically unpaved, strengthened by thick walls and high towers, and seats of government and power.

- In terms of their spiritual meaning as outlined in Scripture, cities were associated with human rebellion and idolatry (e.g., Enoch, the city of Cain), with independence and arrogance (as in the case of the Tower of Babel), and with evil and godlessness (as with Babylon). Cities were judged by God for their sinfulness (e.g., Sodom and Gomorrah, Jericho, Nineveh), and denounced for their false sense of security and power (specifically, Jerusalem).

- Although associated with the rebellion of humankind, the Scriptures teach that God adopted the city as symbol of his dwelling place and blessing. In spite of the fact that David won the city in battle, God selected Jerusalem for himself, and determined to make her a praise in the earth. Divine irony is present here; God transforms the secular image of self-dependence and rebellion into an image of *refuge* (i.e., the cities of Refuge), as well as the image of *reconciliation*, a place which can know and experience his forgiveness and blessing (i.e., Jonah and the experience of Nineveh).

- Because of the mercy and grace of Almighty God in Christ, hope exists for any city which repents in the face of his judgment, yields in the face of his demands, and seeks his mercy in the face of his punishment.

3

I. Biblical Foundations: Defining the City

Video Segment 1
Outline

· ·

The City as Sign of Independence and Rebellion

Early Genesis thus establishes a general worldview in which the image of the city is an anti-God state of affairs that attempts to thwart God's rule over the world. It is a place where culture subverts religion for its own purposes rather than advancing the glory of God. Genesis provides this background to an Israel living in the midst of a futile creation, a theme developed in the Exodus account of Israel's oppressive servitude to an Egyptian city-building program (Exod. 1.8–14; 5.5–21). God's original intent for his image bearers was to build society for the glory of God. They were to multiply and spread out over the earth, extending the rule of God over creation as God's vice-regents (Gen. 1.26–28). Because they exercised autonomy [independence from God], the first man and woman were cursed and driven out of God's presence to await the fulfillment of God's promise to deliver them from that curse (Gen. 3, esp. vv. 15 and 24). All efforts at city building from this point on are reassertions of that original autonomy.

~ Leland Ryken. **The Dictionary of Biblical Imagery**. (electronic ed.). Downers Grove, IL: InterVarsity Press, 2000. p. 151.

· ·

A. Word usage and general definitions

    1. Hebrew, *îr* (pronounced 'eer')

    2. Critical difference between a city and a village: *cities were a collection of houses and buildings surrounded by walls.*

       a. Lev. 25.29-31

       b. 1 Sam. 6.18

c. Ezek. 38.11

3. Biblical cities, although impossible to measure with our modern cities, were still significant and impressive for their time.

    a. Jericho, archeology reveals it to be impressive, walls 17 feet high (1995 *Grolier Multimedia Encyclopedia*)

    b. Hazor (northern Israel, 1700 B.C.) walls nearly 50 feet high, up to 290 feet thick, and the perimeter of the enclosed area over two miles around (Joel F. Drinkard, Jr. "Cities and Urban Life." Holman Bible Dictionary. Nashville: Holman Bible Publishers, 1991. Electronic Edition, *Quick Verse for Windows 5.1*, Parsons Technology. © 1999.)

4. Population of a typical city was between 1,000 and 10,000 people. (Jerusalem probably never grew larger than 25,000 at its peak during OT period.)

5. It appears that "cities and their villages" mentioned in Scripture suggests that some villages belonged to and were dependent upon cities (Josh. 13.23, 28; 15.32, 36, 41), and some villages grew because of population and importance into cities (e.g., Hazaraddar, Num. 34.4 which was Hezron and Addar, Josh. 15.3).

B. Characteristics of ancient cities

1. Relatively small, built with narrow, crooked streets, where markets and courts existed (Eccles. 12.4; Song of Sol. 3.2; Gen. 23.10; Ruth 4.1)

3

2. Few streets were paved, although Josephus says that Solomon had the roads leading to Jerusalem paved (*Antiquities of Josephus*, 8.7).

3. The chief towns and cities were strengthened by thick walls with battlements (2 Chron. 26.6; Zeph. 1.16).

4. High towers were raised over the gates of the cities (2 Sam. 18.24; 2 Kings 9.17); and at the corners of the walls themselves (2 Chron. 14.7; 32.5).

5. Ditches were dug and ramparts built outside the walls, 2 Sam. 20.15; Isa. 26.1.

6. Cities are an old idea: cities such as Ur, Nippur, Kish, Eridu, Lagash, Nineveh, Asshur and others have been excavated, with archeologists setting the dates of them to 3,000 B.C.E. and earlier.

II. Biblical Interpretations: Discerning the Spiritual Meaning of the City

A. The city is associated with human rebellion and idolatry: Cain and the city of Enoch

1. The biblical record, Gen. 4.16-17

2. Cain foregoes wandering, builds a city, and names it after his son. (Enoch means *initiation*, or *inauguration*, in other words, "a new beginning.")

3. The idea of the city is not founded or started by God, but rather the one who murders his brother and builds the city as a place of *permanence* and *security*.

B. The city is associated with independence and arrogance: the Tower of Babel, Gen. 11.1-9.

1. The city and its tower are built for the purpose of "making a name for ourselves, lest we be dispersed over the face of the whole earth," Gen. 11.4.

2. The two-fold purpose

   a. *To make a name for ourselves*: to establish our own way of determining our destiny and achievement

   b. *Lest we be dispersed*: a way to consolidate and reinforce the coordinated power of these independent and arrogant persons

3. Tower of Babel is a powerful symbol of the city as naked rejection of reliance on God, and arrogant dependence on human initiative and strength.

4. God's judgment: dispersing and leaving off the work of building the city, and *God making a name for them*, "Babel" (confusion)

5. *Babel* (Babylon), the symbol of godless human arrogance

3

C. The city is associated with evil and godlessness: Babylon

1. Isaiah's judgment against Babylon as a lover of pleasures and a casual acceptance of its own security, Isa. 47.7-8.

2. Babylon associated with the prophetic vision of the demonic rebellion itself.

   a. Isa. 14.3-4

   b. Isa. 14.12-14

   c. Isa. 13.19

3. Daniel's portrayal of Nebuchadnezzar as an arrogant, self-reliant ruler who ignores God's part in his work or glory, Dan. 4.29-32

4. Babylon is the apocalyptic symbol of godlessness, where the kings of the earth commit adultery, seeking security in the might of the city and not in God, Rev. 18.1-21; cf. Rev. 18.1-3.

D. The city is a place where the judgment of God is manifest and demonstrated: Sodom and Gomorrah, Jericho, Jerusalem, and Nineveh.

1. Sodom and Gomorrah suffered the wrath of God's judgment because of its unbridled immorality and oppression, Deut. 32.32-33; Ezek. 16.49-50; cf. Gen. 19.24-29.

2. Jericho is destroyed by God in the Canaan warfare he waged, and a curse is laid upon those who retake to *rebuild its foundations and gates* (symbolizing the need to completely reject as a people any attempt to reignite the flames of idolatry and rebellion against God).

   a. Josh. 6.26

   b. 1 Kings 16.34

3. Israel's construction of its own cities results in the same kinds of attitudes and behaviors associated with those who built cities in defiance to God.

   a. Abraham and the patriarchs were wanderers, living in tents, not building cities, Heb. 11.9-10.

   b. A clear relationship seems to exist between reliance on the security of the city and abandoning the security of the Lord: Rehoboam.

      (1) 2 Chron. 11.5-12

      (2) 2 Chron. 12.1 - When the rule of Rehoboam was established and he was strong, he abandoned the law of the Lord, and all Israel with him.

   c. The prophets preach constantly against the tendency to depend upon walled cities for help rather than God.

      (1) Ps. 9.6-9

      (2) Jer. 5.17

      (3) Jer. 21.13

4. Jerusalem, the city that God chooses, is judged because of its immorality and godlessness.

    a. Its pride, Jer. 13.9

    b. Compared to Sodom and Gomorrah, Jer. 23.14

    c. Called a city of oppressors, Zeph. 3.1-2

    d. Unfaithful to God by playing as a harlot with foreign gods, Isa. 1.21

    e. Compared to Samaria and found to be even more immoral than her, Ezek. 16.1-2, 48, 51

    f. The one who kills the prophets and stones those whom God sends, Luke 13.34

5. Nineveh and Samaria receive God's harshest condemnations and pronouncements because of their injustice, bloodiness, and transgression against him, Jon. 1.1-2; Nah. 3.1; Mic. 1.5.

6. Jesus denounced the hardness of heart of Jerusalem and other cities which were not receptive to God's message of the Kingdom in himself.

    a. Matt. 11.20

    b. Luke 13.34

The New Jerusalem as the Ultimate Vindication of the City

The ultimate vindication of the city comes in the apocalyptic vision of New Jerusalem, which descends from heaven (Rev. 21.2), symbolic of its divine origin and its transcendence of human and earthly reality. With the appearance of this heavenly city, "the kingdom of the world has become the kingdom of our Lord and of his Christ" (Rev. 11.15). Its ancient rival, Babylon, which attempts to subvert it, will ultimately be destroyed and cast down (Rev. 18). This New Jerusalem will have no temple, "for its temple is the Lord God the Almighty and the Lamb" (Rev. 21.22 RSV), and it will need no sun, since God's glory will be its eternal light (v. 23). Furthermore, "The kings of the earth shall bring their glory into it" (v. 24 RSV). The curse of the Fall will be removed and, along with it, the injustice and futility that characterized life in the city of man.
~ *Leland Ryken.* The Dictionary of Biblical Imagery. *(electronic ed.). Downers Grove, IL: IVP, 2000. p 153.*

III. God's Adoption of the City: the Heart of the Lord for Cities

A. Jerusalem in God's heart

    1. God chose the city of Jerusalem for himself, even though David captured Zion in his warfare.

        a. David's capture of Zion in battle, 2 Sam. 5.4-10

        b. God's selection of Jerusalem

            (1) 2 Chron. 12.13

            (2) Ps. 48.1

            (3) Ps. 78.68-70

            (4) Ps. 132.13

            (5) Isa. 14.32

    2. The Lord established Jerusalem and has determined to make her a praise in the earth.

        a. Isa. 62.6-7

        b. Isa. 62.12

    3. Divine irony: God selected something which humankind created (this is the same as the idea of *kingship*; although God's people chose a king against God's will, God adopted it and expanded it for his own divine purpose).

3

a. God's people desire for a king not God's explicit will, 1 Sam. 8.4-9

b. God adopting the idea of king for his own purpose and glory

(1) Isa. 9.6-7

(2) Jer. 23.5-6

B. God transforms the city as a symbol of *rebellion* into a city of *refuge*.

1. Six towns were designated in Israel as a place where one might flee from vengeance.

   a. Associated with priests, Num. 35.6

   b. To avoid death, Num. 35.12

   c. For the stranger and sojourner as well, Num. 35.15

2. Cities viewed as places of violence and blood now are envisioned as places of security and safety.

C. God forgives the city which chooses to repent.

1. God sends his prophets to declare his burdens of woe against the cities because of their wickedness and transgressions, Jon. 1.2, Jon. 3.2, Isa. 58.1, Amos 7.15, Zech. 1.14.

2. God promises woe and destruction to the unrepentant city, Jon. 3.4.

3. The judgment of God, however, is stayed if a city turns from its wicked ways and repents.

    a. Jer. 18.7-10

    b. Jon. 3.10

4. God takes no pleasure in the destruction of cities, but will relent and forgive if they show the signs of humility and repentance.

    a. Jon. 4.2

    b. Exod. 34.6-7

D. Implications of God's work: *there is hope for the city, because our God is a good and forgiving God, not willing that these masses perish!*

1. He will restrain his anger upon those who are repentant, including the bloody city, Ps. 78.38.

2. His mercy triumphs over judgment in the face of the repentant, Hos. 11.8-9.

3

Conclusion

» The concept of the ancient city is born from its connection to self-reliance, arrogance, and rebellion against God. In case after case from Nineveh to Jerusalem, God has judged the city because of its wickedness and transgression.

» Through his gracious and sovereign election of the city, God has adopted the concept of the city associating it with his own presence, transforming the city into a place of refuge, repentance, and restoration.

Please take as much time as you have available to answer these and other questions that the video brought out. In this section we saw the origins and development of the concept of the city. Born in the rebellion and arrogance of Cain, the ancient city was conceived spiritually in deep connection to self-reliance, arrogance, and rebellion against God. In numerous cases, God judged the city because of its idolatry, injustice, and wickedness. Yet, through God's mercy and love, God sovereignly elected the city as his own concept, transforming it into his own dwelling place, and refashioning it as a place of refuge, repentance, and restoration. As an urban Christian leader, you ought to understand these concepts well, and, where appropriate, support your answers with Scripture.

Segue 1

**Student Questions
and Response**

1. Give an overview of the some of the general characteristics of the ancient city. From a biblical point of view, where did the concept originate? How were ancient cities distinguished from villages?

2. Why is the association of the creation of cities with Cain such an important spiritual concept? What can we learn from the incident at the Tower of Babel about the nature of the city? Similarly, how does the city of Babylon inform our understanding of the spiritual godlessness of cities in general?

3. What were some cities mentioned in the Bible that incurred God's judgment because of their sinfulness and lack of repentance? Why was Jerusalem denounced especially for its own false sense of security and power?

4. Although the city was associated with the rebellion of humankind, how did God adopt the city as symbol of his dwelling place and blessing? How does the example of Zion (Jerusalem) reveal this gracious and sovereign selection

of God? What has God determined specifically about Jerusalem in regard to his own presence and glory?

5. Explain the nature of the "divine irony" associated with God, the secular image of the city, and his transformation of it into a new and different symbol?

6. How does God's designation of the six cities of refuge, and his forgiveness of Nineveh, transform completely our view of the secular and unredeemable city? Explain.

7. To what can we attribute the fact that, for any city that repents before God, its inhabitants can garner his attention and mercy, even in the face of certain judgment and death?

8. Read Ryken's analysis below of our Christian responsibility in light of his transformation of the city from object of rebellion to place of his presence. What do you think of his views of how we are now to act in light of God's transformed image of the city?

3

How Should God's Transformation of the City Affect Our Lives Today?

In light of the complex that makes up the image of the city, the Christian life is to display certain characteristics. First, the Christian is a citizen of God's city through righteousness based on faith, not on the works of the law. By analogy, Paul compares these two outlooks to the "Jerusalem above" and the "present Jerusalem" (Gal. 4.22–26; cf. Phil. 3.20). People who attempt on their own to justify themselves before God are citizens of the latter, while those who look to Christ in faith are citizens of the former.

Second, the Christian life is marked by respect for human government as God's provisional source of order since the Fall and prior to the consummation (Matt. 22.21; Rom. 13.1–7; 1 Pet. 2.13–17); therefore, the believer is to live like a Joseph or a Daniel in relating to the surrounding world. The ancient Epistle of Diognetus, a defense of Christianity, describes Christians as those who "dwell in their own countries, but only as sojourners; they bear their share of all responsibilities as citizens, and they endure all hardships as strangers. Every foreign country is a homeland to them, and every homeland is foreign.... Their existence is on earth, but their citizenship is in heaven" (Epistle to Diognetus 5.1–9).

Third, the life of faith is to be a life of confidence in God's promise to establish his city. Hebrews speaks of the faith by which Abraham "sojourned in the land of promise, as in a foreign land, living in tents.... For he looked forward to the city which has foundations, whose builder and maker is God" (Heb 11.9–10 RSV). Heavenly citizenship is to be the ground of confidence in life's trials, the goal toward which life is directed.

But a significant difference distinguishes the NT believers from their OT counterparts. Of the latter we are told, "All these people were still living by faith when they died. They did not receive the things promised; they only saw them and welcomed them from a distance" (Heb. 11.13 NIV). While the Christian is to continue in this alien mode until the consummation (1 Pet. 1.1; 2.11), in a very profound and real sense the pilgrimage has ended because of Christ's atoning work (Eph. 2.19). Through the persevering, substitutionary faithfulness of Jesus (Heb. 12.2), Christians "have come to Mount Zion and to the city of the living God, the heavenly Jerusalem" (Heb. 12.22 RSV). So while the geopolitical manifestation of God's city is yet future, it has been eternally established in the heavens through Jesus' work, and believers in Jesus have already taken up residence there (John 14.1–3) through union with him (Eph. 2.6).

Therefore the Church of Jesus lives in the world now as God's holy "city set on a hill" (Matt. 5.14). Augustine described it thus. "The humble City is the society of holy men and good angels; the proud city is the society of wicked men and evil angels. The one City began with the love of God; the other had its beginnings in the love of self" (City of God 14.13).

~ Leland Ryken. **The Dictionary of Biblical Imagery.** (electronic ed.). Downers Grove, IL: InterVarsity Press, 2000. p. 153-154.

Christian Mission and the City

Segment 2: Rationale for Vital Urban Mission

Rev. Dr. Don L. Davis

Summary of Segment 2

Three critical reasons exist to sufficiently show why urban mission must be a priority for all mission activity today: the city is the seat of influence, power, and spiritual activity in the world, it is steadily becoming a magnet for the oppressed, the broken, and the poor, and the city is seen as the picture of our spiritual destiny and inheritance. The city played an important role in the ministry of Jesus and the apostles. Jesus' own ministry of kingdom proclamation was rooted in city work, and his proclamation mandate centered around Jerusalem. Furthermore, Christianity was birthed in a city, and spread through the Roman empire in the first century via the great urban centers of the time (in places such as Damascus, Antioch, Corinth, Philippi, Thessalonica, Athens, and Rome itself). Many of the same problems and opportunities connected with the cities of Jesus and the apostles' day exist in today's urban populations. The modern cities of the world are numerous in size, scope, and population, and serve as the national and world centers of government, education, health-care, information, entertainment, trade, commerce, business, industry, jurisprudence, the military, and religion.

Cities are known today by their identity and focus, whether they are cultural, political and administrative, industrial, commercial, symbolic, or primary cities. The modern cities of the world serve as magnets for the oppressed, the broken, and the poor. The Bible reveals a clear and compelling witness concerning God's heart for the poor, and if God is concerned for the poor, he likewise is concerned about the American inner city because of its staggering number of underclass and poor families. The city is the picture and symbol of our spiritual destiny and inheritance, the New Jerusalem, where God dwells and Christ is adored. The explicit goal of mission is to *rob the cities of the world* in order to *fill up and populate* the New Jerusalem, the true mother of all believers (*God's final urban renewal project*). Because of the significance of the city both in Scripture and in the modern world, the city must remain at the hub of all missionary enterprise.

Our objective for this segment, *Rationale for Vital Urban Mission*, is to enable you to see that:

- Three critical reasons exist to sufficiently show why urban mission must be a priority for all mission activity today: the city is the seat of influence,

3

power, and spiritual activity in the world; it is quickly becoming a magnet for the oppressed, the broken, and the poor, and the city is seen as the picture of our spiritual destiny and inheritance.

• The city played an important role in the ministry of Jesus and the apostles. Jesus' own ministry of kingdom proclamation was rooted in city work, and his proclamation mandate centered around Jerusalem. Furthermore, Christianity was birthed in a city, and spread through the Roman empire in the first century via the great urban centers of the time (in places such as Damascus, Antioch, Corinth, Philippi, Thessalonica, Athens, and Rome itself).

• The ministry of the apostles after Christ were anchored in strategic outreach to the cities of the Roman empire, beginning with Jerusalem, moving to Samaria and Judea, to the very far flung corners of the Roman empire. Paul's journeys as recorded in Acts were virtually totally urban in character, occurring in centers which proved to be the gateways to the larger Roman empire.

• Many of the same problems and opportunities connected with the cities of Jesus and the apostles' day exist in today's urban populations. The modern cities of the world are numerous in size, scope, and population, and serve as the national and world centers of government, education, health-care, information, entertainment, trade, commerce, business, industry, jurisprudence, the military, and religion.

• Anthropologists categorize cities in terms of their identity and focus. There are *cultural cities* (which lead the world in fashion, trends, and ideas), *political and administrative cities* (centers of worldwide decision making bodies, or those containing governments and their bureaucracies), *industrial cities* (noisy, blue-collar, factory centers host to central manufacturing industries) *commercial cities* (giant marketplaces or bazaars where goods and services are exchanged on worldwide basis), *symbolic cities* (cities where great historical struggles are fought, settled, and symbolized), and *primary cities* (those which combine all of the characteristics together).

• The modern cities of the world serve as magnets for the oppressed, the broken, and the poor. The Bible reveals a clear and compelling witness concerning God's heart for the poor, and the trend of urbanization (and its concentration on the poor) represents the most powerful characteristic of modern times. The argument is logical and plain: if God is concerned for the poor, he likewise is concerned about the American inner city because of its staggering number of underclass and poor families.

- The Bible clearly shows how the city is the picture and symbol of our spiritual destiny and inheritance. The hope of the saints is to dwell with God in the New Jerusalem, not a place where God is absent and where arrogance rules, but rather the home of the righteous where God is present, and Jesus is adored as Lord of all.

- The explicit goal of mission is to *rob the cities of the world in order to fill up and populate* the New Jerusalem, the true mother of all believers (*God's final urban renewal project*).

- Because of the significance of the city both in Scripture and in the modern world, the city must remain at the hub of all missionary enterprise. Our praying, giving, and sending of laborers must focus on reaching unreached cities, we must recruit more missionaries to serve in the city, strategize how to affect unreached cities with the Gospel, and pray for the city and seek its safety, finding our safety in its preservation.

3

Video Segment 2 Outline

I. The City Is a Seat of Influence, Power, and Spiritual Activity

Matt. 9.35-38 - And Jesus went throughout all the cities and villages, teaching in their synagogues and proclaiming the gospel of the kingdom and healing every disease and every affliction. [36] When he saw the crowds, he had compassion for them, because they were harassed and helpless, like sheep without a shepherd. [37] Then he said to his disciples, "The harvest is plentiful, but the laborers are few; [38] therefore pray earnestly to the Lord of the harvest to send out laborers into his harvest."

Mission does what Jesus did. Jesus went to where the people were, and wherever people exist you will find a strategic need to display the light and power of the Kingdom of God.

A. Jesus and the apostles carried out their kingdom ministry in an itinerant ministry to the cities.

1. The ministry of Jesus was rooted in city work, Matt. 4.23-25.

   a. Word for city (*polis*) is used 39 times in Luke in connection to the ministry context of Jesus.

   b. Luke 7.37

   c. Luke 8.1-4

   d. Luke 10.1

   e. Luke 18.2-3

2. Jesus' work of kingdom proclamation and display was rooted in a mandate to proclaim the Kingdom to Jerusalem, Luke 19.41-44.

   a. Jesus' ministry was to usher in the kingdom reign with Jerusalem being a significant part of that display.

   b. Because of its spiritual ignorance, his reign over Jerusalem was rejected.

3. Christianity was birthed in a city, Jerusalem, and spread via the great urban centers of the Roman world in the first century. Ours is an urban religion, which took root in cities such as Damascus, Antioch, Corinth, Philippi, Thessalonica, Athens, and even Rome.

4. Paul's missionary journeys were completely urban in character.

   a. His ministry included going to many different cities covering a broad region.

      (1) Acts 20.23

      (2) Rom. 15.19-23

   b. "The preoccupation with cities was not peculiar to Paul. . . . within a decade of the crucifixion of Jesus, the village culture of Palestine had been left behind, and the Greco-Roman city became the dominant environment of the Christian movement" (Wayne A. Meeks. *The First Urban Christians: The Social World of the Apostle Paul.* New Haven, CT: Yale University Press, 1983, p. 9-11).

5. Proclaiming Christ and his Kingdom (the heart of mission) occurred in urban areas, in cities, which served as gateways to the larger Roman empire.

   a. Acts 8.5-6

   b. Acts 13.44

   c. Acts 14.20-22

   d. Acts 16.14

   e. Acts 18.8-10

B. City populations today resemble the same traits as the crowds which Christ observed as he went through the cities and villages of his time.

The city populations of today are as Jesus viewed them, distracted and distressed, as those without a shepherd.

Matt. 9.36-37 - When he saw the crowds, he had compassion for them, because they were harassed and helpless, like sheep without a shepherd. [37] Then he said to his disciples, "The harvest is plentiful, but the laborers are few; [38] therefore pray earnestly to the Lord of the harvest to send out laborers into his harvest."

1. In the northern hemisphere, the urban poor live predominantly within inner cities. In the southern hemisphere, they cluster mainly around the cities.

2. Most of those in the northern hemisphere would be classified as relatively poor, whereas almost all in the southern hemisphere are absolutely poor.

3. Despite many differences in the groupings of the poor, the Brandt Report and research by UNA and the WHO clearly indicate that urban poor worldwide have in common: feelings of powerlessness, persistent sense of insignificance, frustration, and despair, fearfulness of the future, low health expectation, inadequate housing, unemployment or underemployment, insufficient money, poor provision for education, a higher rate of crime, and political turmoil.

4. There are large, long-established reservoirs of the poor in the inner cities of Europe and North America; floods of work-seeking rural dwellers pouring into the cities of Latin America, Asia, and Africa; increasing streams of refugees from natural disaster and political repression.

5. The urban poor are found in the *callampas* (mushroom cities) of Chile, the *bustees* of India, the *gourbevilles* of Tunisia, the *secekindu* (built after dusk and before dawn) of Turkey, the *ghettos* of the U.S.A., and the *slums* of Australia.

C. The harvest of souls in our world cities is staggering, nearly mind-boggling.

1. Recall what God said to reluctant Jonah about the bloody city of Nineveh, which he spared because of his great compassion, Jon. 4.11.

2. By analogy, if God spared Nineveh because of its 120 thousand, just think of the burden of the Lord for the great cities of the world!

3. A snapshot of the world today paints a remarkable portrait of the urban centers of this time.

   a. 3 billion are under the age of 25

   b. 960 million illiterate adults (two thirds of which are female)

   c. 767 million people live in Africa

   d. 190 million have mobile phones

   e. 66 million are over the age of 80

   f. 33.4 million are infected with AIDS/HIV. – Timothy Monsma. "The Urbanization of our World" in *Cities: Missions' New Frontier*.

3

4. World Urbanization Prospects (United Nations) "It is projected that just after the turn of the millennium, in a few years, for the first time in history urban dwellers will outnumber those in traditional rural areas ... By 2006, half of the world population are expected to be urban dwellers. The urban population is growing three times faster than its rural counterpart. By 2030, three of every five persons will be living in urban areas."

5. This has now become a reality: there are more urban dwellers than any other dweller in the earth.

D. Cities are the centers of service and dominance.

1. They are the centers of government, education, health-care, information, entertainment, trade, commerce, business, industry, jurisprudence and the courts, the military, and religion.

2. Impossible to think reasonably of modern civilization without referring to the great cities of the world—Washington, New York, Seoul, Cairo, Brasilia, Istanbul, Moscow, Stockholm, London, Paris, Buenos Aires, Amsterdam, Los Angeles, and so on. Cities are significant because of their strategic import.

   a. *Cultural cities* (leading the world in fashion, trends, and ideas) e.g., Paris, Oxford, Boston, San Francisco

   b. *Political and Administrative cities* (centers of worldwide decision making bodies, or which contain governments and their bureaucracies) e.g., Washington, Moscow, New Delhi

c. *Industrial cities* (noisy, blue-collar, factory centers host to central manufacturing industries) e.g., Bombay, Sao Paulo, Chicago-Gary area

d. *Commercial cities* (giant marketplaces or bazaars where goods and services are bartered and exchanged on a worldwide basis) e.g., New York, Hong Kong

e. *Symbolic cities* (cities where great struggles are fought and settled and symbolized, or which represent issues of division, oppression, warfare, religious hatred, or freedom within their countries or to the rest of the world) e.g., Soweto, Belfast, Berlin, Beirut, Jerusalem

f. *Primary cities* (cites which combine all of the preceding characteristics, and can be said to be the greatest of the great cities) e.g., Bangkok, Mexico City, London

3

3. Where do most city dwellers live? The fifteen largest urban agglomerations, ranked by population size by 2015. Currently, twelve of the largest cities are in Asia, three in South America, two in the USA and one in Africa (World Urbanization Prospects; the 1996 Revision. New York: The United Nations, 1998) [population totals as of 1998].

a. Tokyo, Japan 28.9

b. Bombay, India 26.2

c. Lagos, Nigeria 24.6

d. Sao Paulo, Brazil 20.3

e. Dhaka, Bangladesh 19.5

f. Karachi, Pakistan 19.4

g. Mexico City, Mexico 19.2

h. Shanghai, China 18.0

i. New York, US 17.6

j. Calcutta, India 17.3

k. Delhi, India 16.9

l. Beijing, China 15.6

m. Metro-Manila, Philippines 14.7

n. Cairo, Egypt 14.4

o. Los Angeles, US 14.2

God loves the city because that is where the teeming millions of his compassion reside.

As goes the city, so goes the nation and the world!

II. The City Is a Magnet for the Oppressed, the Broken, and the Poor

A. God's heart for the poor: a spiritual mandate

1. The Scriptures reveal the God and Father of our Lord Jesus as a God who loves and has called the poor to himself, and the cities of the world are brimming with masses of people who are poor, and weak, and despised.

2. Jesus said in Luke 6 that the poor, those who wept and were hungry, those who were hated on account of his name were the truly blessed ones in this life.

3. 1 Corinthians 1.29 says God chose the foolish to shame the wise, the weak to shame the strong, and the things despised to shame the things considered great.

4. Religion that is pure and undefiled in the Father's sight is to visit widows and orphans in their distress and keep oneself unspotted from the world, James 1.27.

5. Psalm 10.14 says that God is the helper of the helpless, and that he does justice for the fatherless and the oppressed, and the true fast according to Isaiah 58 is to bring the homeless and hungry into your midst and minster to them.

6. James 2.5 says that God has chosen the poor to be rich in faith, and heirs of the Kingdom which he has promised to those who love him.

3

B. The trend of life today: urbanization as the most powerful characteristic of modern times

1. Harvie Conn, "Urban Mission." *Toward the 21st Century in Christian Mission*. (Grand Rapids: Eerdmans, 1993). "As we move into the twenty-first century the needs will grow . . . Our globe will have 433 mega-cities with over 1 million people in each. Our urban population will increase by 1.6 million people per week. Poverty in our urban areas will continue to expand, producing a "planet of urban slums." To meet those needs, new churches must be planted on a radically accelerated scale. The day of church planting for the world's cities has yet to dawn. The invisible, unreached peoples of the world's cities must be found–the poor, the industrial workers, the government employees, the new ethnic and tribal groups settling in urban areas. If we are to reach the world of the twenty-first century, we must reach its cities."

2. David B. Barrett. "Annual Statistical Table on Global Missions: 1999." *International Bulletin of Missionary Research*. Vol. 23, No. 1, Jan. 1999.

    a. By the year 2025, the urban poor will number over 3 billion people and comprise over one-third of the world's population. Over two billion of that number will be concentrated in urban slums.

    b. World wide today, non-Christian urban dwellers are increasing at a rate of 136,000 people per day. A figure that is projected to rise to 360,000 per day by 2025.

    c. In 1900 we had about 100 million poor people in the world. One century later that number had grown to 1.92 billion poor, and by 2025 there will be over 3 billion poor people in the world.

3. The biblical argument: *if God is concerned for the poor, he must be concerned about the American inner city!*

    a. Poverty in America continues to increase; the most recent information available from the US Census Bureau for 2001, which shows an increase to 32.9 million in poverty in America, which may also reflect an increase in the poverty figures for the inner city. For the first time in almost a decade, poverty in the United States rose last year, while median income fell. According to the Census Bureau, both negative economic indicators coincided with a recession. The poverty rate rose to 11.7 percent in 2001, up from 11.3 percent in 2000. It was the first year-to-year increase in poverty since 1991 - 92. At the same time, median household income declined 2.2 percent overall from its 2000 level to $42,288.

    b. The numbers of poor continue to rise; the Census reports 1.3 million more people were poor in 2001 than in 2000 - 32.9 million compared to 31.6 million.

C. If mission is about the city, then it will also have to be about the poor, because the vast majority of individuals in the city are poor.

1. God judged his people because of the immorality of their cities and the oppression of their poor, Amos 2.6-8.

2. The teeming millions abroad and the growing numbers at home show that our cities are magnets for the poorest of the poor in our world today.

3. Mission must be about the cities because those whom God cherishes reside in them.

III. The City Is the Picture and Symbol of our Spiritual Destiny and Inheritance

A. The hope of the saints and the sages: a city whose maker and builder is God

    1. The old Negro song of expectation, "There's plenty good room, plenty good room, plenty good room in my Father's Kingdom . . . choose your seat, and sit down!"

    2. We are sojourners, pilgrims, aliens, having here no lasting citizenship, home, or identity. We belong to a coming age, a new order under the reign of God, in a city designed for us, 1 Pet. 2.11-12.

    3. The nature of faith is to have no permanent place in this world but look for the city built by God, Heb. 11.10.

    4. God has prepared for his holy ones a city.

        a. Rev. 21.9-10

        b. Heb. 11.13-16

B. The symbol and reality of our eternal destiny is to dwell in a *New Jerusalem*, not where God is absent and arrogance rules, but where God is present and Jesus is adored as Lord of all.

    1. Rev. 21.2

All the Hopes of Israel and the Church Are Found in a City

All in all, we find the fulfilment of Israel's hopes, the realization of God's promises to her; the manifestation, in a city which has the glory of God, of the reality already declared by the heavens and the firmament; and the answer to all aesthetic yearnings and national aspirations in the place to which the kings of the earth bring their glory. Of this city the reborn are citizens, and to it all pilgrims of faith tend. The city is also described as the Lamb's bride; it is in another aspect his church for which he died, the pattern and goal of all human society. In the last analysis this chief of scriptural cities is men, not walls: just men made perfect, the city of the living God.
~ J. N. Birdsall. "City." *The New Bible Dictionary*. 3rd ed. (electronic ed.). Downers Grove, IL: InterVarsity Press, 1996. p. 209.

2. Jesus is the Cosmic Contractor, who by his own design and power is designing a city for us to live in. Human life began in a garden, but it will end, ultimately, in the city of God built by our Lord, John 14.1-4.

3. Our true identity and citizenship is associated with this city of God, Phil. 3.20-21.

C. The explicit goal of mission (evangelizing, discipling, and church planting) is to rob the cities of the lost in order to fill up the rolls of and populate the New Jerusalem, which is the true mother of all believers.

1. Jerusalem above is our true mother, Gal. 4.26.

2. The roll call above is the most significant one we can belong to, Ps. 87.3-6.

3. The word of the Lord will go from Jerusalem.

   a. Isa. 2.2-3

   b. Mic. 4.1-2

4. Gladness and joy will never leave its precincts, Isa. 65.18.

5. God himself will dwell with his people in the *final urban renewal project*, Joel 3.17.

3

IV. Implications for Urban Ministry

A. In all our mission praying, giving, and sending, we must focus upon the cities.

   1. Because of their strategic importance

   2. Because of their missionary significance

   3. Because of their spiritual centrality

B. Be proud and thankful for our responsibility to represent the Lord in the city.

C. Be strategic and cunning in how we might affect numerous regions through first generation contacts in members of a globalized network of contacts (*oikos, oikia*).

D. Pray for the city, and seek its health, for in its safety is our safety, Jer. 29.4-7.

Conclusion

» Three convincing reasons exist for the Church's involvement in urban mission.

» Cities are the world's seats of influence, power, and spiritual activity, are the magnets for the oppressed, the broken, and the poor, and are the primary picture and symbol of our spiritual destiny and inheritance.

Segue 2

Student Questions and Response

The following questions were designed to help you review the material in the second video segment. In this section we considered three claims about the city's importance in mission in the 21st millennium. First, cities are the seats of influence, power, and spiritual activity in the world today; through urbanization and immigration, they are also becoming the magnets for the world's oppressed, broken, and poor populations. Lastly, the Scriptures make plain that the city is the definitive and final picture and symbol of our spiritual destiny and inheritance. These reasons provide a clear rationale for a concentrated and strategic outreach to the cities of the world. Review the central ideas surrounding these reasons through the questions below.

1. List out the three reasons to show why urban mission must be a priority for all mission activity today. Of the three, which one do you believe is the *most compelling reason*? Explain your answer.

2. What part did the city play in the ministries of Jesus and the apostles? What role did Jerusalem play in their Kingdom advancing work? How did the Christian message spread through the Roman empire, how was this illustrated especially in the journeys of Paul?

3. What part did the following great centers of the Roman empire play in the advance of the Gospel in the early Church (e.g., Damascus, Antioch, Corinth, Philippi, Thessalonica, Athens, and Rome itself)?

4. How do the problems encountered in the ancient cities of old compare with the opportunities and problems we encounter today in the modern cities? How do cities today vary in size, scope, influence, and population? In what sense can we say that the modern cities "serve as the national and world centers of government, education, health-care, information, entertainment, trade, commerce, business, industry, jurisprudence, the military, and religion?"

5. List out the various categories that anthropologists use today to identify cities. List the characteristics of the following categories, with definitions and examples of each: *cultural cities, political and administrative cities, industrial cities, commercial cities, symbolic cities* and *primary cities.*

6. In the modern world what is causing such great numbers of the oppressed, the broken, and the poor to migrate to urban areas? In what sense can we say that urbanization represents "the most powerful characteristic of modern times?"

3

7. How does the Bible reveal "a clear and compelling witness" concerning God's heart for the poor? If it is true that God has a special concern for the poor, why then can we probably assert that he is also concerned with the American inner city, and the great cities of the world?

8. In what sense does the reality of the New Jerusalem reveal God's choice of the city as the picture and symbol of our spiritual destiny and inheritance? How does the New Jerusalem differ from the sense of the secular city displayed in the great cities of the past?

9. What is the explicit goal of mission as it relates to the cities of this lost world over against the dwelling place of the righteous, the New Jerusalem?

10. Finally, why must we always keep urban ministry and mission at the very center of all of our praying, giving, going, and sending others to serve in the city? According to the Lord's own Word, how do we ensure our own welfare as we dwell in the midst of a needy and hurting urban community?

3

In View of the City's Need, What Is the Mission of the Church?

The church's mission can be summed up in five general tasks. The order in which they are listed is not intended to suggest priorities. Biblically speaking each is vitally important. By stressing one more than the others, different groups of Christians have tended to see them as alternatives. God, however, allows us no choice.

1. ***It is to be involved in stewarding the material resources of creation.*** *This means encouraging a wise and harmonious use of the natural order created by God, by engaging in the numerous aspects of conservation and the elimination of pollution. The church will point to the creator's gift of life for all which implies renouncing greed, and a restrained enjoyment of material goods by all in such a way that future generations will find life sustainable on earth.*

2. ***It is to serve human beings without distinction and whatever their need.*** *It has a compassionate task to aid refugees and the victims of drought and famine and to help set up development schemes, literacy campaigns, health education and housing programmes. It has a particular responsibility to minister to the needs of the handicapped, old*

people, the bereaved, children at risk and families in tension, and to rehabilitate offenders against the law, alcoholics, drug-addicts and chronic gamblers.

3. ***It must bear witness to "the truth as it is in Jesus" (Eph. 4.21).*** *This includes a number of tasks, sometimes separated into apologetics, pre-evangelism and evangelism. Bearing witness means both the verbal communication of the apostolic gospel and visual demonstration of its power to bring new life and hope to human relationships and communities.*

4. ***It should be engaged in seeing that God's justice is done in society.*** *In particular, the church will be active in promoting and defending the integrity of family life against easy divorce, abortion, casual or abnormal sexual relationships, pornography, the exploitation of women and children, and experimentation on early human life. It will also seek alternatives to policies which give rise to more homeless, badly educated, undernourished and unemployed people. It will fight for human rights and against human discrimination. Finally, it will challenge the inexorable build-up of weapons of mass destruction and the increasing arms trade between rich and poor nations.*

5. ***It has a responsibility to show what it means in practice to be a reconciled and liberated community in the midst of a corrupt, distressed and despairing world.*** *It is sent to demonstrate the reality of God's unmerited grace by practising forgiveness, the sharing of goods and resources, by eliminating prejudice and suspicion, and by exercising power as servanthood, not as domination and control. The church is to be both a sign and an agent of God's purpose to create a new order where his peace and justice will reign.*

~ J. A. Kirk. "Missiology." **The New Dictionary of Theology**.
S. B. Ferguson, ed. (electronic ed.).
Downers Grove, IL: InterVarsity Press, 2000. p. 435.

3

This lesson focuses upon the city and its strategic role in mission. On account of the city's primacy both in terms of God's selection of the city as a symbol of transformation and safety, as well as its significance in the modern world, it must remain a priority in all Christian ministry and kingdom advancement. Take the time to carefully review the central truths in this lesson through the concepts listed below.

Summary of Key Concepts

- The concept of the city is central within the Old and New Testaments, and provides us with a simple overview of their ancient characteristics. Cities in the ancient world were different than villages in that they were a collection of houses and buildings surrounded by walls, were significant and impressive for their time, and some were dependent for protection and supply upon others. A common reality in the ancient world, cities of old were relatively small, typically unpaved, strengthened by thick walls and high towers, and seats of government and power.

- In terms of their spiritual meaning as outlined in Scripture, cities were associated with human rebellion and idolatry (e.g., Enoch, the city of Cain), with independence and arrogance (as in the case of the Tower of Babel), and with evil and godlessness (as with Babylon). Cities were judged by God for their sinfulness (e.g., Sodom and Gomorrah, Jericho, Nineveh), and denounced for their false sense of security and power (specifically, Jerusalem).

- Although associated with the rebellion of humankind, the Scriptures teach that God adopted the city as a symbol of his dwelling place and blessing. In spite of the fact that David won the city in battle, God selected Jerusalem for himself, and determined to make her a praise in the earth. Divine irony is present here; God transforms the secular image of self-dependence and rebellion into an image of *refuge* (i.e., the cities of Refuge), as well as the image of *reconciliation*, a place which can know and experience his forgiveness and blessing (i.e., Jonah and the experience of Nineveh).

- Because of the mercy and grace of Almighty God in Christ, hope exists for any city which repents in the face of his judgment, yields in the face of his demands, and seeks his mercy in the face of his punishment.

- Three critical reasons exist to sufficiently show why urban mission must be a priority for all mission activity today: the city is the seat of influence, power, and spiritual activity in the world, it is becoming a magnet for the oppressed, the broken, and the poor, and the city is seen as the picture of our spiritual destiny and inheritance.

➼ The city played an important role in the ministry of Jesus and the apostles. Jesus' own ministry of kingdom proclamation was rooted in city work, and his proclamation mandate centered around Jerusalem. Furthermore, Christianity was birthed in a city, and spread through the Roman empire in the first century via the great urban centers of the time (in places such as Damascus, Antioch, Corinth, Philippi, Thessalonica, Athens, and Rome itself).

➼ The ministry of the apostles after Christ were anchored in strategic outreach to the cities of the Roman empire, beginning with Jerusalem, moving to Samaria and Judea, to the very far flung corners of the Roman empire. Paul's journeys, as recorded in Acts, were virtually totally urban in character, occurring in centers which proved to be the gateways to the larger Roman empire.

➼ Many of the same problems and opportunities connected with the cities of Jesus and the apostles' day exist today in urban populations. The modern cities of the world are numerous in size, scope, and population, and serve as the national and world centers of government, education, health-care, information, entertainment, trade, commerce, business, industry, jurisprudence, the military, and religion.

➼ Anthropologists categorize cities in terms of their identity and focus. There are *cultural cities* (which lead the world in fashion, trends, and ideas), *political and administrative cities* (centers of worldwide decision making bodies, or those containing governments and their bureaucracies), *industrial cities* (noisy, blue-collar, factory centers host to central manufacturing industries) *commercial cities* (giant marketplaces or bazaars where goods and services are exchanged on worldwide basis), *symbolic cities* (cities where great historical struggles are fought, settled, and symbolized), and *primary cities* (those which combine all of the characteristics together).

➼ The modern cities of the world serve as magnets for the oppressed, the broken, and the poor. The Bible reveals a clear and compelling witness concerning God's heart for the poor, and the trend of urbanization (and its concentration on the poor) represents the most powerful characteristic of modern times. The argument is logical and plain: if God is concerned for the

3

poor, he likewise is concerned about the American inner city because of its staggering number of underclass and poor families.

↪ The Bible clearly shows how the city is the picture and symbol of our spiritual destiny and inheritance. The hope of the saints is to dwell with God in the New Jerusalem, not a place where God is absent and where arrogance rules, but rather the home of the righteous where God is present, and Jesus is adored as Lord of all.

↪ The explicit goal of mission is to *rob the cities of the world in order to fill up and populate* the New Jerusalem, the true mother of all believers (*God's final urban renewal project*).

↪ Because of the significance of the city both in Scripture and in the modern world, the city must remain at the hub of all missionary enterprise. Our praying, giving, and sending of laborers must focus on reaching unreached cities; we must recruit more missionaries to serve in the city, strategize how to affect unreached cities with the Gospel, and pray for the city and seek its safety, finding our safety in its preservation.

3

Now is the time for you to discuss with your fellow students your questions about the city and its place in mission today. Here is your opportunity to discuss your own ideas about the city, and the particular issues that you have about mission and the city in light of the material you have just studied. The priority here is on *your* questions; use the questions below to discover your own list of issues and concerns.

Student Application and Implications

* What is your opinion of the city–where did you grow up, and how did your family and the people who lived in your community view the city? How would you characterize your feeling about the city today?

* Is it easy for you to see the links between human rebellion, idolatry, independence, and arrogance and the modern American city? Do you think that God will judge the modern American city even as he did the ancient cities on account of their sinfulness and hardness of heart? Explain.

* Do you associate any city with the sense that we discovered in our lesson today, that is, as a symbol of God's dwelling place and blessing? Can this be said only of the New Jerusalem, or are we to strive to see our cities today in this way? Explain.

* If you could live in any city in the country, which one would it be and why? What are your current "blind spots" about the city, in other words, do you fail to see things (whether good or evil) with cities because of your *biases* either in favor or against them?

* Would you consider doing urban mission, planting churches and making disciples in an urban community? What about an urban *poor* community–do you presently have any biases or burdens against or for doing ministry in the city?

* How do you normally see people in the city–are they victims of oppression, or are they simply receiving the just desserts of their own actions and neglect? Explain your answer.

* Why do you think so few Christians in America seem concerned about the growing number of urban underclass who have no access to the Church in their own culture and language? Why do so many blame the conditions of many suffering urban dwellers on their own lack of moral integrity and personal responsibility?

* Complete the following sentence: "Before I would feel the freedom to go and do mission in the city, the Lord would have to . . ."

* Do you ever wish that God would *judge* some of the cities that exist today? Explain. Do you think that modern cities can count on the same response that God gave to the Ninevites if they were to repent and humble themselves, even as they did?

* Many think of cities only as places to visit on vacation or during a break. How would you say that you currently view your relationship to cities, and the people that live in them–what is your personal responsibility and calling concerning the city, and your call to serve in it?

* Do you pray for the cities of the world? If not, why not? Do you pray for your own city, its leaders and rulers, its population and needs, its opportunities, and spiritual hunger? How might you begin to pray more seriously on behalf of those who live in your urban community? Do you give and support urban mission locally? Globally? Where? (See "Let God Arise" in the appendix of this module.)

3

*   Does it thrill you that Jesus is building us a city to dwell in forever? Be as honest as possible in your response. Do *you understand* mission as *robbing the cities of the world in order to fill up and populate* the New Jerusalem, the true mother of all believers?

CASE STUDIES

Being a Chaplain or Playing Compromise?

1

The notion of the Church as the chaplain of the city is rooted in the instruction of the Lord through Jeremiah to the people of Judah before their captivity into Babylon. Rather than have them be discouraged and despondent in Babylon, God instructed them to raise their families within it, and to seek its welfare: "Thus says the Lord of hosts, the God of Israel, to all the exiles whom I have sent into exile from Jerusalem to Babylon: [5] Build houses and live in them; plant gardens and eat their produce. [6] Take wives and have sons and daughters; take wives for your sons, and give your daughters in marriage, that they may bear sons and daughters; multiply there, and do not decrease. [7] But seek the welfare of the city where I have sent you into exile, and pray to the Lord on its behalf, for in its welfare you will find your welfare" (Jer. 29.4-7). This case of the Babylonian captivity raises questions regarding the stance that believers ought to take in regard to a wicked and ungodly city. Rather than oppose it and stir up trouble within it, God advocates that his people build their families in the midst of the city, raise their families there, and to even multiply and grow there. The command to seek its welfare seems controversial; how can the well-being of the people of God be directly tied to the safety and security of Babylon, the symbol of idolatrous and rebelliousness before God? What does God's instruction to the Israelites tell us about the nature of the people of God to the city, and what lessons can we learn from this for our application today?

Staying Put or Moving Up and Out?

2

A major and growing African-American urban church is struggling with a decision about whether to stay in its current location, or move to a more advancing and upscale part of the community. With a dynamic pastor who is committed to the Word and the advance of the Kingdom, the church has steadily grown in number, influence, and resources. With a strong cache of leaders who are capable and submissive, and a congregation eager to serve, the leaders are seriously considering if they should move. Landlocked because of the property situation they are in, they cannot build in their current site. They have a number of ministries in the community which target the neediest members of it; the church has been there for decades, and is now in the midst of genuine renewal. With their pastor becoming more and more a city- and nationwide person of influence, the leaders are convinced that by moving and building, they could greatly increase their ministry opportunities and impact on the city. Others, who see the church as the salt and light of their current impoverished urban neighborhood, struggle with the idea of the church leaving a place where it is greatly needed to go to a community which is affluent and "safe." If you were called to advise the pastor and leaders on their upcoming decision, what principles and perspectives would you give them about the direction you think they ought to take?

That Kind of Good News Ain't Encouraging– Nothing's Changing around Here!

A conflict has arisen in an urban church that recently initiated a series of evangelistic outreaches in an extremely poor and isolated part of an inner city in a major Midwestern city. Motivated by a deep passion to go to places where other churches and ministries were unwilling or afraid to go, the pastor trained and commissioned an outreach team to go into the apartment complexes with the Gospel. The receptivity of many of the apartment's residents was amazing, including even managers of the building, which allowed the team access to certain unused apartments. With a fair amount of interest and participation, it was not long before the team had started its own Bible study, and saw fruit—some of the families and individuals in attendance came to Christ. During one of the studies one evening, an invited guest and resident of the apartment shared her feelings about the outreach team and the church who sent them. "I don't know you people, and honestly you seem to be okay. But, I don't understand how you can say God sent you in here to share the Good News 'bout Jesus, but nothing has changed in the neighborhood. The gangs are still crazy, ain't no jobs anywhere, and most of us are struggling just to get by. How can God send you guys in here just to tell us about salvation without saving us from the neighborhood? I just don't understand that. That kind of Good News ain't encouraging—nothing's changing around here!" How would you answer this dear sister's analysis and doubts?

An Evangelical Conspiracy against the American Inner City?

(Based on a true story). A prestigious Christian graduate school was establishing and funding a number of initiatives to reach unreached populations around the world, including Muslims, Chinese, and Slavic peoples. Many scholarships were offered to international students with a burden for ministry, and the school has equipped hundreds of qualified spiritual laborers serving Christ in fields all across the world. However, less than 25 minutes away, lay one of the largest ghettos in the United States. Over a million people live in substandard housing in violent, gang and drug infested neighborhoods, and virtually no Christian groups minister in their midst. When confronted with the disparity in the school's investment of thousands of dollars and hours in foreign mission but none in their own local community, the director of the school lamented how difficult it was to find donors to fund initiatives among America's urban poor. He found it easier to raise funds for the training of people in Honduras than in Houston, in Jamaica than in Jersey City. How do you explain the overall neglect of evangelicals to the needs and potential of the city? Why would it be easier for the director of the school to raise substantial funds for ministry overseas, and yet find it nearly impossible to get people to underwrite the equipping of workers for urban America?

The concept of the city is central within the Old and New Testaments, and provides us with a simple overview of their ancient characteristics. Cities in the ancient world were different than villages in that they were a collection of houses and buildings surrounded by walls, were significant and impressive for their time, and some were dependent for protection and supply upon others. A common reality in the ancient world, cities of old were relatively small, typically unpaved, strengthened by thick walls and high towers, and seats of government and power. In terms of their spiritual meaning as outlined in Scripture, cities were associated with human rebellion and idolatry (e.g., Enoch, the city of Cain), with independence and arrogance (as in the case of the Tower of Babel), and with evil and godlessness (as with Babylon). Cities were judged by God for their sinfulness (e.g., Sodom and Gomorrah, Jericho, Nineveh), and denounced for their false sense of security and power (specifically, Jerusalem). Although associated with the rebellion of humankind, the Scriptures teach that God adopted the city as symbol of his dwelling place and blessing. In spite of the fact that David won the city in battle, God selected Jerusalem for himself, and determined to make her a praise in the earth. Divine irony is present here; God transforms the secular image of

Restatement of the Lesson's Thesis

self-dependence and rebellion into an image of *refuge* (i.e., the cities of Refuge), as well as the image of *reconciliation*, a place which can know and experience his forgiveness and blessing (i.e., Jonah and the experience of Nineveh). Because of the mercy and grace of Almighty God in Christ, hope exists for any city which repents in the face of his judgment, yields in the face of his demands, and seeks his mercy in the face of his punishment.

Three critical reasons exist to sufficiently show why urban mission must be a priority for all mission activity today: the city is the seat of influence, power, and spiritual activity in the world, it is becoming a magnet for the oppressed, the broken, and the poor, and the city is seen as the picture of our spiritual destiny and inheritance. The city played an important role in the ministry of Jesus and the apostles. Jesus' own ministry of kingdom proclamation was rooted in city work, and his proclamation mandate centered around Jerusalem. Furthermore, Christianity was birthed in a city, and spread through the Roman empire in the first century via the great urban centers of the time (in places such as Damascus, Antioch, Corinth, Philippi, Thessalonica, Athens, and Rome itself). Many of the same problems and opportunities connected with the cities of Jesus and the apostles' day exist today in urban populations. The modern cities of the world are numerous in size, scope, and population, and serve as the national and world centers of government, education, health-care, information, entertainment, trade, commerce, business, industry, jurisprudence, the military, and religion.

Cities are known today by their identity and focus, whether they are cultural, political and administrative, industrial, commercial, symbolic, or primary cities. The modern cities of the world serve as magnets for the oppressed, the broken, and the poor. The Bible reveals a clear and compelling witness concerning God's heart for the poor, and if God is concerned for the poor, he likewise is concerned about the American inner city because of its staggering number of underclass and poor families. The city is the picture and symbol of our spiritual destiny and inheritance, the New Jerusalem, where God dwells and Christ is adored. The explicit goal of mission is to *rob the cities of the world in order to fill up and populate* the New Jerusalem, the true mother of all believers (*God's final urban renewal project*). Because of the significance of the city both in Scripture and in the modern world, the city must remain at the hub of all missionary enterprise.

3

If you are interested in pursuing some of the ideas of *Christian Mission and the City,* you might want to give these books a try:

Bakke, Ray, and Jim Hart. *The Urban Christian: Effective Ministry in Today's Urban World.* Downers Grove, IL: InterVarsity Press, 1987.

Conn, Harvie M., and Manuel Ortiz. *Urban Ministry: The Kingdom, the City, and the People of God.* Downers Grove, IL: InterVarsity Press, 2001.

Lupton, Robert D. *Theirs Is the Kingdom: Celebrating the Gospel in Urban America.* New York: HarperCollins Publishers, 1989.

Perkins, John. *Restoring At-Risk Communities: Doing It Together and Doing It Right.* Grand Rapids: Baker Books, 1995.

Seeking to relate these truths concerning the city and your role as an urban leader in your own ministry through your church represents the heart of this work. How God might want you to change or alter your ministry approach based on these truths is largely dependent on your ability to hear what the Holy Spirit is saying to you about where you are, where your pastoral leadership is, where the members of your church are, and what specifically God is calling you to do right now, if anything, about these truths. Plan to spend good time this week meditating on the divine irony of God selecting the city as his image of refuge, reconciliation, and restoration, and consider how your own ministry might be impacted through God's perspective on the significance and power of the city.

As you consider your ministry project for this module, you can possibly use it to connect to these insights on mission and the city in a direct way to a group you minister to on a regular basis. Seek the face of God for insight, and come back next week ready to share your insights with the other learners in your class.

Always take the time to pray about your lessons, even at those times when it appears that no specific burden or insight seems to grasp your mind and heart. The *discipline of prayer* is essential in learning the lessons which the Holy Spirit desires to give you from the intellectual work you have done to mine them from your study of this material. Calvin comments on this need for discipline in prayer, regardless of the feelings or leadings you may have:

*Wherefore, although it is true that while we are listless or insensible to our wretchedness, he wakes and watches for us and sometimes even assists us unasked; it is very much for our interest to be **constantly supplicating him**; first, that our heart may always be inflamed with a serious and ardent desire of seeking, loving and serving him, while we accustom ourselves to have recourse to him as a sacred anchor in every necessity; secondly, that no desires, no longing whatever, of which we are ashamed to make him the witness, may enter our minds, while we learn to place all our wishes in his sight, and thus pour out our heart before him; and, lastly, that we may be prepared to receive all his benefits with true gratitude and thanksgiving, while our prayers remind us that they proceed from his hand.*

~ John Calvin. **Institutes of the Christian Religion.**
Trans. of **Institutio Christianae Religionis**. Reprint, with new introd.
Originally published: Edinburgh: Calvin Translation Society, 1845-1846. (III, xx, 3).
(electronic ed.). Oak Harbor, WA: Logos Research Systems, Inc., 1997.

. . . .

Lift your heart up to God, and pray for yourself and your fellow students, and ask God to lead you into a deeper, clearer understanding of his will and word on mission, the city, and your calling to both.

3

ASSIGNMENTS ►

Scripture Memory

Hebrews 11.13-16

Reading Assignment

To prepare for class, please visit *www.tumi.org/books* to find next week's reading assignment, or ask your mentor.

Other Assignments

As usual you ought to come with your reading assignment sheet containing your summary of the reading material for the week. Also, you must have selected the text for your exegetical project, and turn in your proposal for your ministry project.

In this lesson we learned how the concept of the ancient city is born from its connection to self-reliance, arrogance, and rebellion against God, and how God adopted the concept of the city for his own purpose, using it as the symbol of refuge, repentance, and restoration. We also considered three convincing reasons for the Church's involvement in urban mission. Cities are the seats of influence, power, and spiritual activity, they are magnets for the oppressed, the broken, and the poor, and finally cities are the picture and symbol of our spiritual destiny and inheritance.

In our next lesson, we will move from a consideration of the city to the poor, our final concept in our study of the foundations for mission. We will examine the concept of the poor and mission through the lens of the rich biblical concept of *shalom*, or wholeness. As the covenant community of Yahweh, God called the people of Israel to live faithfully to his covenant. In so doing, poverty and injustice would be replaced with justice and righteousness. This mandate represents a blueprint for the people of God today. Jesus is Lord and Head of the Church, the new covenant community advancing the Kingdom today. God calls his people to live in *shalom* and demonstrate to its members and to the world his justice and mercy, especially on behalf of the poor and oppressed among us today.

Looking Forward to the Next Lesson

3

Name _____

Date _____

For each assigned reading, write a brief summary (one or two paragraphs) of the author's main point. (For additional readings, use the back of this sheet.)

Reading 1

Title and Author: _____ Pages _____

Reading 2

Title and Author: _____ Pages _____

LESSON
4

Christian Mission and the Poor

Lesson Objectives

Welcome in the strong name of Jesus Christ! After your reading, study, discussion, and application of the materials in this lesson, you will be able to:

- Define the concept of the poor in light of the biblical vision of *shalom*, or wholeness: *shalom* is the Hebrew term for "fullness of human community in fellowship with God and with one another."

- Outline the elements of *shalom* including its experience of health and wellness, safety and protection, harmony between neighbors, prosperity and material sufficiency, and the absence of malice and conflict–genuine peace. This also includes the idea of *shalom* as God's gracious provision, as connected with the coming of the Messiah who is the Prince of *shalom*, as well as *shalom* as the standard for the people of God.

- Explain how poverty is the denial of God's *shalom*, how his blessing was to prevent the occurrence of poverty, and the commands to the covenant community were designed to ensure justice and righteousness among Yahweh's people, and that faithfulness to the covenant was designed for the continuation of *shalom* among the Israelites as they obeyed his voice and met its conditions.

- Show how God is identified with the poor, i.e., it is his design to lift and bless them from their state, to punish those who oppress them, and to demand that his people demonstrate the same concern that he has on behalf of the broken, poor, and the oppressed. The Exodus is a key event which embodies God's identification with the poor and the oppressed, revealing his heart of justice, the creation of his covenant community which was called to be a reflection of his holiness, a model of justice and mercy, and a beacon for the nations.

- Lay out the biblical causes of poverty, including natural disaster and calamity (e.g., famine, drought, storm, etc.), personal laziness and slothfulness (e.g., bad decisions, immoral character, idleness, hard-heartedness, etc.), and oppression and injustice from the hands of the powerful (e.g., mistreatment, exploitation, defrauding wages, etc.). The

4

term "the poor" in the Scriptures is linked to a number of different concepts which serve as synonyms, including "the widow," "the fatherless," and the "stranger."

- List the standards God gave to his covenant people in regard to the generous and just treatment of the poor as a witness. These include special provisions for the care of the poor which were factored into the harvest and gleaning stipulations of the Law, justice in the courts where all matters, measures, and transactions were to be done honestly and rightly, regardless of person, and resources were to be shared in the Sabbatical year, with the poor provided a share of the produce of the fields and vineyards.

- Further list out the standards, including how the people of God were forbidden to charge interest to the poor, fair timely payment for a day's work (i.e., wages to be paid the same day with no oppression or defrauding allowed), with radical hospitality to be practiced to the poor (an "open hand policy"), and resources to be set aside for them (i.e., certain portions of the tithe and bounty to be given to the most needy and vulnerable in the midst of the community). The poor were to be included in all celebrations, and in the year of Jubilee, the poor were to recover their property, with provision made for those whose funds were short or absent.

- Note the implications of these standards for God's covenant community: God's people were in all their dealings to reflect God's identification with the poor, informed by God's deliverance of them at the Exodus, and were to demonstrate the Lord's *shalom* in all their relationships and dealings with others.

- Give evidence how Jesus' founding of the Church is God's new covenant kingdom community, called to demonstrate the same *shalom* in the midst of the people of God.

- Explain how Jesus' Messiahship was inaugurated in acts of healing the oppressed and preaching Good News to the poor, who were the object of his attention, calling, ministry, and purpose, and authenticated his Messiahship to John the Baptist through works of justice and preaching to the poor. Further show how he verified and confirmed the salvation of others by their treatment of the poor, and how he identified without reservation to the "least of these" (i.e., the hungry, thirsty, the stranger, the naked, the sick, and the prisoner).

- Show the connection between Christ's kingdom community, the Church, and its responsibility to demonstrate mercy and justice in the kingdom community, i.e., it is called to proclaim the Good News to the poor as the body of Christ in the world, and how it is called to give evidence of the life of the Age to Come in its display of justice on behalf of the poor. Also demonstrate that in the life and mission of the Church, empowered by the Holy Spirit, the *shalom* of God's OT covenant community is enjoyed and displayed.

- Demonstrate how the new community displays radical generosity and hospitality to the needy within the community, especially to the widows, fatherless, and poor in our midst, as well as makes provision for other churches during times of calamity and distress.

- Lay out how the new community is called to be an advocate for the poor, which is a hallmark of authentic Christian mission. This advocacy includes not being partial or bigoted on account of class or difference among the members of the body, possessing a commitment to be a community of good works on behalf of the poor and vulnerable, and working to help meet the practical needs of the hurting, especially those in the household of God.

- Discern the implications of the Church as the new community of the Kingdom for urban mission, including the demand to proclaim the Good News to the poor (i.e., respecting the poor as those who have been chosen by God, with whom Jesus identified, who are never to be patronized but dealt with justly and compassionately with full expectation of their transformation and contribution).

- Summarize further implications of this vision, including that the Church must act in accordance with God's choice of the poor (i.e., defending their cause, maintaining their rights, providing advocacy for them, and showing no partiality in our affairs in the Church); we are to be generous and hospitable in meeting the needs of the poor, sharing our own goods, being hospitable to strangers and to the imprisoned, and showing love as we have been shown.

- Lay out the final (and perhaps the most important) implication which is that the Church must seek justice and equity in dealing with the poor in our midst and in the world; we are not merely to meet necessities but strive to impact structures and relationships that will lead to a more just situation. As

4

the Lord in the OT demanded that the covenant community give the poor resources, so the Church is to "live the true prosperity Gospel," by seeking justice and equity on behalf of the poor in all dealings and issues.

Tell Me, Are You the One?

Luke 7.18-23 - The disciples of John reported all these things to him. And John, [19] calling two of his disciples to him, sent them to the Lord, saying, "Are you the one who is to come, or shall we look for another?" [20] And when the men had come to him, they said, "John the Baptist has sent us to you, saying, 'Are you the one who is to come, or shall we look for another?'" [21] In that hour he healed many people of diseases and plagues and evil spirits, and on many who were blind he bestowed sight. [22] And he answered them, "Go and tell John what you have seen and heard: the blind receive their sight, the lame walk, lepers are cleansed, and the deaf hear, the dead are raised up, the poor have good news preached to them. [23] And blessed is the one who is not offended by me."

The ministry of Jesus as Messiah came on the scene in Judea with much excitement and anticipation, but it was not immediately obvious to all that he was the Messiah, and this is true even of John the Baptist. The remarkable nature of the miracles and mighty works of Jesus steadily gained audience in the latter days of John the Baptist. As the ministry of John decreased, so Jesus increased in both scope and influence (cf. John 3.30). John baptized the nation for repentance in anticipation of the unveiling of Jesus' declaration of the Kingdom of God, and Jesus demonstrated its power in his miracles, his sermons, and the nature of his own character and life. Every part of who Jesus was and what he did communicated to the validity of his claims: Jesus of Nazareth was the Messiah of God, proclaiming the Kingdom present in his incarnation in the world.

As the report went all throughout Judea and the surrounding region of Jesus' mighty works, the disciples of John heard of his works, and went and reported them to John. John sent two of his disciples to Jesus with the very straightforward question: "Are You the Coming one, or do we look for another?" There was enough evidence in Jesus' works and standing to reveal, at the very least, a prophetic calling upon the life of the Nazarene. John's question need not be interpreted as evidence of his own doubt or misunderstanding: his question reveals John's desire for truth and plainness, especially in the sense of Jesus' own testimony of his identity.

Luke tells us that in the very hour that Jesus heard the question from John's disciples, he began to cure people of their many infirmities and afflictions, and cast out demons. To the blind he gave sight. What a flurry of evidences Jesus must have provided for John regarding his identity! Both in terms of number and diversity, we can easily suppose that Jesus was fully convincing to the disciples of John that in him the power of the Kingdom of God was present, and that God was working through him to demonstrate deeds of deliverance, healings, and miracles.

After this powerful demonstration of his own kingdom authority and power, Jesus answers John's two disciples with his commentary on the meaning of what he had just accomplished. Jesus instructs them to go and tell John the things that they personally beheld Jesus to do—tell John specifically of the works that they had witnessed him accomplish. "The blind see, the lame walk, the lepers are cleansed, the deaf hear, the dead are raised, and the poor have the gospel preached to them." And Jesus closes with the very marvelous saying that the one who is not offended by him is blessed.

Here we have in shorthand the clearest sense of Jesus' own verification of his identity. How did Jesus know that John would understand the meaning of his acts of miracles and healings as a sign of his Messiahship? Why was he convinced that to tell John that the poor are having the Gospel of the Kingdom preached to them would be unmistakable evidence that he, in fact, was the Messiah of God. Maybe a few texts might show why:

> Isa. 32.3-4 - Then the eyes of those who see will not be closed, and the ears of those who hear will give attention. [4] The heart of the hasty will understand and know, and the tongue of the stammerers will hasten to speak distinctly.

> Isa. 35.5-6 - Then the eyes of the blind shall be opened, and the ears of the deaf unstopped; [6] then shall the lame man leap like a deer, and the tongue of the mute sing for joy. For waters break forth in the wilderness, and streams in the desert

> Isa. 42.6-7 - I am the Lord; I have called you in righteousness; I will take you by the hand and keep you; I will give you as a covenant for the people, a light for the nations, [7] to open the eyes that are blind, to bring out the prisoners from the dungeon, from the prison those who sit in darkness.

> Isa. 42.16 - And I will lead the blind in a way that they do not know, in paths that they have not known I will guide them. I will turn the darkness before them into light, the rough places into level ground. These are the things I do, and I do not forsake them.

4

Isa. 61.1-3 - The Spirit of the Lord God is upon me, because the Lord has anointed me to bring good news to the poor; he has sent me to bind up the brokenhearted, to proclaim liberty to the captives, and the opening of the prison to those who are bound; [2] to proclaim the year of the Lord's favor, and the day of vengeance of our God; to comfort all who mourn; [3] to grant to those who mourn in Zion- to give them a beautiful headdress instead of ashes, the oil of gladness instead of mourning, the garment of praise instead of a faint spirit; that they may be called oaks of righteousness, the planting of the Lord, that he may be glorified.

Jesus' answer shows what the Messiah would be, and why his own works and actions correspond perfectly to that image. Jesus' healings and preaching the Good News to the poor are signs of the Messianic era, that the Kingdom of God has come, and most importantly, that Jesus of Nazareth is the Messiah of the Kingdom. We know that Jesus is the One by what he did with (and said to) the poor.

How, then, do we reveal our connection to the Messiah? By loving the hungry, thirsty, naked, stranger, prisoner, and the sick as if they were him, as if he were them, for in fact, what we do (or don't do) to them, we are doing it to him (Matt. 25.31-46). The Messianic era (and the Messianic community) will be known by its justice and righteousness done on behalf of the broken and the needy.

This is significant for us today. The true Messiah proved his spiritual credential by virtue of his love, generosity, care, and healing of the most vulnerable, unlovely, and needy persons in Israelite society, and by his preaching to the poor the Good News of God's Kingdom come. Now his followers must demonstrate their authenticity by fleshing out the same works to the same people as he. Indeed, those who claim to be abiding in him ought to walk, even as he walked (1 John 2.6).

Jesus is certainly the One that we all are looking for. By the way, are you a member of his new forever-to-live Messianic community? As the campfire tune suggests, "And they'll know we are Christians by our love, by our love, yes, they'll know we are Christians by our love."

Nicene Creed and Prayer

After reciting and/or singing the Nicene Creed (located in the Appendix), pray the following prayer:

O God, you invite the poor and the sinful to take their place in the festive assembly of the new covenant. May your church always honor the presence of the Lord in the humble and the suffering, and may we learn to recognize each other as brothers and sisters, gathered together around your table. We ask this through our Lord Jesus Christ, who lives and reigns with you in the unity of the Holy Spirit, one God, forever and ever. Amen.

~ Presbyterian Church (U.S.A.) and Cumberland Presbyterian Church. The Theology and Worship Ministry Unit. **Book of Common Worship**. Louisville, KY: Westminister/John Knox Press, 1993. p. 372.

Quiz

Put away your notes, gather up your thoughts and reflections, and take the quiz for Lesson 3, *Christian Mission and the City*.

Scripture Memorization Review

Review with a partner, write out and/or recite the text for last class session's assigned memory verse: Hebrews 11.13-16.

Assignments Due

Turn in your summary of the reading assignment for last week, that is, your brief response and explanation of the main points that the authors were seeking to make in the assigned reading (Reading Completion Sheet).

4

How Can They Live that Way?

 In a society that values hard work, industry, and personal responsibility, the "truly needy" poor have a difficult time showing that they merit help and support. Generally, there is a tendency not to define or sketch out the poor on the basis of historical oppressions, systemic social policies that make it hard for them to participate in the larger society, or mistreatment by those in power. Rather, in American mainstream culture, a poor person is poor because of a lack of initiative, hard work, personal dignity, and moral failure. Admittedly, many actually are poor because of their own moral failure, bad personal decisions, addictions, or slothfulness. However, these are deemed to be the vast majority of the poor; and oftentimes, policies and responses to the poor are based on what is viewed as poor people's lack of discipline and determination to better their situation. It is quite fashionable, even in Christian settings, to blame them for their situations. This view would claim that there are plenty of opportunities available for anyone who truly wants to better themselves and their condition. If a person is poor for a long time, it is their own fault—there is no reason that anyone needs to live that way. What do you make of this position, which is so popular among many non-Christian, middle class cultures, and even among Christians as well?

True Religion

In discussing the issue of faith and salvation, a major question has remained through Christian history: What truly is "saving faith?" How do we know that a person has legitimately repented from their sin and idolatry, and believed in the Lord Jesus Christ? In the history of evangelical tradition, we have usually relied on outside indicators at the time of salvation to serve as evidence of authentic faith. A hand that goes up at the end of preaching, someone standing up to indicate their desire for salvation, going down front and praying with the pastor, and praying the "Sinner's Prayer" have all been used as solid evidences of saving faith. However, more of the biblical evidences occur long after the initial claim to faith: does the person love their brothers and sisters in Christ (John 13.34-35), have they demonstrated a real heart for those who lack basic food and clothes (James 2.14-16), and have they opened their heart of compassion to those who need help (1 John 3.16-18)? True religion, according to James, is to meet the needs of widows and orphans in their distress, and to keep oneself unspotted from the world (James 1.27). How do you think the traditional evangelical evidences of saving faith line up with what the Bible says here and elsewhere about our conduct toward the poor being the proof of our relationship with God?

Give Them a Fishing Line

The old adage, "If you give a person a fish you feed them for a day, but if you give them a fishing line, you feed them for a lifetime" is taken nearly universally to be good social policy for our treatment of the poor. Many actually believe that the welfare systems have failed for this very reason; unbroken financial support with little or no stipulation as to how the money is spent is seen as aiding dependence and undermining personal responsibility. Unfortunately, many who have received aid actually have come to see the government as their provider, spawning some to forego employment in favor of the support (as limited as it is). Now, many state and local agencies are setting hard limits on the length of time that a person can receive government aid, and are making job training and participation mandatory. They argue that aid is for temporary support not permanent care. Those who argue against these kinds of approaches claim that while these initiatives look good, they do not address the more fundamental issues of a living wage at a job that actually can support a growing family. The short term gain of getting a person on welfare off the rolls only undermines the more fundamental question as to whether or not you can quickly reshape a social situation that took years to develop. In your opinion what ought to be a defensible Christian view about the role of government in supporting the lives of its most needy citizens?

CONTENT ► **Christian Mission and the Poor**

Segment 1: *Shalom* in the Covenant Community

Rev. Dr. Don L. Davis

Summary of Segment 1

The concept of the poor is built on the biblical vision of *shalom,* or wholeness: *shalom* is the Hebrew term for "fullness of human community in fellowship with God and with one another." The biblical elements of *shalom* include the experience of health and wellness, safety and protection from harm, harmony between neighbors, prosperity and material sufficiency, and the absence of malice and conflict–genuine peace. It also includes the idea of *shalom* as God's gracious provision, as is connected with the coming of the Messiah who is the Prince of *shalom,* as well as *shalom* as the standard for the people of God. Poverty is the denial of God's *shalom*; his blessing and provision were given to prevent the occurrence of poverty, and the commands to the covenant community were designed to ensure justice and righteousness among Yahweh's people. The Exodus embodies God's identification with the poor and the oppressed, revealing his heart of justice and creating his covenant community which was called to be a reflection of his holiness, a model of justice and mercy, and a beacon for the nations.

The Scriptures define several causes of poverty, including natural disaster and calamity (e.g., famine, drought, storm, etc.), personal laziness and slothfulness (e.g., bad decisions, immoral character, idleness, hard-heartedness, etc.), and oppression and injustice from the hands of the powerful (e.g., mistreatment, exploitation, defrauding wages, etc.). The term "the poor" in the Scriptures is linked to a number of different concepts which serve as synonyms, including "the widow," "the fatherless," and the "stranger." God's covenant standards give witness of his heart for them, including such things as the harvest and gleaning stipulations of the Law, justice in the courts where all matters, measures, and transactions were to be done honestly and rightly, and resources of the people were to be shared in the Sabbatical year, with the poor being provided a share of the produce of the fields and vineyards. The implications of these standards for God's covenant community are plain: God's people were in all their actions to reflect God's identification with the poor, informed by God's deliverance of them at the Exodus, and were to demonstrate the Lord's *shalom* in all their relationships and dealings with others.

Our objective for this segment, *Shalom in the Covenant Community*, is to enable you to see that:

- The concept of the poor is built on the biblical vision of *shalom*, or wholeness: *shalom* is the Hebrew term for "fullness of human community in fellowship with God and with one another."

- The biblical elements of *shalom* include the experience of health and wellness, safety and protection from harm, harmony between neighbors, prosperity and material sufficiency, and the absence of malice and conflict–genuine peace. It also includes the idea of *shalom* as God's gracious provision, as is connected with the coming of the Messiah who is the Prince of *shalom*, as well as *shalom* as the standard for the people of God.

- Poverty is the denial of God's *shalom*; his blessing and provision was given to prevent the occurrence of poverty, and the commands to the covenant community were designed to ensure justice and righteousness among Yahweh's people. Faithfulness to the covenant was designed for the continuation of *shalom* among Israel as they obeyed his voice and met its conditions.

- God identifies with the poor, i.e., it is his design to lift and bless them from their state, to punish those who oppress them, and to demand that his people demonstrate the same concern that he has for the broken, poor, and the oppressed. The Exodus is a key event which embodies God's identification with the poor and the oppressed, revealing his heart of justice and creating his covenant community which was called to be a reflection of his holiness, a model of justice and mercy, and a beacon for the nations.

4

- The Scriptures define several causes of poverty, including natural disaster and calamity (e.g., famine, drought, storm, etc.), personal laziness and slothfulness (e.g., bad decisions, immoral character, hard idleness, heartedness, etc.), and oppression and injustice from the hands of the powerful (e.g., mistreatment, exploitation, defrauding wages, etc.). The term "the poor" in the Scriptures is linked to a number of different concepts which serve as synonyms including "the widow," "the fatherless," and the "stranger."

- God's covenant standards of generous and just treatment of the poor serve as a witness to his own heart for them. He made special provisions for the care of the poor which were factored into the harvest and gleaning stipulations of the Law, and justice in the courts where all matters, measures, and transactions were to be done honestly and rightly. The resources of the people were to be shared in the Sabbatical year, with the poor being provided a share of the produce of the fields and vineyards.

- The people of God were forbidden to charge interest to the poor, and instructed to pay a just and timely payment for a day's work (i.e., wages to be paid the same day with no oppression or defrauding allowed). Radical hospitality was to be practiced to the poor (an "open hand policy") and resources were to be set aside for them (i.e., certain portions of the tithe and bounty to be given to the most needy and vulnerable in the midst of the community). The poor were to be included in all celebrations, and in the year of Jubilee, the poor were to recover their property, with provision made for those whose funds were short or absent.

- The implications of these standards for God's covenant community are plain: God's people were in all their actions to reflect God's identification with the poor, informed by God's deliverance of them at the Exodus, and were to demonstrate the Lord's *shalom* in all their relationships and dealings with others.

I. The Concept of the Poor in the OT

Video Segment 1
Outline

A. God's kingdom community and wholeness (*shalom*)

1. *Shalom* (wholeness) is the Hebrew term for the fullness of human community in fellowship with God and one another.

Poverty Has Never Been God's Will

2. Wholeness or *shalom* is a pregnant concept, inclusive of a rich fullness of realities and blessings.

   a. It includes the experience of health and wellness, Gen. 43.28.

   b. It involves safety (protection from pain and harm), Ps. 4.8.

   c. It involves harmony and agreeableness between neighbors, 1 Sam. 16.4.

   d. It involves prosperity and material sufficiency, Ps. 73.3.

   e. It involves the absence of malice and conflict, genuine peace, Ps. 120.7.

3. *Shalom is directly associated with the covenant community's experience of right relationship with God. It is a result of his gracious provision.*

4. Messiah would be a Prince of *shalom* bringing everlasting *shalom* to the Kingdom of God under his righteous reign, Isa. 9.6-7.

Poverty as a social reality is never idealized in the OT. Poverty is need, distress and suffering, and contrary to the will of God. "There will be no poor among you, for the Lord will bless you in the land which the Lord your God gives you for an inheritance to possess" (Deut. 15.4, RSV). Poverty is a curse; stability and prosperity are blessings from God. But the experience of God's blessing should result in generosity and in care for the poor (Deut. 15.7–11).
~ Hans Kvalbein. "Poverty." *The New Dictionary of Biblical Theology.* T. D. Alexander, ed. (electronic ed.). Downers Grove, IL: InterVarsity Press, 2001.

4

5. God's standard for his people, therefore, is to stand against and repel anything that would interfere with his desire for *shalom* among his people.

B. Poverty as the denial of God's *shalom*

1. The blessing of the Lord was to prevent the occurrence of poverty among his people, Deut. 15.4-5.

2. Obedience to the commands and standards of God would have ensured justice and righteousness in the covenant community.

    a. Isa. 58.10-11

    b. Prov. 28.27

C. Faithfulness to the covenant: the duty of the people of God for the continuation of *shalom*

1. The *shalom* of the Lord was a gift, but the effort to pursue the well-being of others was based on their responsible obedience to God's will, Deut. 28.1-8.

2. Obeying God's voice and keeping the covenant was the *condition* of experiencing God's blessing and care, Exod. 19.5-6.

3. This separation to the will and standard of the Lord was directly related to the covenant community's relationship to God, Lev. 11.44-45.

II. God's Identity with the Poor

A. General texts as to God's identification with the poor

1. The Sovereign God of history works to lift and bless the poor and the oppressed, Exod. 3.7-8; 6.5-7; Deut. 6.6-8.

2. God will work against the oppressor to liberate and bless those who are oppressed and destroyed on account of their burden.

   a. Ps. 12.5

   b. Ps. 10.12

   c. Cf. Jer. 5.26-29; Ps. 10; Isa. 3.14-25; Jer. 22.13-19; Amos 5.11; 6.4; 7.11, etc.

3. God's identification with the poor is dramatically strong, Prov. 14.31; 19.17.

4. God demands that the covenant community demonstrate the same concern on behalf of the broken, poor, and oppressed, Exod. 22.21-24, cf., Deut. 15.13-15.

God's Identifies with the Poor

The prophetic books frequently accuse the rich of oppressing the poor (Amos 8.4–6; Isa. 10.1–4; 32.6–7; Mic. 3.1–4; Jer. 5.26–29; Ezek. 18.12–13). True piety includes care for the poor and real fasting includes sharing bread with the hungry (Isa. 58.5–10). The wisdom literature contains both proclamations of God's blessing for those who care for the helpless (Prov. 14.21, 31; 19.17; 22.9; 28.8; 31.20; Eccles. 11.1) and warnings against closing ear and hand to the need of the poor (Prov. 21.13; 28.27). God is their protector, and those who mock or oppress the poor insult their creator (Prov. 14.31; 17.5).
~ Hans Kvalbein. "Poverty." *The New Dictionary of Biblical Theology*. T. D. Alexander, ed. (electronic ed.). Downers Grove, IL: IVP, 2001.

B. The Exodus as key event: *in light of God's rescue and deliverance of Israel when they were sojourners and slaves, they should show mercy to those within the covenant community.*

    1. Exod. 22.21

    2. Exod. 23.9

    3. Deut. 10.18-19

    4. Deut. 24.17-18

C. The creation of God's kingdom community

    1. A reflection of God's of holiness, Exod. 19

    2. A model of justice and mercy, Exod. 19.5-6

    3. A beacon for the nations, Deut. 26.18-19

III. Causes of Poverty in the Scriptures

A. Natural disaster and calamity

    1. The exigencies of life: "becoming poor"

a. Lev. 25.25

b. Lev. 25.35

c. Lev. 25.36-39

2. Famine, Acts 11.27-29

3. Things lying outside of one's control, e.g., Job

a. Job 1.1-3

b. Job 1.13-19

B. Personal laziness and slothfulness

1. Poverty comes powerfully and suddenly upon the person who refuses to work, Prov. 6.6-11.

2. Slothfulness tends to place the person so afflicted under the control of another, Prov. 12.24.

3. Hunger is the legacy of an idle person, Prov. 19.15.

4. Slothfulness affects every part of the life, Prov. 19.24.

5. A desire for leisure and rest brings to poverty, Prov. 20.13.

6. The property of a lazy person is in constant disrepair, Eccles. 10.18.

C. Oppression and injustice from the hands of the powerful

1. Oppression and mistreatment are harshly warned against by the Lord, Exod. 22.21-27

2. It is sinful and immoral to oppress the poor, Deut. 24.15, 17-19.

3. God will hold the oppressor personally accountable for their mistreatment of the vulnerable and weak, Ps. 82.1-4.

4. God is personally insulted at the mistreatment of a poor person, and is honored by the person who shows respect to the poor, Prov. 14.31.

5. To crush the poor is to welcome the judgment of God, Isa. 3.13-15.

6. Oppression frustrates and sabotages all attempts toward intimacy with God, Isa. 58.1-3.

7. Cf. Ps. 14.6; 12.5; 35.10; Prov. 13.23; Job 24.2-4; Eccl. 5.8; Jer. 22.11-17

4

D. Summary

"In the Old Testament, 'poor' can be translated by six major and three other terms—totaling about 300 references, and revealing a broad understanding of the causes, reality, and consequences of poverty. The poor person is the downtrodden, humiliated, oppressed; the man pleading and crying out for justice; the weak or helpless; the destitute; the needy, dependent person; and the one forcibly subjected to the powerful oppressor. The wide range of terms shows that 'the poor' must be seen from many perspectives. Clustering around 'the poor' are linked words like 'the widow,' 'the fatherless' and 'the stranger.'"

~ "Christian Witness to the Urban Poor."
**Report of the Consultation of World Evangelization
Mini-Consultation on Reaching the Urban Poor.**
Lausanne Committee for World Evangelization, 1980.

IV. The Standards of God's Covenant Community: Giving Witness as the People of God

As God's own covenant community, the people of Israel were under obligation to display the freedom, wholeness, and justice of the Lord God, whose righteous laws were for the protection, wellness, and blessedness (shalom) of God's people.

A. *Provision made for the poor*: the fields were not to be fully harvested to allow the poor to glean the fields.

  1. Do not reap to the edge of your fields for the poor's sake, Lev. 19.9-10.

  2. Do not return to (re-reap) your fields, Deut. 24.19-22.

B. *Justice in the courts*: God's covenant community was to exact justice in all business and legal dealings.

OT Commands Designed to Combat Poverty

Many commandments in the law are explicitly intended to help the poor. In Deuteronomy the Sabbath commandment is socially motivated: the right to rest on the Sabbath is also for servants and strangers (Deut. 5.12–15). During the harvest the corner of the field and the gleanings should be left for the poor (Lev. 19.9–10; Deut. 24.17–22). The law prohibits a creditor from taking interest or a garment from the indebted poor (Exod. 22.25–27; Deut. 24.12–13). In Deuteronomy 14.28–29 and 26.12 there are prescriptions for a special tithe for the poor, for the benefit of the Levite, the sojourner, the fatherless and the widows. In the sabbatical year the land was left fallow so that the poor could eat from it (Lev. 25.1–7; Deut. 15.1–11).
~ Hans Kvalbein. "Poverty." *The New Dictionary of Biblical Theology.* T. D. Alexander, ed. (electronic ed.). Downers Grove, IL: IVP, 2001.

1. Honest courts dealing with the truth of the matter, regardless of a person's place or station, Exod. 23.2-3, Lev. 19.15; Deut. 10.17-18

2. Honest weights and measures in all business transactions and commercial dealings, Lev. 19.35-36, Prov. 11.1, Amos 8.5

C. *Shared resources*: in the Sabbatical year, the poor were provided a share of the produce of the fields and vineyards.

1. No sojourner was to be oppressed or harmed in the covenant community, Exod. 23.9-11.

2. For the Sabbath year, provision was to be made for servants and sojourners as well as family, Lev. 25.3-6.

D. *Interest forbidden*: the people of God were forbidden to charge usury (interest), and garments pledged had to be returned before the sun went down.

1. No interest to be exacted from the poor person, Exod. 22.25-27

2. The pledge of clothing was to be returned the same day "as the sun sets," Deut. 24.10-13.

E. *Fair, timely payment for a day's work*: wages were to be paid to the day laborer before the sun went down.

1. Wages to be paid on the same day, before the sun sets, Deut. 24.14-15

4

2. No oppression or robbing is permitted, Lev. 19.13

F. *Open hands, open hearts always to the poor*: radical generosity was to be practiced to anyone found to be poor or needy, Deut. 15.7-11.

  1. No hardness of heart or spite in regard to the poor in the land.

  2. The internal motivation is addressed here: you shall open wide your hand to your brother, to the needy and poor in your land, Deut. 15.11.

G. *Resources set aside for the poor*: certain portions of the tithe were to be given to the poor, which was tied directly to God's blessing on their lives and produce.

  1. Tithes and provisions to be brought out to meet the needs of the priests, along with the "sojourner, fatherless, and widow" (i.e., the most vulnerable people in the covenant community), Deut. 14.28-29

  2. Setting aside bounty for the vulnerable was directly linked to one's relationship to God and the covenant community itself, Deut. 26.12-15.

H. *Celebration and Festivals, too*: the poor were to be included in the feasts and festivals with the people of God.

  1. The Feast of Weeks, Deut. 16.10-12

  2. The Feast of Booths, Deut. 16.13-14

I.   *Access to productive resources again*: in the year of Jubilee, the poor were to recover their property.

1.   The restoration of the property was to be done justly and fairly, Lev. 25.13-17.

2.   Provision is made for those whose funds and resources were short or non-existent, Lev. 25.25-28.

V.   The Implications for God's Standard in the Covenant Community: Live out the *Shalom* of God in the midst of the Covenant Community

. . . .

The Poor in the OT: A Summary

The impression is sometimes given that God prospered the righteous with material possessions (Ps. 112.1–3). While it is true that the benefits of industry and thrift to individuals and to the nation are clearly seen, and that God promises to bless those who keep his commandments (Deut. 28.1–14), there were numbers of poor people in Israel at every stage of the nation's history. Their poverty might have been caused through natural disasters leading to bad harvests, through enemy invasion, through oppression by powerful neighbors or through extortionate usury. There was an obligation on the wealthier members of the community to support their poorer brethren (Deut. 15.1–11). Those who were most likely to suffer poverty were the fatherless and the widows and the landless aliens (gerim). They were often the victims of oppression (Jer. 7.6; Amos 2.6–7a), but Yahweh was their vindicator (Deut. 10.17–19; Ps. 68.5–6). The law commanded that provision should be made for them (Deut. 24.19–22), and with them were numbered the Levites (Deut. 14.28–29) because they had no holding of land. A man could sell himself into slavery, but if he were a Hebrew he had to be treated differently from a foreigner (Lev. 25.39–46).

~ R. E. Nixon. "Poverty." **The New Bible Dictionary**. D. R. W. Wood, ed. 3rd ed. (electronic ed.). Downers Grove, IL: InterVarsity Press, 1996. p. 945.

. . . .

4

A. God's people are to reflect God's own identification with the poor, informed by their historical experience in the Exodus event.

B. God will demonstrate *shalom* as we follow the Lord and his commands.

Conclusion

> The concept of poverty can be understood through the biblical lens of *shalom*, or the wholeness of God's covenant community.

> Although Israel was unfaithful in demonstrating God's justice and righteousness, the biblical foundation reveals that God identified with the poor in their plight, and asked his people to demonstrate that *shalom* in their dealings with one another as a light to the nations.

Please take as much time as you have available to answer these and other questions that the video brought out. In this section we saw how the concept of poverty is related to the biblical notion of *shalom*, or the wholeness of God's covenant community. In all of God's covenant demands and stipulations, he desired that his people demonstrate his own deep love and commitment to the poor. While Israel did not always obey his will in demonstrating justice and righteousness to the poor, his demands were plain. God identified himself with the poor in their plight, and demanded that his people demonstrate his love for justice, his *shalom*, in their dealings with one another as his covenant community. Review these important truths, and their implication for mission, by answering the questions below.

Segue 1

Student Questions and Response

1. What is the definition of *shalom*, and how does it relate to the biblical definition and understanding of poverty?

2. What are some of the critical biblical elements that fill out the concept of *shalom* in the midst of God's people? Why can *shalom* never be understood as the work of people alone, but always as a product of God's gracious provision? How is it connected with the coming of the Messiah?

3. Explain how poverty (and its effects) is a denial of God's *shalom*. How were God's blessing, provisions, and commands of the covenant designed to overcome poverty and ensure justice and righteousness among his people?

4. In what sense can we say that God identifies with the poor in their plight and condition? How does the Exodus event embody and give shape to God's identification with the poor and the oppressed? How was Israel meant to be a "reflection of his holiness, a model of justice and mercy, and a beacon for the nations" through the covenant?

5. What are the three major causes of poverty in the Scriptures, and how do they relate to one another? How is the term "the poor" in Scripture linked to other concepts which serve as its synonyms, for example, "the widow," "the fatherless," and the "stranger?"

6. List out some of God's standards for treatment of the poor in the OT covenant community. How do these standards serve as a witness, both to his heart for the poor, as well as his applied wisdom to his people for the elimination of poverty among them?

7. List two of the covenant standards God gave to his people and thoroughly discuss them in light of their meaning and implication for *shalom*. How might these standards inform our treatment of the poor today? Be specific.

8. In looking at these standards for God's covenant community, what are the key implications of them? How do these standards inform our thinking about our foundations for doing justice, discipleship, and mission today?

4

Christian Mission and the Poor

Segment 2: Missional Principles and Implications for Doing Ministry in the City

Rev. Dr. Don L. Davis

**Summary of
Segment 2**

Jesus is both the founder and head of the Church, God's new covenant kingdom community, which is called to demonstrate God's *shalom* in the midst of the people of God today. Jesus identified himself as the Messiah of the OT prophets and promise. He inaugurated his Messianic ministry with acts of healing the oppressed and preaching good news to the poor, authenticated his Messiahship to John the Baptist through works of justice and preaching to the poor, verified and confirmed the salvation of others by their treatment of the poor, and identified without reservation to the "least of these" (i.e., the hungry, thirsty, the stranger, the naked, the sick, and the prisoner). The Church is God's kingdom community. It is called to proclaim the Good News of the Kingdom to the poor, to act as the body of Christ with one another, and to give evidence of the life of the Age to Come in its display of justice in the world. In the life and mission of the Church, empowered by the Holy Spirit, the *shalom* of God's OT covenant community is enjoyed and displayed. As Christ's body in the world, the Church is called to be an advocate for the poor, which is a hallmark of authentic Christian mission. Regarding urban mission, the Church is called to proclaim the Good News to the poor, which includes respecting them as chosen by God and those with whom Christ identified. We are never to patronize them but deal with them justly and compassionately, confident of their ability to be transformed and to contribute to the Kingdom's advance. We are not merely to meet surface needs but strive to impact structures and relationships that will lead to a more just situation, living the true "prosperity Gospel," which is to seek justice and equity on behalf of the most vulnerable among us.

Our objective for this segment, *Missional Principles and Implications for Doing Ministry in the City*, is to enable you to see that:

- Jesus is both the founder and Head of the Church, God's new covenant kingdom community, which is called to demonstrate God's *shalom* in the midst of the people of God today.

- Jesus identified himself as the Messiah of the OT prophets and promise. He inaugurated his Messianic ministry with acts of healing the oppressed and preaching good news to the poor, who were the object of his attention, calling, ministry, and purpose, and authenticated his Messiahship to John the Baptist through works of justice and preaching to the poor. Furthermore, Jesus verified and confirmed the salvation of others by their treatment of the poor, and identified without reservation to the "least of these" (i.e., the hungry, thirsty, the stranger, the naked, the sick, and the prisoner).

- The Church is God's kingdom community. It is called to proclaim the Good News of the Kingdom to the poor, to act as the body of Christ with one another, and to give evidence of the life of the Age to Come in its display of justice in the world. In the life and mission of the Church, empowered by the Holy Spirit, the *shalom* of God's OT covenant community is enjoyed and displayed.

- The Church is called to display radical generosity and hospitality to the needy, with special priority and provision for those within the community, especially to the widows, fatherless, and the poor. We are also responsible to make provision for other churches during times of calamity and distress.

- As Christ's body in the world, the Church is called to be an advocate for the poor, which is a hallmark of authentic Christian mission. This advocacy includes being just (i.e., neither partial nor bigoted on account of class or difference) in the body, possessing a commitment to good works on behalf of the poor and vulnerable, and working to help meet the practical needs of others, especially those in the household of God.

- Regarding urban mission, the Church is called to proclaim the Good News to the poor, which includes respecting them as chosen by God and those with whom Christ identified. We are never to patronize them but deal with them justly and compassionately, confident of their ability to be transformed and to contribute to the Kingdom's advance.

- The Church must act in accordance with God's choice of the poor, which means she must defend their cause, maintain their rights, provide advocacy, and show no partiality in our dealings with them. We are to be generous and hospitable in meeting their needs, sharing our own goods with others, being hospitable to strangers and to the imprisoned, and showing love as we have been shown.

- In all our giving and caring, we are to seek justice and equity for the poor, wherever we find them. We are not merely to meet surface needs but strive to impact structures and relationships that will lead to a more just situation, living the true "prosperity Gospel," which is to seek justice and equity on behalf of the most vulnerable among us.

4

I.   Jesus and the Founding of the Church: God's *New Covenant* Kingdom Community

Video Segment 2
Outline

· ·

Early Christian Church Was Made Up of Poor People

Care for the poor was a concern laid upon Paul and Barnabas by their agreement with James, Peter and John (Gal. 2.10). The poor among the Christian Jews in Jerusalem were in need of support and the Gentile Christians had an obligation to them in return for the spiritual blessings received from Jerusalem (Rom. 15.26–27). The collection is mentioned in all Paul's principal letters; he strongly recommends the Corinthian church to participate (1 Cor. 16.1–4; 2 Cor. 8–9). The reason for the collection is evidently the social need among Christians in Jerusalem, possibly caused by hostility and persecution from the broader Jewish community. The collection also had a political function as a symbol of love and solidarity from the Pauline churches. The majority of those in Paul's churches were poor people of humble origins (1 Cor. 1.26–28), but Paul stresses the abundance they had received in the gospel, 'as poor, yet making many rich, as having nothing, and yet possessing all things' (2 Cor. 6.10). When encouraging participation in the collection Paul also plays on the broader meaning of the words 'rich' and 'poor'. In 2 Corinthians 8.9 the 'rich' Christ has become 'poor' – a reference to the incarnation (cf. Phil 2.6) – so that believers can be rich and share with one another. Christ provides a new standard of values (Phil. 3.8), and the treasure of the gospel creates generosity in sharing with the needy (1 Tim. 6.17–19).

~ Hans Kvalbein. "Poverty." The New Dictionary of Biblical Theology.
T. D. Alexander, ed. (electronic ed.). Downers Grove, IL: InterVarsity Press, 2001.

· ·

A.   God's heart is revealed in Jesus' inauguration of his ministry in his annunciation of his Messiahship (*Jesus' inaugural sermon at Nazareth*), Luke 4.16-21.

1.   Jesus is the *Messiah whose ministry is inaugurated by his anointing from God to preach to the poor*, John 1.41, He first found his own brother Simon and said to him, "We have found the Messiah" (which means Christ).

4

2. It is an anointing of righteousness, Ps. 45.7, cf. Heb. 1.9.

3. The King to come would be a *lover of justice and equity*, Ps. 99.4.

4. Jesus preached the Good News of forgiveness and *shalom* to the poor, Luke 6.20.

5. The Messianic prophecies speak of One who would cause the poor of humankind to exult in God, Isa. 29.19-20.

6. *Ministry to the poor is undeniable proof of Jesus' Messiahship.*

   a. The object of his *attention*: his choice of texts (Messianic Servant)

   b. The object of his *calling*: the anointing of the Holy Spirit

   c. The objects of his *ministry*: the poor, the captive, the blind, the oppressed

   d. The object of his *purpose*: to proclaim the year of the Lord's favor

B. Jesus *authenticates* his Messiahship to John the Baptist through works of justice and preaching to the poor, Luke 7.18-23.

   1. John the Baptist's doubts: *are you the One who is to come, or shall we look for another?*, v. 19.

2. Jesus' response: healed many diseases and plagues, expelled demons, healed the blind

3. *Jesus' show-and-tell*: Go and tell John what you have seen and heard (i.e., the blind receive sight, the lame walk, lepers are cleansed, the deaf hear, the dead are raised up, and the *poor have the Good News preached to them*, v. 22).

4. Signs of the end of time and demonstration of the Kingdom present: *Jesus' signs are indisputable evidence that he is the Messiah of the Hebrew Scriptures!*

5. *Ministry to the poor is undeniable proof of the Messiah's identity.*

C. Jesus *verifies* and *confirms* the salvation of others by how they treat the poor, Luke 19.1-9.

1. Zacchaeus as a betrayer of the covenant community: loyalist to the Roman empire and extorter of God's people (*i.e., a rich tax collector*)

2. His interaction with Jesus Christ and open display of a heart change

    a. Half of my goods I give to the *poor* (token of authentic heart change).

    b. If I have defrauded anyone of anything, I restore it *fourfold* (radical generosity and restitution).

4

3. Zacchaeus' generosity not the *means* of salvation, but the *evidence* of salvation, cf. 1 John 4.7-8; 1 John 3.16; James 2.14-16.

4. Jesus' reply: *today salvation has come to this house, since he is also a son of Abraham*, Luke 19.9.

5. *Ministry to the poor is evidence to Messiah Jesus of salvation before God.*

D. Jesus *identifies* without reservation to "the least of these" among us, Matt. 25.34-40.

1. The Judgment Seat of the King, Matt. 25.31-45

2. *The characters*: two sets of people—sheep and goats

3. *The responses*: two orientations of the King, one to the sheep, one to the goats (one blessed and embraced, the other judged and rejected)

4. *Two destinies*: the sheep in the Kingdom inherited an eternal home prepared from the foundation of the world, the goats inherited the eternal fire prepared for the devil and his angels.

5. *Transactions with the same group of people*: the hungry, the thirsty, the stranger, the naked, the sick, the prisoner

6. *Two different kinds of reaction*: one was hospitable, charitable, generous; the other apathetic, heartless, negligent.

7. The King in judgment uses the same standard to determine the fate of both groups; *way you treated or mistreated these people, those on the underside of life, so you responded to me.*

8. *Messiah Jesus' identity with the poor is total and complete, and relationship with them serves as the basis of relationship with him.*

II. Demonstrating Mercy and Justice in the Kingdom Community

A. Proclamation of the Good News to the poor

1. The Church is the *body of Christ*, the new covenant kingdom community called to continue his work in the world through mission and justice.

   a. The members are sealed and anointed by the same Spirit which indwelt Jesus, Eph. 1.13; 4.30; 2 Cor. 1.20-22 with Luke 4.18-19.

   b. They are his members in the world called to demonstrate the *character of the Kingdom, first in their own midst, and then in connection to the world.*

2. The apostles proclaimed Jesus as the Messiah, whose presence ushered in the presence of the future, the inauguration of the fulfillment of the Kingdom of God.

3. Jesus of Nazareth is the Messiah of God, John 1.41-45; John 4.25-26.

The Gospel Addresses the Poor, the Recipients of the Kingdom

In some very important sayings the "poor" are those addressed by the gospel or the recipients of the kingdom. The expression "good news is preached to the poor" in Jesus' answer to John the Baptist (Matt. 11.5; cf. Luke 7.22) is borrowed from Isaiah 61.1, which is the text for Jesus' inaugural sermon in Nazareth (Luke 4.18). In Nazareth it is applied to the congregation in the synagogue; in the answer to John the Baptist it concludes a list of Jesus' healing miracles which includes terms used in Isaiah to refer to the salvation of Israel.
~ Hans Kvalbein. "Poverty." The New Dictionary of Biblical Theology. T. D. Alexander, ed. (electronic ed.). Downers Grove, IL: IVP, 2001.

4

4. In his person, the righteous *shalom* of the Kingdom of God was displayed in every way.

    a. Acts 10.36-38

    b. Luke 7.21-23

5. *Jesus founded a new covenant community which he intends to be the living display of the love and justice of the Kingdom in this day and hour: the Church of Jesus Christ*, 1 Cor. 12.27.

6. The life of the Age to Come is now experienced and displayed in the good works and proclamation of the Good News by the Church: Mission is integrally connected to displaying justice on behalf of the poor *in and through the Church*!

    a. The Holy Spirit in the Church is the literal down payment of the *full inheritance to come*, Eph. 1.13; 4.30; 2 Cor. 1.20-22.

    b. The gathering of Jews and Gentiles into one community through faith is a token of the *shalom* to come over all the world at the consummation of the Kingdom of God, Eph. 3.3-10; Rom. 16.24ff.; Col. 1.26-27.

    c. The *acts of righteousness done* in and through the Church are signs of the Kingdom's presence right here-and-now, Acts 2 with Joel 2.

7. The Church is now the new Israel of God, called to demonstrate through its preaching and good works the standard of God's kingdom reign, Gal. 6.16.

4

8. In this community both Jews and Gentiles gather as heirs of the Abrahamic promise, and joint heirs with Christ.

   a. Gal. 3.14

   b. Gal. 3.28-29

9. Now, in the life and mission of the Church of Jesus Christ, and the empowerment of the Holy Spirit, the *shalom* of God's OT covenant community may be displayed and enjoyed.

   a. 1 Pet. 2.9-10

   b. Ps. 33.12

   c. 1 Pet. 1.2

   d. 1 Cor. 3.16-17

B. Equity and mercy: generosity and hospitality addressing the basic needs of life

   1. *Pentecost*: the new community is born through the Word of God and the power of the Holy Spirit, Acts 2.1-4, 39-39.

   2. The love and justice (*shalom*) of God's covenant community is demonstrated on the first day of its existence, Acts 2.42-47.

The Content of the Gospel Is Directed to the Poor

The content of the gospel will be best displayed in its reality among the poor. In the gospels Jesus said that the groups which best demonstrated the gospel in its fullness are the poor and the "sinners." The self-righteous Pharisees would learn the true nature of the gospel only as they too ate with "sinners," and learnt what the gospel meant to them. Only as they experienced helplessness and alienation themselves would they be transformed by the gospel and experience its true power.
~ C. M. N. Sugden. "Poverty and Wealth." *The New Dictionary of Theology*. S. B. Ferguson, ed. (electronic ed.). Downers Grove, IL: InterVarsity Press, 2000. p. 524.

3. Continued fillings and empowerment from the Holy Spirit display the justice, righteousness, and unity of the covenant people of God.

   a. Acts 4.31-35

   b. The Church displays the *shalom* of the covenant community of God, Deut. 15.4-6, cf. Deut. 2.7, Ps. 34.9.

4. The Church makes provisions to meet the needs of the widows and the poor in its midst, cf. Acts 6.1-6 with 1 Timothy 5.

   a. Radical displays of generosity, Acts 4.35

   b. Official registries were kept to meet the needs of those who were poor and lacked good, 1 Tim. 5.9.

5. *Wealth sharing*: provision was made by all the churches in Macedonia and beyond to aid the Jerusalem church during a time of famine, Acts 11.27-30, cf. 2 Cor. 8-9.

C. Advocacy for the poor: a hallmark of authentic Christian mission

   1. No partiality in treatment of the poor from the rich, James 2.1-7; 5.1-4

      a. God has made the poor rich in faith and heirs of the Kingdom of God, James 2.5.

4

b. The rich will be sent away empty in the Kingdom to come, Luke 1.51-53.

2. Pure religion was defined in the community in terms of how the poor were treated.

   a. James 1.27

   b. Job 29.12-13

3. The community is created for good works, and maintains and perseveres in doing good to the broken and the poor.

   a. Gal. 5.6

   b. Gal. 6.9-10

   c. 1 John 3.17-19

4. Practical help meeting the needs of those inside and outside of the Church is the standard of *true membership* in the covenant community of God.

   a. 1 John 4.7-8

   b. Gal. 5.22

c. John 13.34-35

III. Implications for a Biblical Understanding of Urban Mission

. . . .

Do the Poor Need the Wealthy, or Vice Versa?

When those who are 'righteous' and 'rich' do experience the content of the gospel as defined by what it means to the poor, then the power of the gospel is shown. When the rich young ruler turned away, Jesus commented: 'How hard it is for rich people to enter the kingdom of God ... What is impossible for man is possible for God' (Luke 19.24–27). This biblical perspective confronts the view that the poor need the generosity of the wealthy as endless receivers of aid. Rather the wealthy need the poor, to learn from them the nature and meaning of the deliverance God brings to both. The basis of the sharing is when those separated by distorted relationships discover that they both equally need each other. Only Jesus Christ can bring this about. 'Accept one another as Christ has accepted you' (Rom. 15.7).

~ C. M. N. Sugden. "Poverty and Wealth." **The New Dictionary of Theology.** S. B. Ferguson, ed. (electronic ed.). Downers Grove, IL: InterVarsity Press, 2000. p. 524.

. . . .

A. Proclaim the Good News to the poor: *imitate the ministry of Jesus by proclaiming the Good News to the poor.*

1. Respect them as those who have been chosen by God as heirs of the Kingdom, James 2.5.

2. Serve them as those whom Jesus has unqualified identification with: the hungry, the thirsty, the stranger, the sick, the imprisoned, the naked, Matt. 25.31-46.

3. Do not patronize nor lionize the poor; know that those who deal justly with them are *lending to the Lord*, Prov. 19.17.

4. Expect the poor to be completely transformed by their rebirth in the faith and regeneration of the Holy Spirit.

    a. Eph. 4.28

    b. 1 Cor. 6.9-11

B. The Church as God's covenant community is to act in accordance with God's choice of the poor.

    1. Defending their cause and maintaining their rights, Ps. 82.3.

    2. Advocating for them when they are voiceless and vulnerable, Deut. 24.12-15.

    3. Show no partiality in the affairs of our Christian communities, James 2.1-7.

C. We are to be generous and hospitable in meeting the needs of the poor.

    1. We are to love in word and deed, not just words alone, James 2.14-16; 1 John 3.16-19.

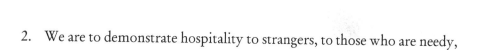

2. We are to demonstrate hospitality to strangers, to those who are needy, to those imprisoned.

    a. Heb. 13.1-3

    b. Rom. 12.13

    c. 1 Pet. 4.9

3. We are to show love as we have been shown love by God, Deut. 10.18-19.

D. We are to transcend generosity by seeking for justice and equity.

1. We are not merely to meet the bare necessities, but strive to impact others lives by working for justice (*enabling the poor to gain access to those resources that will allow them to produce for themselves*).

2. In the OT God demanded his covenant community give to the poor the means to produce, as the Lord had blessed them, Deut. 15.12-14.

3. *Live the true prosperity Gospel*: expect the Lord to strengthen your cause, however small, when done with justice for the poor and the broken in mind, Ps. 41.1-3.

Conclusion

» Jesus identified himself intimately with the poor, both in his calling as Messiah of God and Head of the Church.

» As the Suffering Servant who fulfilled the Messianic prophecy, Jesus has created a new community, the Church, whose mission it is to proclaim the Good News of the Kingdom to the poor and strive to demonstrate the life of that Kingdom to its members and its neighbors.

» May God grant us the Holy Spirit, the One who alone can make *shalom* a reality in the midst of the people of God today. Amen, and amen.

May the Entire Church Be Marshaled to Contribute to Mission, While Time Remains

The entire church is Marshaled to contribute to mission. The church worships God directly (1 Pet. 2.9; Heb. 12.28, 29; Rom. 15.5–12), ministers to the saints (Eph. 4.12–16) and to the world (Luke 24.48; Acts 5.32; Phil. 2.14–18). The means of ministry include: the ministry of the word; the ministry of order, by which Christian living is subjected to the law of love; and the ministry of mercy, manifesting the compassion of Christ. These means of ministry are common to all believers as they seek to fulfil their calling. Some members of Christ's body have gifts in one or more of these areas to an unusual degree. There are administrative gifts that require public recognition for their proper exercise. The NT therefore describes offices in the church: apostles and prophets to lay the foundation and launch the mission (Eph. 2.20; 3.5); evangelists, pastors and teachers to proclaim the revealed word with authority (Eph. 4.11;); others with gifts for government to join them in ruling the church (Rom. 12.8; 1 Cor. 12.28; 1 Tim. 5.17); and deacons to administer the service of mercy (1 Tim. 3.8–13). Those who govern are given to the church by Christ to serve in his name, under his lordship. Church power is spiritual (2 Cor. 10.3–6), ministerial (1 Pet. 5.3; Matt. 20.25–28), and only declarative (Mark 7.8; Rev. 21.18, 19). Yet it is authoritative (Matt. 16.19; 18.17–20; 10.14-15; Heb. 13.17).

~ E. P. Clowney. "Church." **The New Dictionary of Theology.** S. B. Ferguson, ed. (electronic ed.). Downers Grove, IL: InterVarsity Press, 2000. p. 142.

Segue 2

Student Questions and Response

The following questions were designed to help you review the material in the second video segment. In this last section we discovered how Jesus without qualification connected his own life and ministry intimately with the poor. As Messiah and Head of the Church, he demonstrated in all his ministry and teaching his commitment to the broken, the lost, and the vulnerable of his day. This orientation is also likely connected to his role as the Suffering Servant who fulfilled the Messianic prophecy, the one commissioned to rescue the captive and poor, to proclaim the Good News of the Kingdom, to establish his own Messianic community which would demonstrate the life of that Kingdom to its members and its neighbors. As you review the various main points of the lesson through the questions below, consider the ways in which God may be calling us to display in our lives and ministries the same kingdom *shalom* that was so clearly evident in the life and teaching of Jesus. As usual, always be clear and concise in your answers, and where possible, support with Scripture!

1. What is Jesus' connection to the Church as God's new kingdom community?

2. Explain how Jesus' role of Messiah was inaugurated, authenticated, confirmed, and identified in every way by the poor and their treatment. What does this suggest to us about the priority the poor must always have in the work of the Church?

3. What does it mean to say that the Church is "God's kingdom community?" In its role as the body of Christ, how is the Church called to imitate and fulfill the ministry of Christ in the world today? How does the Church in its works, words, and witness give evidence of the life of the Age to Come in the world today?

4. In what sense can we say that through the life and mission of the Church, as it is empowered by the Holy Spirit, that the very *shalom* of God is both enjoyed and displayed right here and right now?

5. Why are generosity and hospitality to the needy (especially to widows, the fatherless, and the poor) so important in the witness of the Church to Kingdom?

6. In what way are the people of God to be an advocate for the poor and those without a voice in society and in life? What are the characteristics of such an advocacy, and why can we say that "standing in the gap" for the poor is a hallmark of authentic Christian mission?

4

7. Why ought the poor never be patronized but always respected and dignified in all our dealings with them? In what sense is it necessary for those who serve the poor to be confident of God's ability to transform their condition, as well as for them to become major contributors to the advancement of God's Kingdom?

8. Explain the statement: "The Church must act in accordance with God's choice of the poor." In what sense can we say that God has chosen the poor to be rich in faith (James 2.5)? Why must we always be especially careful to show generosity to strangers and the imprisoned?

9. Why must our caring and ministry to the poor always go beyond meeting surface needs seeking to engage and change structures and relationships that will lead to a more just situation for them? Explain.

10. Why is helping the poor according to God's standards of *shalom* the best definition of the "prosperity Gospel?" What can we be confident that God will do on our behalf if we truly sacrifice ourselves on behalf of the poor?

The Poor in the NT

In the teaching of Jesus material possessions are not regarded as evil, but as dangerous. The poor are often shown to be happier than the rich, because it is easier for them to have an attitude of dependence upon God. It was to them that he came to preach the gospel (Luke 4.18; 7.22). It is they who are the first to be blessed and to be assured of the possession of the Kingdom of God (Luke 6.20), if their poverty is the acknowledgment of spiritual bankruptcy (Matt. 5.3). A poor person's offering may be of much greater value than a rich man's (Mark 12.41-44). The poor must be shown hospitality (Luke 14.12-14), and given alms (Luke 18.22), though charity was to be secondary to worship (John 12.1-8). The early Church made an experiment in the communal holding of wealth (Acts 2.41-42; 4.32). This led at first to the elimination of poverty (Acts 4.34-35), but it has often been held that it was responsible for the later economic collapse of the church at Jerusalem. Much of the ministry of Paul was concerned with raising money in the Gentile churches to assist the poor Christians in Jerusalem (Rom. 15.25-29; Gal. 2.10). These churches were also taught to provide for their own poor members (Rom. 12.13, etc.). James is especially vehement against those who allowed distinctions of wealth in the Christian community (James 2.1-7). The poor were called by God and their salvation brought glory to him (1 Cor. 1.26–31). The material wealth of the church of Laodicea was in sad contrast with her spiritual poverty (Rev. 3.17).

The most systematic exposition about poverty and wealth in the Epistles is found in 2 Cor. 8–9, where Paul sets the idea of Christian charity in the context of the gifts of God and especially that of his Son who, 'though he was rich, yet for your sake he became poor, so that by his poverty you might become rich'. In the light of that, running the risk of material poverty will lead to spiritual blessing, just as the apostles were poor but made many rich (2 Cor. 6.10).

~ R. E. Nixon. "Poverty." **The New Bible Dictionary**. D. R. W. Wood, ed. 3rd ed.
(electronic ed.). Downers Grove, IL: InterVarsity Press, 1996. p. 945.

. . . .

**Summary of
Key Concepts**

This lesson focuses upon the relationship of the poor and Christian mission. We explored this concept through the lens of God's *shalom*, mentioned first in the OT in terms of God's covenant community Israel and its dealings with the poor, and expanded our discussion to the role of the Church. The following concepts highlight the key insights in this lesson.

☞ The concept of the poor is built on the biblical vision of *shalom*, or wholeness: *shalom* is the Hebrew term for "fullness of human community in fellowship with God and with one another."

☞ The biblical elements of *shalom* include the experience of health and wellness, safety and protection from harm, harmony between neighbors, prosperity and material sufficiency, and the absence of malice and conflict–genuine peace. It also includes the idea of *shalom* as God's gracious provision, as is connected with the coming of the Messiah who is the Prince of *shalom*, as well as *shalom* as the standard for the people of God.

☞ Poverty is the denial of God's *shalom*; his blessing and provision were given to prevent the occurrence of poverty, and the commands to the covenant community were designed to ensure justice and righteousness among Yahweh's people. Faithfulness to the covenant was designed for the continuation of *shalom* among Israel as they obeyed his voice and met its conditions.

4

- God identifies with the poor, i.e., it is his design to lift and bless them from their state, to punish those who oppress them, and to demand that his people demonstrate the same concern that he has on behalf of the broken, poor, and the oppressed. The Exodus is a key event which embodies God's identification with the poor and the oppressed, revealing his heart of justice, the creation of his covenant community which was called to be a reflection of his holiness, a model of justice and mercy, and a beacon for the nations.

- The Scriptures define several causes of poverty, including natural disaster and calamity (e.g., famine, drought, storm, etc.), personal laziness and slothfulness (e.g., bad decisions, immoral character, idleness, hard-heartedness, etc.), and oppression and injustice from the hands of the powerful (e.g., mistreatment, exploitation, defrauding wages, etc.). The term "the poor" in the Scriptures is linked to a number of different concepts which serve as synonyms, including "the widow," "the fatherless," and the "stranger."

- God's covenant standards of generous and just treatment of the poor serve as a witness to his own heart for them. He made special provisions for the care of the poor which were factored into the harvest and gleaning stipulations of the Law, and justice in the courts where all matters, measures, and transactions were to be done honestly and rightly. The resources of the people were to be shared in the Sabbatical year, with the poor being provided a share of the produce of the fields and vineyards.

- The people of God were forbidden to charge interest to the poor, and instructed to pay a just and timely payment for a day's work (i.e., wages to be paid the same day with no oppression or defrauding allowed). Radical hospitality was to be practiced to the poor (an "open hand policy") and resources were to be set aside for them (i.e., certain portions of the tithe and bounty to be given to the most needy and vulnerable in the midst of the community). The poor were to be included in all celebrations, and in the year of Jubilee, the poor were to recover their property, with provision made for those whose funds were short or absent.

- The implications of these standards for God's covenant community are plain: God's people were in all their actions to reflect God's identification with the poor, informed by God's deliverance of them at the Exodus, and were to demonstrate the Lord's *shalom* in all their relationships and dealings with others.

4

- Jesus is both the founder and head of the Church, God's new covenant kingdom community, which is called to demonstrate God's *shalom* in the midst of the people of God today.

- Jesus identified himself as the Messiah of the OT prophets and promise. He inaugurated his Messianic ministry with acts of healing the oppressed and preaching good news to the poor, who were the object of his attention, calling, ministry, and purpose, and authenticated his Messiahship to John the Baptist through works of justice and preaching to the poor. Furthermore, Jesus verified and confirmed the salvation of others by their treatment of the poor, and identified without reservation to the "least of these" (i.e., the hungry, thirsty, the stranger, the naked, the sick, and the prisoner).

- The Church is God's kingdom community. It is called to proclaim the Good News of the Kingdom to the poor, to act as the body of Christ with one another, and to give evidence of the life of the Age to Come in its display of justice in the world. In the life and mission of the Church, empowered by the Holy Spirit, the *shalom* of God's OT covenant community is enjoyed and displayed.

- The Church is called to display radical generosity and hospitality to the needy, with special priority and provision for those within the community, especially to the widows, fatherless, and the poor. We are also responsible to make provision for other churches during times of calamity and distress.

- As Christ's body in the world, the Church is called to be an advocate for the poor, which is a hallmark of authentic Christian mission. This advocacy includes being just (i.e., neither partial nor bigoted on account of class or difference) in the body, possessing a commitment to good works on behalf of the poor and vulnerable, and working to help meet the practical needs of others, especially those in the household of God.

- Regarding urban mission, the Church is called to proclaim the Good News to the poor, which includes respecting them as chosen by God and those with whom Christ identified. We are never to patronize them but deal with them justly and compassionately, confident of their ability to be transformed and to contribute to the Kingdom's advance.

- The Church must act in accordance with God's choice of the poor, which means she must defend their cause, maintain their rights, provide advocacy,

4

and show no partiality in our dealings with them. We are to be generous and hospitable in meeting their needs, sharing our own goods with others, being hospitable to strangers and to the imprisoned, and showing love as we have been shown.

↪ In all our giving and caring, we are to seek justice and equity for the poor, wherever we find them. We are not merely to meet surface needs but strive to impact structures and relationships that will lead to a more just situation, living the true "prosperity Gospel," which is to seek justice and equity on behalf of the most vulnerable among us.

Now is the time for you to discuss with your fellow students your questions about Christian mission and the poor. The following questions are meant to trigger your own questions about your own personal opinions and conviction about the poor, and your relationship to them. Generate your own questions as you ponder and share with your fellow students your concerns and observations.

Student Application and Implications

* What is your own personal understanding of *shalom* now, having gone through this introduction to the concept? Why might this concept be important for your own life and ministry where you live and serve the Lord right now?

* In what way have you experienced *shalom* in the midst of your family and local church since you accepted Christ (i.e., think in terms of *shalom's* key characteristics: health and wellness, safety and protection from harm, harmony between neighbors, prosperity and material sufficiency, and the absence of malice and conflict–genuine peace).

* Did you grow up poor, or did you know someone who grew up poor? How has that experience shaped your understanding of your own Christian experience today?

* Why would you say that poverty is the denial of God's *shalom*? If you grew up poor, how did you experience this reality, personally? Explain.

* Of the three causes of poverty mentioned in Scripture (i.e., natural disaster and calamity, personal laziness and slothfulness, and oppression and injustice from the hands of the powerful) which do you think brings about the most shame in the poor? Which do you think gets the most attention in the Church? Which gets the least attention?

* Complete the following statement: "If I had to describe my current attitude about the poor with a single word or phrase, it would be . . ."

* How involved have you been personally in ministries that serve the poor? What were your attitudes as you interacted with them? Have you found it difficult to love and serve the poor? Why or why not?

* Are you currently involved in a ministry with one in Jesus' group of the "least of these, my brethren," (i.e., the hungry, thirsty, the stranger, the naked, the sick, and the prisoner)? What are the kinds of attitudes and understandings required to minister effectively among them?

* Would those who know you characterize you as both generous and hospitable? Why do you think these traits are given such attention in connection with the kingdom ethic in the NT?

* If a person is stingy and selfish, what is the best way for them to learn how to become generous and hospitable? Why is it important to find the widows, fatherless, and the poor to serve, even if locating them is difficult and "off our beaten path?"

* Do you find it easy to believe in the transformation of poor people–what kind of attitude do you communicate to others about those who are poor? Are you accustomed to blaming the poor for their problems, or do you rather tend to respect them as those who are chosen by God?

* Complete the following sentence: "If God could just one thing in my own attitude and life to make me more effective in caring for others who are poor, I would ask him to . . ."

4

CASE STUDIES

The Problem of Katrina

1 ▶ The entire United States watched in horror when Katrina hit the great southern city of New Orleans, and affected the thousands of urban poor who were stranded without food, water, or aid. To see so many elderly, young, and needy people suffer miserably in substandard living situations was deeply painful; no amount of excuses, blame shifting, or promises about "next time" could bring relief or comfort to the many who still, to this day, suffer without jobs, financial support, or any idea of the next steps in their lives. The lack of service to the poor has been attributed to many

reasons: "The people were poor and black, and this population has never counted much in American history," "These people did not heed the call to leave the city when they had a chance," "The government agencies were slow in dealing with the problem and incompetent once it arrived"—these and other reasons have been offered to make sense of the terrible natural disaster that has affected so many lives. In thinking about the possibility of calamity and natural disaster, what is your opinion about who is responsible for care during and after these events: the people themselves, the government agencies and authorities, the Church and other helping agencies, or all of them, in some kind of combination or another?

Liberation Theology and the Poor

Liberation theology is arguably the most important theological development in the 20th century. The various types of liberation theology focus on the primary commitment of the God of the Scriptures being the God of the poor and the oppressed. All biblical materials and theological disciplines are weighed as to how they make known this fundamental identification of God with the poor, the ostracized, the broken, the disadvantaged, and the needy. In a church, a key leader and teacher, has been deeply affected by his reading of several books in the liberation theological field dealing with the poor. He is convinced that although some of the material argues things not in Scripture, there are parts that provide keen insight into the nature of oppression, the poor, and the city. Their own urban church, caring for families plagued by addictions, drugs, or abuse, could use some of the insights and encouragements offered in the book, the leader suggests. He determines to bring some of this material into his College Age adult study class, not to produce controversy but to stretch the minds of the students to consider God more in the sense of the Exodus—the liberating God of the poor. Some of the other teachers are concerned about the effect of this material on the minds of the students, especially those who are still young in the faith and susceptible to error. If you were the pastor of such a church, how would you handle this situation? Given the teacher's sincere desire to teach the students about God's heart for the poor, what procedure or alternatives would you suggest to him?

Co-dependence or Compassion?

3 (Based on a true story). A dear sister (whom we will call Sharon) who had been saved from a troubled past of drug and alcohol addiction had recently joined the fellowship. She was genuinely saved, desirous to grow in Christ, but still a very immature Christian. Most of the relationships that she possessed in her past life were essentially those of people offering Sharon aid and support from crisis to crisis. In some ways, the sister continued to relate to people in this way, and given her desire for change, many actually found this kind of helping relationship proper. It all changed when this sister began to come to church high and drunk, and many neither said nor did anything about it. Sharon was deeply beloved, cherished by all, and everyone was "pulling for her;" no one wanted to be so judgmental or discouraging that she might be tempted to return to her life of debauchery. The pastor, who like everyone else was concerned for Sharon but also desirous to see her mature in Christ, mentioned the situation of coming to church drunk as unacceptable as a Christian. Now that she belongs to Christ, she must discipline herself in him to abstain from these kinds of things, and if necessary, go to extremes to get the help she needs, even to the point of committing herself to a drug and alcohol treatment program. On hearing this advice, the dear sister was offended, and shared with a number of members the lack of understanding and patience the pastor had shown. Other members confronted the pastor, reminding him of the need for patience and love and not to be judgmental and harsh. With what you know about the situation here, what would be your advice to the church as they sought to care for Sharon? Whose approach is compassionate, and whose is leading toward co-dependence?

Advertising By the Poor

4 One of the most common practices today by relief organizations and ministries dealing with the poor is to display disturbing pictures of the conditions that they live in for the sake of moving people to give. This practice has become the rule of thumb in many places; testimonies of the poor are used as a means to raise funds for legitimate work of aid, support, and emergency care. The problem with these kinds of tactics is the way in which the poor are seen. Perhaps without knowing it consciously, such practices can easily lead to reinforcing certain stereotypes about the poor which are not necessarily true. Most poor in America, for instance, are white, not Black or Brown, and many of them hold jobs. The frequency of the images of the poor, Black welfare mom is so present everywhere that it becomes the accepted norm and rule. One mission agency, in an attempt to change these kinds of practices, shifted its advertising. Rather than concentrating on the worst situations of the neediest families in their more dire situations, this agency determined to speak of the ways in which the Lord was transforming the lives of the poor. The focus would no longer be on the past, but on the future. Some in the organization are not convinced that this will help. They argue that the depiction of the real lives of the poor in their materials is simply telling the plain truth; it is being clear about what is really happening. Furthermore, they argue, that unless people see needs and have a way to help, they won't care much about the "success stories" we provide. They will be happy for us, but they won't financially support us. How would you advise this social agency if they asked your opinion about how they ought to communicate their work about the poor? Is there a way to communicate the need of the people without selling the poor out, forcing them to lose their dignity in the ways we raise resources to support them?

The concept of the poor is built on the biblical vision of *shalom,* or wholeness: *shalom* is the Hebrew term for "fullness of human community in fellowship with God and with one another." The biblical elements of *shalom* include the experience of health and wellness, safety and protection from harm, harmony between neighbors, prosperity and material sufficiency, and the absence of malice and conflict–genuine peace. It also includes the idea of *shalom* as God's gracious provision, as is connected with the coming of the Messiah who is the Prince of *shalom,* as well as *shalom* as the standard for the people of God. Poverty is the denial of God's *shalom;* his blessing and provision were given to prevent the occurrence of poverty, and the commands to the covenant community were designed to ensure justice and righteousness among Yahweh's people. The Exodus embodies God's identification with the poor and the oppressed, revealing his heart of justice and creating his covenant community which was called to be a reflection of his holiness, a model of justice and mercy, and a beacon for the nations.

The Scriptures define several causes of poverty, including natural disaster and calamity (e.g., famine, drought, storm, etc.), personal laziness and slothfulness (e.g., bad decisions, immoral character, idleness, hard-heartedness, etc.), and oppression and injustice from the hands of the powerful (e.g., mistreatment, exploitation, defrauding wages, etc.). The term "the poor" in the Scriptures is linked to a number of different concepts which serve as synonyms, including "the widow," "the fatherless," and the "stranger." God's covenant standards give witness of his heart

Restatement of the Lesson's Thesis

4

for them, including such things as the harvest and gleaning stipulations of the Law, justice in the courts where all matters, measures, and transactions were to be done honestly and rightly, and resources of the people were to be shared in the Sabbatical year, with the poor being provided a share of the produce of the fields and vineyards. The implications of these standards for God's covenant community are plain: God's people were in all their actions to reflect God's identification with the poor, informed by God's deliverance of them at the Exodus, and were to demonstrate the Lord's *shalom* in all their relationships and dealings with others.

Jesus is both the founder and Head of the Church, God's new covenant kingdom community, which is called to demonstrate God's *shalom* in the midst of the people of God today. Jesus identified himself as the Messiah of the OT prophets and promise. He inaugurated his Messianic ministry with acts of healing the oppressed and preaching good news to the poor, authenticated his Messiahship to John the Baptist through works of justice and preaching to the poor, verified and confirmed the salvation of others by their treatment of the poor, and identified without reservation to the "least of these" (i.e., the hungry, thirsty, the stranger, the naked, the sick, and the prisoner). The Church is God's kingdom community. It is called to proclaim the Good News of the Kingdom to the poor, to act as the body of Christ with one another, and to give evidence of the life of the Age to Come in its display of justice in the world. In the life and mission of the Church, empowered by the Holy Spirit, the *shalom* of God's OT covenant community is enjoyed and displayed.

As Christ's body in the world, the Church is called to be an advocate for the poor, which is a hallmark of authentic Christian mission. Regarding urban mission, the Church is called to proclaim the Good News to the poor, which includes respecting them as chosen by God and those with whom Christ identified. We are never to patronize them but deal with them justly and compassionately, confident of their ability to be transformed and to contribute to the Kingdom's advance. We are not merely to meet surface needs, but to strive to impact structures and relationships that will lead to a more just situation, living the true "prosperity Gospel," which is to seek justice and equity on behalf of the most vulnerable among us.

4

If you are interested in pursuing some of the ideas of *Christian Mission and the Poor,* you might want to give these books a try:

Gordon, Wayne L. *Real Hope in Chicago*. Grand Rapids: Zondervan, 1995.

Greenway, Roger S., ed. *Discipling the City: A Comprehensive Approach to Urban Mission*. 2nd ed. Grand Rapids: Baker Books, 1992.

Perkins, John. *With Justice for All*. Glendale, CA: Regal Books, 1982.

Phillips, Keith. *No Quick Fix*. Ventura, CA: Regal Books, 1985.

Sherman, Amy L. *Restorers of Hope: Reaching the Poor in Your Community with Church-based Ministries that Work*. Wheaton, IL: Crossway Books, 1997.

Sider, Ronald J. *Just Generosity: A New Vision for Overcoming Poverty In America*. Grand Rapids: Baker Books, 1999.

Resources and Bibliographies

You will be responsible to now apply the insights of your module in a practicum that you and your mentor agree to. The ramifications of the concept of the poor for Christian mission is clear. We simply cannot afford to miss such a central concept, especially as it relates to the very legitimacy of our professed faith.

In your sharing of the insights of this lesson in your ministry project you will want to think practically about how your teaching can influence the devotional life, prayers, and spiritual ministry you currently have in your church. How might the insights covered in this lesson influence your attitude at work, your relationship with your spouse or friends, or affect your attitude about where you live? What makes the Word come alive in our experience is our ability to correlate teaching with our lives and in our ministries. Your ministry project is an opportunity to make this connection. In the next days you will have the opportunity to share these insights in real-life, actual ministry environments. Pray that God will give you insight into his ways as you share your insights in your projects.

Ministry Connections

In this, the last lesson in this module, search your heart before the Lord: are there any remaining issues, persons, situations, or opportunities that you need the Spirit's leading and direction to respond to? Were there specific insights about the poor and our responsibility to them in this lesson that you need help and support in, things to change, to learn, to stop, to start? What particular issues or people has God laid

Counseling and Prayer

4

upon your heart that require focused supplication and prayer for in this lesson? Whatever the Lord says to you, take the necessary time to pray for yourself and your fellow students, trusting him for wisdom, courage, and power to apply his Word to your life and ministry.

ASSIGNMENTS ▶

Scripture Memory

No assignment due.

Reading Assignment

No assignment due.

Other Assignments

Your ministry project and your exegetical project should now be outlined, determined, and accepted by your instructor. Make sure that you plan ahead, so you will not be late in turning in your assignments.

Final Exam Notice

The final will be a take home exam, and will include questions taken from the first three quizzes, new questions on material drawn from this lesson, and essay questions which will ask for your short answer responses to key integrating questions. Also, you should plan on reciting or writing out the verses memorized for the course on the exam. When you have completed your exam, please notify your mentor and make certain that they get your copy.

Please note: Your module grade cannot be determined if you do not take the final exam and turn in all outstanding assignments to your mentor (ministry project, exegetical project, and final exam).

The Last Word about this Module

In this lesson we considered the concept of poverty through the lens of the concept *shalom,* or the wholeness of God's covenant community. We saw that even though Israel proved unfaithful in keeping God's covenant call to display his justice and righteousness, the image of *shalom* in the covenant was beautiful and true. God Almighty identifies with the poor in their plight, and asks his people to demonstrate that *shalom* in their dealings with one another as a light to the nations. In the person of Jesus Christ, the righteousness of God was fulfilled, and a new community was brought into being by the Holy Spirit. The Church, has now been called to fulfill the *shalom* anticipated in the OT, with Jesus as its founder and head.

4

As the Suffering Servant who fulfilled the Messianic prophecy of God regarding Messiah, he now has created a new community, the Church, whose mission it is to proclaim the Good News of the Kingdom to the poor and strive to demonstrate the life of that Kingdom to its members and its neighbors. The vision of mission (as sacred drama, as divine romance, as fulfillment of the promise, and as war of the spheres) is made plain when we, as members of the Church, awaken to our call to display the Kingdom of God in the earth. And, of all the places needing this display in the world today, the cities cry out for a living witness to Christ and his Kingdom.

Our sincere desire is that we will embrace this call to join God in his sacred plot, in his divine romance, as children of the promise and warriors of Christ, and do all we can to advance his Kingdom to the ends of the earth. May our God grant you a heart for the world, as his servant, and may he through his Holy Spirit lead you to the ministry where you can make your unique contribution to make *shalom* a reality in the midst of the people of God today.

To his glory, Amen, and amen!

4

Appendices

APPENDIX 1

The Nicene Creed

We believe in one God,   *(Deut. 6.4-5; Mark 12.29; 1 Cor. 8.6)*
the Father Almighty,   *(Gen. 17.1; Dan. 4.35; Matt. 6.9; Eph. 4.6; Rev. 1.8)*
Maker of heaven and earth   *(Gen 1.1; Isa. 40.28; Rev. 10.6)*
and of all things visible and invisible.   *(Ps. 148; Rom. 11.36; Rev. 4.11)*

We believe in one Lord Jesus Christ, the only Begotten Son of God,
begotten of the Father before all ages,
God from God, Light from Light, True God from True God,
begotten not created,
of the same essence as the Father,   *(John 1.1-2; 3.18; 8.58; 14.9-10; 20.28; Col. 1.15, 17; Heb. 1.3-6)*
through whom all things were made.   *(John 1.3; Col. 1.16)*

Who for us men and for our salvation came down from heaven
and was incarnate by the Holy Spirit and the virgin Mary
and became human.   *(Matt. 1.20-23; John 1.14; 6.38; Luke 19.10)*
Who for us too, was crucified under Pontius Pilate,
suffered, and was buried.   *(Matt. 27.1-2; Mark 15.24-39, 43-47; Acts 13.29; Rom. 5.8; Heb. 2.10; 13.12)*
The third day he rose again
according to the Scriptures,   *(Mark 16.5-7; Luke 24.6-8; Acts 1.3; Rom. 6.9; 10.9; 2 Tim. 2.8)*
ascended into heaven,
and is seated at the right hand of the Father.   *(Mark 16.19; Eph. 1.19-20)*
He will come again in glory
to judge the living and the dead,
and his Kingdom will have no end.
   (Isa. 9.7; Matt. 24.30; John 5.22; Acts 1.11; 17.31; Rom. 14.9; 2 Cor. 5.10; 2 Tim. 4.1)

We believe in the Holy Spirit, the Lord and life-giver,
   (Gen. 1.1-2; Job 33.4; Ps. 104.30; 139.7-8; Luke 4.18-19; John 3.5-6; Acts 1.1-2; 1 Cor. 2.11; Rev. 3.22)
who proceeds from the Father and the Son,   *(John 14.16-18, 26; 15.26; 20.22)*
who together with the Father and Son
is worshiped and glorified,   *(Isa. 6.3; Matt. 28.19; 2 Cor. 13.14; Rev. 4.8)*
who spoke by the prophets.   *(Num. 11.29; Mic. 3.8; Acts 2.17-18; 2 Pet. 1.21)*

We believe in one holy, catholic, and apostolic Church.
   (Matt. 16.18; Eph. 5.25-28; 1 Cor. 1.2; 10.17; 1 Tim. 3.15; Rev. 7.9)

We acknowledge one baptism for the forgiveness of sin,   *(Acts 22.16; 1 Pet. 3.21; Eph. 4.4-5)*
And we look for the resurrection of the dead
And the life of the age to come.   *(Isa. 11.6-10; Mic. 4.1-7; Luke 18.29-30; Rev. 21.1-5; 21.22-22.5)*

Amen.

APPENDIX 2

We Believe: Confession of the Nicene Creed (Common Meter*)

Rev. Dr. Don L. Davis, 2007. All Rights Reserved.

* This song is adapted from the Nicene Creed, and set to Common Meter (8.6.8.6.), meaning it can be sung to tunes of the same meter, such as: *O, for a Thousand Tongues to Sing; Alas, and Did My Savior Bleed?; Amazing Grace; All Hail the Power of Jesus' Name; There Is a Fountain; Joy to the World*

The Father God Almighty rules, Maker of earth and heav'n.
Yes, all things seen and those unseen, by him were made, and given!

We hold to one Lord Jesus Christ, God's one and only Son,
Begotten, not created, too, he and our Lord are one!

Begotten from the Father, same, in essence, God and Light;
Through him all things were made by God, in him were given life.

Who for us all, for salvation, came down from heav'n to earth,
Was incarnate by the Spirit's pow'r, and the Virgin Mary's birth.

Who for us too, was crucified, by Pontius Pilate's hand,
Suffered, was buried in the tomb, on third day rose again.

According to the Sacred text all this was meant to be.
Ascended to heav'n, to God's right hand, now seated high in glory.

He'll come again in glory to judge all those alive and dead.
His Kingdom rule shall never end, for he will reign as Head.

We worship God, the Holy Spirit, our Lord, Life-giver known,
With Fath'r and Son is glorified, Who by the prophets spoke.

And we believe in one true Church, God's people for all time,
Cath'lic in scope, and built upon the apostolic line.

Acknowledging one baptism, for forgiv'ness of our sin,
We look for Resurrection day–the dead shall live again.

We look for those unending days, life of the Age to come,
When Christ's great Reign shall come to earth, and God's will shall be done!

APPENDIX 3

The Story of God: Our Sacred Roots

Rev. Dr. Don L. Davis

The Alpha and the Omega	Christus Victor	Come, Holy Spirit	Your Word Is Truth	The Great Confession	His Life in Us	Living in the Way	Reborn to Serve
The LORD God is the source, sustainer, and end of all things in the heavens and earth. All things were formed and exist by his will and for his eternal glory: the triune God, Father, Son, and Holy Spirit, Rom. 11.36.							
THE TRIUNE GOD'S UNFOLDING DRAMA — God's Self-Revelation in Creation, Israel, and Christ				THE CHURCH'S PARTICIPATION IN GOD'S UNFOLDING DRAMA — Fidelity to the Apostolic Witness to Christ and His Kingdom			
The Objective Foundation: The Sovereign Love of God — God's Narration of His Saving Work in Christ				The Subjective Practice: Salvation by Grace through Faith — The Redeemed's Joyous Response to God's Saving Work in Christ			
The Author of the Story	*The Champion of the Story*	*The Interpreter of the Story*	*The Testimony of the Story*	*The People of the Story*	*Re-enactment of the Story*	*Embodiment of the Story*	*Continuation of the Story*
The Father as *Director*	Jesus as *Lead Actor*	The Spirit as *Narrator*	Scripture as *Script*	As Saints, *Confessors*	As Worshipers, *Ministers*	As Followers, *Sojourners*	As Servants, *Ambassadors*
Christian *Worldview*	Communal *Identity*	Spiritual *Experience*	Biblical *Authority*	Orthodox *Theology*	Priestly *Worship*	Congregational *Discipleship*	Kingdom *Witness*
Theistic and Trinitarian Vision	Christ-centered Foundation	Spirit-Indwelt and -Filled Community	Canonical and Apostolic Witness	Ancient Creedal Affirmation of Faith	Weekly Gathering in Christian Assembly	Corporate, Ongoing Spiritual Formation	Active Agents of the Reign of God
Sovereign Willing	Messianic Representing	Divine Comforting	Inspired Testifying	Truthful Retelling	Joyful Excelling	Faithful Indwelling	Hopeful Compelling
Creator True Maker of the Cosmos	**Recapitulation** Typos and Fulfillment of the Covenant	**Life-Giver** Regeneration and Adoption	**Divine Inspiration** God-breathed Word	**The Confession of Faith** Union with Christ	**Song and Celebration** Historical Recitation	**Pastoral Oversight** Shepherding the Flock	**Explicit Unity** Love for the Saints
Owner Sovereign Disposer of Creation	**Revealer** Incarnation of the Word	**Teacher** Illuminator of the Truth	**Sacred History** Historical Record	**Baptism into Christ** Communion of Saints	**Homilies and Teachings** Prophetic Proclamation	**Shared Spirituality** Common Journey through the Spiritual Disciplines	**Radical Hospitality** Evidence of God's Kingdom Reign
Ruler Blessed Controller of All Things	**Redeemer** Reconciler of All Things	**Helper** Endowment and the Power	**Biblical Theology** Divine Commentary	**The Rule of Faith** Apostles' Creed and Nicene Creed	**The Lord's Supper** Dramatic Re-enactment	**Embodiment** Anamnesis and Prolepsis through the Church Year	**Extravagant Generosity** Good Works
Covenant Keeper Faithful Promisor	**Restorer** Christ, the Victor over the powers of evil	**Guide** Divine Presence and Shekinah	**Spiritual Food** Sustenance for the Journey	**The Vincentian Canon** Ubiquity, antiquity, universality	**Eschatological Foreshadowing** The Already/Not Yet	**Effective Discipling** Spiritual Formation in the Believing Assembly	**Evangelical Witness** Making Disciples of All People Groups

APPENDIX 4
The Theology of Christus Victor
A Christ-Centered Biblical Motif for Integrating and Renewing the Urban Church

Rev. Dr. Don L. Davis

	The Promised Messiah	The Word Made Flesh	The Son of Man	The Suffering Servant	The Lamb of God	The Victorious Conqueror	The Reigning Lord in Heaven	The Bridegroom and Coming King
Biblical Framework	Israel's hope of Yahweh's anointed who would redeem his people	In the person of Jesus of Nazareth, the Lord has come to the world	As the promised king and divine Son of Man, Jesus reveals the Father's glory and salvation to the world	As Inaugurator of the Kingdom of God, Jesus demonstrates God's reign present through his words, wonders, and works	As both High Priest and Paschal Lamb, Jesus offers himself to God on our behalf as a sacrifice for sin	In his resurrection from the dead and ascension to God's right hand, Jesus is proclaimed as Victor over the power of sin and death	Now reigning at God's right hand till his enemies are made his footstool, Jesus pours out his benefits on his body	Soon the risen and ascended Lord will return to gather his Bride, the Church, and consummate his work
Scripture References	Isa. 9.6-7 Jer. 23.5-6 Isa. 11.1-10	John 1.14-18 Matt. 1.20-23 Phil. 2.6-8	Matt. 2.1-11 Num. 24.17 Luke 1.78-79	Mark 1.14-15 Matt. 12.25-30 Luke 17.20-21	2 Cor. 5.18-21 Isa. 52-53 John 1.29	Eph. 1.16-23 Phil. 2.5-11 Col. 1.15-20	1 Cor. 15.25 Eph. 4.15-16 Acts. 2.32-36	Rom. 14.7-9 Rev. 5.9-13 1 Thess. 4.13-18
Jesus' History	The pre-incarnate, only begotten Son of God in glory	His conception by the Spirit, and birth to Mary	His manifestation to the Magi and to the world	His teaching, exorcisms, miracles, and mighty works among the people	His suffering, crucifixion, death, and burial	His resurrection, with appearances to his witnesses, and his ascension to the Father	The sending of the Holy Spirit and his gifts, and Christ's session in heaven at the Father's right hand	His soon return from heaven to earth as Lord and Christ: the Second Coming
Description	The biblical promise for the seed of Abraham, the prophet like Moses, the son of David	In the Incarnation, God has come to us; Jesus reveals to humankind the Father's glory in fullness	In Jesus, God has shown his salvation to the entire world, including the Gentiles	In Jesus, the promised Kingdom of God has come visibly to earth, demonstrating his binding of Satan and rescinding the Curse	As God's perfect Lamb, Jesus offers himself up to God as a sin offering on behalf of the entire world	In his resurrection and ascension, Jesus destroyed death, disarmed Satan, and rescinded the Curse	Jesus is installed at the Father's right hand as Head of the Church, Firstborn from the dead, and supreme Lord in heaven	As we labor in his harvest field in the world, so we await Christ's return, the fulfillment of his promise
Church Year	Advent	Christmas	Season after Epiphany Baptism and Transfiguration	Lent	Holy Week Passion	Eastertide Easter, Ascension Day, Pentecost	Season after Pentecost Trinity Sunday	Season after Pentecost All Saints Day, Reign of Christ the King
	The Coming of Christ	*The Birth of Christ*	*The Manifestation of Christ*	*The Ministry of Christ*	*The Suffering and Death of Christ*	*The Resurrection and Ascension of Christ*	*The Heavenly Session of Christ*	*The Reign of Christ*
Spiritual Formation	As we await his Coming, let us proclaim and affirm the hope of Christ	O Word made flesh, let us every heart prepare him room to dwell	Divine Son of Man, show the nations your salvation and glory	In the person of Christ, the power of the reign of God has come to earth and to the Church	May those who share the Lord's death be resurrected with him	Let us participate by faith in the victory of Christ over the power of sin, Satan, and death	Come, indwell us, Holy Spirit, and empower us to advance Christ's Kingdom in the world	We live and work in expectation of his soon return, seeking to please him in all things

APPENDIX 5

Christus Victor

An Integrated Vision for the Christian Life

Rev. Dr. Don L. Davis

For the Church

- The Church is the primary extension of Jesus in the world
- Ransomed treasure of the victorious, risen Christ
- *Laos:* The people of God
- God's new creation: presence of the future
- Locus and agent of the Already/Not Yet Kingdom

For Theology and Doctrine

- The authoritative Word of Christ's victory: the Apostolic Tradition: the Holy Scriptures
- Theology as commentary on the grand narrative of God
- *Christus Victor* as core theological framework for meaning in the world
- The Nicene Creed: the Story of God's triumphant grace

For Spirituality

- The Holy Spirit's presence and power in the midst of God's people
- Sharing in the disciplines of the Spirit
- Gatherings, lectionary, liturgy, and our observances in the Church Year
- Living the life of the risen Christ in the rhythm of our ordinary lives

For Gifts

- God's gracious endowments and benefits from *Christus Victor*
- Pastoral offices to the Church
- The Holy Spirit's sovereign dispensing of the gifts
- Stewardship: divine, diverse gifts for the common good

Christus Victor

Destroyer of Evil and Death
Restorer of Creation
Victor o'er Hades and Sin
Crusher of Satan

For Worship

- People of the Resurrection: unending celebration of the people of God
- Remembering, participating in the Christ event in our worship
- Listen and respond to the Word
- Transformed at the Table, the Lord's Supper
- The presence of the Father through the Son in the Spirit

For Evangelism and Mission

- Evangelism as unashamed declaration and demonstration of *Christus Victor* to the world
- The Gospel as Good News of kingdom pledge
- We proclaim God's Kingdom come in the person of Jesus of Nazareth
- The Great Commission: go to all people groups making disciples of Christ and his Kingdom
- Proclaiming Christ as Lord and Messiah

For Justice and Compassion

- The gracious and generous expressions of Jesus through the Church
- The Church displays the very life of the Kingdom
- The Church demonstrates the very life of the Kingdom of heaven right here and now
- Having freely received, we freely give (no sense of merit or pride)
- Justice as tangible evidence of the Kingdom come

APPENDIX 6

Old Testament Witness to Christ and His Kingdom

Rev. Dr. Don L. Davis

Christ Is Seen in the OT's:	Covenant Promise and Fulfillment	Moral Law	Christophanies	Typology	Tabernacle, Festival, and Levitical Priesthood	Messianic Prophecy	Salvation Promises
Passage	Gen. 12.1-3	Matt. 5.17-18	John 1.18	1 Cor. 15.45	Heb. 8.1-6	Mic. 5.2	Isa. 9.6-7
Example	The Promised Seed of the Abrahamic covenant	The Law given on Mount Sinai	Commander of the Lord's army	Jonah and the great fish	Melchizedek, as both High Priest and King	The Lord's Suffering Servant	Righteous Branch of David
Christ As	Seed of the woman	The Prophet of God	God's present Revelation	Antitype of God's drama	Our eternal High Priest	The coming Son of Man	Israel's Redeemer and King
Where Illustrated	Galatians	Matthew	John	Matthew	Hebrews	Luke and Acts	John and Revelation
Exegetical Goal	To see Christ as heart of God's sacred drama	To see Christ as fulfillment of the Law	To see Christ as God's revealer	To see Christ as antitype of divine typos	To see Christ in the Temple *cultus*	To see Christ as true Messiah	To see Christ as coming King
How Seen in the NT	As fulfillment of God's sacred oath	As *telos* of the Law	As full, final, and superior revelation	As substance behind the historical shadows	As reality behind the rules and roles	As the Kingdom made present	As the One who will rule on David's throne
Our Response in Worship	God's veracity and faithfulness	God's perfect righteousness	God's presence among us	God's inspired Scripture	God's ontology: his realm as primary and determinative	God's anointed servant and mediator	God's resolve to restore his kingdom authority
How God Is Vindicated	God does not lie: he's true to his word	Jesus fulfills all righteousness	God's fulness is revealed to us in Jesus of Nazareth	The Spirit spoke by the prophets	The Lord has provided a mediator for humankind	Every jot and tittle written of him will occur	Evil will be put down, creation restored, under his reign

APPENDIX 7

Summary Outline of the Scriptures

Rev. Dr. Don L. Davis

1. GENESIS - Beginnings
   a. Adam
   b. Noah
   c. Abraham
   d. Isaac
   e. Jacob
   f. Joseph

2. EXODUS - Redemption, (out of)
   a. Slavery
   b. Deliverance
   c. Law
   d. Tabernacle

3. LEVITICUS - Worship and Fellowship
   a. Offerings, sacrifices
   b. Priests
   c. Feasts, festivals

4. NUMBERS - Service and Walk
   a. Organized
   b. Wanderings

5. DEUTERONOMY - Obedience
   a. Moses reviews history and law
   b. Civil and social laws
   c. Palestinian Covenant
   d. Moses' blessing and death

6. JOSHUA - Redemption (into)
   a. Conquer the land
   b. Divide up the land
   c. Joshua's farewell

7. JUDGES - God's Deliverance
   a. Disobedience and judgment
   b. Israel's twelve judges
   c. Lawless conditions

8. RUTH - Love
   a. Ruth chooses
   b. Ruth works
   c. Ruth waits
   d. Ruth rewarded

9. 1 SAMUEL - Kings, Priestly Perspective
   a. Eli
   b. Samuel
   c. Saul
   d. David

10. 2 SAMUEL - David
    a. King of Judah
       (9 years - Hebron)
    b. King of all Israel
       (33 years - Jerusalem)

11. 1 KINGS - Solomon's Glory, Kingdom's Decline
    a. Solomon's glory
    b. Kingdom's decline
    c. Elijah the prophet

12. 2 KINGS- Divided Kingdom
    a. Elisha
    b. Israel (N. Kingdom falls)
    c. Judah (S. Kingdom falls)

13. 1 CHRONICLES - David's Temple Arrangements
    a. Genealogies
    b. End of Saul's reign
    c. Reign of David
    d. Temple preparations

14. 2 CHRONICLES - Temple and Worship Abandoned
    a. Solomon
    b. Kings of Judah

15. EZRA - The Minority (Remnant)
    a. First return from exile - Zerubbabel
    b. Second return from exile - Ezra (priest)

16. NEHEMIAH - Rebuilding by Faith
    a. Rebuild walls
    b. Revival
    c. Religious reform

17. ESTHER - Female Savior
    a. Esther
    b. Haman
    c. Mordecai
    d. Deliverance: Feast of Purim

18. JOB - Why the Righteous Suffer
    a. Godly Job
    b. Satan's attack
    c. Four philosophical friends
    d. God lives

19. PSALMS - Prayer and Praise
    a. Prayers of David
    b. Godly suffer; deliverance
    c. God deals with Israel
    d. Suffering of God's people - end with the Lord's reign
    e. The Word of God (Messiah's suffering and glorious return)

20. PROVERBS - Wisdom
    a. Wisdom versus folly
    b. Solomon
    c. Solomon - Hezekiah
    d. Agur
    e. Lemuel

21. ECCLESIASTES - Vanity
    a. Experimentation
    b. Observation
    c. Consideration

22. SONG OF SOLOMON - Love Story

23. ISAIAH - The Justice (Judgment) and Grace (Comfort) of God
    a. Prophecies of punishment
    b. History
    c. Prophecies of blessing

24. JEREMIAH - Judah's Sin Leads to Babylonian Captivity
    a. Jeremiah's call; empowered
    b. Judah condemned; predicted Babylonian captivity
    c. Restoration promised
    d. Prophesied judgment inflicted
    e. Prophesies against Gentiles
    f. Summary of Judah's captivity

25. LAMENTATIONS - Lament over Jerusalem
    a. Affliction of Jerusalem
    b. Destroyed because of sin
    c. The prophet's suffering
    d. Present desolation versus past splendor
    e. Appeal to God for mercy

26. EZEKIEL - Israel's Captivity and Restoration
    a. Judgment on Judah and Jerusalem
    b. Judgment on Gentile nations
    c. Israel restored; Jerusalem's future glory

27. DANIEL - The Time of the Gentiles
    a. History; Nebuchadnezzar, Belshazzar, Daniel
    b. Prophecy

28. HOSEA - Unfaithfulness
    a. Unfaithfulness
    b. Punishment
    c. Restoration

29. JOEL - The Day of the Lord
    a. Locust plague
    b. Events of the future day of the Lord
    c. Order of the future day of the Lord

30. AMOS - God Judges Sin
    a. Neighbors judged
    b. Israel judged
    c. Visions of future judgment
    d. Israel's past judgment blessings

31. OBADIAH - Edom's Destruction
    a. Destruction prophesied
    b. Reasons for destruction
    c. Israel's future blessing

32. JONAH - Gentile Salvation
    a. Jonah disobeys
    b. Other suffer
    c. Jonah punished
    d. Jonah obeys; thousands saved
    e. Jonah displeased, no love for souls

33. MICAH - Israel's Sins, Judgment, and Restoration
    a. Sin and judgment
    b. Grace and future restoration
    c. Appeal and petition

34. NAHUM - Nineveh Condemned
    a. God hates sin
    b. Nineveh's doom prophesied
    c. Reasons for doom

35. HABAKKUK - The Just Shall Live by Faith
    a. Complaint of Judah's unjudged sin
    b. Chaldeans will punish
    c. Complaint of Chaldeans' wickedness
    d. Punishment promised
    e. Prayer for revival; faith in God

36. ZEPHANIAH - Babylonian Invasion Prefigures the Day of the Lord
    a. Judgment on Judah foreshadows the Great Day of the Lord
    b. Judgment on Jerusalem and neighbors foreshadows final judgment of all nations
    c. Israel restored after judgments

37. HAGGAI - Rebuild the Temple
    a. Negligence
    b. Courage
    c. Separation
    d. Judgment

38. ZECHARIAH - Two Comings of Christ
    a. Zechariah's vision
    b. Bethel's question; Jehovah's answer
    c. Nation's downfall and salvation

39. MALACHI - Neglect
    a. The priest's sins
    b. The people's sins
    c. The faithful few

Summary Outline of the Scriptures (continued)

1. MATTHEW - Jesus the King
   a. The Person of the King
   b. The Preparation of the King
   c. The Propaganda of the King
   d. The Program of the King
   e. The Passion of the King
   f. The Power of the King

2. MARK - Jesus the Servant
   a. John introduces the Servant
   b. God the Father identifies the Servant
   c. The temptation initiates the Servant
   d. Work and word of the Servant
   e. Death, burial, resurrection

3. LUKE - Jesus Christ the Perfect Man
   a. Birth and family of the Perfect Man
   b. Testing of the Perfect Man; hometown
   c. Ministry of the Perfect Man
   d. Betrayal, trial, and death of the Perfect Man
   e. Resurrection of the Perfect Man

4. JOHN - Jesus Christ is God
   a. Prologue - the Incarnation
   b. Introduction
   c. Witness of Jesus to his Apostles
   d. Passion - witness to the world
   e. Epilogue

5. ACTS - The Holy Spirit Working in the Church
   a. The Lord Jesus at work by the Holy Spirit through the Apostles at Jerusalem
   b. In Judea and Samaria
   c. To the uttermost parts of the Earth

6. ROMANS - The Righteousness of God
   a. Salutation
   b. Sin and salvation
   c. Sanctification
   d. Struggle
   e. Spirit-filled living
   f. Security of salvation
   g. Segregation
   h. Sacrifice and service
   i. Separation and salutation

7. 1 CORINTHIANS - The Lordship of Christ
   a. Salutation and thanksgiving
   b. Conditions in the Corinthian body
   c. Concerning the Gospel
   d. Concerning collections

8. 2 CORINTHIANS - The Ministry in the Church
   a. The comfort of God
   b. Collection for the poor
   c. Calling of the Apostle Paul

9. GALATIANS - Justification by Faith
   a. Introduction
   b. Personal - Authority of the Apostle and glory of the Gospel
   c. Doctrinal - Justification by faith
   d. Practical - Sanctification by the Holy Spirit
   e. Autographed conclusion and exhortation

10. EPHESIANS - The Church of Jesus Christ
    a. Doctrinal - the heavenly calling of the Church
       A Body
       A Temple
       A Mystery
    b. Practical - The earthly conduct of the Church
       A New Man
       A Bride
       An Army

11. PHILIPPIANS - Joy in the Christian Life
    a. Philosophy for Christian living
    b. Pattern for Christian living
    c. Prize for Christian living
    d. Power for Christian living

12. COLOSSIANS - Christ the Fullness of God
    a. Doctrinal - In Christ believers are made full
    b. Practical - Christ's life poured out in believers, and through them

13. 1 THESSALONIANS - The Second Coming of Christ:
    a. Is an inspiring hope
    b. Is a working hope
    c. Is a purifying hope
    d. Is a comforting hope
    e. Is a rousing, stimulating hope

14. 2 THESSALONIANS - The Second Coming of Christ
    a. Persecution of believers now; judgment of unbelievers hereafter (at coming of Christ)
    b. Program of the world in connection with the coming of Christ
    c. Practical issues associated with the coming of Christ

15. 1 TIMOTHY - Government and Order in the Local Church
    a. The faith of the Church
    b. Public prayer and women's place in the Church
    c. Officers in the Church
    d. Apostasy in the Church
    e. Duties of the officer of the Church

16. 2 TIMOTHY - Loyalty in the Days of Apostasy
    a. Afflictions of the Gospel
    b. Active in service
    c. Apostasy coming; authority of the Scriptures
    d. Allegiance to the Lord

17. TITUS - The Ideal New Testament Church
    a. The Church is an organization
    b. The Church is to teach and preach the Word of God
    c. The Church is to perform good works

18. PHILEMON - Reveal Christ's Love and Teach Brotherly Love
    a. Genial greeting to Philemon and family
    b. Good reputation of Philemon
    c. Gracious plea for Onesimus
    d. Guiltless illustration of Imputation
    e. General and personal requests

19. HEBREWS - The Superiority of Christ
    a. Doctrinal - Christ is better than the Old Testament economy
    b. Practical - Christ brings better benefits and duties

20. JAMES - Ethics of Christianity
    a. Faith tested
    b. Difficulty of controlling the tongue
    c. Warning against worldliness
    d. Admonitions in view of the Lord's coming

21. 1 PETER - Christian Hope in the Time of Persecution and Trial
    a. Suffering and security of believers
    b. Suffering and the Scriptures
    c. Suffering and the sufferings of Christ
    d. Suffering and the Second Coming of Christ

22. 2 PETER - Warning Against False Teachers
    a. Addition of Christian graces gives assurance
    b. Authority of the Scriptures
    c. Apostasy brought in by false testimony
    d. Attitude toward Return of Christ: test for apostasy
    e. Agenda of God in the world
    f. Admonition to believers

23. 1 JOHN - The Family of God
    a. God is Light
    b. God is Love
    c. God is Life

24. 2 JOHN - Warning against Receiving Deceivers
    a. Walk in truth
    b. Love one another
    c. Receive not deceivers
    d. Find joy in fellowship

25. 3 JOHN - Admonition to Receive True Believers
    a. Gaius, brother in the Church
    b. Diotrephes
    c. Demetrius

26. JUDE - Contending for the Faith
    a. Occasion of the epistle
    b. Occurrences of apostasy
    c. Occupation of believers in the days of apostasy

27. REVELATION - The Unveiling of Christ Glorified
    a. The person of Christ in glory
    b. The possession of Jesus Christ - the Church in the World
    c. The program of Jesus Christ - the scene in Heaven
    d. The seven seals
    e. The seven trumpets
    f. Important persons in the last days
    g. The seven vials
    h. The fall of Babylon
    i. The eternal state

APPENDIX 8

From Before to Beyond Time:

The Plan of God and Human History

Adapted from: Suzanne de Dietrich. **God's Unfolding Purpose.** *Philadelphia: Westminster Press, 1976.*

I. Before Time (Eternity Past) 1 Cor. 2.7
   A. The Eternal Triune God
   B. God's Eternal Purpose
   C. The Mystery of Iniquity
   D. The Principalities and Powers

II. Beginning of Time (Creation and Fall) Gen. 1.1
   A. Creative Word
   B. Humanity
   C. Fall
   D. Reign of Death and First Signs of Grace

III. Unfolding of Time (God's Plan Revealed Through Israel) Gal. 3.8
   A. Promise (Patriarchs)
   B. Exodus and Covenant at Sinai
   C. Promised Land
   D. The City, the Temple, and the Throne (Prophet, Priest, and King)
   E. Exile
   F. Remnant

IV. Fullness of Time (Incarnation of the Messiah) Gal. 4.4-5
   A. The King Comes to His Kingdom
   B. The Present Reality of His Reign
   C. The Secret of the Kingdom: the Already and the Not Yet
   D. The Crucified King
   E. The Risen Lord

V. The Last Times (The Descent of the Holy Spirit) Acts 2.16-18
   A. Between the Times: the Church as Foretaste of the Kingdom
   B. The Church as Agent of the Kingdom
   C. The Conflict Between the Kingdoms of Darkness and Light

VI. The Fulfillment of Time (The Second Coming) Matt. 13.40-43
   A. The Return of Christ
   B. Judgment
   C. The Consummation of His Kingdom

VII. Beyond Time (Eternity Future) 1 Cor. 15.24-28
   A. Kingdom Handed Over to God the Father
   B. God as All in All

From Before to Beyond Time
Scriptures for Major Outline Points

I. Before Time (Eternity Past)

1 Cor. 2.7 (ESV) - But we impart a secret and hidden wisdom of God, *which God decreed before the ages* for our glory (cf. Titus 1.2).

II. Beginning of Time (Creation and Fall)

Gen. 1.1 (ESV) - *In the beginning,* God created the heavens and the earth.

III. Unfolding of Time (God's Plan Revealed Through Israel)

Gal. 3.8 (ESV) - And the Scripture, foreseeing that God would justify the Gentiles by faith, *preached the Gospel beforehand to Abraham,* saying, "In you shall all the nations be blessed" (cf. Rom. 9.4-5).

IV. Fullness of Time (The Incarnation of the Messiah)

Gal. 4.4-5 (ESV) - *But when the fullness of time had come,* God sent forth his Son, born of woman, born under the law, to redeem those who were under the law, so that we might receive adoption as sons.

V. The Last Times (The Descent of the Holy Spirit)

Acts 2.16-18 (ESV) - But this is what was uttered through the prophet Joel: "'*And in the last days it shall be,*' God declares, 'that I will pour out my Spirit on all flesh, and your sons and your daughters shall prophesy, and your young men shall see visions, and your old men shall dream dreams; even on my male servants and female servants in those days I will pour out my Spirit, and they shall prophesy.'"

VI. The Fulfillment of Time (The Second Coming)

Matt. 13.40-43 (ESV) - Just as the weeds are gathered and burned with fire, *so will it be at the close of the age.* The Son of Man will send his angels, and they will gather out of his kingdom all causes of sin and all lawbreakers, and throw them into the fiery furnace. In that place there will be weeping and gnashing of teeth. Then the righteous will shine like the sun in the Kingdom of their Father. He who has ears, let him hear.

VII. Beyond Time (Eternity Future)

1 Cor. 15.24-28 (ESV) - Then comes the end, when he delivers the Kingdom to God the Father after destroying every rule and every authority and power. For he must reign until he has put all his enemies under his feet. The last enemy to be destroyed is death. For "God has put all things in subjection under his feet." But when it says, "all things are put in subjection," it is plain that he is excepted who put all things in subjection under him. When all things are subjected to him, then the Son himself will also be subjected to him who put all things in subjection under him, that God may be all in all.

APPENDIX 9

"There Is a River"

Identifying the Streams of a Revitalized Authentic Christian Community in the City[1]

Rev. Dr. Don L. Davis • Psalm 46.4 (ESV) - There is a river whose streams make glad the city of God, the holy habitation of the Most High.

Tributaries of Authentic Historic Biblical Faith			
Recognized Biblical Identity	*Revived Urban Spirituality*	*Reaffirmed Historical Connectivity*	*Refocused Kingdom Authority*
*The Church Is **One***	*The Church Is **Holy***	*The Church Is **Catholic***	*The Church Is **Apostolic***
A Call to Biblical Fidelity *Recognizing the Scriptures as the anchor and foundation of the Christian faith and practice*	A Call to the Freedom, Power, and Fullness of the Holy Spirit *Walking in the holiness, power, gifting, and liberty of the Holy Spirit in the body of Christ*	A Call to Historic Roots and Continuity *Confessing the common historical identity and continuity of authentic Christian faith*	A Call to the Apostolic Faith *Affirming the apostolic tradition as the authoritative ground of the Christian hope*
A Call to Messianic Kingdom Identity *Rediscovering the story of the promised Messiah and his Kingdom in Jesus of Nazareth*	A Call to Live as Sojourners and Aliens as the People of God *Defining authentic Christian discipleship as faithful membership among God's people*	A Call to Affirm and Express the Global Communion of Saints *Expressing cooperation and collaboration with all other believers, both local and global*	A Call to Representative Authority *Submitting joyfully to God's gifted servants in the Church as undershepherds of true faith*
A Call to Creedal Affinity *Embracing the Nicene Creed as the shared rule of faith of historic orthodoxy*	A Call to Liturgical, Sacramental, and Catechetical Vitality *Experiencing God's presence in the context of the Word, sacrament, and instruction*	A Call to Radical Hospitality and Good Works *Expressing kingdom love to all, and especially to those of the household of faith*	A Call to Prophetic and Holistic Witness *Proclaiming Christ and his Kingdom in word and deed to our neighbors and all peoples*

[1] *This schema is an adaptation and is based on the insights of the **Chicago Call** statement of May 1977, where various leading evangelical scholars and practitioners met to discuss the relationship of modern evangelicalism to the historic Christian faith.*

APPENDIX 10
A Schematic for a Theology of the Kingdom and the Church

The Urban Ministry Institute

The Reign of the One, True, Sovereign, and Triune God, the LORD God, Yahweh, God the Father, Son, and Holy Spirit

The Father	The Son	The Spirit
Love - 1 John 4.8 Maker of heaven and earth and of all things visible and invisible	Faith - Heb. 12.2 Prophet, Priest, and King	Hope - Rom. 15.13 Lord of the Church
Creation All that exists through the creative action of God.	**Kingdom** The Reign of God expressed in the rule of his Son Jesus the Messiah.	**Church** The one, holy, apostolic community which functions as a witness to (Acts 28.31) and a foretaste of (Col. 1.12; James 1.18; 1 Pet. 2.9; Rev. 1.6) the Kingdom of God.

Rom. 8.18-21

The eternal God, sovereign in power, infinite in wisdom, perfect in holiness, and steadfast in love, is the source and goal of all things.

Rom. 8.18-21 →

O, the depth of the riches and wisdom and knowledge of God! How unsearchable are his judgments, and how inscrutable his ways! For who has known the mind of the Lord, or who has been his counselor? Or who has given a gift to him, that he might be repaid?" For from him and through him and to him are all things. To him be glory forever! Amen! - Rom. 11.33-36 (ESV) (cf. 1 Cor. 15.23-28; Rev.)

Freedom (Slavery)

Jesus answered them, "Truly, truly, I say to you, everyone who commits sin is a slave to sin. The slave does not remain in the house forever; the son remains forever. So if the Son sets you free, you will be free indeed." - John 8.34-36 (ESV)

The Church is an Apostolic Community Where the Word is Rightly Preached, Therefore it is a Community of:

Calling - For freedom Christ has set us free; stand firm therefore, and do not submit again to a yoke of slavery. - Gal. 5.1 (ESV) (cf. Rom. 8.28-30; 1 Cor. 1.26-31; Eph. 1.18; 2 Thess. 2.13-14; Jude 1.1)

Faith - ". . . for unless you believe that I am he you will die in your sins" . . . . So Jesus said to the Jews who had believed in him, "If you abide in my word, you are truly my disciples, and you will know the truth, and the truth will set you free." - John 8.24b, 31-32 (ESV) (cf. Ps. 119.45; Rom. 1.17; 5.1-2; Eph. 2.8-9; 2 Tim. 1.13-14; Heb. 2.14-15; James 1.25)

Witness - The Spirit of the Lord is upon me, because he has anointed me to proclaim good news to the poor. He has sent me to proclaim liberty to the captives and recovering of sight to the blind, to set at liberty those who are oppressed, to proclaim the year of the Lord's favor. - Luke 4.18-19 (ESV) (cf. Lev. 25.10; Prov. 31.8; Matt. 4.17; 28.18-20; Mark 13.10; Acts 1.8; 8.4, 12; 13.1-3; 25.20; 28.30-31)

Rev. 21.1-5 →

But he was wounded for our transgressions; he was crushed for our iniquities; upon him was the chastisement that brought us peace, and with his stripes we are healed. - Isa. 53.5 (ESV)

Wholeness (Sickness)

The Church is One Community Where the Sacraments are Rightly Administered, Therefore it is a Community of:

Worship - You shall serve the Lord your God, and he will bless your bread and your water, and I will take sickness away from among you. - Exod. 23.25 (ESV) (cf. Ps. 147.1-3; Heb. 12.28; Col. 3.16; Rev. 15.3-4; 19.5)

Covenant - And the Holy Spirit also bears witness to us; for after the saying, "This is the covenant that I will make with them after those days, declares the Lord: I will put my laws on their hearts, and write them on their minds," then he adds, "I will remember their sins and their lawless deeds no more." - Heb. 10.15-17 (ESV) (cf. Isa. 54.10-17; Ezek. 34.25-31; 37.26-27; Mal. 2.4-5; Luke 22.20; 2 Cor. 3.6; Col. 3.15; Heb. 8.7-13; 12.22-24; 13.20-21)

Presence - In him you also are being built together into a dwelling place for God by his Spirit. - Eph. 2.22 (ESV) (cf. Exod. 40.34-38; Ezek. 48.35; Matt. 18.18-20)

Isa. 11.6-9 →

Behold, my servant whom I have chosen, my beloved with whom my soul is well pleased. I will put my Spirit upon him, and he will proclaim justice to the Gentiles. He will not quarrel or cry aloud, nor will anyone hear his voice in the streets; a bruised reed he will not break, and a smoldering wick he will not quench, until he brings justice to victory. - Matt. 12.18-20 (ESV)

Justice (Selfishness)

The Church is a Holy Community Where Discipline is Rightly Ordered, Therefore it is a Community of:

Reconciliation - For he himself is our peace, who has made us both one and has broken down in his flesh the dividing wall of hostility by abolishing the law of commandments and ordinances, that he might create in himself one new man in place of the two, so making peace, and might reconcile us both to God in one body through the cross, thereby killing the hostility. And he came and preached peace to you who were far off and peace to those who were near. For through him we both have access in one Spirit to the Father. - Eph. 2.14-18 (ESV) (cf. Exod. 23.4-9; Lev. 19.34; Deut. 10.18-19; Ezek. 22.29; Mic. 6.8; 2 Cor. 5.16-21)

Suffering - Since therefore Christ suffered in the flesh, arm yourselves with the same way of thinking, for whoever has suffered in the flesh has ceased from sin, so as to live for the rest of the time in the flesh no longer for human passions but for the will of God. - 1 Pet. 4.1-2 (ESV) (cf. Luke 6.22; 10.3; Rom. 8.17; 2 Tim. 2.3; 3.12; 1 Pet. 2.20-24; Heb. 5.8; 13.11-14)

Service - But Jesus called them to him and said, "You know that the rulers of the Gentiles lord it over them, and their great ones exercise authority over them. It shall not be so among you. But whoever would be great among you must be your servant, and whoever would be first among you must be your slave even as the Son of Man came not to be served but to serve, and to give his life as a ransom for many." - Matt. 20.25-28 (ESV) (cf. 1 John 4.16-18; Gal. 2.10)

APPENDIX 11

Living in the Already and the Not Yet Kingdom

Rev. Dr. Don L. Davis

The Spirit: The pledge of the inheritance (***arrabon***)

The Church: The foretaste (***aparche***) of the Kingdom

"In Christ": The rich life (***en Christos***) we share as citizens of the Kingdom

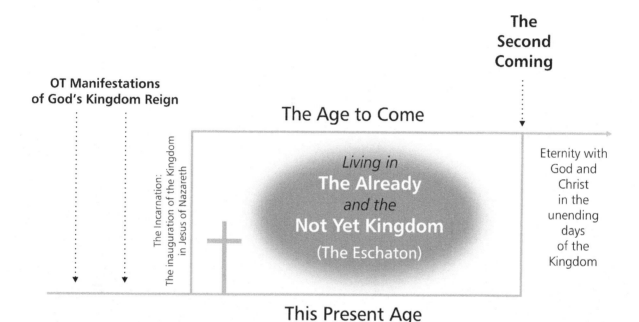

Internal enemy: The flesh (*sarx*) and the sin nature

External enemy: The world (*kosmos*) the systems of greed, lust, and pride

Infernal enemy: The devil (*kakos*) the animating spirit of falsehood and fear

Jewish View of Time

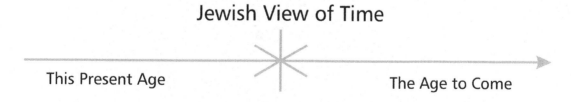

This Present Age   The Age to Come

The Coming of Messiah

The restoration of Israel

The end of Gentile oppression

The return of the earth to Edenic glory

Universal knowledge of the Lord

APPENDIX 12
Jesus of Nazareth: The Presence of the Future
Rev. Dr. Don L. Davis

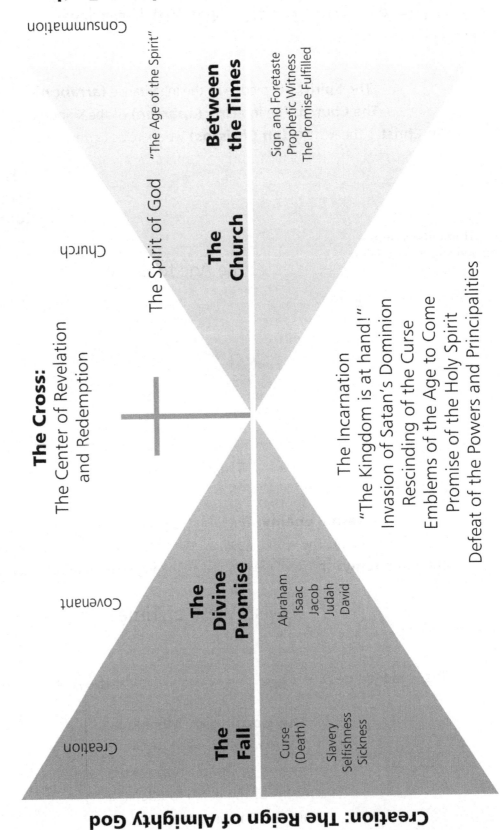

Glorification: New Heavens and New Earth

Consummation

Between the Times

"The Age of the Spirit"

Sign and Foretaste
Prophetic Witness
The Promise Fulfilled

The Church

The Spirit of God

Church

The Cross:
The Center of Revelation
and Redemption

The Incarnation
"The Kingdom is at hand!"
Invasion of Satan's Dominion
Rescinding of the Curse
Emblems of the Age to Come
Promise of the Holy Spirit
Defeat of the Powers and Principalities

The Divine Promise

Covenant

Abraham
Isaac
Jacob
Judah
David

The Fall

Curse
(Death)

Slavery
Selfishness
Sickness

Creation

Creation: The Reign of Almighty God

APPENDIX 13

Traditions
(Paradosis)

Dr. Don L. Davis and Rev. Terry G. Cornett

Strong's Definition

Paradosis. Transmission, i.e. (concretely) a precept; specifically, the Jewish traditionary law

Vine's Explanation

denotes "a tradition," and hence, by metonymy, (a) "the teachings of the rabbis," . . . (b) "apostolic teaching," . . . of instructions concerning the gatherings of believers, of Christian doctrine in general . . . of instructions concerning everyday conduct.

1. The concept of tradition in Scripture is essentially positive.

Jer. 6.16 (ESV) - Thus says the Lord: "Stand by the roads, and look, and ask for the ancient paths, where the good way is; and walk in it, and find rest for your souls. But they said, 'We will not walk in it'" (cf. Exod. 3.15; Judg. 2.17; 1 Kings 8.57-58; Ps. 78.1-6).

2 Chron. 35.25 (ESV) - Jeremiah also uttered a lament for Josiah; and all the singing men and singing women have spoken of Josiah in their laments to this day. They made these a rule in Israel; behold, they are written in the Laments (cf. Gen. 32.32; Judg. 11.38-40).

Jer. 35.14-19 (ESV) - The command that Jonadab the son of Rechab gave to his sons, to drink no wine, has been kept, and they drink none to this day, for they have obeyed their father's command. I have spoken to you persistently, but you have not listened to me. I have sent to you all my servants the prophets, sending them persistently, saying, 'Turn now every one of you from his evil way, and amend your deeds, and do not go after other gods to serve them, and then you shall dwell in the land that I gave to you and your fathers.' But you did not incline your ear or listen to me. The sons of Jonadab the son of Rechab have kept the command that their father gave them, but this people has not obeyed me. Therefore, thus says the

Traditions (continued)

Lord, the God of hosts, the God of Israel: Behold, I am bringing upon Judah and all the inhabitants of Jerusalem all the disaster that I have pronounced against them, because I have spoken to them and they have not listened, I have called to them and they have not answered." But to the house of the Rechabites Jeremiah said, "Thus says the Lord of hosts, the God of Israel: Because you have obeyed the command of Jonadab your father and kept all his precepts and done all that he commanded you, therefore thus says the Lord of hosts, the God of Israel: Jonadab the son of Rechab shall never lack a man to stand before me."

2. Godly tradition is a wonderful thing, but not all tradition is godly.

Any individual tradition must be judged by its faithfulness to the Word of God and its usefulness in helping people maintain obedience to Christ's example and teaching.[1] In the Gospels, Jesus frequently rebukes the Pharisees for establishing traditions that nullify rather than uphold God's commands.

Mark 7.8 (ESV) - You leave the commandment of God and hold to the tradition of men" (cf. Matt. 15.2-6; Mark 7.13).

Col. 2.8 (ESV) - See to it that no one takes you captive by philosophy and empty deceit, according to human tradition, according to the elemental spirits of the world, and not according to Christ.

3. Without the fullness of the Holy Spirit, and the constant edification provided to us by the Word of God, tradition will inevitably lead to dead formalism.

Those who are spiritual are filled with the Holy Spirit, whose power and leading alone provides individuals and congregations a sense of freedom and vitality in all they practice and believe. However, when the practices and teachings of any given tradition are no longer infused by the power of the Holy Spirit and the Word of God, tradition loses its effectiveness, and may actually become counterproductive to our discipleship in Jesus Christ.

Eph. 5.18 (ESV) - And do not get drunk with wine, for that is debauchery, but be filled with the Spirit.

[1] "All Protestants insist that these traditions must ever be tested against Scripture and can never possess an independent apostolic authority over or alongside of Scripture." (J. Van Engen, "Tradition," *Evangelical Dictionary of Theology*, Walter Elwell, Gen. ed.) We would add that Scripture is itself the "authoritative tradition" by which all other traditions are judged. See "Appendix A, The Founders of Tradition: Three Levels of Christian Authority," p. 4.

Gal. 5.22-25 (ESV) - But the fruit of the Spirit is love, joy, peace, patience, kindness, goodness, faithfulness, gentleness, self-control; against such things there is no law. And those who belong to Christ Jesus have crucified the flesh with its passions and desires. If we live by the Spirit, let us also walk by the Spirit.

2 Cor. 3.5-6 (ESV) - Not that we are sufficient in ourselves to claim anything as coming from us, but our sufficiency is from God, who has made us competent to be ministers of a new covenant, not of the letter but of the Spirit. For the letter kills, but the Spirit gives life.

4. **Fidelity to the Apostolic Tradition (teaching and modeling) is the essence of Christian maturity.**

2 Tim. 2.2 (ESV) - and what you have heard from me in the presence of many witnesses entrust to faithful men who will be able to teach others also.

1 Cor. 11.1-2 (ESV) - Be imitators of me, as I am of Christ. Now I commend you because you remember me in everything and maintain the traditions even as I delivered them to you (cf.1 Cor. 4.16-17, 2 Tim. 1.13-14, 2 Thess. 3.7-9, Phil. 4.9).

1 Cor. 15.3-8 (ESV) - For I delivered to you as of first importance what I also received: that Christ died for our sins in accordance with the Scriptures, that he was buried, that he was raised on the third day in accordance with the Scriptures, and that he appeared to Cephas, then to the twelve. Then he appeared to more than five hundred brothers at one time, most of whom are still alive, though some have fallen asleep. Then he appeared to James, then to all the apostles. Last of all, as to one untimely born, he appeared also to me.

5. **The Apostle Paul often includes an appeal to the tradition for support in doctrinal practices.**

1 Cor. 11.16 (ESV) - If anyone is inclined to be contentious, we have no such practice, nor do the churches of God (cf. 1 Cor. 1.2, 7.17, 15.3).

Traditions (continued)

1 Cor. 14.33-34 (ESV) - For God is not a God of confusion but of peace. As in all the churches of the saints, the women should keep silent in the churches. For they are not permitted to speak, but should be in submission, as the Law also says.

6. When a congregation uses received tradition to remain faithful to the "Word of God," they are commended by the apostles.

1 Cor. 11.2 (ESV) - Now I commend you because you remember me in everything and maintain the traditions even as I delivered them to you.

2 Thess. 2.15 (ESV) - So then, brothers, stand firm and hold to the traditions that you were taught by us, either by our spoken word or by our letter.

2 Thess. 3.6 (ESV) - Now we command you, brothers, in the name of our Lord Jesus Christ, that you keep away from any brother who is walking in idleness and not in accord with the tradition that you received from us.

Appendix A

The Founders of Tradition: Three Levels of Christian Authority

Exod. 3.15 (ESV) - God also said to Moses, "Say this to the people of Israel, 'The Lord, the God of your fathers, the God of Abraham, the God of Isaac, and the God of Jacob, has sent me to you.' This is my name forever, and thus I am to be remembered throughout all generations."

1. The Authoritative Tradition: the Apostles and the Prophets (The Holy Scriptures)

Eph. 2.19-21 (ESV) - So then you are no longer strangers and aliens, but you are fellow citizens with the saints and members of the household of God, built on the foundation of the apostles and prophets, Christ Jesus himself being the cornerstone, in whom the whole structure, being joined together, grows into a holy temple in the Lord.

~ The Apostle Paul

Traditions (continued)

Those who gave eyewitness testimony to the revelation and saving acts of Yahweh, first in Israel, and ultimately in Jesus Christ the Messiah. This testimony is binding for all people, at all times, and in all places. It is the authoritative tradition by which all subsequent tradition is judged.

[2] See Appendix B, "Defining the Great Tradition."

2. The Great Tradition: the Ecumenical Councils and their Creeds[2]

What has been believed everywhere, always, and by all.

~ Vincent of Lerins

The Great Tradition is the core dogma (doctrine) of the Church. It represents the teaching of the Church as it has understood the Authoritative Tradition (the Holy Scriptures), and summarizes those essential truths that Christians of all ages have confessed and believed. To these doctrinal statements the whole Church, (Catholic, Orthodox, and Protestant)[3] gives its assent. The worship and theology of the Church reflects this core dogma, which finds its summation and fulfillment in the person and work of Jesus Christ. From earliest times, Christians have expressed their devotion to God in its Church calendar, a yearly pattern of worship which summarizes and reenacts the events of Christ's life.

[3] Even the more radical wing of the Protestant reformation (Anabaptists) who were the most reluctant to embrace the creeds as dogmatic instruments of faith, did not disagree with the essential content found in them. "They assumed the Apostolic Creed—they called it 'The Faith,' Der Glaube, as did most people." See John Howard Yoder, Preface to Theology: Christology and Theological Method. Grand Rapids: Brazos Press, 2002. pp. 222-223.

3. Specific Church Traditions: the Founders of Denominations and Orders

The Presbyterian Church (U.S.A.) has approximately 2.5 million members, 11,200 congregations and 21,000 ordained ministers. Presbyterians trace their history to the 16th century and the Protestant Reformation. Our heritage, and much of what we believe, began with the French lawyer John Calvin (1509-1564), whose writings crystallized much of the Reformed thinking that came before him.

~ The Presbyterian Church, U.S.A.

Christians have expressed their faith in Jesus Christ in various ways through specific movements and traditions which embrace and express the Authoritative Tradition and the Great Tradition in unique ways. For instance,

Traditions (continued)

Catholic movements have arisen around people like Benedict, Francis, or Dominic, and among Protestants people like Martin Luther, John Calvin, Ulrich Zwingli, and John Wesley. Women have founded vital movements of Christian faith (e.g., Aimee Semple McPherson of the Foursquare Church), as well as minorities (e.g., Richard Allen of the African Methodist Episcopal Church or Charles H. Mason of the Church of God in Christ, who also helped to spawn the Assemblies of God), all which attempted to express the Authoritative Tradition and the Great Tradition in a specific way consistent with their time and expression.

The emergence of vital, dynamic movements of the faith at different times and among different peoples reveal the fresh working of the Holy Spirit throughout history. Thus, inside Catholicism, new communities have arisen such as the Benedictines, Franciscans, and Dominicans; and outside Catholicism, new denominations have emerged (Lutherans, Presbyterians, Methodists, Church of God in Christ, etc.). Each of these specific traditions have "founders," key leaders whose energy and vision helped to establish a unique expression of Christian faith and practice. Of course, to be legitimate, these movements must adhere to and faithfully express both the Authoritative Tradition and the Great Tradition. Members of these specific traditions embrace their own unique practices and patterns of spirituality, but these unique features are not necessarily binding on the Church at large. They represent the unique expressions of that community's understanding of and faithfulness to the Authoritative and Great Traditions.

Specific traditions seek to express and live out this faithfulness to the Authoritative and Great Traditions through their worship, teaching, and service. They seek to make the Gospel clear within new cultures or sub-cultures, speaking and modeling the hope of Christ into new situations shaped by their own set of questions posed in light of their own unique circumstances. These movements, therefore, seek to contextualize the Authoritative tradition in a way that faithfully and effectively leads new groups of people to faith in Jesus Christ, and incorporates those who believe into the community of faith that obeys his teachings and gives witness of him to others.

Appendix B

Defining the "Great Tradition"

The Great Tradition (sometimes called the "classical Christian tradition") is defined by Robert E. Webber as follows:

> *[It is] the broad outline of Christian belief and practice developed from the Scriptures between the time of Christ and the middle of the fifth century*

> ~ Webber. **The Majestic Tapestry**.
> Nashville: Thomas Nelson Publishers, 1986. p. 10.

This tradition is widely affirmed by Protestant theologians both ancient and modern.

> *Thus those ancient Councils of Nicea, Constantinople, the first of Ephesus, Chalcedon, and the like, which were held for refuting errors, we willingly embrace, and reverence as sacred, in so far as relates to doctrines of faith, for they contain nothing but the pure and genuine interpretation of Scripture, which the holy Fathers with spiritual prudence adopted to crush the enemies of religion who had then arisen.*

> ~ John Calvin. **Institutes**. IV, ix. 8.

> *. . . most of what is enduringly valuable in contemporary biblical exegesis was discovered by the fifth century.*

> ~ Thomas C. Oden. **The Word of Life**.
> San Francisco: HarperSanFrancisco, 1989. p. xi

> *The first four Councils are by far the most important, as they settled the orthodox faith on the Trinity and the Incarnation.*

> ~ Philip Schaff. **The Creeds of Christendom**. Vol. 1.
> Grand Rapids: Baker Book House, 1996. p. 44.

Our reference to the Ecumenical Councils and Creeds is, therefore, focused on those Councils which retain a widespread agreement in the Church among Catholics, Orthodox, and Protestants. While Catholic and Orthodox share common agreement on the first seven councils, Protestants tend to affirm and use primarily the first four. Therefore, those councils which continue to be shared by the whole Church are completed with the Council of Chalcedon in 451.

Traditions (continued)

It is worth noting that each of these four Ecumenical Councils took place in a pre-European cultural context and that none of them were held in Europe. They were councils of the whole Church and they reflected a time in which Christianity was primarily an eastern religion in it's geographic core. By modern reckoning, their participants were African, Asian, and European. The councils reflected a church that ". . . has roots in cultures far distant from Europe and preceded the development of modern European identity, and [of which] some of its greatest minds have been African" (Oden, *The Living God*, San Francisco: HarperSanFrancisco, 1987, p. 9).

Perhaps the most important achievement of the Councils was the creation of what is now commonly called the Nicene Creed. It serves as a summary statement of the Christian faith that can be agreed on by Catholic, Orthodox, and Protestant Christians.

The first four Ecumenical Councils are summarized in the following chart:

Name/Date/Location	Purpose
First Ecumenical Council *325 A.D.* *Nicea, Asia Minor*	Defending against: *Arianism* Question answered: *Was Jesus God?* Action: *Developed the initial form of the Nicene Creed to serve as a summary of the Christian faith*
Second Ecumenical Council *381 A.D.* *Constantinople, Asia Minor*	Defending against: *Macedonianism* Question answered: *Is the Holy Spirit a personal and equal part of the Godhead?* Action: *Completed the Nicene Creed by expanding the article dealing with the Holy Spirit*
Third Ecumenical Council *431 A.D.* *Ephesus, Asia Minor*	Defending against: *Nestorianism* Question answered: *Is Jesus Christ both God and man in one person?* Action: *Defined Christ as the Incarnate Word of God and affirmed his mother Mary as **theotokos** (God-bearer)*
Fourth Ecumenical Council *451 A.D.* *Chalcedon, Asia Minor*	Defending against: *Monophysitism* Question answered: *How can Jesus be both God and man?* Action: *Explained the relationship between Jesus' two natures (human and Divine)*

APPENDIX 14

Jesus and the Poor

Don L. Davis

Thesis: The heart of Jesus' ministry of the Kingdom was the transformation and renewal of the those on the underside of life, the poor. He demonstrated his personal heart vision in how he inaugurated his ministry, authenticated his ministry, defined the heart and soul of ministry, identifying himself directly with the poor.

I. Jesus Inaugurated His Ministry with an Outreach to the Poor.

A. The inaugural sermon at Nazareth, Luke 4.16-21

Luke 4.16-21 (ESV) - And he came to Nazareth, where he had been brought up. And as was his custom, he went to the synagogue on the Sabbath day, and he stood up to read. [17] And the scroll of the prophet Isaiah was given to him. He unrolled the scroll and found the place where it was written, [18] "The Spirit of the Lord is upon me, because he has anointed me to proclaim good news to the poor. He has sent me to proclaim liberty to the captives and recovering of sight to the blind, to set at liberty those who are oppressed, [19] to proclaim the year of the Lord's favor." [20] And he rolled up the scroll and gave it back to the attendant and sat down. And the eyes of all in the synagogue were fixed on him. [21] And he began to say to them, "Today this Scripture has been fulfilled in your hearing."

B. The meaning of this inauguration

1. The object of his attention: his choice of texts

2. The object of his calling: his Spirit anointing

Jesus and the Poor (continued)

3. The objects of his love:

a. Good news to the poor

b. Release to the captives

c. Recovery of sight to the blind

d. Letting the oppressed go free

4. The object of his ministry: the Year of the Lord's favor

C. *Ministry to the poor as the cornerstone of his inaugural ministry*

II. Jesus Authenticated His Ministry by His Actions toward the Poor.

A. John's query regarding Jesus' authenticity, Luke 7.18-23

Luke 7.18-23 (ESV) - The disciples of John reported all these things to him. And John, [19] calling two of his disciples to him, sent them to the Lord, saying, "Are you the one who is to come, or shall we look for another?" [20] And when the men had come to him, they said, "John the Baptist has sent us to you, saying, 'Are you the one who is to come, or shall we look for another?'" [21] In that hour he healed many people of diseases and plagues and evil spirits, and on many who were blind he bestowed sight. [22] And he answered them, "Go and tell John what you have seen and heard: the BLIND RECEIVE THEIR SIGHT, the lame walk, lepers are cleansed, and the deaf hear, the dead are raised up, the POOR HAVE GOOD NEWS PREACHED TO THEM. [23] And blessed is the one who is not offended by me."

B. Will the real Messiah please stand up?

1. The question of John, 19-20

2. The actions of Jesus, 21 (the show-side of "show-and-tell")

3. The explanation of his identity, 22-23

   a. Go and tell John what you have seen and heard.

   b. Blind seeing, lame walking, lepers cleansed, deaf hearing, dead being raising, the poor hearing the Gospel

C. *Ministry to the poor is undeniable proof of the Messiah's identity.*

III. Jesus Verified Salvation in Relation to One's Treatment of the Poor.

A. The story of Zaccheus, Luke 19.1-9

Luke 19.1-9 (ESV) - He entered Jericho and was passing through. [2] And there was a man named Zacchaeus. He was a chief tax collector and was rich. [3] And he was seeking to see who Jesus was, but on account of the crowd he could not, because he was small of stature. [4] So he ran on ahead and climbed up into a sycamore tree to see him, for he was about to pass that way. [5] And when Jesus came to the place, he looked up and said to him, "Zacchaeus, hurry and come down, for I must stay at your house today." [6] So he hurried and came down and received him joyfully. [7] And when they saw it, they all grumbled, "He has gone in to be the guest of a man who is a sinner." [8] And Zacchaeus stood and said to the Lord, "Behold, Lord, the half of my goods I give to the poor. And if I have defrauded anyone of anything, I restore it fourfold." [9] And Jesus said to him, "Today salvation has come to this house, since he also is a son of Abraham."

1. The palpitations of Zaccheus

2. The salutation of Zaccheus (to Jesus)

3. The declaration of Zaccheus

   a. Half of all I own I give to the poor.

   b. I restore those wrongly treated by me four-fold.

Jesus and the Poor (continued)

4. The salvation of Zaccheus, vv.9-10

B. Plucking Grain on the Sabbath, Matt.12.1-8

Matt. 12.1-8 (ESV) - At that time Jesus went through the grainfields on the Sabbath. His disciples were hungry, and they began to pluck heads of grain and to eat. [2] But when the Pharisees saw it, they said to him, "Look, your disciples are doing what is not lawful to do on the Sabbath." [3] He said to them, "Have you not read what David did when he was hungry, and those who were with him: [4] how he entered the house of God and ate the bread of the Presence, which it was not lawful for him to eat nor for those who were with him, but only for the priests? [5] Or have you not read in the Law how on the Sabbath the priests in the temple profane the Sabbath and are guiltless? [6] I tell you, something greater than the temple is here. [7] And if you had known what this means, 'I DESIRE MERCY, AND NOT SACRIFICE,' you would not have condemned the guiltless. [8] For the Son of Man is lord of the Sabbath."

1. Disciples snacking on corn on the Sabbath

2. The Pharisees disputation: "Look, your disciples are doing what is not lawful to do on the sabbath."

3. Jesus' retort: "I desire mercy and not sacrifice."

   a. Mercy to the poor and broken, not ritual faithfulness

   b. Compassion for the broken, not religious discipline

C. *Ministry to the poor is the litmus test of authentic salvation.*

IV. Jesus Identifies Himself Unreservedly with the Poor.

A. Those who cannot repay you, Luke 14.11-15

Luke 14.11-14 (ESV) - "For everyone who exalts himself will be humbled, and he who humbles himself will be exalted." [12] He said also to the man who had invited him, "When you give a dinner or a banquet, do not invite your friends or your brothers or your relatives or rich neighbors, lest they also invite you in return and you be repaid. [13] But when you give a feast, invite the poor, the crippled, the lame, the blind, [14] and you will be blessed, because they cannot repay you. You will be repaid at the resurrection of the just."

B. The Judgment Seat of the King, Matt. 25.31-45

Matt. 25.34-40 (ESV) - Then the King will say to those on his right, "Come, you who are blessed by my Father, inherit the kingdom prepared for you from the foundation of the world. [35] For I was hungry and you gave me food, I was thirsty and you gave me drink, I was a stranger and you welcomed me, [36] I was naked and you clothed me, I was sick and you visited me, I was in prison and you came to me." [37] Then the righteous will answer him, saying, "Lord, when did we see you hungry and feed you, or thirsty and give you drink? [38] And when did we see you a stranger and welcome you, or naked and clothe you? [39] And when did we see you sick or in prison and visit you?" [40] And the King will answer them, "Truly, I say to you, as you did it to one of the least of these my brothers, you did it to me."

1. Two sets of people: sheep and goats

2. Two responses: one blessed and embraced, one judged and rejected

3. Two destinies: the sheep in the Kingdom inherited, prepared from the foundation of the world, the goats in the eternal fire prepared for the devil and his angels

4. Two reactions: one was hospitable, charitable, generous; the other apathetic, heartless, negligent

Jesus and the Poor (continued)

5. The same group of people: the hungry, the thirsty, the stranger, the naked, the sick, the prisoner

6. *The same standard: in the way you treated or mistreated these people, those on the underside of life, so you responded to me.*

C. Jesus made it appear as those who were least deserving but repentant would become heirs of the Kingdom.

Matt. 21.31 (ESV) - "Which of the two did the will of his father?" They said, "The first." Jesus said to them, "Truly, I say to you, the tax collectors and the prostitutes go into the kingdom of God before you."

Mark 2.15-17 (ESV) - And as he reclined at table in his house, many tax collectors and sinners were reclining with Jesus and his disciples, for there were many who followed him. [16] And the scribes of the Pharisees, when they saw that he was eating with sinners and tax collectors, said to his disciples, "Why does he eat with tax collectors and sinners?" [17] And when Jesus heard it, he said to them, "Those who are well have no need of a physician, but those who are sick. I came not to call the righteous, but sinners."

D. Ministry to the poor is ministry to the Lord Jesus - his identification with them is complete.

Conclusion: The heart and soul of Jesus' ministry was directed toward the transformation and liberation of those who were most vulnerable, most forgotten, most neglected. As disciples, may we demonstrate the same.

APPENDIX 15

Paul's Partnership Theology

Our Union with Christ and Partnership in Kingdom Ministry

Adapted from Brian J. Dodd. **Empowered Church Leadership**. *Downers Grove: InterVarsity Press, 2003.*

The apostolic fondness for Greek terms compounded with the prefix syn (with or co-)

English Translation of the Greek Term	Scripture References
Co-worker (*Synergos*)	Rom 16.3, 7, 9, 21; 2 Cor. 8.23; Phil. 2.25; 4.3; Col. 4.7, 10, 11, 14; Philem. 1, 24
Co-prisoner (*Synaichmalotos*)	Col. 4.10; Philem. 23
Co-slave (*Syndoulous*)	Col. 1.7; 4.7
Co-soldier (*Systratiotes*)	Phil. 2.25; Philem. 2
Co-laborer (*Synathleo*)	Phil. 4.2-3

APPENDIX 16

Six Kinds of New Testament Ministry for Community

Rev. Dr. Don L. Davis

Type	Greek	Text	Task
Proclamation	*evanggelion*	Rom. 1.15-17	Preaching the Good News
Teaching	*didasko*	Matt. 28.19	To make disciples of Jesus
Worship	*latreuo*	John 4.20-24	Ushering into God's presence
Fellowship	*agape*	Rom. 13.8-10	The communion of saints
Witness	*marlyria*	Acts 1.8	Compelling testimony to the lost
Service	*diakonia*	Matt. 10.43-45	Caring for the needs of others

APPENDIX 17

Spiritual Gifts Specifically Mentioned in the New Testament

Rev. Terry G. Cornett

Administration	1 Cor. 12.28	The ability to bring order to Church life.
Apostleship	1 Cor. 12.28; Eph. 4.11	The ability to establish new churches among the unreached, nurture them to maturity, and exercise the authority and wisdom necessary to see them permanently established and able to reproduce; and/or A gift unique to the founding of the Church age which included the reception of special revelation and uniquely binding leadership authority
Discernment	1 Cor. 12.10	The ability to serve the Church through a Spirit-given ability to distinguish between God's truth (his presence, working, and doctrine) and fleshly error or satanic counterfeits
Evangelism	Eph. 4.11	The passion and the ability to effectively proclaim the Gospel so that people understand it
Exhortation	Rom. 12.8	The ability to give encouragement or rebuke that helps others obey Christ
Faith	1 Cor. 12.9	The ability to build up the Church through a unique ability to see the unrealized purposes of God and unwaveringly trust God to accomplish them
Giving	Rom. 12.8	The ability to build up a church through taking delight in the consistent, generous sharing of spiritual and physical resources
Healing	1 Cor. 12.9; 12.28	The ability to exercise faith that results in restoring people to physical, emotional, and spiritual health
Interpretation	1 Cor. 12.10	The ability to explain the meaning of an ecstatic utterance so that the Church is edified
Knowledge	1 Cor. 12.8	The ability to understand scriptural truth, through the illumination of the Holy Spirit, and speak it out to edify the body; and/or The supernatural revelation of the existence, or nature, of a person or thing which would not be known through natural means

Spiritual Gifts Specifically Mentioned in the New Testament (continued)

Leadership	Rom. 12.8	Spiritually-inspired courage, wisdom, zeal, and hard work which motivate and guide others so that they can effectively participate in building the Church
Mercy	Rom. 12.8	Sympathy of heart which enables a person to empathize with and cheerfully serve those who are sick, hurting, or discouraged
Ministering (or Service, or Helping, or Hospitality)	Rom. 12.7; 1 Pet. 4.9	The ability to joyfully perform any task which benefits others and meets their practical and material needs (especially on behalf of the poor or afflicted)
Miracles	1 Cor. 12.10; 12.28	The ability to confront evil and do good in ways that make visible the awesome power and presence of God
Pastoring	Eph. 4.11	The desire and ability to guide, protect, and equip the members of a congregation for ministry
Prophecy	1 Cor. 12.28; Rom. 12.6	The ability to receive and proclaim openly a revealed message from God which prepares the Church for obedience to him and to the Scriptures
Teaching	1 Cor. 12.28; Rom. 12.7; Eph. 4.11	The ability to explain the meaning of the Word of God and its application through careful instruction
Tongues	1 Cor. 12.10; 12.28	Ecstatic utterance by which a person speaks to God (or others) under the direction of the Holy Spirit
Wisdom	1 Cor. 12.8	Spirit-revealed insight that allows a person to speak godly instruction for solving problems; and/or Spirit-revealed insight that allows a person to explain the central mysteries of the Christian faith

APPENDIX 18

Checklist of Narrative Elements

Adapted from Leland Ryken. How to Read the Bible as Literature.

I. What Is the *Setting* of the Story?

   A. Physical surroundings

   B. Historical environment

   C. Cultural situation

   D. Interpersonal relationships and situation

II. Who Are the *Characters* in the Story?

   A. Who are the main/supporting players in the story?

   B. Who is the "protagonist?" Who is the "antagonist?"

   C. How does the author describe the character's development?

   D. What is the final outcome of the character's life and choices?

III. What Plot *Conflicts* Exist within the Story?

   A. What are the central conflicts with God?

   B. What are the central conflicts with others?

   C. What are the central conflicts within the characters themselves?

   D. What are the central conflicts between the character and their situation?

IV. What Are the Aspects of *Narrative Suspense* Revealed in the Story?

   A. What influences make us sympathize with the characters?

   B. What produces disgust and aversion between us and the characters?

   C. How are we made to approve of what the characters did?

   D. What events or happenings cause us to disapprove of the characters?

Checklist of Narrative Elements (continued)

V. What Insight Do the Characters Give Us as a *"Commentary on Living"*?

   A. Reality: What is the view of reality portrayed in the story and the character?

   B. Morality: What constitutes good and bad in the context of this story?

   C. Value: What is of ultimate concern and value in the story?

VI. How Does the Story *Unify* Itself in its Various Parts?

   A. How does the organization of the story contribute to its unity?

   B. What is the sequence of events in this story? (Beginning, Middle, and End)

   C. In what way does the story's end resolve the questions raised at the beginning?

VII. How Are the Characters *Tested*, and What *Choices* Do They Make?

   A. What is the dilemma/problem/conflict the protagonist is seeking to overcome?

   B. What character quality is tested in the protagonist?

   C. What alternative life choices are open to the characters in the story?

   D. Which decisions do the characters make, and what is the result of their decisions?

VIII. How Do the Characters *Progress and Grow* (or Decline and Fall) in the Story?

   A. Where do the characters begin in the story?

   B. How do the experiences of the character affect their development?

   C. Where do the individual characters eventually wind up as a result of their experiences, and the choices they made within them?

IX. What *Foils, Dramatic Irony, and Poetic Justice* Are Used in the Story?

A. Foils: what characters are set against each other as foes in the story?

B. Dramatic irony: When is the reader informed of situations and realities that the characters themselves are unaware of?

X. What Items Are *Repeated, Highlighted, and Foregrounded* in the Story?

A. Repetition: what phrases, items, themes, issues, or actions are repeated?

B. Highlighting: what things in the characters and events are emphasized above other things?

C. Foregrounding: what things are made to stand out "center stage" in the flow of the story?

XI. What Is the *Point of View* of the Author of the Story?

A. What comments does the author give us about the characters and events in the story?

B. What feelings do you believe the story is intending to generate?

C. How are the materials and details arranged to communicate the author's viewpoint clearly?

APPENDIX 19

Translating the Story of God

Rev. Dr. Don L. Davis

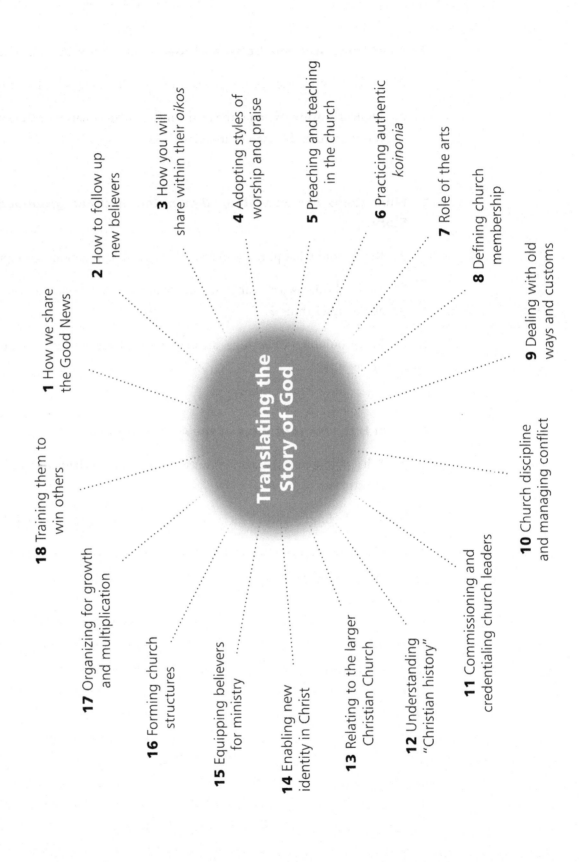

Translating the Story of God

1 How we share the Good News

2 How to follow up new believers

3 How you will share within their *oikos*

4 Adopting styles of worship and praise

5 Preaching and teaching in the church

6 Practicing authentic *koinonia*

7 Role of the arts

8 Defining church membership

9 Dealing with old ways and customs

10 Church discipline and managing conflict

11 Commissioning and credentialing church leaders

12 Understanding "Christian history"

13 Relating to the larger Christian Church

14 Enabling new identity in Christ

15 Equipping believers for ministry

16 Forming church structures

17 Organizing for growth and multiplication

18 Training them to win others

World Impact's Vision: Toward a Biblical Strategy to Impact the Inner City

World Impact, Inc.

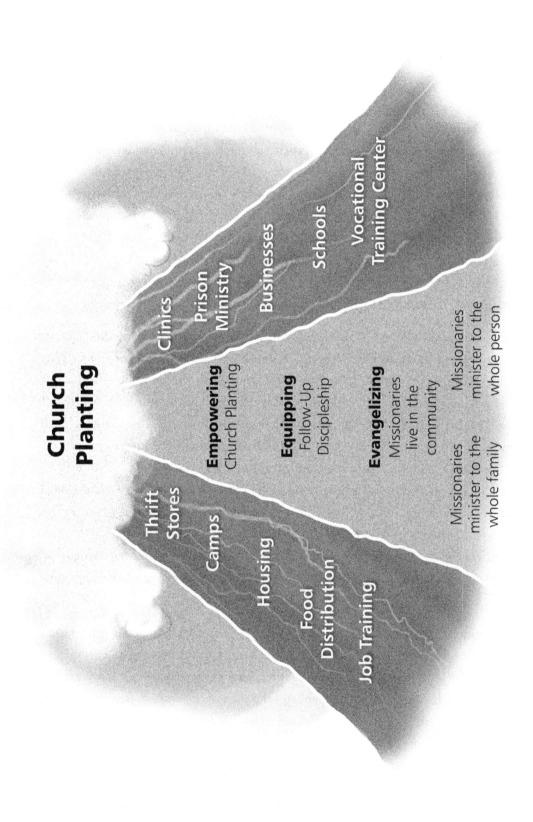

Church Planting

Clinics

Prison Ministry

Businesses

Schools

Vocational Training Center

Empowering
Church Planting

Equipping
Follow-Up
Discipleship

Evangelizing
Missionaries
live in the
community

Missionaries
minister to the
whole person

Missionaries
minister to the
whole family

Thrift Stores

Camps

Housing

Food Distribution

Job Training

APPENDIX 21

The Role of Women in Ministry

Dr. Don L. Davis

While it is plain that God has established a clearly designed order of responsibility within the home, it is equally clear that women are called and gifted by God, led by his own Spirit to bear fruit worthy of their calling in Christ. Throughout the NT, commands are directed specifically to women to submit, with the particular Greek verb *hupotasso*, occurring frequently which means "to place under" or "to submit" (cf. 1 Tim. 2.11). The word also translated into our English word "subjection" is from the same root. In such contexts these Greek renderings ought not to be understood in any way except as positive admonitions towards God's designed framework for the home, where women are charged to learn quietly and submissively, trusting and working within the Lord's own plan.

This ordering of the woman's submission in the home, however, must not be misinterpreted to mean that women are disallowed from ministering their gifts under the Spirit's direction. Indeed, it is the Holy Spirit through Christ's gracious endowment who assigns the gifts as he wills, for the edification of the Church (1 Cor. 12.1-27; Eph. 4.1-16). The gifts are not given to believers on the criteria of gender; in other words, there is no indication from the Scriptures that some gifts are for men only, and the others reserved for women. On the contrary, Paul affirms that Christ provided gifts as a direct result of his own personal victory over the devil and his minions (cf. Eph. 4.6ff.). This was his own personal choice, given by his Spirit to whomever he wills (cf. 1 Cor. 12.1-11). In affirming the ministry of women we affirm the right of the Spirit to be creative in all saints for the well-being of all and the expansion of his Kingdom, as he sees fit, and not necessarily as we determine (Rom. 12.4-8; 1 Pet. 4.10-11).

Furthermore, a careful study of the Scriptures as a whole indicates that God's ordering of the home in no way undermines his intention for men and women to serve Christ as disciples and laborers together, under Christ's leading. The clear NT teaching of Christ as head of the man, and the man of the woman (see 1 Cor. 11.4) shows God's esteem for godly spiritual representation within the home. The apparent forbidding of women to hold teaching/ruling positions appears to be an admonition to protect God's assigned lines of responsibility and authority within the home. For instance, the particular Greek term in the highly debated passage in 1 Timothy 2.12, *andros*, which has often times been translated "man," may also be translated "husband." With such a translation, then, the teaching would be that a wife ought not to rule over her husband.

This doctrine of a woman who, in choosing to marry, makes herself voluntarily submissive to "line up under" her husband is entirely consistent with the gist of the NT teaching on the role of authority in the Christian home. The Greek word *hupotasso*, which means to "line up under" refers to a wife's voluntary submission to her own husband (cf. Eph. 5.22, 23; Col. 3.18; Titus 2.5; 1 Pet. 3.1). This has nothing to do with any supposed superior status or capacity of the husband; rather, this refers to God's design of godly headship, authority which is given for comfort, protection, and care, not for destruction or domination (cf. Gen. 2.15-17; 3.16; 1 Cor. 11.3). Indeed, that this headship is interpreted in light of Christ's headship over the Church signifies the kind of godly headship that must be given, that sense of tireless care, service, and protection required from godly leadership.

Of course, such an admonition for a wife to submit to a husband would not in any way rule out that women be involved in a teaching ministry (e.g., Titus 2.4), but, rather, that in the particular case of married women, that their own ministries would come under the protection and direction of their respective husbands (Acts 18.26). This would assert that a married woman's ministry in the Church would be given serving, protective oversight by her husband, not due to any notion of inferior capacity or defective spirituality, but for the sake of, as one commentator has put it, "avoiding confusion and maintaining orderliness" (cf. 1 Cor. 14.40).

In both Corinth and Ephesus (which represent the contested Corinthian and Timothy epistolary comments), it appears that Paul's restriction upon women's participation was prompted by occasional happenings, issues which grew particularly out of these contexts, and therefore are meant to be understood in those lights. For instance, the hotly-contested test of a women's "silence" in the church (see both 1 Cor. 14 and 1 Tim. 2) does not appear in any way to undermine the prominent role women played in the expansion of the Kingdom and development of the Church in the first century. Women were involved in the ministries of prophecy and prayer (1 Cor. 11.5), personal instruction (Acts 18.26), teaching (Titus 2.4,5), giving testimony (John 4.28, 29), offering hospitality (Acts 12.12), and serving as co-laborers with the apostles in the cause of the Gospel (Phil. 4.2-3). Paul did not relegate women to an inferior role or hidden status but served side-by-side with women for the sake of Christ "I urge Euodia and I urge Syntyche to live in harmony in the Lord. Indeed, true companion, I ask you also to help these women

The Role of Women in Ministry (continued)

who have shared my struggle in *the cause of* the Gospel, together with Clement also and the rest of my fellow workers, whose names are in the book of life" (Phil. 4.2-3).

Furthermore, we must be careful in subordinating the personage of women *per se* (that is, their nature as women) versus their subordinated role in the marriage relationship. Notwithstanding the clear description of the role of women as heirs together of the grace of life in the marriage relationship (1 Pet. 3.7), it is equally plain that the Kingdom of God has created a dramatic shift in how women are to be viewed, understood, and embraced in the kingdom community. It is plain that in Christ there is now no difference between rich and poor, Jew and Gentile, barbarian, Scythian, bondman and freemen, as well as man and woman (cf. Gal. 3.28; Col. 3.11). Women were allowed to be disciples of a Rabbi (which was foreign and disallowed at the time of Jesus), and played prominent roles in the NT church, including being fellow laborers side by side with the apostles in ministry (e.g., see Euodia and Syntyche in Phil. 4.1ff.), as well as hosting a church in their houses (cf. Phoebe in Rom. 16.1-2, and Apphia in Philem. 1).

In regards to the issue of pastoral authority, I am convinced that Paul's understanding of the role of equippers (of which the pastor-teacher is one such role, cf. Eph. 4.9-15) is not gender specific. In other words, the decisive and seminal text for me on the operation of gifts and the status and function of offices are those NT texts which deal with the gifts (1 Cor. 12.1-27; Rom. 12.4-8; 1 Pet. 4.10-11, and Eph. 4.9-15). There is no indication in any of these formative texts that gifts are gender-specific. In other words, for the argument to hold decisively that women were never to be in roles that were pastoral or equipping in nature, the simplest and most effective argument would be to show that the Spirit simply would never even consider giving a woman a gift which was not suited to the range of callings which she felt a calling towards. Women would be forbidden from leadership because the Holy Spirit would never grant to a woman a calling and its requisite gifts because she was a woman. Some gifts would be reserved for men, and women would never receive those gifts.

A careful reading of these and other related texts show no such prohibition. It appears that it is up to the Holy Spirit to give any person, man or woman, any gift that suits him for any ministry he wishes them to do, as he wills (1 Cor. 12.11 "But one and the same Spirit works all these things, distributing to each one individually as he wills"). Building upon this point, Terry Cornett has even written a fine theological essay showing how the NT Greek for the word "apostle" is unequivocally applied to women, most clearly shown in the rendering of the female noun, "Junia" applied to "apostle" in Romans 16.7, as well as allusions to co-laboring, for instance, with the twins, Tryphena and Tryphosa, who "labored" with Paul in the Lord (16.12).

Believing that every God-called, Christ-endowed, and Spirit-gifted and led Christian ought to fulfill their role in the body, we affirm the role of women to lead and instruct under godly authority that submits to the Holy Spirit, the Word of God, and is informed by the tradition of the Church and spiritual reasoning. We ought to expect God to give women supernatural endowments of grace to carry out his bidding on behalf of his Church, and his reign in the Kingdom of God. Since men and women both reflect the *Imago Dei* (i.e., image of God), and both stand as heirs together of God's grace (cf. Gen. 1.27; 5.2; Matt. 19.4; Gal. 3.28; 1 Pet. 3.7), they are given the high privilege of representing Christ together as his ambassadors (2 Cor. 5.20), and through their partnership to bring to completion our obedience to Christ's Great Commission of making disciples of all nations (Matt. 28.18-20).

APPENDIX 22

Discerning the Call: The Profile of a Godly Christian Leader

Rev. Dr. Don L. Davis

	Commission	Character	Community	Competence
Definition	Recognizes the call of God and replies with prompt obedience to his lordship and leading	Reflects the character of Christ in their personal convictions, conduct, and lifestyle	Regards multiplying disciples in the body of Christ as the primary role of ministry	Responds in the power of the Spirit with excellence in carrying out their appointed tasks and ministry
Key Scripture	2 Tim. 1.6-14; 1 Tim. 4.14; Acts 1.8; Matt. 28.18-20	John 15.4-5; 2 Tim. 2.2; 1 Cor. 4.2; Gal. 5.16-23	Eph. 4.9-15; 1 Cor. 12.1-27	2 Tim. 2.15; 3.16-17; Rom. 15.14; 1 Cor. 12
Critical Concept	The Authority of God: God's leader acts on God's recognized call and authority, acknowledged by the saints and God's leaders	The Humility of Christ: God's leader demonstrates the mind and lifestyle of Christ in his or her actions and relationships	The Growth of the Church: God's leader uses all of his or her resources to equip and empower the body of Christ for his/her goal and task	The Power of the Spirit: God's leader operates in the gifting and anointing of the Holy Spirit
Central Elements	A clear call from God Authentic testimony before God and others Deep sense of personal conviction based on Scripture Personal burden for a particular task or people Confirmation by leaders and the body	Passion for Christlikeness Radical lifestyle for the Kingdom Serious pursuit of holiness Discipline in the personal life Fulfills role-relationships as bondslave of Jesus Christ Provides an attractive model for others in their conduct, speech, and lifestyle (the fruit of the Spirit)	Genuine love for and desire to serve God's people Disciples faithful individuals Facilitates growth in small groups Pastors and equips believers in the congregation Nurtures associations and networks among Christians and churches Advances new movements among God's people locally	Endowments and gifts from the Spirit Sound discipling from an able mentor Skill in the spiritual disciplines Ability in the Word Able to evangelize, follow up, and disciple new converts Strategic in the use of resources and people to accomplish God's task
Satanic Strategy to Abort	Operates on the basis of personality or position rather than on God's appointed call and ongoing authority	Substitutes ministry activity and/or hard work and industry for godliness and Christlikeness	Exalts tasks and activities above equipping the saints and developing Christian community	Functions on natural gifting and personal ingenuity rather than on the Spirit's leading and gifting
Key Steps	Identify God's call Discover your burden Be confirmed by leaders	Abide in Christ Discipline for godliness Pursue holiness in all	Embrace God's Church Learn leadership's contexts Equip concentrically	Discover the Spirit's gifts Receive excellent training Hone your performance
Results	Deep confidence in God arising from God's call	Powerful Christlike example provided for others to follow	Multiplying disciples in the Church	Dynamic working of the Holy Spirit

Selecting a Credible Criteria for Independence
Navigating Toward a Healthy Transition
Don L. Davis

In order to establish a smooth transition from a missionary-led community to an indigenous, independent church community, we must identify and agree upon a clear criteria which would help us know when the transition is complete. In other words, everything depends on all of the key players' ability (i.e., missionaries, elders, and church community) to be crystal clear regarding our assumptions about what the transition involves and what we are seeking to accomplish. If, for any reason, we are unclear as to our expectations and directions together, we can easily misunderstand one another, and prolong the process, or even make the transition period unnecessarily painful.

The following categories are given as a guide, a criteria which may help you as leaders critically assess whether you have covered all necessary areas of transition. The list is suggestive, not exhaustive, and is not meant to be a final summary, but a tickler to help you think carefully through all of the issues necessary to make your period of transition an open and supportive one.

1. **A Faithful Group of Converted, Gathered, Maturing Disciples of Jesus**

   a. Solid conversions to Jesus Christ as Lord and Savior

   b. Self-identity as a separate Christian assembly with its own passionate spirituality, inspiring worship, and presence in the community

   c. Possess a clear sense of membership, ownership, belonging; able to bring new members in easily through strong orientation and loving relationships

   d. Clear sense of entering membership, disciplining members, restoring them

   e. Incorporating people smoothly into the life of the body (i.e., small group life, friendships, large group fellowship, etc.)

2. **Identified, Commissioned, and Released Indigenous Leaders**

   a. Selected by and for the body publicly and prayerfully

   b. Determiners of the church's direction and operation

   c. Accountable to the church's membership for their life and ministry

Selecting a Credible Criteria for Independence (continued)

    d. The body exercising wisdom as it determines which leaders to fund (i.e., how many it can afford to fund fully or partially), while at the same time relying on lay leaders and members to meet its needs as God leads

    e. Acknowledged separately from missionary leadership as authority of the body

3. Selection of its Own Pastor and Pastoral Staff

    a. Creation of a charter/by-laws/constitution/covenant delineating role of pastor(s) and relationship to body

    b. Installation of a pastor duly ratified by membership and endorsed by leadership

    c. Formal recognition of pastor's authority and responsibility

    d. Affirmation of community's support and submission to pastoral leadership

4. Limited and Decreasing Oversight, Participation, and Direction

    a. Missionaries have surrendered all significant positions and authority

    b. Clear understanding of the role of the missionaries presently serving our body

    c. Distinct lines between missionaries and indigenous leaders in decision-making and direction setting of the church

    d. Encouragement for missionaries to seek God's leading regarding new communities to target for new outreaches of the Gospel

5. Distinctive and Unique Burden-Driven, Gift-Oriented Ministries of the Church

    a. Clear mission and vision of the church's purpose and goals to mature and grow in number as God leads

    b. Reproducing new assemblies built into the DNA of our church (i.e., to fund and support other efforts of church planting around our city and beyond)

    c. Open doorways for members to explore ministry opportunities that coincide with the body's vision to mobilize its members to minister in their community.

d. Ongoing equipping of the body members by the pastoral staff to enable members to do the work of the ministry

e. Regular programming for worship, teaching, fellowship, and mission funded and directed by the church's personnel and members

6. **Generating Non-Missionary Ministry Resources and Operating Income**

a. Deep conviction within the congregation that they will look to God alone as the source of supply to implement their vision

b. Development of a plan to make the congregation financially free and independent of outside missionary support

c. Clear guidelines under which support and aid can be given to the body

d. Identifying independent sources for ongoing access to cash resources that would help support the effort

7. **Acquisition and Stewardship of the Church's Equipment, Resources, and Facilities**

a. Functional, user-friendly structures created to administer the church's business and stewardship

b. Careful, ongoing inventory of the church's resources

c. Clear record keeping of the church's funds and finances, purchases, and allocations

d. Responsible purchase and upkeep of the church's equipment and facilities

8. **Development of its Own New Friends, Siblings, Volunteers, and Partners**

a. Recognition from other Christian communities, inside and outside community

b. New relationships with outside churches or other organizations who would continue to support the effort with work groups and short term help

c. New affiliation with church denominations or groups whose vision resonates with the church

d. Associations to increase the effectiveness of the church's outreach and mission

APPENDIX 24

Salvation as Joining the People of God

Terry Cornett

I.   The Most Significant Way to Define Salvation in the Biblical Context Is to Describe it as Being Joined to the People of God.

A. Old Testament

1. The prototype Old Testament image of salvation is the Exodus where God "saved" his people from bondage and slavery in Egypt.

   a. To be saved meant to be joined to the people of God who were being delivered together out of bondage and placed directly under God's lordship, laws, protection, provision, and presence.

   b. Exod. 6.7 (ESV) - *I will take you as my own people*, and I will be your God. Then you will know that I am the LORD your God, who brought you out from under the yoke of the Egyptians (cf. Lev. 26.12; Deut. 4.20, Hos. 13.4).

2. God's selection of Israel as "his people" gave them a unique position among all the peoples of the earth.

   a. Deut. 7.6 (ESV) - For you are a people holy to the LORD your God. *The LORD your God has chosen you out of all the peoples on the face of the earth to be his people, his treasured possession* (cf. Deut. 14.2, 26.18, 33.29).

   b. Deut. 27.9 (ESV) - Then Moses and the priests, who are Levites, said to all Israel, "Be silent, O Israel, and listen! *You have now become the people of the LORD your God.*"

3. The means of salvation for anyone outside of Israel was to join themselves to the people of God.

   a. Exod. 12.37-38, 48a (ESV) - The Israelites journeyed from Rameses to Succoth. There were about six hundred thousand men on foot, besides women and children. *Many other people went up with*

Salvation as Joining the People of God (continued)

them, as well as large droves of livestock, both flocks and herds. . . . *"An alien living among you who wants to celebrate the LORD'S Passover must have all the males in his household circumcised; then he may take part like one born in the land."*

b. Isa. 56.3-8 (ESV) - *Let no foreigner who has bound himself to the LORD say,"The LORD will surely exclude me from his people."* And let not any eunuch complain,"I am only a dry tree." For this is what the LORD says: "To the eunuchs who keep my Sabbaths, who choose what pleases me and hold fast to my covenant-to them I will give within my temple and its walls a memorial and a name better than sons and daughters; I will give them an everlasting name that will not be cut off. And foreigners who bind themselves to the LORD to serve him, to love the name of the LORD, and to worship him, *all who keep the Sabbath without desecrating it and who hold fast to my covenant-these I will bring to my holy mountain and give them joy in my house of prayer. Their burnt offerings and sacrifices will be accepted on my altar;* for my house will be called a house of prayer for all nations." *The Sovereign LORD declares-he who gathers the exiles of Israel: "I will gather still others to them besides those already gathered."*

4. The New Testament suggests that even Moses (an ethnic Hebrew but raised culturally as an Egyptian and therefore a foreigner) had to make a conscious choice to join himself to the people of God in faith so that he could experience salvation.

Heb. 11.25 (ESV) - *He* [Moses] *chose to be mistreated along with the people of God* rather than to enjoy the pleasures of sin for a short time.

5. Summary: [In the Old Testament] salvation came, not by the man's mere merit, but because the man belonged to a nation peculiarly chosen by God ("Salvation," *International Standard Bible Encyclopedia* [Electronic ed.]. Cedar Rapids: Parsons Technology, 1998.).

Salvation as Joining the People of God (continued)

B. New Testament

"...who gave himself for us to redeem us from all wickedness *and to purify for himself a people that are his very own, eager to do what is good*" (Titus 2.14).

1. Both Peter and Paul suggest that the New Testament view of salvation is equally concerned as the Old Testament with God calling out a people but that the people "called out" are bound to Christ and his Church rather than to a political or ethnic "nation."

   a. 1 Pet. 2.9-10 (ESV) - *But you are a chosen people, a royal priesthood, a holy nation, a people belonging to God*, that you may declare the praises of him who called you out of darkness into his wonderful light. *Once you were not a people, but now you are the people of God; once you had not received mercy, but now you have received mercy.*

   b. Acts 15.14 (ESV) - Simon has described to us how God at first showed his concern *by taking from the Gentiles a people for himself.*

   c. Eph. 2.13, 19 (ESV) - But now in Christ Jesus you who once were far away have been brought near through the blood of Christ. . . . Consequently, you are no longer foreigners and aliens, *but fellow citizens with God's people* and members of God's household.

   d. Rom. 9.24-26 (ESV) - Even us, whom he also called, *not only from the Jews but also from the Gentiles*? As he says in Hosea: *"I will call them 'my people' who are not my people*; and I will call her 'my loved one' who is not my loved one," and, *"It will happen that in the very place where it was said to them,'You are not my people,' they will be called 'sons of the living God.'"*

2. "On the other hand, while the [Gospel] message involved in every case is strict individual choice, yet the individual who accepted it entered into social relations with the others who had so chosen. *So salvation involved admission to a community of service* (Mark 9.35, etc.)" (*International Standard Bible Encyclopedia* [Electronic Edition]).

II. The Metaphors of Salvation: Joined to a People.

In human society, belonging to a "people" (family, clan, nation) happens through either:

* birth,

* adoption, or

* marrying into a family group

Thus, the New Testament language of salvation draws from these three primary metaphors to describe what happens at salvation.

A. Birth

1. John 1.12-13 (ESV) - Yet to all who received him, to those who believed in his name, he gave the right to become children of God - *children born not of natural descent*, nor of human decision or a husband's will, *but born of God.*

2. John 3.3 (ESV) - In reply Jesus declared, "I tell you the truth, *no one can see the Kingdom of God unless he is born again.*"

3. 1 Pet. 1.23 (ESV) - *For you have been born again*, not of perishable seed, but of imperishable, through the living and enduring word of God.

4. 1 Pet. 1.3 (ESV) - Praise be to the God and Father of our Lord Jesus Christ! *In his great mercy he has given us new birth* into a living hope through the resurrection of Jesus Christ from the dead.

B. Adoption

1. Rom. 8.23 (ESV) - Not only so, but we ourselves, who have the firstfruits of the Spirit, groan inwardly *as we wait eagerly for our adoption as sons*, the redemption of our bodies.

2. Eph. 1.4-6 (ESV) - For he chose us in him before the creation of the world to be holy and blameless in his sight. *In love he predestined us to be adopted as his sons through Jesus Christ*, in accordance with his pleasure and will - to the praise of his glorious grace, which he has freely given us in the One he loves.

Salvation as Joining the People of God (continued)

3. Gal. 4.4-7 (ESV) - But when the time had fully come, God sent his Son, born of a woman, born under law, to redeem those under law, *that we might receive the full rights of sons.* Because you are sons, God sent the Spirit of his Son into our hearts, the Spirit who calls out, "Abba, Father." *So you are no longer a slave, but a son; and since you are a son, God has made you also an heir.*

C. Marriage

1. John 3.29 (ESV) - *The bride belongs to the bridegroom.* The friend who attends the bridegroom waits and listens for him, and is full of joy when he hears the bridegroom's voice. That joy is mine, and it is now complete. *[Spoken by John the Baptist in reference to Christ.]*

2. Eph. 5.31-32 (ESV) - "For this reason *a man will leave his father and mother and be united to his wife, and the two will become one flesh.*" This is a profound mystery - *but I am talking about Christ and the Church.*

3. Rev. 19.7 (ESV) - Let us rejoice and be glad and give him glory! *For the wedding of the Lamb has come, and his bride has made herself ready.*

APPENDIX 25

A Theology of the Church

Don L. Davis and Terry Cornett ©1996 World Impact Press

The Church Is an Apostolic Community
Where the Word Is Rightly Preached

I. A Community of Calling

A. The essential meaning of Church is *Ekklesia*: those who have been "*called out*" in order to be "*called to*" a New Community.

1. Like the Thessalonians, the Church is called out from idolatry to serve the living God and *called to* wait for his Son from heaven.

2. The Church is *called out* in order that it may belong to Christ (Rom. 1.6). Jesus speaks of the Church as "my *ekklesia*" that is the "called out ones" who are his unique possession (Matt. 16.18; Gal. 5.24; James 2.7).

3. The components of God's call:

    a. The foundation is God's desire to save (John 3.16, 1 Tim. 2.4).

    b. The message is the good news of the Kingdom (Matt. 24.14).

    c. The recipients are "whosoever will" (John 3.15).

    d. The method is through faith in the shed blood of Christ and acknowledgment of his lordship (Rom. 3.25; 10.9-10; Eph. 2.8).

    e. The result is regeneration and placement into the body of Christ (2 Cor. 5.17; Rom. 12.4-5; Eph. 3.6; 5.30).

B. The Church is *called out*.

1. Called out of the world:

    a. The world is under Satan's dominion and stands in opposition to God.

    b. Conversion and incorporation in Christ's Church involves repentance (*metanoia*) and a transfer of kingdom allegiances.

A Theology of the Church (continued)

    c.   The Church exists as strangers and aliens who are "in" but not "of" this world system.

  2. Called out from sin:

    a.   Those in the Church are being sanctified, set apart for holy action, so that they may live out their calling as saints of God (1 Cor. 1.2; 2 Tim. 1.9, 1 Pet. 1.15).

    b.   The Church must be available for God's purpose and use (Rom. 8.28-29; Eph. 1.11; Rom. 6.13).

    c.   The Church must bring glory to God alone (Isa. 42.8; John 13.31-32; 17.1; Rom. 15.6; 1 Pet. 2.12).

    d.   The Church must now be characterized by obedience to God (2 Thess. 1.8; Heb. 5.8-9; 1 John 2.3).

C. The Church is *called to*:

  1. Salvation and new life

    a.   Forgiveness and cleansing from sin (Eph. 1.7; 5.26; 1 John 1.9).

    b.   Justification (Rom. 3.24; 8.30; Titus 3.7) in which God pronounces us guiltless as to the penalty of his divine law.

    c.   Regeneration (John 3.5-8; Col. 3.9-10) by which a "new self" is birthed in us through the Spirit.

    d.   Sanctification (John 17.19; 1 Cor. 1.2) in which we are "set apart" by God for holiness of life.

    e.   Glorification and Life Eternal (Rom. 8.30, 1 Tim. 6.12; 2 Thess. 2.14) in which we are changed to be like Christ and prepared to live forever in the presence of God (Rom. 8.23; 1 Cor. 15.51-53; 1 John 3.2).

A Theology of the Church (continued)

2. Participation in a new community of God's chosen people (1 Pet. 2.9-10)

   a. Members of Christ's body (1 Cor. 10.16-17; 12.27).

   b. Sheep of God's flock under one Shepherd (John 10; Heb. 13.20; 1 Pet. 5.2-4).

   c. Members of God's family and household (Gal. 6.10; 1 Tim. 3.15).

   d. Children of Abraham and recipients of covenant promise (Rom. 4.16; Gal. 3.29; Eph. 2.12).

   e. Citizens of the New Jerusalem (Phil. 3.20; Rev. 3.12).

   f. The firstfruits of the Kingdom of God (Luke 12.32; James 1.18).

3. Freedom (Gal. 5.1, 13)

   a. Called out of the dominion of darkness which suppresses freedom (Col. 1.13-14).

   b. Called away from sin which enslaves (John 8.34-36).

   c. Called to God the Father who is the Liberator of his people (Exod. 6.6).

   d. Called to God the Son who gives the truth which sets free (John 8.31-36).

   e. Called to God the Spirit whose presence creates liberty (2 Cor. 3.17).

II. A Community of Faith

A. The Church is a community of faith, which has, by faith, confessed Jesus as Lord and Savior.

Faith refers both to *the content of our belief* and to *the act of believing* itself. Jesus is the object (content) of our faith and his life is received through faith (our belief) in him and his word. In both of these senses, the Church is a community of faith.

A Theology of the Church (continued)

1. The Church places its faith:

   a. in the Living Word (Jesus the Messiah),

   b. who is revealed in the written Word (Sacred Scripture),

   c. and who is now present, teaching and applying his Word to the Church (through the ministry of the Holy Spirit).

2. The Church guards the deposit of faith, given by Christ and the apostles, through sound teaching and the help of the Holy Spirit who indwells its members (2 Tim. 1.13-14).

B. Because it is a community of faith, the Church is also a community of grace.

   1. The Church exists by grace-through faith rather than through human merit or works (Gal. 2.21; Eph. 2.8).

   2. The Church announces, in faith, the grace of God to all humanity (Titus 2.11-15).

   3. The Church lives by grace in all actions and relationships (Eph. 4.1-7).

C. The Church is a community where the Scriptures are preached, studied, meditated upon, memorized, believed, and obeyed (Ezek. 7.10; Jos. 1.8; Ps. 119; Col. 3.16; 1 Tim. 4.13; James 1.22-25).

   1. The Church preaches the Gospel of the Kingdom, as revealed in Scripture, and calls people to repentance and faith which leads to obedience (Matt. 4.17; 28.19-20; Acts 2.38-40).

   2. The Church studies and applies the Scriptures through teaching, rebuking, correcting, and training in righteousness so that all members of the community are equipped to live godly lives characterized by good works (2 Tim. 3.16-17; 4.2).

   3. The Church intentionally reflects on the Scriptures in light of reason, tradition, and experience, learning and doing theology as a means of more fully understanding and acting upon truth (Ps. 119.97-99; 1 Tim. 4.16; 2 Tim. 2.15).

4. The Church functions as a listening community which is aware of the Spirit's presence and relies upon him to interpret and apply the Scriptures to the present moment (John 14.25-26).

D. The Church contends for the faith that was once for all entrusted to the saints (Jude 3).

III. A Community of Witness

A. The Church witnesses to the fact that in the incarnation, life, teaching, death and resurrection of Jesus the Christ, God's Kingdom has begun (Mark 1.15; Luke 4.43; 6.20; 11.20; Acts 1.3; 28.23; 1 Cor. 4.20; Col. 1.12-13).

1. The Church proclaims Jesus as *Christus Victor* whose reign will:

   a. Rescind the curse over creation and humankind (Rev. 22.3).

   b. Defeat Satan and the powers and destroy their work (1 John 3.8).

   c. Reverse the present order by defending and rewarding the meek, the humble, the despised, the lowly, the righteous, the hungry, and the rejected (Luke 1.46-55; 4.18-19; 6.20-22).

   d. Propitiate God's righteous anger (Gal. 3.10-14; 1 John 2.1-2).

   e. Create a new humanity (1 Cor. 15.45-49; Eph. 2.15; Rev. 5.9-10).

   f. Destroy the last enemy- death (1 Cor. 15.26).

2. Ultimately, the very Kingdom itself will be turned over to God the Father, and the freedom, wholeness, and justice of the Lord will abound throughout the universe (Isa. 10.2-7; 11.1-9; 53.5; Mic. 4.1-3; 6.8; Matt. 6.33; 23.23; Luke 4.18-19; John 8.34-36; 1 Cor. 15.28; Rev. 21).

A Theology of the Church (continued)

B.   The Church witnesses by:

1.   Functioning as a sign and foretaste of the Kingdom of God; the Church is a visible community where people see that:

   a.   Jesus is acknowledged as Lord (Rom. 10.9-10).

   b.   The truth and power of the Gospel is growing and producing fruit among every kindred, tribe, and nation (Acts 2.47; Rom. 1.16; Col. 1.6; Rev. 7.9-10).

   c.   The values of God's Kingdom are accepted and acted upon (Matt. 6.33).

   d.   God's commands are obeyed on earth as they are in heaven (Matt. 6.10; John 14.23-24).

   e.   The presence of God is experienced (Matt. 18.20; John 14.16-21).

   f.   The power of God is demonstrated (1 Cor. 4.20).

   g.   The love of God is freely received and given (Eph. 5.1-2; 1 John 3.18; 4.7-8).

   h.   The compassion of God is expressed in bearing each other's burdens, first within the Church, and then, in sacrificial service to the whole world (Matt. 5.44-45; Gal. 6.2, 10; Heb. 13.16).

   i.   The redemptiveness of God transcends human frailty and sin so that the treasure of the Kingdom is evident in spite of being contained in earthen vessels (2 Cor. 4.7).

2.   Performing signs and wonders which confirm the Gospel (Mark 16.20; Acts 4.30; 8.6,13; 14.3; 15.12; Rom. 15.18-19; Heb. 2.4)

3.   Accepting the call to mission

   a.   Going into all the world to preach the Gospel (Matt. 24.14; 28.18-20; Acts 1.8, Col. 1.6).

   b.   Evangelizing and making disciples of Christ and his Kingdom (Matt. 28.18-20; 2 Tim. 2.2).

    c.   Establishing churches among those unreached by the Gospel (Matt. 16.18; 28.19; Acts 2.41-42; 16.5; 2 Cor. 11.28; Heb. 12.22-23).

    d.   Displaying the excellencies of Christ's Kingdom by engendering freedom, wholeness, and justice in his Name (Isa. 53.5; Mic. 6.8; Matt. 5.16; 12.18-20; Luke 4.18-19; John 8.34-36; 1 Pet. 3.11).

4.   Acting as a prophetic community

    a.   Speaking the Word of God into situations of error, confusion, and sin (2 Cor. 4.2; Heb. 4.12; James 5.20; Titus 2.15).

    b.   Speaking up for those who cannot speak up for themselves so that justice is defended (Prov. 31.8-9).

    c.   Announcing judgment against sin in all its forms (Rom. 2.5; Gal. 6.7-8; 1 Pet. 4.17).

    d.   Announcing hope in situations where sin has produced despair (Jer. 32.17; 2 Thess. 2.16; Heb. 10.22-23; 1 Pet. 1.3-5).

    e.   Proclaiming the return of Jesus, the urgency of the hour, and the reality that soon every knee will bow and every tongue confess that Jesus is Lord to the glory of God the Father (Matt. 25.1-13; Phil. 2.10-11; 2 Tim. 4.1, Titus 2.12-13).

The Church Is One Community
Where the Sacraments Are Rightly Administered

IV. A Community of Worship

A. The Church recognizes that worship is the primary end of all creation.

1.   The worshiper adores, praises, and gives thanks to God for his character and actions, ascribing to him the worth and glory due his Person. This worship is directed to:

    a.   The Father Almighty who is the Maker of all things visible and invisible.

A Theology of the Church (continued)

    b. The Son who by his incarnation, death, and resurrection accomplished salvation and who is now glorified at the Father's right hand.

    c. The Spirit who is the Lord and Giver of Life.

2. Worship is the primary purpose of the material heavens and earth, and all life therein (Pss. 148-150; Luke 19.37-40; Rom. 11.36; Rev. 4.11; 15.3-4).

3. Worship is the central activity of the angelic hosts who honor God in his presence (Isa. 6; Rev. 5).

4. Worship is the chief vocation of the "community of saints," all true Christians, living and dead, who seek to glorify God in all things (Ps. 29.2; Rom. 12.1-2; 1 Cor. 10.31; Col. 3.17).

B. The Church offers acceptable worship to God. This means:

1. The worshipers have renounced all false gods or belief systems that lay claim to their allegiance and have covenanted to serve and worship the one true God (Exod. 34.14; 1 Thess. 1.9-10).

2. The worshipers worship:

    a. In Spirit - as regenerated people who, through saving faith in Jesus Christ, are filled with the Holy Spirit and under his direction.

    b. In Truth - understanding God as he is revealed in Scripture and worshiping in accordance with the teaching of the Word.

    c. In Holiness - Living lives that demonstrate their genuine commitment to serve the Living God.

C. The Church worships as a royal priesthood, wholeheartedly offering up sacrifices of praise to God and employing all its creative resources to worship him with excellence.

1. The Christian Church is a people who worship, not a place of worship.

2. The entire congregation ministers to the Lord, each one contributing a song, a word, a testimony, a prayer, etc. according to their gifts and capacities (1 Cor. 14.26).

3. The Church worships with the full range of human emotion, intellect, and creativity:

   a. Physical expression- raising of hands, dancing, kneeling, bowing, etc.

   b. Intellectual engagement- striving to understand God's nature and works.

   c. Artistic expression- through music and the other creative arts.

   d. Celebratory expression- the Church plays in the presence of God (Prov. 8.30-31) experiencing "Sabbath rest" through festivals, celebrations, and praise.

4. The Church worships liturgically by together reenacting the story of God and his people.

   a. The Church proclaims and embodies the drama of God's redemptive action in its ritual, tradition, and order of worship.

   b. The Church, like the covenant people Israel, orders its life around the celebration of the Lord's Supper and Baptism which reenact the story of God's salvation (Deut. 16.3; Matt. 28.19; Rom. 6.4; 1 Cor. 11.23-26).

   c. The Church remembers the worship and service of saints through the ages, learning from their experiences with the Spirit of God (Deut. 32.7; Pss. 77.10-12; 143.5; Isa. 46.9; Heb. 11).

5. The Church worships in freedom:

   a. Constantly experiencing new forms and expressions of worship which honor God and allow his people to delight in him afresh (Pss. 33.3; 40.3; 96.1; 149.1; Isa. 42.9-10; Luke 5.38; Rev. 5.9).

A Theology of the Church (continued)

      b. Being led by the Spirit so that its worship is responsive to God himself (2 Cor. 3.6; Gal. 5.25; Phil. 3.3).

      c. Expressing the unchanging nature of God in forms that are conducive to the particular cultures and personalities of the worshipers (Acts 15).

  6. The Church worships in right order, making sure that each act of worship edifies the body, and stands in accordance with the Word of God (1 Cor. 14.12, 33, 40; Gal. 5.13-15, 22-25; Eph. 4.29; Phil. 4.8).

D. The Church's worship leads to wholeness:

  1. Health and blessing attend the worshiping community (Exod. 23.25; Ps. 147.1-3).

  2. The community takes on the character of the One who is worshiped (Exod. 29.37; Ps. 27.4; Jer. 2.5; 10.8; Matt. 6.21; Col. 3.1-4; 1 John 3.2).

V. A Community of Covenant

A. The Church is the gathering of those who participate in the New Covenant. This New Covenant:

  1. Is mediated by Jesus Christ, the Great High Priest, and is purchased and sealed by his blood (Matt. 26.28; 1 Tim. 2.5; Heb. 8.6; 4.14-16).

  2. Is initiated and participated in only through the electing grace of God (Rom. 8.29-30; 2 Tim. 1.9; Titus 1.1; 1 Pet. 1.1).

  3. Is a covenant of peace (*Shalom*) which gives access to God (Ezek. 34.23-31; Rom. 5.1-2; Eph. 2.17-18; Heb. 7.2-3).

  4. Is uniquely celebrated and experienced in the Lord's Supper and Baptism (Mark 14.22-25; 1 Cor. 10.16; Col. 2.12; 1 Pet. 3.21).

5. By faith, both imputes and imparts righteousness to the participants so that God's laws are put in the hearts and written on their minds (Jer. 31.33; Rom. 1.17; 2 Cor. 5.21; Gal. 3.21-22; Phil. 1.11; 3.9; Heb. 10.15-17; 12.10-11; 1 Pet. 2.24).

B. The Covenant enables us to understand and experience Christian sanctification:

1. Righteousness: right relationships with God and others (Exod. 20.1-17; Mic. 6.8; Mark 12.29-31; James 2.8).

2. Truth: right beliefs about God and others (Ps. 86.11; Isa. 45.19; John 8.31-32, 17.17; 1 Pet. 1.22).

3. Holiness: right actions toward God and others (Lev. 11.45; 20.8; Eccles. 12.13; Matt. 7.12; 2 Cor. 7.1; Col. 3.12; 2 Pet. 3.11).

C. The purpose of the New Covenant is to enable the Church to be like Christ Jesus:

1. Jesus is the new pattern for humanity:

    a. The second Adam (Rom. 5.12-17; 1 Cor. 15.45-49).

    b. The likeness into which the Church is fashioned (Rom. 8.29; 1 John 3.2).

    c. His life, character, and teaching are the standard for faith and practice (John 13.17; 20.21; 2 John 6, 9, 1 Cor. 11.1).

2. This covenant is made possible by the sacrifice of Christ himself (Matt. 26.27-29; Heb. 8-10).

3. The apostolic ministry of the new covenant is meant to conform believers to the image of Christ (2 Cor. 3; Eph. 4.12-13).

A Theology of the Church (continued)

D. The Covenant binds us to those who have gone before.

1. It recognizes that the Church is one (Eph. 4.4-5).

2. It reminds us that we are surrounded by a cloud of witnesses who have participated in the same covenant (Heb. 12.1).

3. It reminds us that we are part of a sacred chain:

   God-Christ-Apostles-Church.

4. It reminds us that we share the same:

   a. Spiritual parentage (John 1.13; 3.5-6; 2 Cor. 1.2; Gal. 4.6; 1 John 3.9).

   b. Family likeness (Eph. 3.15; Heb. 2.11).

   c. Lord, faith and baptism (Eph. 4.5).

   d. Indwelling Spirit (John 14.17; Rom. 8.9; 2 Cor. 1.22).

   e. Calling and mission (Eph. 4.1; Heb. 3.1; 2 Pet. 1.10).

   f. Hope and destiny (Gal. 5.5; Eph. 1.18; Eph. 4.4; Col. 1.5).

5. Causes us to understand that since we share the same covenant, administered by the same Lord, under the leadership of the same Spirit with those Christians who have come before us, we must necessarily reflect upon the creeds, the councils, and the actions of the Church throughout history in order to understand the apostolic tradition and the ongoing work of the Holy Spirit (1 Cor. 11.16).

VI. A Community of Presence

A. "Where Jesus Christ is, there is the Church" - Ignatius of Antioch (Matt. 18.20).

B. The Church is the dwelling place of God (Eph. 2.19-21):

1. His nation

2. His household

3. His temple

C. The Church congregates in eager anticipation of God's presence (Eph. 2.22).

1. The Church now comes into the presence of God at every gathering:

    a. Like the covenant people in the Old Testament, the Church gathers in the presence of God (Exod. 18.12; 34.34; Deut. 14.23; 15.20; Ps. 132.7; Heb. 12.18-24).

    b. The gathered Church makes manifest the reality of the Kingdom of God by being in the presence of the King (1 Cor. 14.25).

2. The Church anticipates the future gathering of the people of God when the fullness of God's presence will be with them all (Ezek. 48.35; 2 Cor. 4.14; 1 Thess. 3.13; Rev. 21.13).

D. The Church is absolutely dependent on the presence of the Spirit of Christ.

1. Without the presence of the Holy Spirit there is no Church (Acts 2.38; Rom. 8.9; 1 Cor. 12.13; Gal. 3.3; Eph. 2.22; 4.4; Phil. 3.3).

2. The Holy Spirit creates, directs, empowers, and teaches congregations of believers (John 14.16-17, 26; Acts 1.8; 2.17; 13.1; Rom. 15.13, 19; 2 Cor. 3.18).

3. The Holy Spirit gives gifts to the Church so that it can accomplish its mission, bringing honor and glory to God (Rom. 12.4-8; 1 Cor. 12.1-31; Heb. 2.4).

4. The Holy Spirit binds the Church together as the family of God and the body of Christ (2 Cor. 13.14; Eph. 4.3).

A Theology of the Church (continued)

E. The Church is a Kingdom of priests which stands in God's presence (1 Pet. 2.5, 9):

1. Ministering before the Lord (Ps. 43.4; Ps. 134.1-2).

2. Placing God's blessing on his people (Num. 6.22-27; 2 Cor. 13.14).

3. Bringing people before the attention of God (1 Thess. 1.3; 2 Tim. 1.3).

4. Offering themselves and the fruit of their ministry to God (Isa. 66.20, Rom. 12.1; 15.16).

F. The Church lives in God's presence through prayer.

1. Prayer as access to the Holy of Holies (Rev. 5.8).

2. Prayer as communion with God (Ps. 5.3; Rom. 8.26-27).

3. Prayer as intercession.

   a. For the world (1 Tim. 2.1-2).

   b. For the saints (Eph. 6.18-20, 1 Thess. 5.25).

4. Prayer as thanksgiving (Phil. 4.6; Col. 1.3).

5. Prayer as the warfare of the Kingdom.

   a. Binding and loosing (Matt. 16.19).

   b. Engaging the principalities and powers (Eph. 6.12,18).

The Church Is a Holy Community
Where Discipline Is Rightly Ordered

VII. A Community of Reconciliation

A. The Church is a community that is reconciled to God: all reconciliation is ultimately dependent on God's reconciling actions toward humanity.

1. God's desire to reconcile is evidenced by sending his prophets and in the last days by his Son (Heb. 1.1-2).

2. The incarnation, the life, the death, and the resurrection of Jesus are the ultimate acts of reconciliation from God toward humanity (Rom. 5.8).

3. The Gospel is now a message of reconciliation, made possible by Christ's death, that God offers to humanity (2 Cor. 5.16-20).

B. The Church is a community of individuals and peoples that are reconciled to each other by their common identity as one body.

1. By his death Christ united his people who are born of the same seed (1 John 3.9), reconciled as fellow citizens and members of a new humanity (Eph. 2.11-22).

2. The Church community treats all members of God's household with love and justice in spite of differences in race, class, gender, and culture because they are organically united by their participation in the body of Christ (Gal. 3.26-29; Col. 3.11).

C. The Church is a community that is concerned for reconciliation among all peoples.

1. The Church functions an ambassador that invites all people to be reconciled to God (2 Cor. 5.19-20). This task of mission lays the foundation for all the reconciling activities of the Church.

2. The Church promotes reconciliation with and between all people.

    a. Because the Church is commanded to love its enemies (Matt. 5.44-48).

    b. Because the Church is an incarnational community which seeks, like Christ, to identify with those alienated from itself.

A Theology of the Church (continued)

    c. Because the Church embodies and works for the vision of the Kingdom of God in which peoples, nations, and nature itself will be completely reconciled and at peace (Isa. 11.1-9; Mic. 4.2-4; Matt. 4.17; Acts 28.31).

    d. Because the Church recognizes the eternal plan of God to reconcile all things in heaven and on earth under one head, the Lord Jesus Christ, in order that the Kingdom may be handed over to God the Father who will be all in all (Eph. 1.10; Rom. 11.36; 1 Cor. 15.27-28; Rev. 11.15, 21.1-17).

D. The Church is a community of friendship: friendship is a key part of reconciliation and spiritual development.

    1. Spiritual maturity results in friendship with God (Exod. 33.11; James 2.23).

    2. Spiritual discipleship results in friendship with Christ (John 15.13-15).

    3. Spiritual unity is expressed in friendship with the saints (Rom. 16.5, 9, 12; 2 Cor. 7.1; Phil. 2.12; Col. 4.14; 1 Pet. 2.11; 1 John 2.7; 3 John 1.14).

VIII. A Community of Suffering

A. The Church community suffers because it exists in the world as "sheep among wolves" (Luke 10.3).

    1. Hated by those who reject Christ (John 15.18-20).

    2. Persecuted by the world system (Matt. 5.10; 2 Cor. 4.9; 2 Tim. 3.12).

    3. It is uniquely the community of the poor, the hungry, the weeping, the hated, the excluded, the insulted, and the rejected (Matt. 5.20-22).

    4. It is founded on the example and experience of Christ and the apostles (Isa. 53.3; Luke 9.22; Luke 24.46; Acts 5.41; 2 Tim. 1.8; 1 Thess. 2.2).

B. The Church community imitates Christ in his suffering.

1. Because it purifies from sin (1 Pet. 4.1-2).

2. Because it teaches obedience (Heb. 5.8).

3. Because it allows them to know Christ more fully (Phil. 3.10).

4. Because those who share in Christ's suffering will also share in his comfort and glory (Rom. 8.17-18; 2 Cor. 1.5; 1 Pet. 5.1).

C. The Church community suffers because it identifies with those who suffer.

1. The body of Christ suffers whenever one of its members suffers (1 Cor. 12.26).

2. The body of Christ suffers because it voluntarily identifies itself with the despised, the rejected, the oppressed, and the unlovely (Prov. 29.7; Luke 7.34; Luke 15.1-2).

D. The cross of Christ is both the instrument of salvation and the pattern for Christian life. The cross embodies the values of the Church community.

1. The cross of Christ is the most fundamental Christian symbol. It serves as a constant reminder that the Church is a community of suffering.

2. The basic requirement of discipleship is a willingness to take up the cross daily and follow Jesus (Mark 8.34; Luke 9.23; Luke 14.27).

IX. A Community of Works

A. "Works of Service" are the hallmark of Christian congregations as they do justice, love mercy, and walk humbly with God.

1. The leadership of the Church is charged with preparing God's people for "works of service" (Eph. 4.12).

2. These good works are central to the new purpose and identity which is given us during the new birth. "For we are his workmanship, created in

A Theology of the Church (continued)

Christ Jesus for good works, which God prepared beforehand, that we should walk in them" (Eph. 2.10).

3. These works of service reveal God's character to the world and lead people to give him praise (Matt. 5.16; 2 Cor. 9.13).

B. Servanthood characterizes the Christian's approach to relationships, resources, and ministry.

1. The Church community serves based on the example of Christ who came "not to be served but to serve" (Matt. 20.25-28; Luke 22.27; Phil. 2.7).

2. The Church community serves based on the command of Christ and the apostles (Mark 10.42-45; Gal. 5.13; 1 Pet. 4.10).

3. The Church community serves, first of all, "the least of these" according to the mandates of Christ's teaching (Matt. 18.2-5; Matt. 25. 34-46; Luke 4.18-19).

C. Generosity and hospitality are the twin signs of kingdom service.

1. Generosity results in the giving of one's self and one's good for the sake of announcing and obeying Christ and his kingdom reign.

2. Hospitality results in treating the stranger, the foreigner, the prisoner, and the enemy as one of your very own people (Heb. 13.2).

3. These signs are the true fruit of repentance (Luke 3.7-14; Luke 19.8-10; James 1.27)

D. Stewardship is the foundational truth which governs the way the Church uses resources in order to do "Works of Service."

1. Our resources (time, money, authority, health, position, etc.) belong not to ourselves but to God.

    a. We answer to God for our management of the things entrusted to us personally and corporately (Matt. 25.14-30).

    b. Money should be managed in such as way that treasures are laid up in heaven (Matt. 6.19-21; Luke 12.32-34; Luke 16.1-15; 1 Tim. 6.17-19).

    c. Seeking first the Kingdom of God is the standard by which our stewardship is measured and the basis upon which more will be entrusted (Matt. 6.33).

2. Proper stewardship should contribute to equality and mutual sharing (2 Cor. 8.13-15).

3. Greed is indicative of dishonest stewardship and a repudiation of God as the owner and giver of all things (Luke 12.15; Luke 16.13; Eph. 5.5; Col. 3.5; 1 Pet. 5.2).

E. Justice is a key goal of the Church as it serves God and others.

1. Doing justice is an essential part of fulfilling our service to God (Deut. 16.20; 27.19; Pss. 33.5; 106.3; Prov. 28.5; Mic. 6.8; Matt. 23.23).

2. Justice characterizes the righteous servant but is absent from the hypocrite and the unrighteous (Prov. 29.7; Isa. 1.17; 58.1-14; Matt. 12.18-20; Luke 11.42).

APPENDIX 26

Culture, Not Color: Interaction of Class, Culture, and Race

World Impact Inc.

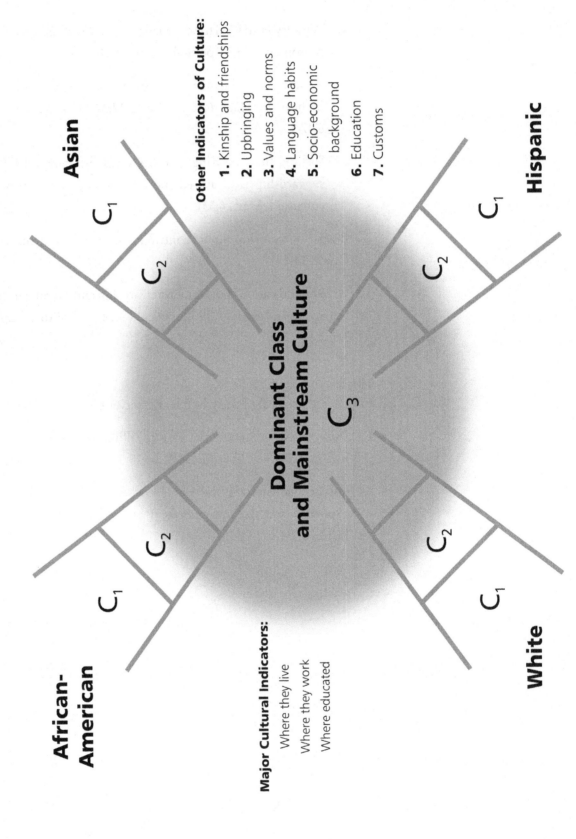

Other Indicators of Culture:

1. Kinship and friendships
2. Upbringing
3. Values and norms
4. Language habits
5. Socio-economic background
6. Education
7. Customs

Major Cultural Indicators:

Where they live
Where they work
Where educated

Asian

Hispanic

African-American

White

Dominant Class and Mainstream Culture

C_3

C_1 C_2

APPENDIX 27

That We May Be One
Elements of an Integrated Church Planting Movement Among the Urban Poor
Rev. Dr. Don L. Davis

Church Planting Movements among the Urban Poor = an integrated and aggressive advance of the Kingdom of God among the urban poor resulting in a significant increase of indigenous churches which fundamentally share in common a constellation of elements which provides them with a distinct and unique identity, purpose, and practice.

Ministry among the urban poor must be grounded in a vision and understanding of the liberty we have in Christ to conceive of coherent, integrated movements of followers of Jesus who because of shared experience, proximity, culture, and history *determine to reflect their unique faith and practice in a way consistent with the historic faith but distinct to their life and times.* This is not an arbitrary act; movements cannot ignore the nature of the one (unity), holy (sanctity), catholic (universality), and apostolic (apostolicity) Church, the one true people of God.

Nevertheless, as was affirmed by the emerging leaders of the then American Episcopal Church, the freedom that we have in Christ allows for different forms and usages of worship in the body of Christ without any offense whatsoever, as long as we are faithful to the historic orthodox beliefs of the Church as taught to us by the prophets and apostles of our Lord. Doctrine must remain anchored and complete; discipline, however, can be based on the contingencies and exigencies of the people who embrace them, as long as all that is shaped and conceived builds up the body of Christ, and glorifies God our Father through our Lord Jesus Christ.

"The congregations in an Integrated Church Planting Movement Among the Urban Poor *will exhibit together:*"

1. *A shared history and identity* (i.e., *a common name and heritage*). CPMs among the urban poor will seek to link themselves to and identify themselves by a well defined and joyfully shared history and persona that all members and congregations share.

That We May Be One (continued)

2. *A shared liturgy and celebration* (i.e., *a common worship*). CPMs among the urban poor should reflect a shared hymnody, practice of the sacraments, theological focus and imagery, aesthetic vision, vestments, liturgical order, symbology, and spiritual formation that enables us to worship and glorify God in a way that lifts up the Lord and attracts urbanites to vital worship.

3. *A shared membership, well-being, welfare, and support* (i.e., *a common order and discipline*). CPMs among the urban poor must be anchored in evangelical and historically orthodox presentations of the Gospel that result in conversions to Jesus Christ and incorporation into local churches.

4. *A shared catechism and doctrine* (i.e., *a common faith*). CPMs among the urban poor must embrace a common biblical theology and express it practically in a Christian education that reflects their commonly-held faith.

5. *A shared church government and authority* (i.e., *a common polity*). CPMs among the urban poor must be organized around a common polity, ecclesial management, and submit to flexible governing policies that allow for effective and efficient management of their resources and congregations.

6. *A shared leadership development structure* (i.e., *a common pastoral strategy*). CPMs among the urban poor are committed with supplying each congregation with godly undershepherds, and seek to identify, equip, and support its pastors and missionaries in order that their members may grow to maturity in Christ.

7. *A shared financial philosophy and procedure* (i.e., *a common stewardship*). CPMs among the urban poor strive to handle all of their financial affairs and resources with wise, streamlined, and reproducible policies that allow for the good management of their monies and goods, locally, regionally, and nationally.

8. *A shared care and support ministry* (i.e., *a common service*). CPMs among the urban poor seek to practically demonstrate the love and justice of the Kingdom among its members and towards others in the city in ways that allow individuals and congregations to love their neighbors as they love themselves.

9. *A shared evangelism and outreach* (i.e., *a common mission*): CPMs among the urban poor network and collaborate among their members in order to clearly present Jesus and his Kingdom to the lost in the city in order to multiply new congregations in unreached urban areas as quickly as possible.

10. *A shared vision for connection and association* (i.e., *a common partnership*). CPMs among the urban poor must seek to make fresh connections, links, and relationships with other movements for the sake of regular communication, fellowship, and mission.

These principles of belonging, camaraderie, and identity lay the foundation for a new paradigm of authentic ecumenical unity, the kind that can lead to partnerships and collaboration of grand scope and deep substance. Below is a short overview of the TUMI biblical basis for the kind of partnerships which can fuel and sustain credible church planting movements among the urban poor.

God's Partners and Fellow Workers

1 Cor. 3.1-9 (ESV) - But I, brothers, could not address you as spiritual people, but as people of the flesh, as infants in Christ. [2] I fed you with milk, not solid food, for you were not ready for it. And even now you are not yet ready, [3] for you are still of the flesh. For while there is jealousy and strife among you, are you not of the flesh and behaving only in a human way? [4] For when one says, "I follow Paul," and another, "I follow Apollos," are you not being merely human? [5] What then is Apollos? What is Paul? Servants through whom you believed, as the Lord assigned to each. [6] I planted, Apollos watered, but God gave the growth. [7] So neither he who plants nor he who waters is anything, but only God who gives the growth. [8] He who plants and he who waters are one, and each will receive his wages according to his labor. [9] For we are God's fellow workers. You are God's field, God's building.

To Facilitate Pioneer Church Planting Movements Among America's Unreached C_1 Communities

As a ministry of World Impact, TUMI is dedicated to generating and strategically facilitating dynamic, indigenous C_1 church planting movements targeted to reach the 80% Window of America's inner cities. In order to attain this purpose, we will help form strategic alliances between and among urban missionaries and pastors, theologians and missiologists, churches and denominations, and other kingdom-minded individuals and organizations in order to trigger robust pioneer

That We May Be One (continued)

church planting movements that multiply thousands of culturally-conducive evangelical C_1 churches among America's urban poor. We will offer our expertise to assure that these churches in every way glorify God the Father in their Christ-centered identity, Spirit-formed worship and community life, historically orthodox doctrine, and kingdom-oriented practice and mission.

I. Partnership Involves Recognizing our Fundamental Unity in Christ: We Share the Same Spiritual DNA.

A. *Our faith in Jesus has made us one together.*

1. 1 John 1.3 (ESV) - that which we have seen and heard we proclaim also to you, so that you too may have fellowship with us; and indeed our fellowship is with the Father and with his Son Jesus Christ.

2. John 17.11 (ESV) - And I am no longer in the world, but they are in the world, and I am coming to you. Holy Father, keep them in your name, which you have given me, that they may be one, even as we are one.

B. *The organic unity between the Father and Son, and the people of God,* John 17.21-22 (ESV) - that they may all be one, just as you, Father, are in me, and I in you, that they also may be in us, so that the world may believe that you have sent me. [22] The glory that you have given me I have given to them, that they may be one even as we are one.

C. *Our unity leads to a common effort in glorifying God the Father of our Lord,* Rom. 15.5-6 (ESV) - May the God of endurance and encouragement grant you to live in such harmony with one another, in accord with Christ Jesus, [6] that together you may with one voice glorify the God and Father of our Lord Jesus Christ.

D. *God's will for the body is unity in mind and judgment,* 1 Cor. 1.10 (ESV) - I appeal to you, brothers, by the name of our Lord Jesus Christ, that all of you agree and that there be no divisions among you, but that you be united in the same mind and the same judgment.

E. *The Holy Spirit's baptism has made us of one spiritual body and spirit,* 1 Cor. 12.12-13 (ESV) - For just as the body is one and has many members, and all the members of the body, though many, are one body, so it is with Christ.

[13] For in one Spirit we were all baptized into one body— Jews or Greeks, slaves or free—and all were made to drink of one Spirit.

F. *The very essence of biblical faith is unity*, Eph. 4.4-6 (ESV) - There is one body and one Spirit—just as you were called to the one hope that belongs to your call [5] one Lord, one faith, one baptism, [6] one God and Father of all, who is over all and through all and in all.

G. *Our bond of partnership precludes unity with those not united to Christ*, 2 Cor. 6.14-16 (ESV) - Do not be unequally yoked with unbelievers. For what partnership has righteousness with lawlessness? Or what fellowship has light with darkness? [15] What accord has Christ with Belial? Or what portion does a believer share with an unbeliever? [16] What agreement has the temple of God with idols? For we are the temple of the living God; as God said, "I will make my dwelling among them and walk among them, and I will be their God, and they shall be my people.

II. Partnership Involves the Sharing of Monies, Persons, and Resources to Fund a Common Cause: We Share a Common Source, Table, and Pot.

A. *The partnership between those who share the Word and receive it involves concrete blessing and giving.*

1. *The taught share with the teacher*, Gal. 6.6 (ESV) - One who is taught the word must share all good things with the one who teaches.

2. *Illustrated in the relationship of the Jew to the Gentile in the body*, Rom. 15.27 (ESV) - They were pleased to do it, and indeed they owe it to them. For if the Gentiles have come to share in their spiritual blessings, they ought also to be of service to them in material blessings.

B. *The power of unity extends to those who are appointed by God to serve his people*, Deut. 12.19 (ESV) - Take care that you do not neglect the Levite as long as you live in your land.

C. *Those who labor deserve the generous supply of those who benefit from that labor.*

1. *Christ's exhortation to the disciples*, Matt. 10.10 (ESV) - No bag for your journey, nor two tunics nor sandals nor a staff, for the laborer deserves his food.

That We May Be One (continued)

2. *Illustrated from OT Scripture and analogy*, 1 Cor. 9.9-14 (ESV) - For it is written in the Law of Moses, "You shall not muzzle an ox when it treads out the grain." Is it for oxen that God is concerned? [10] Does he not speak entirely for our sake? It was written for our sake, because the plowman should plow in hope and the thresher thresh in hope of sharing in the crop. [11] If we have sown spiritual things among you, is it too much if we reap material things from you? [12] If others share this rightful claim on you, do not we even more? Nevertheless, we have not made use of this right, but we endure anything rather than put an obstacle in the way of the gospel of Christ. [13] Do you not know that those who are employed in the temple service get their food from the temple, and those who serve at the altar share in the sacrificial offerings? [14] In the same way, the Lord commanded that those who proclaim the gospel should get their living by the gospel.

3. *Double honor: respect and sharing of resources*, 1 Tim. 5.17-18 (ESV) - Let the elders who rule well be considered worthy of double honor, especially those who labor in preaching and teaching. [18] For the Scripture says, "You shall not muzzle an ox when it treads out the grain," and, "The laborer deserves his wages."

D. *The Philippian relationship with Paul is a prototype of this kind of essential partnership.*

1. *From the beginning they shared tangibly with Paul*, Phil. 1.3-5 (ESV) - I thank my God in all my remembrance of you, [4] always in every prayer of mine for you all making my prayer with joy, [5] because of your partnership in the gospel from the first day until now.

2. *Epaphroditus was their messenger to transport their aid to Paul*, Phil. 2.25 (ESV) - I have thought it necessary to send to you Epaphroditus my brother and fellow worker and fellow soldier, and your messenger and minister to my need

3. *The Philippians were completely engaged in the support of Paul's ministry from the first*, Phil. 4.15-18 (ESV) - And you Philippians yourselves know that in the beginning of the gospel, when I left Macedonia, no church entered into partnership with me in giving and receiving, except you only. [16] Even in Thessalonica you sent me help for my needs once

and again. [17] Not that I seek the gift, but I seek the fruit that increases to your credit. [18] I have received full payment, and more. I am well supplied, having received from Epaphroditus the gifts you sent, a fragrant offering, a sacrifice acceptable and pleasing to God.

III. Partnership Involves Collaborating Together as Co-workers and Co-laborers in the Work of Advancing the Kingdom: We Share a Common Cause and Task.

A. *Partnership assumes that each person and congregation brings their unique experience, perspective, and gifting to the table for use,* Gal. 2.6-8 (ESV) - And from those who seemed to be influential (what they were makes no difference to me; God shows no partiality)—those, I say, who seemed influential added nothing to me. [7] On the contrary, when they saw that I had been entrusted with the gospel to the uncircumcised, just as Peter had been entrusted with the gospel to the circumcised [8] (for he who worked through Peter for his apostolic ministry to the circumcised worked also through me for mine to the Gentiles).

B. *Authentic partnerships involve discerning the Lord's leading, opportunity, and blessing on those who are called to represent his interests in the places where he has led them,* Gal. 2.9-10 (ESV) - and when James and Cephas and John, who seemed to be pillars, perceived the grace that was given to me, they gave the right hand of fellowship to Barnabas and me, that we should go to the Gentiles and they to the circumcised. [10] Only, they asked us to remember the poor, the very thing I was eager to do.

C. *Partnership in terms of co-working and co-laboring involves a shared vision and commitment to a common cause,* e.g., Timothy, Phil. 2.19-24 (ESV) - I hope in the Lord Jesus to send Timothy to you soon, so that I too may be cheered by news of you. [20] For I have no one like him, who will be genuinely concerned for your welfare. [21] They all seek their own interests, not those of Jesus Christ. [22] But you know Timothy's proven worth, how as a son with a father he has served with me in the gospel. [23] I hope therefore to send him just as soon as I see how it will go with me, [24] and I trust in the Lord that shortly I myself will come also.

That We May Be One (continued)

    D. *Paul's unique words for his partners in the Gospel*

        1. Co-worker (*synergos*), Rom. 16.3, 7, 9, 21; 2 Cor. 8.23; Phil. 2.25; 4.3; Col. 4.7, 10, 11, 14; Philem. 1, 24.

        2. Co-prisoner (*synaichmalotos*), Col. 4.10; Philem. 23

        3. Co-slave (*syndoulos*), Col. 1.7, 4.7

        4. Co-soldier (*systratiotes*) Phil. 2.25; Philem. 2

        5. Co-laborer (*synatheleo*), Phil. 4.2-3

    E. A brief listing of Paul's partners in ministry (these accompanied him at every phase and effort of the work, with diverse backgrounds, giftings, tasks, and responsibilities along the way of his ministry)

        1. John Mark (Col. 4.10; Philem. 24)

        2. Artistarchus (Col. 4.10; Philem. 24)

        3. Andronicus and Junia (Rom. 16.7)

        4. Philemon (Philem. 1)

        5. Epaphroditus (same as Epaphras) (Col. 1.7; Philem. 23; Phil. 2.25)

        6. Clement (Phil. 4.3)

        7. Urbanus (Rom. 16.9)

        8. Jesus (Justus) (Col. 4.11)

        9. Demas (who later apostocized in the world), (Col. 4.14; Philem. 24; 2 Tim. 4.20)

       10. Tychicus (Col. 4.7; Phil. 4.3)

       11. Archippus (Philem. 2)

       12. Euodia (Phil. 4.2-3)

       13. Syntyche (Phil. 4.2-3)

       14. Tertius (Rom. 16.22)

15. Phoebe (Rom. 16.1)

16. Erastus (Rom. 16.23)

17. Quartus (Rom. 16.23)

18. Tryphaena (Rom. 16.12)

19. Tryphosa (Rom. 16.12)

20. Persis (Rom. 16.12)

21. Mary (Rom. 16.6)

22. Onesiphorus (2 Tim. 1.16-18)

IV. Implications of Partnership Principles in Light of TUMI's Visions

To Facilitate Pioneer Church Planting Movements Among America's Unreached C_1 Communities

As a ministry of World Impact, TUMI is dedicated to generating and strategically facilitating dynamic, indigenous C_1 church planting movements targeted to reach the 80% Window of America's inner cities. In order to attain this purpose, we will help form strategic alliances between and among urban missionaries and pastors, theologians and missiologists, churches and denominations, and other kingdom-minded individuals and organizations in order to trigger robust pioneer church planting movements that multiply thousands of culturally-conducive evangelical C_1 churches among America's urban poor. We will offer our expertise to assure that these churches in every way glorify God the Father in their Christ-centered identity, Spirit-formed worship and community life, historically orthodox doctrine, and kingdom-oriented practice and mission.

A. *TUMI will help form strategic alliances to trigger urban church plant movements.*

B. *TUMI seeks to support dynamic movements which produce and sustain healthy C_1 churches.*

That We May Be One (continued)

C. Clear implications of this for us

1. We don't recruit people to ourselves, but to participate in Christ's kingdom advance.

2. We don't own the vision, it is God's desire to impact the world, and we contribute alongside others.

3. Our contribution is no better or worse than others: we are co-laborers with others.

4. The work that others do will probably be more critical and fruitful than our own.

Bottom Line

There is virtually no limit to what we can accomplish if we as a team are willing to give our all for the sake of our common cause, if we do not care what role we have to play in order to win, nor care who gets the credit after the victory.

APPENDIX 28

Ethics of the New Testament: Living in the Upside-Down Kingdom of God
True Myth and Biblical Fairy Tale
Dr. Don L. Davis

The Principle of Reversal

The Principle Expressed	Scripture
The poor shall become rich, and the rich shall become poor	Luke 6.20-26
The law breaker and the undeserving are saved	Matt. 21.31-32
Those who humble themselves shall be exalted	1 Pet. 5.5-6
Those who exalt themselves shall be brought low	Luke 18.14
The blind shall be given sight	John 9.39
Those claiming to see shall be made blind	John 9.40-41
We become free by being Christ's slave	Rom. 12.1-2
God has chosen what is foolish in the world to shame the wise	1 Cor. 1.27
God has chosen what is weak in the world to shame the strong	1 Cor. 1.27
God has chosen the low and despised to bring to nothing things that are	1 Cor. 1.28
We gain the next world by losing this one	1 Tim. 6.7
Love this life and you'll lose it; hate this life, and you'll keep the next	John 12.25
You become the greatest by being the servant of all	Matt. 10.42-45
Store up treasures here, you forfeit heaven's reward	Matt. 6.19
Store up treasures above, you gain Heaven's wealth	Matt. 6.20
Accept your own death to yourself in order to live fully	John 12.24
Release all earthly reputation to gain Heaven's favor	Phil. 3.3-7
The first shall be last, and the last shall become first	Mark 9.35
The grace of Jesus is perfected in your weakness, not your strength	2 Cor. 12.9
God's highest sacrifice is contrition and brokenness	Ps. 51.17
It is better to give to others than to receive from them	Acts 20.35
Give away all you have in order to receive God's best	Luke 6.38

APPENDIX 29

Empowering People for Freedom, Wholeness, and Justice

Theological and Ethical Foundations for World Impact's Development Ministries

Don Davis and Terry Cornett

A Theology of Development

Love of God and love of neighbor have been pivotal themes of both Old and New Testament theology from their inception. From the time of the early Church forward, there has been a concern to demonstrate God's love and character to the world in word and deed, through faith and works, by both evangelistic proclamation and acts of justice and mercy.

Starting with its forerunners in Puritan, Pietistic, Moravian, and Wesleyan reform and revival movements, and extending into the modern Protestant missions movement, evangelical missionaries have combined a strong emphasis on evangelism and the establishment of churches with a serious attempt to engage in action that would foster justice and righteousness, especially on behalf of the poor and oppressed.

Evangelical reformers and missionaries have started schools and hospitals aimed at being accessible to the least advantaged segments of society, formed orphanages and worked for the reform of child labor laws, established businesses and cooperative ventures among the poor, supported legislation to abolish slavery and to ensure the protection of human rights, worked to upgrade the status of women in society, and mediated conflicts between warring groups and nations.[1]

Although Christians generally agree that evangelism and social action are important responsibilities of the Church, there is considerable variation in both the terms that are used to designate these responsibilities, and the way in which they are defined and placed in relation to one another. As a missions agency which is engaged in both of these activities, it is important to establish our definition of terms and a statement of the theological relationship which exists between these two tasks.

Prologue

[1] *See Paul E. Pierson's article, "Missions and Community Development: A Historical Perspective," (Elliston 1989, 1-22) for an introduction to the history of development work in evangelical missions and Donald W. Dayton's book "Discovering an Evangelical Heritage" (Dayton, 1988) for a helpful look at evangelical reform movements.*

1. The Kingdom of God as the Basis of Evangelism, Church Planting and Development

2 See George Eldon Ladd (1974, 45-134), for an introduction to a biblical theology of the Kingdom.

3 That is, the One who in his own person fully embodies the rule of God.

1.1 The Kingdom of God as the Basis for Mission

"Missiology is more and more coming to see the Kingdom of God as the hub around which all of mission work revolves" (Verkuyl 1978, 203). Evangelism, church-planting and development work are not based on a few isolated "proof-texts," but are an abiding response to the theme of the Kingdom which is woven throughout the scriptural record. The Kingdom of God embodies the essence of what God's mission (*Missio Dei*) in the world is and provides a basis for seeing how our own activities are intended to fit into God's overall plan.[2]

1.2 The Kingdom as Restoration

The Scriptures assert what human experience everywhere reveals; something has gone dramatically wrong with the world. The Bible teaches that the basis of this problem is humanity's rejection of God's rulership. The Genesis account of the Fall shows humanity repudiating God's right to give direction and boundaries to their decisions. From that time forward, evil filled the void left by the absence of God's loving rule. The world ceased to function correctly; death replaced life; disease replaced health; enmity replaced friendship; domination replaced cooperation; and scarcity replaced abundance. All human relationships with God and with each other were poisoned by the inner desire of each individual and social group to replace God's authority with their own rule.

In a response of grace to this situation, God decided not to reject and destroy the world, but to redeem it. He set in motion a plan to liberate the world from its bondage to evil powers, and to restore all things to perfection under his Kingly rule. Throughout the Scriptures this plan of reclamation is described as the "*Kingdom of God,*" and insight into its nature and means of coming are progressively revealed.

Johannes Verkuyl summarizes the message of the Kingdom in this fashion:

> *The heart of the message of the Old and New Testament is that God . . . is actively engaged in the reestablishment of His liberating dominion over the cosmos and all of humankind. In seeking out Israel, He sought all of us and our entire world, and in Jesus Christ He laid the foundation of the Kingdom. Jesus Christ the Messiah "promised to the fathers," is the **auto basileia**[3]: in Him the Kingdom has both come, and is coming in an absolutely unique way and with exceptional clarity. In His preaching Jesus divulges the riches, the **thesaurus** of that Kingdom: reconciliation,*

Empowering People for Freedom, Wholeness, and Justice (continued)

the forgiveness of sins, victory over demonic powers. Standing within the tradition of the Mosaic law, He expounds the core message of . . . the prophets; He accomplishes the reconciliation of the world to God; He opens the way to the present and future Kingdom which demands decisions of us in all aspects of life (Verkuyl 1993, 72).

1.3 Responsibilities for Those Who Seek God's Kingdom

The implications of the Kingdom of God for mission can be delineated in three central truths. A kingdom-centered theology and missiology will be concerned for:

- Evangelizing so that people are converted to Christ as Lord.

- Creating churches where people are discipled and bear fruit.

- Helping the Church live out its commitment to bring freedom, wholeness, and justice in the world.

Thus:

A truly Kingdom-centered theology . . . can never neglect the call for the conversion of persons among all peoples and religious communities. To everyone of whatever religious persuasion the message must be repeated: "The Kingdom of God is at hand; repent, and believe in the Gospel.". . . Kingdom-centered theology entails a call to recognition of the lordship of the King and new orientation to the constitution of His Kingdom. In the absence of this aspect, proclamation of the good news of the Gospel is impossible. A theology and missiology informed by the biblical notion of the rule of Christ will never fail to identify personal conversion as one of the inclusive goals of God's Kingdom . . .

The Church . . . is raised up by God among all nations to share in the salvation and suffering service of the Kingdom . . . The Church constitutes the firstling, the early harvest of the Kingdom. Thus, although not limited to the Church, the Kingdom is unthinkable without the Church. Conversely, growth and expansion of the Church should not be viewed as ends but rather as means to be used in the service of the Kingdom. . . . The keys of the Kingdom have been given to the Church. It does not fulfill its mandate by relinquishing those keys but rather by using them to open up the avenues of approach to the Kingdom for all peoples and all population groups at every level of human society . . .

Finally, the gospel of the Kingdom addresses itself to all immediate human need, both physical and mental. It aims to right what is wrong on earth. It enjoins engagement in the struggle for racial, social, cultural, economic, and political justice. . . . The good news of the Kingdom has to do with all of these things. For this reason missiology must bend its efforts to the erection of a multiplicity of visible signs of God's Kingdom throughout the length and breadth of this planet (Verkuyl 1993, 72-73).

Evangelism, church planting and development spring from a common theological base: a desire to live out the implications of the Kingdom of God which has broken into this present age in the person of Jesus Christ, the King of kings. This Kingdom is both *already* and *not yet*. It is currently *forcefully advancing* and *spreading like yeast through dough*, but also awaiting the return of Christ *when every knee will bow* and there will be a *new heaven and a new earth*. Our evangelism and our development work acknowledge God's kingly rule, now, during a time when the world, as a whole, does not. We announce the good news of the in-breaking Kingdom of peace and justice, call people to repentance and salvation through faith in its King, hope in its inevitable complete triumph, and live out obedience to its commands and values in the present moment.

2. Kingdom Work

Since evangelism/church planting and development work are intimately related, those who engage in them often find that their roles and projects overlap. While this is both normal and good, a clear beginning definition of each role may help to minimize the confusion which can sometimes result from this process.

2.1 Missionaries

Missionaries are called to pioneer new outreaches that focus on the evangelization of peoples in unreached (or under-reached) areas, social classes, or cultural groups.

Therefore, we assert that:

Missionaries cross class and cultural barriers to evangelize and disciple unreached groups so that reproducing churches are formed among them and placed at the service of God's kingdom rule.

Empowering People for Freedom, Wholeness, and Justice (continued)

2.2 Development Workers

Development workers are called to confront conditions and structures in the world that do not submit themselves to the rule of God.

Therefore, we assert that:

> *Development workers enable individuals, churches and communities to experience movement toward the freedom, wholeness, and justice of the Kingdom of God.*

2.3 The Common Link

Both missionaries and Christian development workers are united in their common commitment to further God's kingdom rule in all areas of life.

Missionary activity is centered around the proclamation of "good news" that calls people into the Kingdom of God through an experience of salvation and regeneration. It focuses on bringing unreached peoples, cultures, and subcultures into the community of the redeemed (i.e., "bringing the world into the Church"). All of this is done with an eye toward creating churches which can disciple their members to acknowledge God's rulership and live out the values of his Kingdom in their individual and corporate life.

Missionary activity also encompasses development that seeks to call every area of life into conformity with God's kingdom rule. It evaluates every concrete life-situation in light of the Lord's Prayer ("thy Kingdom come, thy will be done, on earth as it is in heaven") and engages in deeds of compassion, love, and justice that demonstrate the nature of God's divine plan for all peoples. It focuses on bringing God's rule to bear on every human relationship and structure (i.e., "bringing the Church into the world").

3.1 A Partnership Relationship

Missionary evangelism and church-planting and Christian development work are partners in the process of proclaiming, demonstrating, and extending the rule of the King. Both are responses to the fact that God has announced his desire to reconcile the world to himself through the gift of his Son. Although each is a legitimate response to God's plan for the world, neither is a sufficient response in and of itself.

3. Theological Relationship between Evangelism and Development

Empowering People for Freedom, Wholeness, and Justice (continued)

Both word and deed are necessary components of the Church's announcement of, and faithfulness to, the Kingdom of God.

3.2 Interdependence and Interconnectedness

The relationship between Missions and Development is not a simple one. Their interconnectedness has many facets.

- *They are connected by a common goal.*

  Neither missionaries nor development workers are satisfied until God's reconciliation with man and man's reconciliation with man is completely realized. We believe that this makes both missions and development work Christocentric in orientation, since it is "in Christ" that God is reconciling the world to himself. Christ is the King. It is his sacrificial, reconciling death that provides the objective basis for reconciliation between humanity and God, and within human relationships and structures. It is his kingly authority and presence that allows the Kingdom to break into this present age destroying the works of darkness and creating authentic communities gathered under God's rule.

- *They retain a degree of independence from each other.*

  Evangelism and church-planting can sometimes be done without any immediate focus on development work. Conversely, development work can be sometimes be done without accompanying church-planting activity. Because both are authentic responses to God's activity in the world, they can, when appropriate, operate independently from each other. While each is a legitimate activity in its own right, it will obviously be healthier and more normal to find them occurring together.

- *They need each other for lasting effectiveness.*

  Without evangelism, there are no changed lives, no reconcilers who understand God's plan for man and society, and who undertake change in the power of the Spirit. Without development, the churches established by mission become withdrawn, and do not function as "salt and light" within their local and national communities. Missionary efforts are undermined when the existing church does not make visible in its life the effects of God's

Empowering People for Freedom, Wholeness, and Justice (continued)

kingdom rule. The integration of the two is aptly expressed in Ephesians 2:8-10 which states, "For by grace you have been saved through faith. And this is not your own doing; it is the gift of God, [9] not a result of works, so that no one may boast. [10] For we are his workmanship, created in Christ Jesus for good works, which God prepared beforehand, that we should walk in them."

These facets may be summarized as "a threefold relationship between evangelism and social activity. First, Christian social activity [development] is a *consequence* of evangelism, since it is the evangelized who engage in it. Second it is a *bridge* to evangelism, since it expresses God's love and so both overcomes prejudice and opens closed doors. Third, it is a *partner* of evangelism, so that they are 'like two blades of a pair of scissors or the two wings of a bird'" (Stott 1995, 52).

3.3 The Need for Specialization

Modern missions have seen the rise of both mission and development agencies. This occurs as organizations specialize in one component of the overall task God has given. This recognition of the need for specialization arose early on in the life of the Church.

J. Chongham Cho comments:

> *In Acts 6 . . . a distinction between evangelism and social action was made. This was not a division in essence but for the sake of practical efficacy of the church's mission and as the solution to a problem which arose in the church. This is a necessary deduction from the nature of the church as Christ's body. Although we should resist polarization between evangelism and social action, we should not resist specialization (Cho 1985, 229).*

As a missions agency, our primary focus is evangelism and discipleship which results in the planting of indigenous churches. The fact that evangelism, church-planting and development are interconnected means that missions agencies, especially those who focus on the poor and oppressed, will engage in some form of development work. However, the mission agency must be careful to structure its development work so that it encourages the central task of evangelism and church-planting rather than detracts from it.[4] We should engage in development work which fosters the formation, health, growth, and reproducibility of indigenous churches among the poor.

[4] *See Appendix A for a variety of perspectives on how improperly implemented development work can adversely affect missionary work.*

Empowering People for Freedom, Wholeness, and Justice (continued)

Specialization allows organizations to maximize the training and resources that can be committed to a specific part of the overall task of mission. The development agency may engage in many good and necessary projects that have no immediate connection to evangelism and the planting and nurturing of emerging churches. The missions agency appreciates the many development agencies that engage in this type of work. Although the mission agency will want to network with them (and pray that God will vastly increase their number and effectiveness), the mission agency itself will focus on development projects that assist the task of evangelism, discipleship, and the establishment of indigenous churches. Without this commitment to specialization, the mission agency will lose its ability to accomplish its part of the larger task.

4. Development Work within Our Mission Agency

4.1 Statement of Purpose

While we recognize the legitimacy of engaging in development work for its own sake as a direct godly response to human need, we believe that we are called to specialize in development work that specifically supports and contributes to the task of evangelism, discipleship and church-planting. In light of this, we affirm the following statement.

The aim of World Impact's development ministries is to support the evangelism, discipleship, and church-planting goals of World Impact by:

* *Demonstrating the Love of Christ*

   Many oppressed people have little basis for understanding God's love for them and the essential justice and compassion of his character. Development work can provide a living witness to the love of Christ and his concern for justice and peace in urban neighborhoods. Holistic ministry can come alongside the verbal proclamation of the Gospel, verifying its credibility and enriching the depth of understanding among its hearers. Development work can function pre-evangelistically to prepare people to genuinely listen to the claims of Christ and his message of salvation.

* *Empowering Emerging Churches*

   Emerging urban churches often have few physical resources with which to face the enormous needs of the city. Development work can partner with the pastors of planted-churches, giving access to resources and programs that can meet immediate needs within their congregation, encourage leadership development, and help their congregations engage in effective holistic outreach to their community.

- *Modeling the Implications of the Gospel*

  We cannot hope to reproduce churches committed to engage in a task they have never seen lived out in practice. We engage in development work because we expect newly planted churches to do likewise. We want to provide a living example that the Gospel will necessarily move from belief to action, from word to deed.

4.2 An Important Reminder

One cautionary note is in order. We cannot, through our own efforts, bring the Kingdom of God. As Paul Hiebert reminds us, "Our paradigms are flawed if we begin missions with human activity. Mission is not primarily what we do. It is what God does" (Hiebert 1993, 158). Evangelism, church-planting and development work all function, first and foremost, at the disposal of the Spirit of God. Knowing what should be done, and how we should do it, is never primarily determined through strategic diagrams or well-thought-out organizational approaches. Our first duty is to be faithful to the King, to listen to his instructions, and to respond to his initiatives.

An Ethic of Development

We have stated that:

> *Development workers enable individuals, churches and communities to experience movement toward the freedom, wholeness, and justice of the Kingdom of God.*

The process by which we move toward this goal, and the decisions we make to achieve these ends must be guided by an ethic which is consistent with God's standard for human relationships.

Ethics has to do with human conduct and character. It is the systematic study of the principles and methods for distinguishing right from wrong and good from bad. A Christian ethic of development helps us make decisions about development issues in

5. Introduction

Empowering People for Freedom, Wholeness, and Justice (continued)

light of biblical revelation and theology. It enables us to think and act clearly so that we can discern what is right to do and how it should be done.

Ethics is concerned that our theology be applied to our behaviors and attitudes. It is not content to simply understand the truth. Instead, it continually seeks to help us discover how to apply the truth (and attempts to motivate us to do so). True ethical behavior means that ethical principles are understood, internalized, and applied to the situation through the development of specific strategies and practices. In an organization, true ethical behavior also requires that strategies and practices undergo regular testing, evaluation and refinement. This ensures that the organization is accomplishing in practice what it affirms in principle.

Finally, it should be noted that our experiences always confront us with paradoxes, anomalies and competing priorities. An ethic of development does not attempt to condense life into a neatly packaged system. Rather, it provides principles that will help us to clarify what is most important in the particular situation that are facing. Each ethical decision must involve discussion about how the various principles outlined below interrelate and about which are the most significant values for a given decision. Only in dialogue and in prayer can the correct decision be discerned.

The ethical principles of the Kingdom of God can be expressed in the values of freedom, wholeness, and justice. These values are the root and the fruit of doing development from a kingdom perspective.

6. World Impact's Development Work is Committed to Freedom

Freedom is the ability to exercise our God-given capacity to make choices that express love. Therefore, development should engender freedom by helping individuals:

- Gain dignity and respect.
- Be empowered to make wise choices.
- Take responsibility for themselves and others.

This process involves helping individuals *understand* and *achieve* what they need to live freely in community as biblically responsible, self-directing, maturing servants of God's Kingdom. It implies the development of relationships characterized neither by dependence nor independence, but by loving *interdependence* that results in partnership, mutuality, and increased freedom.

Empowering People for Freedom, Wholeness, and Justice (continued)

6.1 Development affirms human beings as precious and unique in the sight of God, and believes that they have been granted unique capacities and potentials by God.

Explanation

As beings made in the image of God, every person regardless of station or place, is worthy of dignity and respect. People are to be cherished, nurtured, and provided for according to their intrinsic value and preciousness to God. Biblically based development will never exploit people for the sake of economic purposes or treat people as instruments, but instead will value them as ends-in-themselves, to be loved and respected for their worth before God.

Implications

- *People are to be given priority in every dimension of development.*

  Development should contribute to the potential for self-sufficiency, should enhance the quality of life, and should encourage good stewardship among those participating in the programs.

- *Mutual respect is foundational to authentic development.*

  For the poor, life in the urban community is full of inconvenience, difficulty, and shame. The needy daily experience the indignities of being poor in an affluent society. Oftentimes they are accused of moral laxity, subjected to stifling bureaucracies, and pre-judged as causing their own poverty through incompetence or lack of motivation. Development is sensitive to these messages which are given to the needy in our society. It recognizes that the poor are the objects of God's compassion and good news, chosen to be rich in faith and heirs to the Kingdom of God (James 2.5). Development seeks to demonstrate God's righteous cherishing of the poor through its specific actions and relationships.

  Aid not founded on genuine respect can easily humiliate the poor. Therefore, assistance offered to those in need must affirm their dignity and self-respect. Anything that diminishes the worth and significance of the poor in the development process is sinful and injurious to the well-being of all, both those offering the aid and those receiving it.

Empowering People for Freedom, Wholeness, and Justice (continued)

- *The workplace should operate as a caring community.*

  While an impersonal atmosphere characterizes many business environments, Christian development strives to create a relational framework for trainees and employees. Development workers and those participating in the development project must develop habit patterns of caring for each other beyond the constraints of the project at hand.

6.2 Development should empower people to take full responsibility for their own lives and to care for the needs of others.

<u>Explanation</u>

Development emerges from the conviction that all work is honorable. God has mandated that human beings earn their living with integrity and excellence. This mandate for individual work is grounded in God's initial command given to humankind at creation, and continues on and is reaffirmed in the teachings of the apostles. While God demands that his people be generous and hospitable to the needy and the stranger (2 Cor. 9), God likewise commands all to work honestly with their own hands (1 Thess. 4), and further charges that those who refuse to work ought to correspondingly be denied benevolent aid, that is, "if anyone will not work, neither let him eat," (cf. 2 Thess. 3.10).

Development rejects the notion that the creation of wealth is intrinsically evil. Such a view is simplistic and fails to grapple with the biblical notion of Christian stewardship. Development aims to create abundance, but never for the sake of selfish gain or lustful greed. Rather, development takes seriously the biblical requirement that we work, not merely to meet our own needs, but so that from the abundance God has provided we may use our goods and resources to meet the needs of others, especially those who are our brothers and sisters in the body of Christ (cf. Eph. 4; 2 Cor. 8; Gal. 6). The biblical standard is that those who stole before they entered the Kingdom are to steal no more, but to work honorably in quietness and integrity, in order that they may have sufficient resources to meet their own needs, and have sufficient wealth to care for others. Development not only seeks to honor the needy by ensuring they can participate in the basic human right to work, it also challenges them to trust God to supply their needs through honorable labor that allows them to be providers for themselves and others.

Empowering People for Freedom, Wholeness, and Justice (continued)

Implications

- *Nothing can excuse a worker, leader, or professional from the perils and potentials of personal responsibility.*

  Christian workers are not exempt from the vices of laziness, slothfulness, mismanagement, and greed, and they will not be spared from the consequences of such habits and conduct.

- *It is a primary aim of development to increase the maturity of everyone involved in the process.*

  It is assumed that the maturing individual will be increasingly characterized by vision (establishing and owning life-long purposes, aspirations and priorities), responsibility (acting on those purposes, aspirations and priorities with motivation, perseverance and integrity), and wisdom (increasing in skill, understanding and the ability to discern and do what is right for themselves and others).

  Maturing individuals should move from dependence toward autonomy, from passivity toward activity, from small abilities to large abilities, from narrow interests to broad interests, from egocentricity to altruism, from ignorance toward enlightenment, from self-rejection toward self-acceptance, from compartmentability toward integration, from imitation toward originality and from a need for rigidity toward a tolerance for ambiguity (Klopfenstein 1993, 95-96).

- *Decisions are best handled at the closest point to those affected.*

  National policies and procedures exist to:

  » Provide a framework for effective decision making.

  » Express the values and purposes that are corporately shared.

  » Ensure equity between peoples and projects at many different sites.

  » Provide accountability which safeguards integrity.

  Responsible decision making within a community assumes that there are mature individuals with a commitment to these common purposes and that open communication exists between the people involved. When these elements are present, most decision making should be done by the people

Empowering People for Freedom, Wholeness, and Justice (continued)

who are responsible to implement the decisions. All decisions must take into consideration the local context and the unique people, relationships, and project conditions that are present.

• *Wages should be fair.*

When development work involves employment, the employee should be compensated equitably in relation to their contribution toward the success or profitability of the project.

• *Training programs should include teaching on the importance of stewardship and giving.*

The need for people to give to God, to others and to their community should be made explicit in the development process. Each person's self-identity as a contributor should be reinforced and the intrinsic connection between receiving and giving (Luke 6.38) should be established.

6.3 Development work must discourage the inclination toward dependency.

Explanation

Development emphasizes that each person should be trained and equipped to achieve their potential to be self-sustaining and self-directing. Creating or nurturing dependency undercuts the deep human need to be a co-creator with God in using our gifts to honor him, and finding our significance and place in the world. Dependency can occur from either end of the people-helping relationship; the developer can create a sense of his or her own indispensability which leads to dependency, or the trainee can easily refuse to progress and grow on to interdependence and depth. Dependency pollutes the process of authentic development by creating unhealthy relationships which damage the trainee's initiative and self-motivation.

Implications

• *Trainees must be required to demonstrated initiative.*

The basic rule of thumb is "Don't do for people what they can do for themselves-even if it means that the project (or training) will go slowly" (Hoke and Voorhies 1989, 224). When too much is done for the people who

Empowering People for Freedom, Wholeness, and Justice (continued)

are being assisted, the developer has taken from the trainees the opportunity to learn from their mistakes. Dependency, even when resulting from a spirit of benevolence and sympathy, inevitably stunts the growth of those who are so affected.

- *Development should avoid the extremes of authoritarian paternalism, on the one hand, and non-directive laissez-faire(ism) on the other.*

Developers, by definition, are leaders, and cannot avoid their responsibility to mentor, train, teach, and provide direction to those they serve. Maintaining complete decision-making control, however, does not foster interdependent relationships. While close accountability is essential in the earliest stages of training, development workers must recognize the need to modify strategies and involvement based on the competency and ongoing progress of the learners.[5]

- *Projects should help trainees gain control of their own destiny.*

Projects must be regularly evaluated to insure that they are not keeping people dependent on long-term employment by WIS. Projects which equip people to gain employment with existing businesses or start businesses of their own are the goal.

Wholeness (*Shalom*) is the personal and communal experience of peace, abundance, goodness, soundness, well-being, and belonging. Wholeness is founded on *righteousness* (right relationships with God and man), *truth* (right beliefs about God and man), and *holiness* (right actions before God and man). *Shalom* is a gift of God and a sign of his Kingdom's presence.

7.1 Development should create an environment where cooperative relationships can flourish.

<u>Explanation</u>

Development that leads to wholeness acknowledges that human activity takes place in community. The web of relationships that occurs in the work environment (e.g. trainer to trainee, co-worker to co-worker,etc.), must reflect our values of Christian community.

[5] *For a discussion of the Hersey-Blanchard training model that tailors leadership style to the competencies and attitudes of the trainee see* **Leadership Research** *(Klopfenstein, 1995)*

7. World Impact's Development Work Is Committed to Wholeness.

Empowering People for Freedom, Wholeness, and Justice (continued)

Implications

- *People are not means to an end.*

  Development seeks, first of all, to develop people. This will necessarily involve equipping them (and holding them accountable to) accomplishing tasks. However, it is the maturing of the person, not the completion of the task that is always the primary end of development work.

- *All people in the development process should work for each other as if they are working for Christ himself.*

  Colossians 3.23-24 reminds us that our work is ultimately directed toward and rewarded by Christ. Development projects must operationalize this principle. This suggests that our work must be done with excellence, integrity, diligence, meekness, love and whatever other virtues are necessary for proper service to God.

- *Relational dynamics must be taken seriously.*

  A development project which produces an excellent product and equips people with marketable skills, but which is characterized by disharmony or disunity among its employees has not achieved its goal. The developer must seek to develop genuine community within the workplace.

7.2 Development activities should demonstrate the truth of the Gospel.

Explanation

1 John 3:18 exhorts us to love not merely with words or tongue, "but with actions and in truth." The love of Christ is given not to "souls" but to whole persons. Development activities should minister unashamedly to the whole person and should serve as evangelism by example. Development work functions as a sign of the Kingdom by enabling people, families, and\or communities to experience the love and care of Christ. This suggests that development workers must know Christ intimately and be able to communicate his love to others.

Empowering People for Freedom, Wholeness, and Justice (continued)

Implications

- *Development projects may emphasize mental, physical, social, or economic development.*

  All aspects of human need are of concern to the development worker. As the development worker's love for people takes shape in concrete actions, it should be their intent that people "may see your good deeds and praise your Father in heaven." (Matt. 5.16).

- *Development workers should be maturing disciples of Christ who are actively engaged in ongoing spiritual growth.*

  Who we are is more important than what we do. Only as development workers are actively seeking to live in Christ's love and listen to his Spirit, will they effectively communicate his love to those they work with.

- *Development workers must receive care for their own physical, mental, emotional, and spiritual health and development.*

  Development workers face unique pressures in dealing with human need. They often feel particular stress from standing in between, and identifying with, both the interests of the particular people they serve and the organization they represent (See Hiebert 1989, 83). Physical, emotional or spiritual burn-out is an ever present possibility. Therefore, it is important that development workers give adequate time and attention to maintaining their own health so that they can continue to effectively minister to the needs of others.

- *Development workers need to be specifically equipped in evangelism and an understanding of missions.*

  Christian development workers usually understand that development and evangelism should work in partnership, but are often undertrained in evangelism (See Hoke and Voorhies 1989). Development workers also need to receive general training in missions and management in addition to being trained for their specific task of development (See Pickett and Hawthorne 1992, D218-19) since many of their daily tasks require an understanding of these disciplines.

Empowering People for Freedom, Wholeness, and Justice (continued)

7.3 *Development activities should be above reproach.*

Explanation

Wholeness and holiness are inseparable concepts. The way in which development work is conducted will have a profound impact on its ability to effect transformation. For development work to contribute to the wholeness, soundness, and well-being of people it must take special care to sustain integrity in word and deed.

Implications

- *Development projects should maintain high ethical standards.*

  Lack of adequate funds or personnel and the pressures of immediate human need can tempt us to "cut corners" in the way we develop and administrate projects. This temptation must be resisted. Our product cannot be artificially separated from our process. Development projects must serve as a witness to the government, society at large, and the people they train through adherence to high ethical standards of business conduct.

- *Development projects must work within the framework of our 501(c)(3) non-profit status.*

  State and Federal laws limit the ability of non-profits to create situations where individuals directly receive wealth and resources from the corporation. (This prevents individuals inside and outside of the organization from abusing the non-profit status for personal gain). As programs are created to empower people and share resources, the development workers must make sure that they are structured in such a way that they fall within the legal guidelines.

- *Appeals to donors must not motivate by guilt, overstate the need, promise unrealistic results, or demean the dignity of aid recipients.*

  Compressing the complexity of human need and relationships into an appeal to donors is a difficult and complicated task. It is, however, necessary and important work. Development workers in the field should take personal responsibility for relaying needs and vision in an accurate manner to those involved in publishing printed materials about a project.

Empowering People for Freedom, Wholeness, and Justice (continued)

Justice results from a recognition that all things belong to God and should be shared in accordance with his liberality and impartiality. Biblical justice is concerned both with equitable treatment and with the restoration of right relationship. It abhors oppression, prejudice and inequality because it understands that these separate people from each other and from God. Development which is based on justice is an important step toward repairing damaged relationships between individuals, classes and cultures which may harbor suspicion and ill-will toward one another. Development work seeks to engender right actions which lead to right relationships.

8.1 Development is rooted in a biblical understanding of God as Creator and Ruler of the universe which demands that all things be reconciled in him.

Explanation

God has delegated to humanity the responsibility to be stewards of his world. This understanding manifests itself in concern for three broad categories of relationship: relations with God, relations with others, and relations with the environment (See Elliston 1989, *Transformation*, 176). Although these relationships were broken by the entrance of sin in the world, God's kingdom rule now demands their restoration.

Development recognizes that until the fullness of the Kingdom of Christ is manifested, there will inevitably be poverty, exploitation, and misery caused by sin's perversion of these three areas of relationship. This realization, neither paralyzes nor discourages authentic Christian development. While understanding the nature of moral evil in the world, authentic development seeks to demonstrate models of justice and reconciliation which reflect the justice of Christ's Kingdom.

Implications

- *Development intends to move people toward right relationship with God.*

   Authentic reconciliation between people is based on their mutual reconciliation with God. Although "common grace" and the "image of God" provide a ground for some degree of reconciliation between all people, it is ultimately in right relationship with God through Christ that the most profound and lasting form of reconciliation can occur. Therefore,

8. World Impact's Development Work Is Committed to Justice

development work is eager to assist in preparing people for hearing the Gospel by witnessing to its truth and living out its implications.

• *Reconciliation between individuals, classes, and cultures is a key value.*

Development will inevitably involve new ways of power-sharing, using resources, making decisions, enforcing policy, and relating to others. There is a need to innovate rather than simply imitate existing models. It is extremely important that the viewpoints of peoples from different classes and cultures be represented in the planning of any development project.

• *Development projects must not be wasteful of resources or harmful to the physical environment.*

God's command to humankind is to recognize his ownership, and neither exploit nor destroy his earth, but to tend and care for it. Stewardship involves using the earth's resources to glorify him and meet the needs of our neighbors while keeping in mind our responsibility to future generations. Development must be sustainable, i.e., it must not simply consume resources but cultivate them as well.

8.2 Development recognizes the systemic and institutional foundations of producing wealth and experiencing poverty.

Explanation

The Bible delineates various moral vices that can lead to poverty in the lives of individuals (e.g., laziness, sloth, neglect of responsibility, cf. Prov. 6; Prov. 24, etc.), However, it is also clear that poverty can be caused by large scale societal and economic factors that create conditions of need, oppression, and want (cf. Isa. 1; Isa. 54, Amos 4, 5, etc.). Even a cursory reading of Scripture reveals that throughout biblical history the prophets condemned certain practices of business, politics, law, industry, and even religion that contributed to the imbalances among various groups within society, and led to the oppression of the poor. Development seeks to be prophetic by affirming that God is committed to the poor and the needy, and will not tolerate their oppression indefinitely. Development is not naive. It does not attribute all poverty in society to individual moral vice. On the contrary, struggling against injustice demands that people recognize the ever-present possibility of demonic influence in human structures (1 John 5.19).

Empowering People for Freedom, Wholeness, and Justice (continued)

Implications

- *Spiritual warfare is a key component of the development process.*

  Ephesians 6.12 reminds us that "we do not wrestle against flesh and blood, but against the rulers, against the authorities, against the cosmic powers over this present darkness, against the spiritual forces of evil in the heavenly places." Development work that does not intentionally and regularly set aside time for prayer and other spiritual disciplines is unlikely to effect lasting change. Development workers should have a plan for spiritual warfare that is as significant a focus as the plan for the development work itself.

  Development workers should also realize that their projects will experience spiritual attack. The accumulation of money or power within a project can be entry points for the perversion of that project despite its best intentions. Relationships between development project leaders, or between development workers and those they are training, can be twisted through the stress of conflict, jealousy, miscommunication, and cultural differences. Both personal relationships and institutional programs need to be protected from spiritual forces that would corrupt or destroy them. This requires an ongoing commitment to spiritual warfare, and to personal and corporate holiness.[6]

- *Development work should challenge unjust practices.*

  Development workers must prepare people to speak out against unjust practices in ways which demonstrate both the love and justice of God. While the non-profit organization is not itself a forum for political advocacy, it is responsible to train people to value justice and to make decisions in a moral context. In the marketplace, workers will be confronted by individual and systemic injustices and should be trained to respond to them in a manner which honors Christ and the values of his Kingdom.

- *The role of the Church in development must not be neglected.*

  Ephesians 2.14 records that it is "Christ himself" who is our peace and who has "destroyed the barrier, the dividing wall of hostility" between Jew and Gentiles. Reconciliation is rooted in the person and work of Christ and thus

[6] *See Thomas McAlpine,* **Facing the Powers** *(McAlpine, 1991) for a helpful discussion of ways in which Reformed, Anabaptist, Charismatic, and Social Science perspectives share both differing perspectives and common ground in understanding and confronting spiritual powers.*

Empowering People for Freedom, Wholeness, and Justice (continued)

the importance of Christ's body, the Church, cannot be overlooked. Missionary development projects should both flow out of and result in dynamic churches.

8.3 Development does not seek to guarantee equality of outcome, but equality of opportunity.

Explanation

Development concentrates on providing an environment in which people can learn the importance and disciplines of work, gain skills which enhance the value of their work, and apply the disciplines and skills they acquire. However, no human endeavor is exempt from the moral force of our ability to choose, i.e., to decide whether or not to fully use the gifts, opportunities, and potentials we have been given. Because of variations of motivation, effort and preparation, differences in incomes are inevitable, and ought to be expected. Development programs should both teach and reward initiative.

Implications

- *Each trainee plays a critical role in their own success.*

  While the developers can offer a vast amount of expertise and aid in creating wealth for the trainees, many of the most important attributes necessary for prolonged success are controlled by the trainees. Without the requisite vision, energy, and commitment to do the work for long enough time so profits can be seen, success will not occur. These qualities arise from the drive and conviction of the trainees, not merely from the availability of the developers. Because of this, development cannot guarantee the success of all those involved in the project.

- *Faithful stewardship should lead to increased responsibility.*

  All development projects should have a plan for rewarding faithfulness, skill development, and diligence. Justice demands that increased effort lead to increased reward.

Empowering People for Freedom, Wholeness, and Justice (continued)

8.4 Development workers should respect cultural differences and strive to create a training style that is culturally conducive to those being empowered.

Explanation

Every human culture is "a blueprint that gives the individuals of a society a way of explaining and coping with life. It teaches people how to think, act and respond appropriately in any given situation. It allows people to work together based on a common understanding of reality. It organizes ways of thinking and acting into forms that can be passed on to others" (Cornett 1991, 2). Culture shapes every form of human activity from the observable behaviors (language, dress, food, etc.) to the internal thoughts and attitudes (thinking styles, definitions of beauty and worth, etc.). Understanding how a culture perceives reality, what it values, and how it functions is fundamental information for the development worker.

Although all human cultures are affected by sinful perspectives, attitudes and behaviors which must be confronted by the Gospel, human cultures themselves are celebrated by the Scriptures. The apostles confirmed that becoming a Christian did not entail having to change one's original culture (Acts 15). The vision of God's Kingdom from Old Testament (Micah 4) to New (Rev. 7.9) involves people from every nation, language and ethnicity. Missionaries from Paul onward have contextualized the Gospel, putting eternal truth in forms that could be understood and practiced by people of diverse cultures (See Cornett 1991, 6-9). Development workers, likewise, must respect cultural differences and seek to contextualize their instruction and resources (See Elliston, Hoke and Voorhies 1989).

Development workers have a unique interest in empowering groups that have been marginalized, oppressed or neglected by the larger society. This will frequently involve working with groups or individuals that are distinct from the dominant culture. Development work will effectively empower immigrants, unassimilated people groups, or people who have been victimized by race or class discrimination, only if it understands and respects the cultural distinctives of these groups.

Finally, development workers must prepare people to live and work in a pluralistic society. Learning how to successfully relate to customers and co-workers from other cultures has become a key component of job training. Although development work must start with the cultural context of those being assisted, it must also enable those workers to respect other cultures and to successfully work in the larger society.

Empowering People for Freedom, Wholeness, and Justice (continued)

Implications

- *Development workers should understand the culture(s) and sub-culture(s) of the people they work with.*

  Development workers should, first of all, gain a basic understanding of the nature of human culture and of strategies for developing effective cross-cultural training relationships.[7] They should gain the fundamental skills necessary for working in the cross-cultural environment (language acquisition, etc.). It is highly desirable for the development worker to have a mentor either from the culture or who is an experienced observer of the culture to assist in the training process.

- *The work environment should be functionally appropriate and aesthetically pleasing when viewed from the perspective of the culture(s) that work or do business there.*

  All human cultures desire environments that combine functionality with beauty. There is significant variation, however, in how beauty and functionality are defined, prioritized and applied from one culture to another. The physical environment in which the development project occurs should take cultural concerns into account.

- *Development workers should be sensitive to how conflict is handled by the culture of the people they work among.*

  Conflict is an inevitable part of working together. It can be a healthy opportunity for growth if handled correctly. Cultural differences, however, can sabotage the process of conflict management. The development worker must take cultural attitudes toward directness/indirectness, shame/guilt, individualism/collectivism, etc. seriously and adapt their conflict management style to reflect those concerns. They must also take seriously their responsibility to prepare people from sub-cultures to work within the dominant culture.

- *Development workers should be sensitive to roles or work that is considered degrading by the culture.*

  Although all honest work carries dignity before God, cultural perceptions of role and status have tremendous power to shape attitudes. Whenever possible, work should be chosen that is not repugnant to the culture. If this

[7] *Basic resources for gaining an understanding of culture include* **The Missionary and Culture** *(Cornett 1991),* **Beyond Culture** *(Hall 1976),* **Christianity Confronts Culture** *(Mayers 1974),* **Ministering Cross-Culturally** *(Lingenfelter and Mayers 1986) and* **Cross-Cultural Conflicts: Building Relationships for Effective Ministry** *(Elmer 1993).*

Empowering People for Freedom, Wholeness, and Justice (continued)

is not possible, careful preparation and training should be done to ensure that each person understands the necessity and dignity of the work involved. In some cases it may be necessary to challenge the cultural value system (see Miller, 1989) but this should be done sensitively and with adequate preparation and involvement of the trainees.

- *Developers should prepare trainees for situations that they are likely to encounter in the workplace.*

People from event-oriented cultures, for example, need to understand the time-oriented culture that defines American business practices. Helping workers learn skills and disciplines for success in the larger society is an important part of the training process.

8.5 *The goal of development is to glorify God through excellence and service, not merely to make a profit.*

Explanation

In the ethics of the corporate world, the highest indicator of success is usually the profitability of the business. However, development work that is informed by kingdom values involves a broader vision. Development seeks to emphasize the importance of people-nurturing and training and the production of a quality product that meets human need.

Since producing quality Christian and professional leadership models is a high aim of our development efforts, we must unashamedly emphasize both external profits as well as internal gains. On the one hand, a business, if it is to survive, must be profitable and able to stand on its on. On the other hand, we must strive to produce men and women who are spiritually mature as well as professionally oriented and technically competent. The creation of wealth is not an end in itself; it is a by-product of engaging in business with an eye toward excellence, in the name of Christ.

Empowering People for Freedom, Wholeness, and Justice (continued)

Implications

- *No skill will be taught or product produced simply because it is valued by society or likely to produce a profit.*

  All skills and products must be consistent with the aims of justice, peace and wholeness that characterize the kingdom rule of Christ. Skills and modes of production that degrade human dignity and products that promote injustice, inequity, or human misery are not to be considered fitting for development regardless of their acceptance by the society at large.

- *The aim of development work must not only be to help people obtain and generate resources but also to help them commit to using those resources on behalf of the Kingdom of God.*

  Helping people to obtain education, skills or wealth is ultimately unproductive if these things are not placed at God's service and the service of others. Good development projects will offer people the opportunity to serve God not only with the profits from their labor but through the work itself. Developers must teach and model that work is an opportunity for service to God (Col. 3.23-24).

9. The Need for Application

Each of the points listed above has a section titled "Explanation" and a section titled "Implications." However, for the paper to be complete one more step is necessary. Every implication must be accompanied by a series of *applications*. These applications should be created by development workers in the field, and structured for the unique needs of the local situation.

In creating these applications, the following guidelines should be followed:

- Each local ministry should thoroughly review the "Implications" sections and decide on specific steps which will enable them to apply these principles to their particular development project.

- These steps should be developed in a way that involves the people most affected by each development project.

- Once finalized, the application steps should be committed to writing.

- These applications should be regularly taught and reviewed.

Empowering People for Freedom, Wholeness, and Justice (continued)

- These applications should be included in each regularly scheduled evaluation done by the project.

- Following each scheduled evaluation, there should be a revising and updating of these applications based on what has been learned in experience.

Appendix A

Selected Quotes on the Role of Development Work within the Mission Agency

Christian social transformation differs from secular relief and development in that it serves in an integrated, symbiotic relationship with other ministries of the Church, including evangelism and church planting (Elliston 1989, 172).

My experience with scores of ministries among the poor has taught me that economic projects, when used as entrees into communities, do not facilitate church planting or growth. . . . the two goals—relief and church planting—are different. They are both Christian, and at times compatible. But many times they do not support each other well at all. . . . It appears that where workers enter a community with a priority to proclaim, many deeds of mercy, acts of justice and signs of power will occur. From these the church will be established. But when workers enter with a priority of dealing with economic need, they may assist the people economically very well, but they rarely establish as church. There is a time for both, and there are life callings to do both, but they must be distinguished (Grigg 1992, 163-64).

Avoid institutions if possible at the beachhead stage (community development programs unrelated to church planting, schools, clinics, etc.); they will come later. In Honduras we developed community development work but it grew out of the churches, not vice versa. We taught obedience to the great commandment of loving our neighbor in a practical way. A poverty program can aid church planting if the two are integrated by the Holy Spirit. But churches dependant on charitable institutions are almost always dominated by the foreign missionary and seldom reproduce (Patterson 1992, D-80).

Empowering People for Freedom, Wholeness, and Justice (continued)

All too often native pastors and churches have become preoccupied with ministries that attract Western dollars (such as orphan work) while neglecting more basic pastoral care and evangelism. Even development work, if not wisely administered, can hinder church growth (Ott 1993, 289).

There is a very real danger of recruiting missionary-evangelists primarily on the basis of their abilities and expertise. "Whatever your special interest is, we can use it in our mission"— this is an all-too-common approach to recruitment. As a result, many workers become frustrated when their special ability is not fully utilized; they react by simply "doing their thing" and contributing only indirectly to the task of planting growing churches. Consequently, the so-called secondary or supporting ministries have a way of becoming primary and actually eclipsing the central task! (Hesselgrave 1980, 112).

It is unfortunate that Christian service and witness often seem to be competing concerns in Christian outreach when, in fact, both are biblical and complementary. . . . One reason for this tension is that service enterprises such as hospitals and educational institutions have a way of preempting finances and energies so that evangelism and witness tend to get crowded out (Hesselgrave 1980 p. 328).

Since we believe in the unity of the Bible, we must say that 'The Great Commission is not an isolated command, (but) a natural outflow of the character of God. . . The missionary purpose and thrust of God. . .' Thus, we should not take the Great Commandment and the Great Commission as though they are mutually exclusive. We should take the Great Commandment—to love others—and the Great Commission—to preach—together, integrated in the mission of Jesus Christ, for it is the same Lord, who commanded and commissioned the same disciples and his followers. Therefore, as Di Gangi says, 'to communicate the gospel effectively we must obey the great commandment as well as the great commission' (Cho 1985, 229).

Empowering People for Freedom, Wholeness, and Justice (continued)

Works Cited

Cho, J. Chongham. "The Mission of the Church." See Nicholls, 1985.

Cornett, Terry G., ed. "The Missionary and Culture." *World Impact Ministry Resources*. Los Angeles: World Impact Mission Studies Training Paper, 1991.

Dayton, Donald W. *Discovering an Evangelical Heritage*. 1976. Peabody, MA: Hendrickson, 1988.

Elliston, Edgar J., ed. *Christian Relief and Development: Developing Workers for Effective Ministry*. Dallas: Word Publishing, 1989.

------. "Christian Social Transformation Distinctives." See Elliston, 1989.

Elliston, Edgar J., Stephen J. Hoke, and Samuel Voorhies. "Issues in Contextualizing Christian Leadership." See Elliston, 1989.

Grigg, Viv. "Church of the Poor." *Discipling the City*. 2nd ed. Ed. Roger S. Greenway. Grand Rapids: Baker Book House, 1992.

Hall, Edward T. *Beyond Culture*. Garden City, NY: Anchor Books, 1976.

Hesselgrave, David. *Planting Churches Cross-Culturally: A Guide for Home and Foreign Missions*. Grand Rapids: Baker Book House, 1980.

Hiebert, Paul G. "Evangelism, Church, and Kingdom." See Van Engen, et. al., 1993.

------. "Anthropological Insights for Whole Ministries." See Elliston, 1989.

Hoke, Stephen J. and Samuel J. Voorhies. "Training Relief and Development Workers in the Two-Thirds World." See Elliston, 1989.

Klopfenstein, David E. and Dorothy A. Klopfenstein. "Leadership Research." CityGates. 1 (1995): 21-26.

Klopfenstein, David, Dotty Klopfenstein and Bud Williams. *Come Yourselves Apart: Christian Leadership in the Temporary Community*. Azusa, CA: Holysm Publishing, 1993.

Ladd, George Eldon. *A Theology of the New Testament*. Grand Rapids: Wm. B. Eerdmans, 1974.

Empowering People for Freedom, Wholeness, and Justice (continued)

McAlpine, Thomas H. *Facing the Powers: What are the Options?* Monrovia, CA: MARC-World Vision, 1991.

Miller, Darrow L. "The Development Ethic: Hope for a Culture of Poverty." See Elliston, 1989.

Nicholls, Bruce J., ed. *In Word and Deed: Evangelism and Social Responsibility.* Grand Rapids: Wm. B. Eerdmans, 1985.

Ott, Craig. "Let the Buyer Beware." *Evangelical Missions Quarterly,* 29 (1993): 286-291.

Patterson, George. "The Spontaneous Multiplication of Churches." See Winter and Hawthorne, 1992.

Pickett, Robert C. and Steven C. Hawthorne. "Helping Others Help Themselves: Christian Community Development." See Winter and Hawthorne, 1992.

Stott, John. "Twenty Years After Lausanne: Some Personal Reflections." *International Bulletin of Missionary Research.* 19 (1995): 50-55.

Van Engen, Charles, et. al., eds. *The Good News of the Kingdom: Mission Theology for the Third Millennium.* Maryknoll: Orbis Books, 1993.

Verkuyl, Johannes. *Contemporary Missiology: An Introduction.* Grand Rapids: Wm. B. Eerdmans, 1978.

------. "The Biblical Notion of Kingdom: Test of Validity for Theology of Religion." See Van Engen, et. al., 1993.

Winter, Ralph D. and Steven C. Hawthorne, eds. *Perspectives on the World Christian Movement: A Reader.* Rev. ed. Pasadena: William Carey Library, 1992.

APPENDIX 30

Substitute Centers to a Christ-Centered Vision

Goods and Effects Which Our Culture Substitutes as the Ultimate Concern

Rev. Dr. Don L. Davis

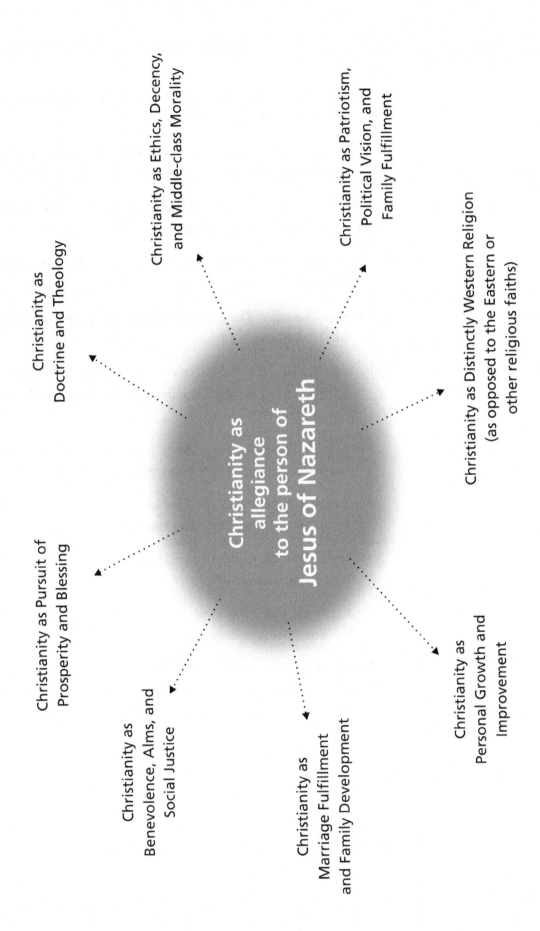

Christianity as
Doctrine and Theology

Christianity as Ethics, Decency,
and Middle-class Morality

Christianity as Patriotism,
Political Vision, and
Family Fulfillment

Christianity as
Distinctly Western Religion
(as opposed to the Eastern or
other religious faiths)

Christianity as
allegiance
to the person of
Jesus of Nazareth

Christianity as Pursuit of
Prosperity and Blessing

Christianity as
Benevolence, Alms, and
Social Justice

Christianity as
Marriage Fulfillment
and Family Development

Christianity as
Personal Growth and
Improvement

APPENDIX 31

Three Contexts of Urban Christian Leadership Development

Rev. Dr. Don L. Davis

Ephesians 4.11 (ESV) - And he himself gave some to be apostles, some prophets, some evangelists, and some pastors and teachers,

12. for the equipping of the saints for the work of ministry, for the edifying of the body of Christ

Three Contexts of Leadership Function

I. Forming, Leading, and Reproducing Dynamic Small Group Life and Ministry
- Inreach (discipling, fellowship, care giving, etc.)
- Outreach (evangelism, service, witness)

II. Facilitating and Reproducing Vital Congregational Life and Ministry

III. Nurturing and Cultivating Inter-congregational Support, Cooperation, and Collaboration

God has appointed leaders in the Church to equip Christians for "the work of the ministry," that they might walk worthy of the Lord in all things, bear abundant fruit in Christ, to win, follow-up, and disciple members within their *oikos* (their family, friends, and associates), and to be zealous in good works to reveal the Kingdom's life

"The Church Assembled"

Small Group

Small Group

Small Group

Congregational Form

According to some biblical linguists, the phrase in the NT for the church in assembly, *en ekklesia*, applies to the local expressions of the people of God when they "come together *as a church*," cf. 1 Cor. 11.18. The people of God can thus be called the "church/assembly," that is, those who by faith in Jesus Christ and his Holy Spirit now represent his called ones in a particular place and locale.

Clusters of churches which band together in partnership for mutual support, refreshment, service, and mission (e.g., Associations, denominations, conferences, etc.)

Small Group

Any recognized part of a larger assembly, e.g., Cell group, Women's study, Prayer group, BibleStudy, Sunday School class, Street Ministry team, Prison outreach team, etc.

The church together as one, from house church to mega-church (i.e., Any distinct gathering of believers who identify with one another, give and serve together, under one pastoral head, where their presence and allegiance are shown and known)

The Locale Church

Congregational Form

Small Group

Small Group

God has given to the Church leaders of unique gifting - apostles, prophets, evangelists, pastors and teachers in order that the "Church Assembled" might be edified and equipped to fulfill its mission and ministry as it scatters, as individuals, into the world. **Luke 10.2-3 (ESV)**, And he said to them, "The harvest is plentiful but the laborers are few. Therefore pray earnestly to the Lord of the harvest to send out laborers into his harvest. **[3]** Go your way; behold, I am sending you out as lambs in the midst of wolves").

Less than all of us

"Us" (My church)

More than all of us

APPENDIX 32

The Complexity of Difference: Race, Culture, Class

Don L. Davis and Terry Cornett

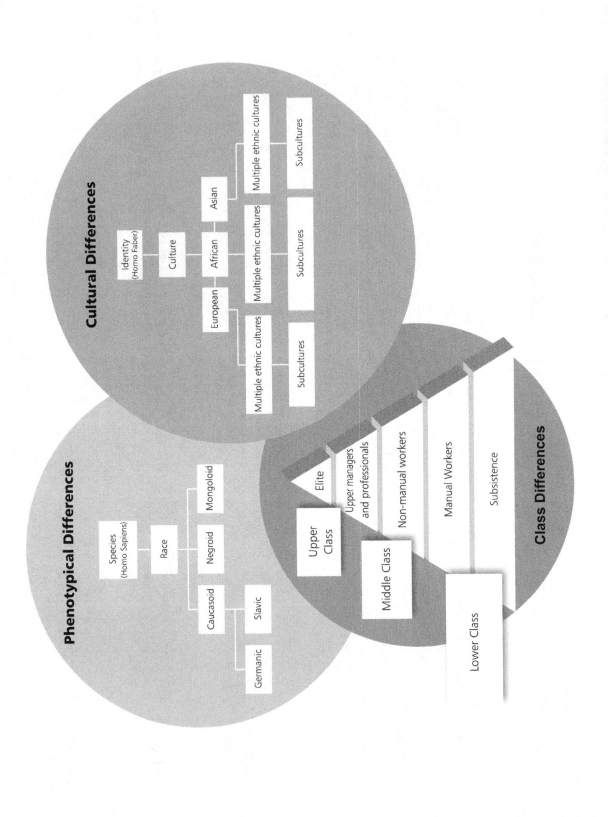

Cultural Differences

Identity (Homo Faber)

Culture

European   African   Asian

Multiple ethnic cultures   Multiple ethnic cultures   Multiple ethnic cultures

Subcultures   Subcultures   Subcultures

Phenotypical Differences

Species (Homo Sapiens)

Race

Caucasoid   Negroid   Mongoloid

Germanic   Slavic

Class Differences

Upper Class — Elite
Upper managers and professionals

Middle Class — Non-manual workers
Manual Workers

Lower Class — Subsistence

A P P E N D I X   3 3

Investment, Empowerment, and Assessment

How Leadership as Representation Provides Freedom to Innovate

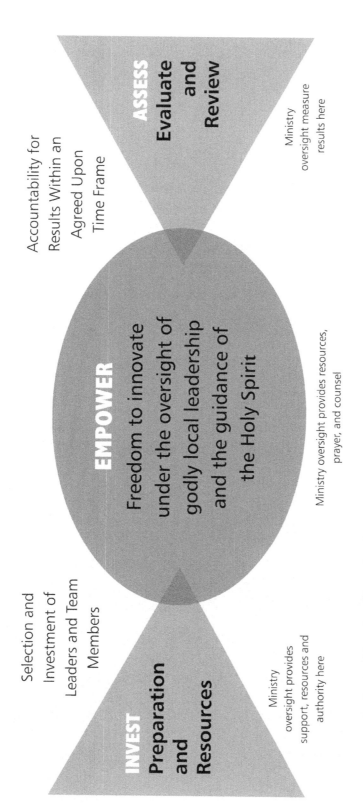

ASSESS

Evaluate and Review

Accountability for Results Within an Agreed Upon Time Frame

Ministry oversight measure results here

EMPOWER

Freedom to innovate under the oversight of godly local leadership and the guidance of the Holy Spirit

Ministry oversight provides resources, prayer, and counsel

Selection and Investment of Leaders and Team Members

Ministry oversight provides support, resources and authority here

INVEST

Preparation and Resources

Evaluation by sending authority
Review of results in light of task
Faithfulness and loyalty assessed
Overall evaluation of plan and strategy
Critical evaluation of leadership performance
Formal determination of operation's "success"
Reassignment in light of evaluation

Formal leadership selection
Acknowledgment of personal call
Determination of task and assignment
Training in spiritual warfare
Authorization to act defined and given
Necessary resources given and logistics planned
Commissioning: deputization formally recognized

APPENDIX 34

The *Oikos* Factor

Spheres of Relationship and Influence

Rev. Dr. Don L. Davis

Survey: 42,000 asked: Who or what
was responsible for your coming to
Christ and your church:

Special need	1-2%
Walk-in	2-3%
Pastor	5-6%
Visitation	1-2%
Sunday School	4-5%
Evangelistic crusade/TV	1/2%
Church program	2-3%
Friend or relative	75-90%!!

--Church Growth, Inc. Monrovia, CA

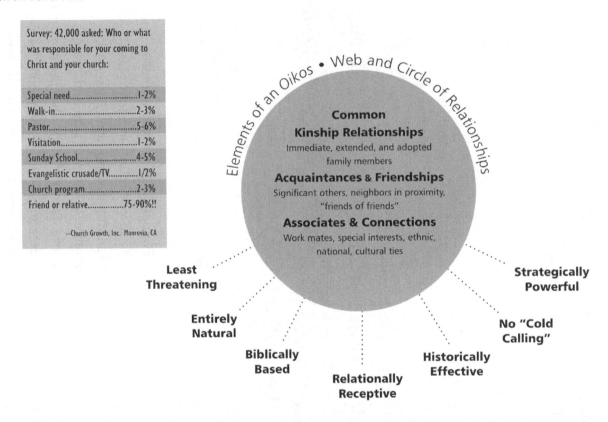

Elements of an Oikos • Web and Circle of Relationships

Common Kinship Relationships
Immediate, extended, and adopted family members

Acquaintances & Friendships
Significant others, neighbors in proximity, "friends of friends"

Associates & Connections
Work mates, special interests, ethnic, national, cultural ties

Least Threatening

Strategically Powerful

Entirely Natural

No "Cold Calling"

Biblically Based

Historically Effective

Relationally Receptive

Oikos (household) in the OT

"A household usually contained four generations, including men, married women, unmarried daughters, slaves of both sexes, persons without citizenship, and "sojourners," or resident foreign workers." *– Hans Walter Wolff, Anthology of the Old Testament.*

Oikos (household) in the NT

Evangelism and disciple making in our NT narratives are often described as following the flow of the relational networks of various people within their *oikoi* (households), that is, those natural lines of connection in which they resided and lived (c.f., Mark 5.19; Luke 19.9; John 4.53; 1.41-45, etc.). Andrew to Simon (John 1.41-45), and both Cornelius (Acts 10-11) and the Philippian jailer (Acts 16) are notable cases of evangelism and discipling through *oikoi*.

Oikos (household) among the urban poor

While great differences exist between cultures, kinship relationships, special interest groups, and family structures among urban populations, it is clear that urbanites connect with others far more on the basis of connections through relationships, friendships, and family than through proximity and neighborhood alone. Often times the closest friends of urban poor dwellers are not immediately close-by in terms of neighborhood; family and friends may dwell blocks, even miles away. Taking the time to study the precise linkages of relationships among the dwellers in a certain area can prove extremely helpful in determining the most effective strategies for evangelism and disciple making in inner city contexts.

APPENDIX 35

Targeting Unreached Groups in Churched Neighborhoods

Mission Frontiers

Many Different Peoples!

Many Homogenous Congregations

**The Extent of Normal "Outreach":
Incorporating and Gathering
According to Culture**

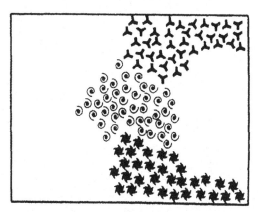

**"So Close and Yet so Far Away":
The Unreached, Unaffected
Neighbors**

APPENDIX 36

Re-presenting Messiah

Don L. Davis

"Gentilization" of modern Christian faith expressions

Contextualization: freedom in Christ to enculturate the gospel
Common modern portrayal of Messianic hope as Gentile faith
Tendency of tradition/culture to usurp biblical authority
Present day eclipse of biblical framework by "captivities"

Strange fires on the altar: examples of socio-cultural captivities

Nationalism
Capitalism
Scientific rationalism
Denominationalism

Personal existentialism
Asceticism/moralism
Ethnocentrism
Nuclear family life

Jesus' critique of socio-cultural captivity

Bondage to religious tradition, Matt. 15.3-9
Ignorance of Scripture and God's power, Matt. 22.29
Zealous effort without knowledge, Romans 10.1-3

Hermeneutic habits that lead toward a syncretistic faith

Selective choice of texts
Tradition viewed as canon
Cultural readings of texts
Preaching and teaching based on eisegesis and audience
Uncritical approaches to one's own doctrine and practice
Apologetics for socio-cultural identity

"Paradigm paralysis" & biblical faith

Blind to one's own historical conditionedness
Limited vantage point and perspective
Privilege and power: political manipulation
Inability to receive criticism
Persecution of opposite viewpoints and new interpretations of faith

Rediscover the Hebraic roots of the biblical Messianic hope (return)

Recognize the socio-cultural captivity of Christian profession (exile)

Re-present Messiah Yeshua with passion and clarity

with fidelity to Scripture in sync with historic orthodoxy without cultural distortion without theological bias

Rediscovery of the Jewish origins of biblical faith, John 4.22

YHWH as God of lovingkindness in covenant faithfulness

Messianic fulfillment in OT: prophecy, type, story, ceremony, and symbol

Hebraic roots of the Promise: YHWH as a Warrior God

People of Israel as community of Messianic hope

Psalms and Prophets emphasize divine rulership of Messiah

Tracing the Seed
Seed of the Woman, Gen. 3.15
Seed of Shem, Gen. 9.26-27
Seed of Abraham, Gen. 12.3
Seed of Isaac and Jacob, Gen. 26.2-5; 28.10-15
Seed of Judah, Gen. 49.10
Seed of David, 2 Sam. 7

Suffering Servant of YHWH: humiliation and lowliness of God's Davidic king

Glimmers of Gentile salvation and global transformation

Live the adventure of NT apocalyptic myth (possession)

Apocalyptic as the "mother tongue and native language" of the apostles and early Church as eschatological community

Yeshua Messiah as the Cosmic Warrior: YHWH as God who wins ultimate victory over his enemies

Messiah Yeshua as Anointed One and Binder of the Strong Man: the Messianic Age to come inaugurated in Jesus of Nazareth

"Already/Not Yet" Kingdom orientation: The Reign of God as both manifest but not consummated

The Evidence and Guarantee of the Age to Come: The Spirit as down payment, first fruits, and seal of God

APPENDIX 37

How to PLANT a Church

Don L. Davis

Evangelize

Mark 16.15-18 (ESV) - And he said to them, "Go into all the world and proclaim the gospel to the whole creation. [16] Whoever believes and is baptized will be saved, but whoever does not believe will be condemned. [17] And these signs will accompany those who believe: in my name they will cast out demons; they will speak in new tongues; [18] they will pick up serpents with their hands; and if they drink any deadly poison, it will not hurt them; they will lay their hands on the sick, and they will recover."

I. Prepare

Luke 24.46-49 (ESV) - and he said to them, "Thus it is written, that the Christ should suffer and on the third day rise from the dead, [47] and that repentance and forgiveness of sins should be proclaimed in his name to all nations, beginning from Jerusalem. [48] You are witnesses of these things. [49] And behold, I am sending the promise of my Father upon you. But stay in the city until you are clothed with power from on high."

A. Form a church-plant team.

B. Pray.

C. Select a target area and population.

D. Do demographic and ethnographic studies.

II. Launch

Gal. 2.7-10 (ESV) - On the contrary, when they saw that I had been entrusted with the gospel to the uncircumcised, just as Peter had been entrusted with the gospel to the circumcised [8] (for he who worked through Peter for his apostolic ministry to the circumcised worked also through me for mine to the Gentiles), [9] and when James and Cephas and John, who seemed to be pillars, perceived the grace that was given to me, they gave the right hand of fellowship to Barnabas and me, that we should go to the Gentiles and they to the circumcised. [10] Only, they asked us to remember the poor, the very thing I was eager to do.

How to PLANT a Church (continued)

A. Recruit and train volunteers.

B. Conduct evangelistic events and door-to-door evangelism.

Eph. 4.11-16 (ESV) - And he gave the apostles, the prophets, the evangelists, the pastors and teachers, [12] to equip the saints for the work of ministry, for building up the body of Christ, [13] until we all attain to the unity of the faith and of the knowledge of the Son of God, to mature manhood, to the measure of the stature of the fullness of Christ, [14] so that we may no longer be children, tossed to and fro by the waves and carried about by every wind of doctrine, by human cunning, by craftiness in deceitful schemes. [15] Rather, speaking the truth in love, we are to grow up in every way into him who is the head, into Christ, [16] from whom the whole body, joined and held together by every joint with which it is equipped, when each part is working properly, makes the body grow so that it builds itself up in love.

Equip

III. Assemble

Acts 2.41-47 (ESV) - So those who received his word were baptized, and there were added that day about three thousand souls. [42] And they devoted themselves to the apostles' teaching and fellowship, to the breaking of bread and the prayers. [43] And awe came upon every soul, and many wonders and signs were being done through the apostles. [44] And all who believed were together and had all things in common. [45] And they were selling their possessions and belongings and distributing the proceeds to all, as any had need. [46] And day by day, attending the temple together and breaking bread in their homes, they received their food with glad and generous hearts, [47] praising God and having favor with all the people. And the Lord added to their number day by day those who were being saved.

A. Form cell groups, Bible studies, etc. to follow up new believers, to continue evangelism, and to identify and train emerging leaders.

B. Announce the birth of a new church to the neighborhood and meet regularly for public worship, instruction and fellowship.

IV. Nurture

1 Thess. 2.5-9 (ESV) - For we never came with words of flattery, as you know, nor with a pretext for greed— God is witness. [6] Nor did we seek glory from people, whether from you or from others, though we could have made demands as apostles of Christ. [7] But we were gentle among you, like a nursing mother taking care of her own children. [8] So, being affectionately desirous of you, we were ready to share with you not only the gospel of God but also our own selves, because you had become very dear to us. [9] For you remember, brothers, our labor and toil: we worked night and day, that we might not be a burden to any of you, while we proclaimed to you the gospel of God.

A. Develop individual and group discipleship.

B. Fill key roles in the church: identify and use spiritual gifts.

Empower

Acts 20.28 (ESV) - Pay careful attention to yourselves and to all the flock, in which the Holy Spirit has made you overseers, to care for the church of God, which he obtained with his own blood.

Acts 20.32(ESV) - And now I commend you to God and to the word of his grace, which is able to build you up and to give you the inheritance among all those who are sanctified.

V. Transition

Titus 1.4-5 (ESV) - To Titus, my true child in a common faith: Grace and peace from God the Father and Christ Jesus our Savior. [5] This is why I left you in Crete, so that you might put what remained into order, and appoint elders in every town as I directed you—

A. Transfer leadership to indigenous leaders so they become self-governing, self-supporting and self-reproducing (appoint elders and pastors).

B. Finalize decisions about denominational or other affiliations.

C. Commission the church.

D. Foster association with World Impact and other urban churches for fellowship, support, and mission ministry.

How to PLANT a Church (continued)

How to PLANT a Church

PREPARE

- Form a church-plant team.

- Pray.

- Select a target area and population.

- Do demographic and ethnographic studies.

LAUNCH

- Recruit and train volunteers

- Conduct evangelistic events and door-to-door evangelism

ASSEMBLE

- Form cell groups, Bible studies, etc. to follow up new believers, to continue evangelism, and to identify and train emerging leaders.

- Announce the birth of a new church to the neighborhood and meet regularly for public worship, instruction and fellowship.

NURTURE

- Develop individual and group discipleship.

- Fill key roles in the church; identify and use spiritual gifts.

TRANSITION

- Transfer leadership to indigenous leaders so they become self-governing, self-supporting and self-reproducing (appoint elders and pastors).

- Finalize decisions about denominational or other affiliations.

- Commission the church.

- Foster association with World Impact and other urban churches for fellowship, support and mission ministry.

Evangelize

Equip

Empower

How to PLANT a Church (continued)

Pauline Precedents From Acts: The Pauline Cycle

1. Missionaries Commissioned: Acts 13.1-4; 15.39-40. Ga. 1.15-16.

2. Audience Contacted: Acts 13.14-16; 14.1; 16.13-15; 17.16-19.

3. Gospel Communicated: Acts 13.17-41; 16.31; Rom. 10.9-14; 2 Tim. 2.8.

4. Hearers Converted: Acts. 13.48; 16.14-15; 20.21; 26.20; 1 Thess. 1.9-10.

5. Believers Congregated: Acts 13.43; 19.9; Rom 16.4-5; 1 Cor. 14.26.

6. Faith Confirmed: Acts 14.21-22; 15.41; Rom 16.17; Col. 1.28; 2 Thess. 2.15; 1 Tim. 1.3.

7. Leadership Consecrated; Acts 14.23; 2 Tim. 2.2; Titus 1.5.

8. Believers Commended; Acts 14.23; 16.40; 21.32 (2 Tim. 4.9 and Titus 3.12 by implication).

9. Relationships Continued: Acts 15.36; 18.23; 1 Cor. 16.5; Eph. 6.21-22; Col. 4.7-8.

10. Sending Churches Convened: Acts 14.26-27; 15.1-4.

The "Pauline Cycle" terminology, stages, and diagram are taken from David J. Hesselgrave, Planting Churches Cross-Culturally, 2nd ed. Grand Rapids: Baker Book House, 2000.

"Evangelize, Equip, and Empower" and "P.L.A.N.T." schemas for church planting taken from Crowns of Beauty: Planting Urban Churches Conference Binder Los Angeles: World Impact Press, 1999.

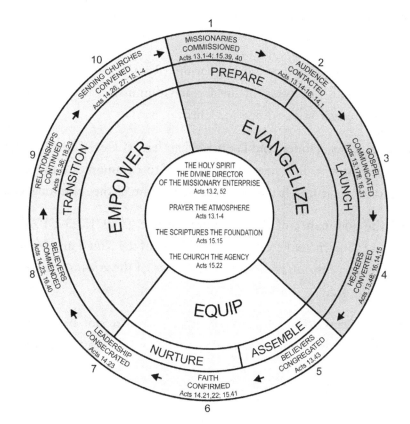

How to PLANT a Church (continued)

Ten Principles of Church Planting

1. **Jesus is Lord.** (Matt. 9.37-38) All church plant activity is made effective and fruitful under the watch care and power of the Lord Jesus, who himself is the Lord of the harvest.

2. **Evangelize, Equip, and Empower unreached people to reach people.** (1 Thess. 1.6-8) Our goal in reaching others for Christ is not only for solid conversion but also for dynamic multiplication; those who are reached must be trained to reach others as well.

3. **Be inclusive: whosoever will may come.** (Rom. 10.12) No strategy should forbid any person or group from entering into the Kingdom through Jesus Christ by faith.

4. **Be culturally neutral: Come just as you are.** (Col. 3.11) The Gospel places no demands on any seeker to change their culture as a prerequisite for coming to Jesus; they may come just as they are.

5. **Avoid a fortress mentality.** (Acts 1.8) The goal of missions is not to create an impregnable castle in the midst of an unsaved community, but a dynamic outpost of the Kingdom which launches a witness for Jesus within and unto the very borders of their world.

6. **Continue to evangelize to avoid stagnation.** (Rom. 1.16-17) Keep looking to the horizons with the vision of the Great Commission in mind; foster an environment of aggressive witness for Christ.

7. **Cross racial, class, gender, and language barriers.** (1 Cor. 9.19-22) Use your freedom in Christ to find new, credible ways to communicate the kingdom message to those farthest from the cultural spectrum of the traditional church.

8. **Respect the dominance of the receiving culture.** (Acts 15.23-29) Allow the Holy Spirit to incarnate the vision and the ethics of the Kingdom of God in the words, language, customs, styles, and experience of those who have embraced Jesus as their Lord.

9. **Avoid dependence.** (Eph. 4.11-16) Neither patronize nor be overly stingy towards the growing congregation; do not underestimate the power of the Spirit in the midst of even the smallest Christian community to accomplish God's work in their community.

How to PLANT a Church (continued)

10. **Think reproducibility.** (2 Tim. 2.2; Phil. 1.18) In every activity and project you initiate, think in terms of equipping others to do the same by maintaining an open mind regarding the means and ends of your missionary endeavors.

Resources for Further Study

Cornett, Terry G. and James D. Parker. *"Developing Urban Congregations: A Framework for World Impact Church Planters."* World Impact Ministry Resources. Los Angeles: World Impact Press, 1991.

Davis, Don L. and Terry G. Cornett. *"An Outline for a Theology of the Church."* Crowns of Beauty: Planting Urban Churches (Training Manual). Los Angeles: World Impact Press, 1999.

Hesselgrave, David J. *Planting Churches Cross Culturally: A Biblical Guide.* Grand Rapids: Baker Book House, 2000.

Hodges, Melvin L. *The Indigenous Church: A Handbook on How to Grow Young Churches.* Springfield, MO: Gospel Publishing House, 1976.

Shenk, David W. And Ervin R. Stutzman. *Creating Communities of the Kingdom: New Testament Models of Church Planting.* Scottsdale, PA: Herald Press, 1988.

Kingdom of God Timeline
Rev. Dr. Don L. Davis

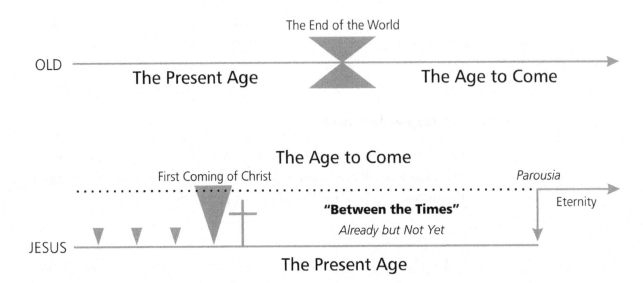

The **"*malkuth*" of Yahweh, the "*basileia tou Theou*."** First century Palestinian Jews saw God as King, of his people Israel and all the earth. Yet, due to the rebellion of humankind and Satan and his angels, God's reign in the earth is **yet future**. It shall be: 1) nationalistic--the salvation and sovereignty of Israel over her enemies, 2) universal knowledge and reign of God, 3) *tsidkenu* (righteousness, justice) and *shalom* (peace), 4) obedience to the Law of God, 5) the final battle with the Gentile nations - Armageddon, 6) occur by a supernatural cataclysm realized at the end of time, 7) transformation of the heavens and earth to pre-Edenic splendor, 8) rule by the son of David-son of Man, 9) rescinding the effects of the curse, 10) the resurrection of the dead, 11) and judgment and destruction of all of God's enemies - sin, death, evil, the "world," the devil and his angels, and 12) eternal life.

Jesus' proclamation: **The Kingdom of God has now appeared in the life, person, and ministry of Messiah Jesus.** In Jesus' words (*kerygma*), his deeds of compassion (*diakinia*), his miracles, his exorcisms of demons, his passion, death, and resurrection, and the sending of the Spirit, **the promised-for Kingdom has come.** The Kingdom is **both** present and future; he announces **the presence of the future.** Present kingdom blessings include 1) the Church as sign and foretaste, 2) the pledge of the Holy Spirit, 3) the forgiveness of sin, 4) the proclamation of the Kingdom worldwide, 5) reconciliation and peace with God, 6) the binding of Satan, with authority given to Christ's disciples.

APPENDIX 39

Models of the Kingdom

Howard A Snyder, March 2002.

1. The Kingdom as Future Hope - the Future Kingdom

This has been a dominant model in the history of the Church. The emphasis is strongly on the future: a final culmination and reconciliation of all things which is more than merely the eternal existence of the soul. The model draws heavily on NT material. While some of the following models also represent future hope, here the note of futurity is determinative.

2. The Kingdom as Inner Spiritual Experience - the Interior Kingdom

A "spiritual kingdom" to be experienced in the heart or soul; "beatific vision." Highly mystical, therefore individualistic; an experience that can't really be shared with others. Examples: Julian of Norwich, other mystics; also some contemporary Protestant examples.

3. The Kingdom as Mystical Communion - the Heavenly Kingdom

The "communion of saints"; the Kingdom as essentially identified with heaven. Less individualistic. Often centers especially in worship and liturgy. Examples: John of Damascus, John Tauler; in somewhat different ways, Wesley and 19th and 20th-century revivalistic and Evangelical Protestantism. Kingdom is primarily other-worldly and future.

4. The Kingdom as Institutional Church - the Ecclesiastical Kingdom

The dominant view of medieval Christianity; dominant in Roman Catholicism until Vatican II. Pope as Vicar of Christ rules on earth in Christ's stead. The tension between the Church and the Kingdom largely dissolves. Traces to Augustine's City of God, but was developed differently from what Augustine believed. Protestant variations appear whenever the Church and Kingdom are too closely identified. Modern "Church Growth" thinking has been criticized at this point.

Models of the Kingdom (continued)

5. The Kingdom as Counter-System - the Subversive Kingdom

May be a protest to #4; sees the Kingdom as a reality which prophetically judges the sociopolitical order as well as the Church. One of the best examples: Francis of Assisi; also 16th century Radical Reformers; "Radical Christians" today; Sojourners magazine. Sees Church as counter-culture embodying the new order of the Kingdom.

6. The Kingdom as Political State - the Theocratic Kingdom

Kingdom may be seen as a political theocracy; Church and society not necessarily to be organized democratically. Tends to work from O.T. models, especially the Davidic Kingdom. Constantinian model; Byzantine Christianity a good example. Calvin's Geneva, perhaps, in a somewhat different sense. Problem of Luther's "two kingdoms" view.

7. The Kingdom as Christianized Society - the Transforming Kingdom

Here also the Kingdom provides a model for society, but more in terms of values & principles to be worked out in society. Kingdom in its fullness would be society completely leavened by Christian values. Post-millennialism; many mid-19th-century Evangelicals; early 20th-century Social Gospel. Kingdom manifested progressively in society, in contrast to premillennialism.

8. The Kingdom as Earthly Utopia - the Earthly Kingdom

May be seen as #7 taken to extreme. This view of the Kingdom is literally utopian. Tends to deny or downplay sin, or see evil as purely environmental. The view of many utopian communities (Cohn, *Pursuit of the Millennium*) including 19th-century U.S. and British examples. In a different way, the view of many of America's Founding Fathers. Most influential 20th-century example: Marxism. Liberation theology, to some degree. In a starkly different way: U.S. Fundamentalist premillennialism, combining this model with #1, #2 and/or #3 -Kingdom has no contemporary relevance, but will be literal utopia in the future. Thus similarities between Marxism and Fundamentalism.

APPENDIX 40

Thy Kingdom Come!
Readings on the Kingdom of God
Edited by Terry G. Cornett and Don L. Davis

Taken from "The Agony and The Ecstasy" in Why We Haven't Changed the World, *by Peter E. Gillquist. Old Tappan, New Jersey: Fleming H. Revell Company, 1982. pp. 47-48.*

A Tale of Two Kingdoms

Hear the parable of a kingdom, a usurper-prince of the realm of this world. By means of a masterful program of clever deception, he has managed to bring millions of subjects under his powerful rule. Granted, he has enticed them from the realm of another Monarch, but he considers them his. After all, they have been under his dominion for some considerable time now, and the Enemy hasn't yet taken them back. Yes, in the mind of this prince, these people are legally his people and this land *his* land. Possession is, after all, he says, nine-tenths of the law.

Suddenly, without much warning, the rival Government takes action. The Son of the Enemy Monarch is dispatched to the prince's very own turf (well, yes, he did steal it, but. . .) to take back those who would resubmit to his reign. The Monarch's plan is to draw these people out from under the prince's authority, philosophy, and life-style.

Most outrageous of all, the Monarch sets up his Government on the prince's own real estate. And instead of immediately removing his restored subjects from the country, he is keeping them there until a disease called *death* (a consequence of the prince's regime which eventually claims everyone) brings about a change in their state of existence. To make the matter even more aggravating, the Son even promises people that he will save them from death, and become the firstfruits by dying and coming back to life again himself.

Unsettled, but undefeated (he thinks), the prince launches an all fronts counterattack. Plainly, he is no match for the other King one on One. So he launches a renewed program of deception, simply lying to his citizens about the other Government. That doesn't always work, for the Monarch's Son keeps taking subjects back. Since they are such weak creatures, however, the prince sees no reason to give up hope for their eventual return. Consequently, even after they become citizens of that other kingdom, he keeps the pressure on.

Falsehood is the prince's most common weapon. He uses it at the most strategic points. Since the most committed people are the most dangerous, he attacks the zealots among his former subjects by spreading rumors about them and

Thy Kingdom Come! Readings on the Kingdom of God (continued)

intimidating them by hints of his power. By and large his successes are few, however, for these people demonstrate an almost supernatural attachment to the Enemy Monarch.

Still, the prince in encouraged by one relatively small, though nonetheless significant, source of help he had not counted on.

There are some servants of the Monarch's Son, mostly honest and well intentioned, who mis-state his promises. These servants are so intent upon winning people back from the realm of the evil prince, that they leave out of their messages some very important facts concerning responsible citizenship in that Domain. They rarely, if ever, mention warfare, or the prince's subversive devices, or the residual effects of the dread diseases caught under his reign. Frankly, they portray the Son's Government as sort of a spiritual welfare state, where there are free goodies for all, with little work or responsibility. One gets the picture of a sort of laid-back paradise, with the Monarch running a giant handout program.

Gleefully, the wicked prince capitalizes on this unexplained chink in their armor. All he has to do is let them preach these omissions, and then cash in on the contradictions the people experience in their daily lives. After all, his best source of returnees just might turn out to be the disappointed hearers who listen to these enthusiastic servants.

The Kingdom as a Key to All of Scripture

Jesus was always full of surprises, even with his disciples. Perhaps the biggest surprise was his news about the Kingdom of God.

Jesus came announcing the Kingdom, creating a stir. Through a brief span of public ministry he kept showing his disciples what the Kingdom was really like. They understood only in part.

Later, risen from the dead, Jesus spent six weeks teaching his disciples more about the Kingdom (Acts 1.3). He explained that his own suffering, death and resurrection were all part of the kingdom plan foretold by Old Testament prophets (Luke 24.44-47).

Now, after the resurrection, his disciples ask, "Are *you finally* going to set up your Kingdom?" (paraphrasing Acts 1.6). How does Jesus respond? He says, in effect,

Excerpted from "Introduction and Chapter One" in A Kingdom Manifesto, *by Howard A. Snyder. Downers Grove: InterVarsity Press, 1985. pp. 11-25*

"The time for the full flowering of the new order still remains a mystery to you; it's in God's hands. But. . . . the Holy Spirit will give you the power to live the kingdom life now. So you are to be witnesses of the Kingdom and its power from here to the very ends of the earth" (Acts 1.7-8).

And so it was, and so it has been. Today we are finally nearing the fulfillment of Jesus' prophecy that "this gospel of the Kingdom will be preached in the whole world as a testimony to all nations" (Matt. 24.14 [NIV]).

And so, as never before, it is time to speak of God's Kingdom now!

This is no attempt to outguess God or pre-empt the sovereign mystery of the Kingdom. The Kingdom still and always remains in God's hands. So this book is not about "times or dates" (Acts 1.7) - a tempting but disastrous detour - but about the plain kingdom teachings which run throughout Scripture. My point is simply this: The Bible is full of teaching on the Kingdom of God, and the Church has largely missed it. But in the providence of God we may now have reached a time when the good news of the Kingdom can be heard and understood as never before. This is due not to any one person, not to any human wisdom or insight, but to God's own working in our day, bringing a new kingdom consciousness.

Thus the theme of this book: The Kingdom of God in Scripture and its meaning for us today.

The Kingdom of God is a key thread in Scripture, tying the whole Bible together. It is not the only unifying theme, nor should it replace other themes which are clearly biblical. Yet it is a critically important theme, especially today. And its recent resurgence in the Church is, I believe, one of the most significant developments of this century!

Once you begin to look in Scripture for the theme of God's reign or Kingdom, it turns up everywhere! Take an example I recently encountered in my own devotional study:

All you have made will praise you, O LORD; your saints will extol you. They will tell of the glory of your kingdom and speak of your might, so that all men may know of your mighty acts and the glorious splendor of your kingdom. Your kingdom is an everlasting kingdom, and your dominion endures through all generations.

~ Psalm 145.10-13 (NIV)

Thy Kingdom Come! Readings on the Kingdom of God (continued)

This one psalm in fact contains a substantial theology of the Kingdom, stressing God's sovereign reign, his mighty acts, his compassion and nearness to those who seek him, his righteousness and justice.

The Kingdom is such a key theme of Scripture that Richard Lovelace can say, "The Messianic Kingdom is not only the main theme of Jesus' preaching; it is the central category unifying biblical revelation." And John Bright comments, "The concept of the Kingdom of God involves, in a real sense, the total message of the Bible. . . . To grasp what is meant by the Kingdom of God is to come very close to the heart of the Bible's gospel of salvation." As E. Stanley Jones wrote over four decades ago, Jesus' message "was the Kingdom of God. It was the center and circumference of all he taught and did. . . . The Kingdom of God is the master-conception, the master-plan, the master-purpose, the master-will that gathers everything up into itself and gives it redemption, coherence, purpose, goal."

True, seeing the Kingdom of God as the only unifying theme of Scripture could be misleading. Personally, I believe the overarching truth is the revelation of the nature and character of God (not merely his existence, which is clear from the created order - Romans 1.20). Here God's love, justice and holiness are central - the character of God's *person* in his tri-unity. Still the reign/rule of God is a key theme of Scripture, for the loving, just, holy God rules consistent with his character and in a way that produces the reflection of his character in all who willingly serve him.

So the Kingdom is indeed a key strand running through the Bible. If it seems less evident in Paul's writings, that is because Paul often speaks of the Kingdom in terms of the sovereign *plan* of God realized through Jesus Christ (as, for example, in Ephesians 1.10), and, for very good reasons, uses less kingdom language. But it is incorrect to say, as some have, that the kingdom theme "disappears" in Paul. . . .

The Bible is full of God's Kingdom. . . . We learn more about the Kingdom when we view all of Scripture as the history of God's "economy" or plan to restore a fallen creation, bringing all God has made - woman, man and their total environment - to the fulfillment of his purposes under his sovereign reign.

One evening my seven-year-old son and I walked through a little patch of woods and came out on an open field. The sun was westering; the sky was serenely laced with blue and gold. Birds flitted in the trees. We talked about peace, the future and the Kingdom of God. Somehow we both sensed, despite our differences in age and understanding, that God desires peace and that what he desires he will bring.

Someday, we said and knew, all the world will be like this magic moment. But not without cost and struggle.

Jesus urges: "Enter through the narrow gate." For "small is the gate and narrow the road that leads to life, and only a few find it" (Matthew 7.13-14). The Kingdom of God is life in abundance (John 10.10), but the way to life is through the narrow gate of faith and obedience to Jesus Christ. If Christians today want to experience the peaceable order of the Kingdom, they must learn and live God's way of peace.

The Preaching and Teaching of Jesus
Summary of Teaching, Vic Gordon

1. The most important thing in life is to be a disciple of Jesus Christ. To do that we must learn from him and then obey what we hear. He must be our Teacher and Lord (Matthew 7.24-27; 11.29; 28.18-20; John 13.13).

2. Obviously, we cannot follow Jesus if we do not know what he taught. The main theme of his preaching and teaching was the Kingdom of God. Most Christians do not know this, yet they call him Lord and Master Teacher!

3. But we are then faced with an immediate problem. As soon as we know the main theme of his teaching, we automatically misunderstand it. Kingdom means something different in the biblical idiom (Hebrew, Aramaic, Greek) than in contemporary English. To us "Kingdom" means "realm" (a place over which a king rules) or "a group of people who live in a king's realm" (the people over whom a king rules). In the Bible, however, the primary meaning of "Kingdom" is "reign" or "rule." The Kingdom of God thus means the reign of God or the rule of God. The Kingdom of God is not a place nor a people, but God's active, dynamic rule. The Kingdom is an act of God, i.e. something he does.

4. The burden and purpose of Jesus' three year public ministry leading up to his death and resurrection was to preach, proclaim and teach about the Kingdom of God (Mark 1.14ff; Matthew 4.17, 23; 9.35; Luke 4.42ff; 8.1; 9.2, 6, 11; 10.1, 9; Acts 1.3; 28.31).

5. Jesus was the original proclaimer of the Gospel, and he proclaimed it originally in terms of the Kingdom of God (Mark 1.14ff; Matthew 4.23; 9.35; 24.14; Luke 20.1). The good news is about God's reign. Of course this is a metaphor, a word picture describing a profound reality.

Thy Kingdom Come! Readings on the Kingdom of God (continued)

6. Jesus' teaching on the Kingdom of God as we will see, determines the basic structure of all his teaching, and indeed the structure of the teaching of the entire New Testament.

7. Why did Jesus choose the word picture "Kingdom of God" to proclaim the good news of God to the world? Two basic reasons:

   a. **It was biblical.** While the exact phrase "Kingdom of God" never occurs in the Old Testament (maybe once in 1 Chronicles 28.5), the idea is everywhere present in the Old Testament. God is always and everywhere King in the Old Testament, especially in the prophets. His kingship is not always realized in this sinful world. In fact the major emphasis in the Old Testament, stated in hundreds of ways and different word pictures, is on God's future, coming reign. The hope of the Old Testament is that God himself will come and bring salvation to his people and judgment/destruction to his enemies. (See e.g. 1 Chronicles 29.11; Psalms 22.28; 96.10-13; 103.19; 145.11-13; Isaiah 25ff; 65ff; Daniel 2.44; 4.3, 34; 6.26; 7.13ff, 27.)

   b. **It was understood and meaningful to the first century Palestinian Jews to whom he proclaimed the Good News.** In fact, the phrase "Kingdom of God" had developed a great deal in the 400 years between the Old Testament and the coming of Jesus. Kingdom of God now summarized the entire Old Testament hope! The first century Jews were expecting God to come as king and reign over the entire world, destroying his enemies and giving all his blessings to his people, Israel. This concept was especially meaningful to the Jews who, on the one hand, strongly believed that their God Yahweh was the one and only true God who ruled over all the universe, and who, on the other, experienced over 700 years of foreign domination at the hands of pagan rulers from Assyria, then Babylon, then Persia, then Greece and finally Rome. Jesus never defines the Kingdom of God for them, because they all knew what it meant. This is a great example for us in our ministries. Jesus went to the people where they were (the incarnation!), was faithful to the biblical message, and spoke it to them in terms they could understand. (See e.g. Luke 1.32ff; 19.11; 23.51; Mark 11.10; 15.43; Acts 1.6.) The phrase Kingdom of God summarized all of the Old

Testament hope and promise. "All that God has said and done in Israel's history is brought to completion in the Kingdom of God" (Dale Patrick).

8. But Jesus offers a new understanding of an already understood concept. He pours his own authoritative meaning into the Kingdom of God and offers a definitive new interpretation of the Old Testament promise and teaching. He makes it certain that the "Kingdom of God" is the interpretive key for the Old Testament. He agrees with the Jews that the Kingdom is God coming into history and reigning by giving salvation to his people and judgment to his enemies. But Jesus goes far beyond this in providing a grand new interpretation of God's reign.

9. Jesus startles and stuns his hearers by saying the Kingdom of God which they have all been waiting for is now present (Mark 1.15). The time of the fulfillment of the Old Testament promises has now arrived. He goes even further than this by teaching that the Kingdom is present in his own person and ministry. (Matthew 11.1-15; 12.28; Luke 10.23ff; 17.20ff.) This teaching that the Kingdom of God has arrived or is here is radically new. No Jewish rabbi had ever taught such a thing (Luke 10.23ff).

10. But Jesus, like most of the Jews of his day, also taught that the Kingdom of God was still future, i.e. it was yet to come (e.g. Matthew 6.10; 8.11ff; 25.31-34; Luke 21.31; 22.17ff. Cf. Matthew 5.3-12; Mark 9.47).

11. The solution to this strange teaching is to realize that Jesus' new perspective on the Kingdom of God contains both elements: the Kingdom is present and future. Jesus taught two comings of the Kingdom. First, the Kingdom came partially in his own person and ministry in history. Second, Jesus taught that there will be a future complete coming of his Kingdom when he returns at the end of human history.

12. Now we can understand what Jesus meant by the "mystery of the Kingdom" (Mark 4.10ff). This strange, new perspective on the Kingdom of God taught that the Old Testament promises could be fulfilled without being consummated. Thus, the mystery of the Kingdom is fulfillment without consummation. **The Kingdom of God has come into history in the person and ministry of Jesus Christ without consummation.** This mystery has been hidden until now revealed in Christ.

Thy Kingdom Come! Readings on the Kingdom of God (continued)

13. In one way or another, all of Jesus' kingdom parables ("The Kingdom of God is like. . .") proclaim and/or explain this mystery. This understanding of the Kingdom is radically new. The first century Palestinian Jews needed to hear this message, understand it and believe it. This is the major concern of Jesus' preaching and teaching.

14. Thus, we can understand Jesus' teaching on the coming of God's Kingdom as being both present and future. The Kingdom is now and it is not yet. Jesus announces the presence of the future.

15. This chart of the Kingdom of God in the teaching of Jesus can help us see more clearly what he is saying. The chart is a time line from Creation into an eternal future (eternal in the Bible means unending time).

    a. The age of the Kingdom is the age to come. We now live in both this age and the age to come.

    b. The Kingdom of God has two moments, each one characterized by a coming of Jesus as the Messianic King to bring God's reign.

16. The Kingdom of God brings the blessings of God. As the people of the Kingdom live now in the tension of both the presence and the future of the Kingdom, some of the blessings have already arrived for us and some await the consummation of the Kingdom in the future.

Present Blessings of the Kingdom

    a. The Gospel is proclaimed.

    b. The forgiveness of sin.

    c. The Holy Spirit indwells God's people.

    d. Sanctification has begun.

Future Blessings of the Kingdom

    a. The Presence of God

    b. Resurrection bodies

    c. Full sanctification

    d. *Shalom*: peace, righteousness, joy, health, wholeness

    e. A new heaven and a new earth

    f. Judgment and destruction of all God's enemies including sin, death, the devil and his demons, all evil

17. Let us not overlook the obvious fact that for Jesus his preaching about the Kingdom is fundamentally a proclamation about God. God brings his Kingdom as a seeking, inviting, gracious Abba Father. He also comes as judge to those who refuse his Kingdom.

18. The Kingdom of God is altogether God's work. He graciously comes into human history in the person of his Son Jesus Christ to bring his rule to the earth. The Kingdom is therefore completely supernatural and gracious. Humans cannot bring, build or accomplish the Kingdom. It is wholly God's act.

19. Jesus' miracles and exorcisms are signs that the Kingdom of God is present in him and his ministry (Matthew 11.1-6; 4.23; 9.35; 10.7ff; Luke 9.1, 2, 6, 11).

20. The Kingdom of God invades the kingdom of Satan when Jesus comes bringing the Kingdom (Matthew 12.22-29; 25.41; Mark 1.24, 34; Luke 10.17ff; 11.17-22).

21. The Kingdom of God is of great value, indeed the greatest thing by far in the whole world (Matthew 13.44-46). Therefore, we must ask, "How should we then respond to this Kingdom?" or "How do we receive this gift of the Kingdom of God?"

APPENDIX 41

Understanding Leadership as Representation

The Six Stages of Formal Proxy

Don L. Davis

Commissioning (1)

Formal Selection and Call to Represent

- Chosen to be an emissary, envoy, or proxy
- Confirmed by appropriate other who recognize the call
- Is recognized to be a member of a faithful community
- Calling out of a group to a particular role of representation
  - Calling to a particular task or mission
  - Delegation of position or responsibility

Equipping (2)

Appropriate Resourcing and Training to Fulfill the Call

- Assignment to a supervisor, superior, mentor, or instructor
- Disciplined instruction of principles underlying the call
- Constant drill, practice, and exposure to appropriate skills
  - Recognition of gifts and strengths
  - Expert coaching and ongoing feedback

Luke 10.1 (ESV) After this the Lord appointed seventy-two others and sent them on ahead of him, two by two, into every town and place where he himself was about to go. . . .

Luke 10.16 (ESV) "The one who hears you hears me, and the one who rejects you rejects me, and the one who rejects me rejects him who sent me."

John 20.21 (ESV) Jesus said to them again, "Peace be with you. As the Father has sent me, even so I am sending you."

Entrustment (3)

Corresponding Authorization and Empowerment to Act

- Delegation of authority to act and speak on commissioner's behalf
- Scope and limits of representative power provided
- Formal deputization (right to enforce and represent)
- Permission given to be an emissary (to stand in stead of)
- Release to fulfill the commission and task received

CONVICTION

CONSCIENCE

CHARACTER

The Revealed Will of God

Leadership As Representation

The Fulfillment of the Task and Mission

Consent of Your Leaders

Mission (4)

Faithful and Disciplined Engagement of the Task

- Subordination of one's will to accomplish the assignment
- Obedience: carrying out the orders of those who sent you
  - Fulfilling the task that was given to you
- Freely acting within one's delegated authority to fulfill the task
  - Maintaining loyalty to those who sent you
  - Using all means available to do one's duty, whatever the cost
- Full recognition of one's answerability to the one(s) who commissioned

Reckoning (5)

Official Evaluation and Review of One's Execution

- Reporting back to sending authority for critical review
- Formal comprehensive assessment of one's execution and results
- Judgment of one's loyalties and faithfulness
- Sensitive analysis of what we accomplishing
- Readiness to ensure that our activities and efforts produce results

Reward (6)

Public Recognition and Continuing Response

- Formal publishing of assessment's results
- Acknowledgment and recognition of behavior and conduct
- Corresponding reward or rebuke for execution
- Review made basis for possible reassignment or recommissioning
- Assigning new projects with greater authority

APPENDIX 42
Readings on the Church

The People of God: Living the Adventure of the *Ekklesia*

1 Pet. 2.9-12 (ESV) - But you are a chosen race, a royal priesthood, a holy nation, a people for his own possession, that you may proclaim the excellencies of him who called you out of darkness into his marvelous light. [10] Once you were not a people, but now you are God's people; once you had not received mercy, but now you have received mercy. [11] Beloved, I urge you as sojourners and exiles to abstain from the passions of the flesh, which wage war against your soul. [12] Keep your conduct among the Gentiles honorable, so that when they speak against you as evildoers, they may see your good deeds and glorify God on the day of visitation.

The identification of Christians as "the people of God" appears a number of times in the New Testament (e.g. Luke 1.17; Acts 15.14; Titus 2.14; Heb. 4.9; 8.10; 1 Pet. 2.9-10; Rev. 18.4; 21.3). But it is used by Paul with special significance in Romans 9.25-26; 11.1-2; 15.10, and 2 Corinthians 6.16 to set the Christian church in the context of the long story of God's dealing with his chosen people Israel. "People of God," a covenant expression, speaks of God's choosing and calling a particular people into covenantal relationship (Exod. 19.5; Deut. 7.6; 14.2; Ps. 135.4; Heb. 8.10; 1 Pet. 2.9-10; Rev. 21.3). They are God's gracious initiative and magnanimous action in creating, calling, saving, judging, and sustaining them. And as God's people, they experience God's presence among them.

~ Richard Longenecker, ed.
Community Formation in the Early Church and in the Church Today.
Peabody, MA: Hendrickson Publishers, 2002. p. 75.

Where Biblical Study of Leadership Begins: The Church as Context for World Change

[A] biblical study on leadership must begin with the story of the church that came into existence on the Day of Pentecost. The term *ekklesia* is used more than one hundred times in the New Testament. In fact, it's virtually impossible to understand God's will for our lives as believers without comprehending this wonderful "mystery of Christ" that has "been revealed by the Spirit to God's holy apostles and prophets" (Eph. 3.4-5).

Readings on the Church (continued)

Beyond the Gospels, most of the NT is the story of "local churches" and how God intended them to function. True, Jesus Christ came to lay the foundation and to build his *ekklesia* (Matt. 16.18) and when he said to Peter, "I will build my *church*," He was certainly thinking more broadly than establishing a "local church" in Caesarea Philippi where this conversation took place (Matt. 16.13-20). . . .

On the other hand, Jesus was also anticipating the multitude of *local churches* that would be established in Judea and Samaria and throughout the Roman Empire--and eventually all over the world as we know it today. This story begins in the book of Acts and spans a significant period during the first century (approximately from A.D. 33 to A.D. 63). Furthermore, during this time frame, most of the New Testament letters were written to these local churches--or to men like Timothy and Titus who were helping to establish these churches.

~ Gene Getz. **Elders and Leaders**.
Chicago: Moody, 2003. pp. 47-48.

A World to Change, a World to Win

If anyone is going to change the world for the better, it may be argued, it ought to be the Christians, not the Communists. For myself, I would say that if we started applying our Christianity to the society in which we live, then it would be we, indeed, who would change the world. Christians, too, have a world to change and a world to win. Had the early Christians gone in for slogans these might well have been theirs. They might be ours too. There is no reason at all why they should be the monopoly of the Communists *[and the Muslims, and the atheists, and the hedonists, and the secular humanists, and the . . .]*

~ Douglas Hyde, **Dedication and Leadership**, pp. 32-33

Those Who Turn the World Upside Down Have Themselves Been Turned Inside Out

The bitterest foe became the greatest friend. The Blasphemer became the preacher of Christ's love. The hand that wrote the indictment of the disciples of Christ when he brought them before magistrates and into prison now penned epistles of God's redeeming love. The heart that once beat with joy when Stephen sank beneath the bloody stones now rejoiced in scourgings and stonings for the sake of Christ.

From this erstwhile enemy, persecutor, blasphemer came the greater part of the New Testament, the noblest statements of theology, the sweetest lyrics of Christian love.

~ C. E. Macartney in **Dynamic Spiritual Leadership** by J. Oswald Sanders. pp. 33-34

APPENDIX 43

Five Views of the Relationship between Christ and Culture

*Based on **Christ and Culture** by H. Richard Niebuhr, New York: Harper and Row, 1951*

Christ against Culture	Christ and Culture in Paradox	Christ the Transformer of Culture	Christ above Culture	The Christ of Culture
Opposition	*Tension*	*Conversion*	*Cooperation*	*Acceptance*
Therefore come out from them and be separate, says the Lord. Touch no unclean thing, and I will receive you. - 2 Cor. 6.17 (cf. 1 John 2.15)	Give to Caesar what is Caesar's, and to God what is God's. - Matt. 22.21 (cf. 1 Pet. 2.13-17)	In putting everything under him, God left nothing that is not subject to him. Yet at present we do not see everything subject to him. - Heb. 2.8 (cf. Col. 1.16-18)	Indeed, when Gentiles, who do not have the law, do by nature things required by the law, they are a law for themselves. - Rom 2.14 (cf. Rom. 13.1, 5-6)	Every good and perfect gift is from above, coming down from the Father of the heavenly lights, who does no change like shifting shadows. - James 1.17 (cf. Phil. 4.8)
Culture is radically affected by sin and constantly opposes the will of God. Separation and opposition are the natural responses of the Christian community which is itself an alternative culture.	Culture is radically affected by sin but does have a role to play. It is necessary to delineate between spheres: Culture as law (restrains wickedness), Christianity as grace (gives righteousness). Both are an important part of life but the two cannot be confused or merged.	Culture is radically affected by sin but can be redeemed to play a positive role in restoring righteousness. Christians should work to have their culture acknowledge Christ's lordship and be changed by it.	Culture is a product of human reason and is part of a God-given way to discover truth. Although culture can discern real truth, sin limits its capacities which must be aided by revelation. Seeks to use culture as a first step toward the understanding of God and his revelation.	Culture is God's gift to help man overcome his bondage to nature and fear and advance in knowledge and goodness. Human culture is what allows us to conserve the truth humanity has learned. Jesus' moral teaching moves human culture upward to a new level.
Tertullian Menno Simons Anabaptists	Martin Luther Lutherans	St. Augustine John Calvin Reformed	Thomas Aquinas Roman Catholic	Peter Abelard Immanual Kant Liberal Protestant

APPENDIX 44
A Theology of the Church in Kingdom Perspective
Terry Cornett and Don Davis

APPENDIX 45
The Picture and the Drama
Image and Story in the Recovery of Biblical Myth
Don L. Davis

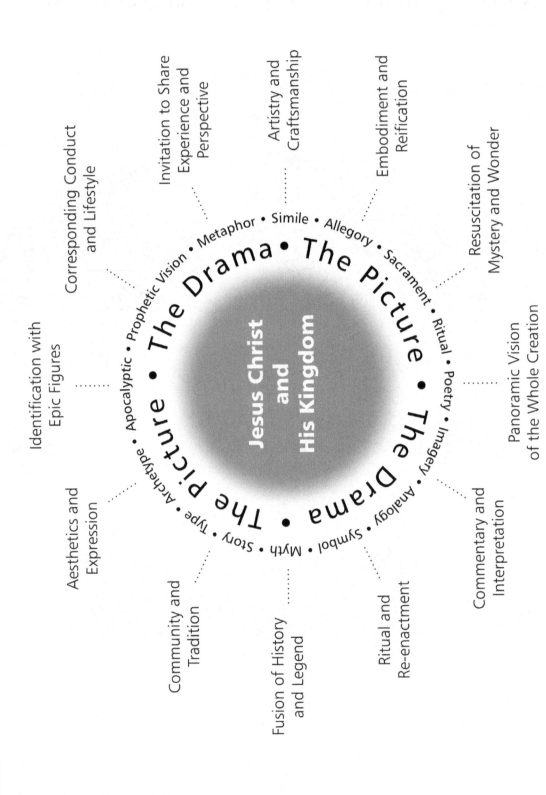

A P P E N D I X 4 6

Fit to Represent

Multiplying Disciples of the Kingdom of God

Rev. Dr. Don L. Davis ● Luke 10.16 (ESV) - The one who hears you hears me, and the one who rejects you rejects me, and the one who rejects me rejects him who sent me.

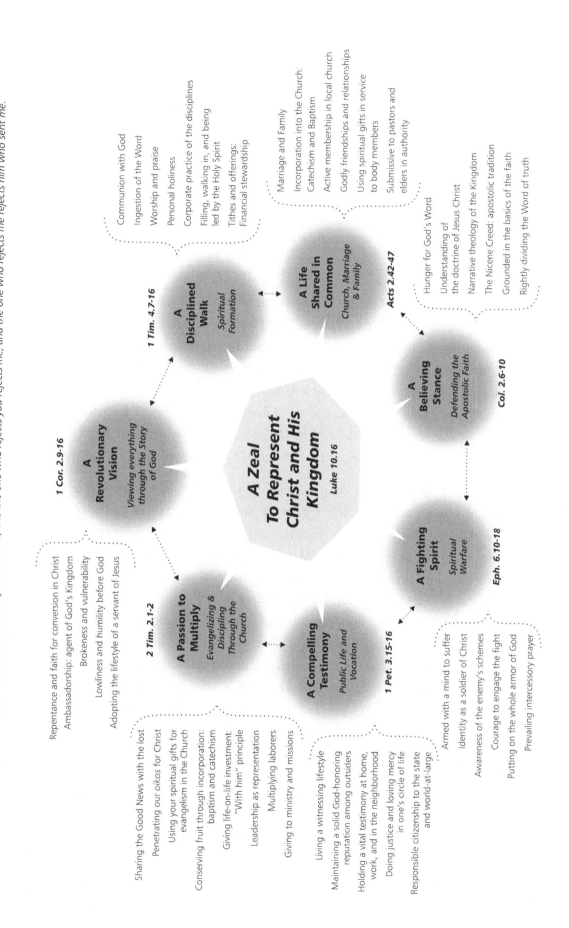

A Zeal
To Represent
Christ and His
Kingdom
Luke 10.16

A
Disciplined
Walk
Spiritual Formation
1 Tim. 4.7-16

- Communion with God
- Ingestion of the Word
- Worship and praise
- Personal holiness
- Corporate practice of the disciplines
- Filling, walking in, and being led by the Holy Spirit
- Tithes and offerings: Financial stewardship

A
Life
Shared in
Common
Church, Marriage & Family
Acts 2.42-47

- Marriage and Family
- Incorporation into the Church: Catechism and Baptism
- Active membership in local church
- Godly friendships and relationships
- Using spiritual gifts in service to body members
- Submissive to pastors and elders in authority

A
Believing
Stance
Defending the Apostolic Faith
Col. 2.6-10

- Hunger for God's Word
- Understanding of the doctrine of Jesus Christ
- Narrative theology of the Kingdom
- The Nicene Creed: apostolic tradition
- Grounded in the basics of the faith
- Rightly dividing the Word of truth

A
Revolutionary
Vision
Viewing everything through the Story of God
1 Cor. 2.9-16

- Repentance and faith for conversion in Christ
- Ambassadorship: agent of God's Kingdom
- Brokeness and vulnerability
- Lowliness and humility before God
- Adopting the lifestyle of a servant of Jesus

A
Passion to
Multiply
Evangelizing & Discipling Through the Church
2 Tim. 2.1-2

- Sharing the Good News with the lost
- Penetrating our oikos for Christ
- Using your spiritual gifts for evangelism in the Church
- Conserving fruit through incorporation: baptism and catechism
- Giving life-on-life investment: "With him" principle
- Leadership as representation
- Multiplying laborers
- Giving to ministry and missions

A
Compelling
Testimony
Public Life and Vocation
1 Pet. 3.15-16

- Living a witnessing lifestyle
- Maintaining a solid God-honoring reputation among outsiders
- Holding a vital testimony at home, work, and in the neighborhood
- Doing justice and loving mercy in one's circle of life
- Responsible citizenship to the state and world-at-large

A
Fighting
Spirit
Spiritual Warfare
Eph. 6.10-18

- Armed with a mind to suffer
- Identity as a soldier of Christ
- Awareness of the enemy's schemes
- Courage to engage the fight
- Putting on the whole armor of God
- Prevailing intercessory prayer

APPENDIX 47

Let God Arise!

A Sober Call to Prevailing Prayer for a Dynamic Spiritual Awakening and the Aggressive Advancement of the Kingdom in America's Inner Cities

Rev. Dr. Don L. Davis, January 1, 2003

> *Written in honor of all those who for these long years have in faith and sacrifice refused to let go of the Lord until he blessed them on behalf of the poor in the city*

What a long title for a short essay! This is my tribute to the wonderful piece penned by the churchman and intellectual Jonathan Edwards, leader in the Awakenings in the northeast in the 18th century regarding the need for intercession to spawn new movements for God. His original title was long as well: "A Humble Attempt to Promote Explicit Agreement and Visible Union of God's People, in Extraordinary Prayer, for the Revival of Religion and the Advancement of Christ's Kingdom on Earth." Edwards wrote his little tract in 1746 after experiencing two remarkable movements of the Spirit of God, in 1734-35 and 1740-42 respectively.

Edwards's tract displayed his deep conviction that when God's people pray fervently, intensely, and powerfully for revival, he would release the power of his Spirit in society. This remarkable visitation would then result in many people repenting and believing in Christ as Lord, and would trigger a worldwide "revival of religion" and an "advancement of the Kingdom on earth." All committed Christians, according to Edwards, have a positive duty to pray for this. Having argued his points primarily from careful reasoning and his exegesis of Zechariah 8.18-23 (among other texts), Edwards sought to support his "humble plea" for a more dedicated and organized movement of prayer pleading to him for his visitation. He was neither the first nor the only Christian leader of the time that was calling for "extraordinary prayer." As a matter of fact, a "Memorial" was written by certain Scottish ministers who circulated their ideas at the time of his tract-writing. This memorial had been circulated throughout many English-speaking churches, but especially in England. It called for a new emphasis of "extraordinary prayer" at certain times, a schedule which Edwards himself endorsed, specifically on "Saturday evenings, Sunday mornings and the first Tuesday of each quarter, for an initial period of seven years."

While history does not record another widespread period of renewal in the English-speaking world until the 1770's (followed by another in the 1790's), Edwards's little tract has been consulted and studied by many a disciple and congregation longing to see a fresh and powerful visitation from God on the Church and in the world.

As I write this morning, I realize that we are presently a long way and time from the 18th century English and Scottish societies wherein Edwards wrote his essay on "revival of religion." As I pen my musings on this subject from my home here in urban America, I am aware that with the turn of a new millennium and the beginning of a new year, we have inherited a world decidedly more dangerous, complex, and frightening than that of Edwards and his contemporaries in Scotland and England. More than six billion people inhabit a planet reeling from pollution and overpopulation. We stand on the brink of war, with reports of terrorist threats and ethnic conflicts shrieking through our airwaves. Millions live with malnourishment and squalor, and vast numbers live in despair and hopelessness in a world that is fundamentally unjust and ungodly. If there ever were a time to renew a humble and sober call for "extraordinary prayer" on behalf of a people, a time, and an hour, it is now.

Of all the hardest and most difficult to reach fields on earth today, America's inner cities are arguably one of the toughest. The levels of poverty, violence, despair, and hopelessness make ordinary efforts fall short and seem completely futile. I am convinced that only if God visits, if the Lord arises and scatters his enemies, as spoken in Psalms 68, will freedom, wholeness, and justice prevail, both within God's people of the city and through them to those who are in desperate need for God's grace and provision.

This tract, like that of Edwards, represents another humble attempt to mobilize believers to cry out day and night to God on behalf of a slumbering Church and those suffering and dying without Christ. The heart cry here, however, is focused on the inner cities of America. This represents an earnest plea to call out a nucleus, an army of godly and available intercessors who will pledge themselves to lay hold of God in prevailing prayer for a breakthrough of God's divine power, for spiritual awakening for his people and advancement of his Kingdom in the city.

A Sober Call to Prevailing Prayer

When Edwards wrote his call to the churches of England and Scotland to pray for revival, he focused on Zechariah 8.18-23 which reads:

> Zech. 8.18-23 (ESV) - And the word of the Lord of hosts came to me, saying, [19] "Thus says the Lord of hosts: The fast of the fourth month and the fast of the fifth and the fast of the seventh and the fast of the tenth shall be to the house of Judah seasons of joy and gladness and cheerful feasts. Therefore love truth and peace. [20] Thus says the Lord of hosts: Peoples shall yet come, even the inhabitants of many cities. [21] The inhabitants of one city shall go to another, saying, 'Let us go at once to entreat the favor of the Lord and to seek the Lord of hosts; I myself am going.' [22] Many peoples and strong nations shall come to seek the Lord of hosts in Jerusalem and to entreat the favor of the Lord. [23] Thus says the Lord of hosts: In those days ten men from the nations of every tongue shall take hold of the robe of a Jew, saying, 'Let us go with you, for we have heard that God is with you.'"

Edwards related this text to prophecies of the very end of time where God would bring dramatic and glorious renewal to the entire earth through the focused intercession of God's people. I do not believe that Edwards was incorrect. Furthermore, I am convinced that God's promise to move in regard to extraordinary prayer by his holy people is a given throughout Scripture, sustained with many examples, both in biblical history and in contemporary life. God Almighty answers prayer.

We make therefore a sober call to all believers who love the Lord Jesus and the cities of America to join us in forming new movements of prayer for the city, for all those who live in them, especially God's people. We are making a call to prevailing prayer in the name of Jesus Christ for God's glory. We are asking that God might send to us his very own Holy Spirit, to break through the darkness, evil, and despair of the city and bring refreshment and revolutionary change among the poorest of America's urban poor.

This is not a call to repeat the "good old days" of the past (i.e., a nostalgic return to the glory days of the great awakening revival meetings, or any other revivals of history). Nor is this a call for the sleepy-headed to simply spend a few more hours in prayer over the unimportant. Nor do we make any pleas here for simply a little more effort in prayer, a kind of seasonal emphasis in prayer for the cities that could be done leisurely and conveniently "every other quarter" or so. Rather, what we advocate here is an entirely new vision of ourselves and the city as powerless without the Lord's intervention. We are asking here for a radical reorientation of our lives toward prayer to God based on a rediscovery and reaffirmation that only God can change the inner cities of America.

Frankly speaking, my deepest conviction continues to be that America's inner cities are simply unwinnable without a new and fresh visitation from God. Nearly sixty million people live in our poorest urban communities, with more than 90% of these residents claiming no knowledge of or relationship to God in Jesus Christ. These tortured communities have been deeply scarred and marred by violence, are severely neglected and exploited economically, and suffer from horrific and severe health-related problems. Our American inner cities are hazardous on a number of different points, and yet they continue to swell from immigrant populations and mind-numbing ethnic and racial diversity. Perhaps the greatest liability of all, America's inner cities suffer from discouragement and nihilistic despair; everyone seems to live in fear and dread, with a keen sense of hopelessness.

Tragically, you can even find Scripture-quoting Christians prophesying alongside the chorus of liberal and conservative nay-sayers who lament the tragedy and demise of the city. Some missiologists suggest that America is already won, and that ethnic and urban churches can finish the job in America's inner cities. Others even doubt whether the city is worth winning, giving a kind of grotesque judgment that those who suffer there are merely reaping what they deliberately have sown. In the face of such physical poverty, broken families, sub-par schools, inferior social services, and general spiritual darkness, most expect little from the city. Their words and demeanor give their deepest beliefs away: they truly wonder if anything good can *really* come out of our inner cities, arguably our 21st century Nazareths.

Despite such low levels of belief, I am convinced that the biblical record is correct when it asserts that nothing is impossible with God (Luke 1.37). Nothing is too hard for God (Jer. 32.26), and he through his power can touch and transform the inhabitants of the city! We stand ever ready and hopeful that God will visit his people in the city, and that through outpourings of his Spirit we can see explosive movements of spiritual awakening and cross-cultural disciple making among the urban poor. These movements will not occur due to human ingenuity and effort, but through times of refreshing that come from the Lord (Acts 3.19). We are convinced that only a breakthrough of God's divine power in remarkable ways and

Let God Arise! (continued)

levels will suffice for the winning of America's inner cities. Only God visiting his people through the presence and power of his Holy Spirit will guarantee a new and fruitful kind of effective urban outreach that can result in the changing of thousands of lives through Christ's power.

As believers and fellow soldiers in kingdom witness, we call for believers everywhere touched by the need of America's inner cities to join us in the *Let God Arise!* movement. We call all who love those who dwell in the city to a new way of living–under the supreme lordship of Jesus Christ. We call all who love the Church in the city to a new way of seeking God–with fervency and passion, who will cry out both day and night to the Lord. Filled with a spirit of longing and humility, we must earnestly seek the Lord's face in intercession, and do so strategically, in an organized and effective manner.

Hear me well, fellow warrior in Christ! The *Let God Arise!* movement, in the same spirit as brother Edwards did in England, is another humble attempt to implore every disciple concerned about the poor in urban America to join us in constant prayer for God to arise and scatter his enemies. We are seeking to facilitate and challenge individuals, small groups, entire congregations in different locales to meet regularly in their homes, in churches, in businesses, in schools–wherever the Lord leads them to pray–to petition God's visitation upon the city.

A Blueprint for Seeking God and Entreating His Favor

Our highest priority in intercession, as the Zechariah text suggests, is that our primary aim would be to "seek the Lord" above all other requests. We must not substitute his blessings or benefits for seeking him first. *Let God Arise!* is primarily a call for disciples of Jesus to recommit to a new level of spirituality, openness, and brokenness before God that will lead to God's special visitation of his people in the city. This sober call to prevailing prayer is anchored in a sense of our impotency without the Lord. This call is not meant as some kind of work where we could claim to earn God's favor, nor are we attempting to bribe God with a manageable and abbreviated season of humbleness before him. On the contrary, our desire is to be transformed by God entirely. We desire that God visit the city, but only if he visits us as well! We desire the transformation of the city, but we desire even more that this awakening begin with the transformation of our very lives under the lordship of Jesus Christ! We are hungry for more of him–more love, more power, more of the Lord. We desire first and foremost to prevail in prayer soberly, openly, humbly, seeking the Lord himself, coming to know him intimately and glorifying him in our very lives–by who we are. Above all else, *Let God Arise!* desires that urban believers seek the person of the Lord first, to know him, to see him, and to experience in new ways his power and blessing in our lives as his disciples.

This means that as a movement, *Let God Arise!* understands the legitimacy of the priorities spelled out throughout Scripture, and especially in the Zechariah chapter 8 text. Verse 22 makes this plain: "Many peoples and strong nations shall come to seek the Lord of hosts in Jerusalem and to entreat the favor of the Lord." We come boldly to the throne of God's grace, not at the earthly Jerusalem, but to the Mount Zion above, where our gracious God dwells. Hebrews chapter 12.22-24 (ESV) underscores this: "But you have come to Mount Zion and to the city of the living God, the heavenly Jerusalem, and to innumerable angels in festal gathering, [23] and to the assembly of the firstborn who are enrolled in heaven, and to God, the judge of all, and to the spirits of the righteous made perfect, [24] and to Jesus, the mediator of a new covenant, and to the sprinkled blood that speaks a better word than the blood of Abel."

Indeed, our first priority, above all else, is to seek the face of the Lord with all our hearts, to know him, and to make him alone our aim and goal in prayer.

Adoration, Admission, and Availability

The following descriptions of the various elements of a *Let God Arise!* prayer session represent a quick summary of the kind of praying and approach to God we seek to have. We are not seeking to be formulaic or wooden in our suggestions, but offer the following merely as a kind of skeleton, a blueprint or road map to guide us along together as we seek God's face and manifestation. Hopefully these elements can give us practical direction as we gather in our homes and churches for prevailing prayer to the Lord.

To begin with, we start our prayer sessions therefore with worship of the Lord, the *Adoration* phase of our prayer concerts. All of our *Let God Arise!* gatherings encourage those present to begin your concert and session of prevailing prayer with a time of adoration and praise, with singing and exaltation, where we delight and enjoy the Lord with clapping, shouts of joy, and heartfelt praise. We must thank

Let God Arise! (continued)

God for his gracious work for us in Christ, and be grateful for the opportunity to come before his presence through the blood of Christ. Above all else (all needs, petitions, and desires), our God is worthy in himself to be worshiped and adored!

Next, we move to the *Admission* portion of our prayer time. After acknowledging the glory and majesty of the God and Father of our Lord Jesus, we then spend ample time admitting our faults and neediness before his mighty hand. Let us learn to bow before the Lord in humble confession of our sin, and the admission that we are powerless, helpless, and defenseless without his oversight, provision, and grace. Let us not hide our sin but readily confess it. Let us not protest our innocence nor boast in our spiritual accomplishment (Luke 18.9-14), but honestly humble ourselves in the sight of the Lord in order that he might lift us up (1 Pet. 5.6). God does in fact resist those who are proud (i.e., those pretending to be sufficient and adequate in their own wisdom, strength, and power) and gives his grace to the humble (i.e., those willing to admit their powerlessness and desperation before the Lord, James 4.6).

Finally, the "*Availability*" portion of our concert focuses on our joyful dedication of our lives to the Lord for his glory and purposes. During this time we dedicate ourselves afresh to the Lord, affirming our death with Christ and our resurrection in him to new life for God's glory and praise (Rom. 6.1-4). We surrender all we are and everything we own to Jesus Christ in order that he might separate us to his causes and interests, and that he might be pleased as a result of all that we are becoming, doing, and achieving in our lives. Paul makes this point when he says to the Corinthians in 2 Cor. 5.9-10 (ESV) "So whether we are at home or away, we make it our aim to please him. [10] For we must all appear before the judgment seat of Christ, so that each one may receive what is due for what he has done in the body, whether good or evil." Our intent and explicit aim is to please the Lord!

In prayer, therefore, let us place no confidence in our own fleshly wisdom or strength. Further, let us abandon all reliance on worldly wisdom, and fully consecrate ourselves in dedication to be and do whatever the Lord Jesus demands, however taxing, difficult, or costly. In humble prayer, may we in the thousands bow our knees to the Lord in authentic surrender, allowing his Spirit the right and privilege to lead us wherever he determines, by whatever path and for whatever purpose he may so ably direct (John 3.8). Only this kind of radical, unconditional availability to God will allow him to use us when he pours his Holy Spirit out upon the inner cities of America!

For a Dynamic Spiritual Awakening

Regardless of the terms used in scholarly literature on God's visitation in revival or awakenings (e.g., revival, renewal, refreshing, revelation, etc.), the reality spoken of within these materials all refer to the same truth. What is this truth? These materials all point toward the need, above all else, of God's presence as the critical factor in all renewal and witness for the Kingdom. America's inner cities today especially demand a fresh visitation from the Lord. God must arise in the city; he must come down and scatter his enemies, and shed abroad his goodness and provision. The Holy Spirit must be outpoured upon the city if it is to be won for Christ.

Nothing short of God's own presence in the city will suffice. No other solutions hold the promise of lasting or comprehensive change occurring in the lives of the millions who languish in the city. None of the typical answers can touch the lives of so many; no solutions of government, social philanthropy, political or jurisprudential reform, or the hiring more policemen and crime fighters or eliminating various kinds of "immoral elements" in impoverished neighborhoods will overcome the spiritual powers and principalities which plague our inner city communities. Spiritual needs must be met with spiritual resources.

Neither will an anemic, sluggish, and worldly-minded church accomplish this task of setting the captives free. We are called as believers to be strong in the Lord and in the power of his might (Eph. 6.10-12). Jesus is the warrior of God who will consummate God's victory on earth at his Second Coming (cf. Revelation 19.8ff). Only when Christ reveals himself, he who alone is able to bind "the strong man of the devil" and set his captives free (cf. Matt. 12.25-30), can we expect the freedom, wholeness, and justice of the Kingdom to liberate the lost in the city.

Entreat the Favor of the Lord for Global and Local Concerns

Because we wholeheartedly believe that God loves all peoples everywhere, we concentrate our prayer efforts with an emphasis on both *global* and *local* concerns.

"Global" concerns mean that every time we gather we do not merely pray for the needs of America's inner cities alone, but for the needs of the entire globe, in cities, nations, and among people groups where the Church of Jesus Christ is bearing witness, as well as for all those who have not yet heard of the saving Gospel of the Lord.

Let God Arise! (continued)

We believe in the Nicene Creed, that there is only one, holy, catholic (universal), and apostolic Church, and that what concerns Christians anywhere ought to concern Christians everywhere. We also believe in the Great Commission of Jesus, that the Church has been called for these last two millennia to bear witness to the Kingdom of God in Jesus Christ among every people group on earth. We therefore pray for the *Awakening* of the Church of Jesus Christ everywhere, pleading to God to act for congregations of believers wherever they gather, in other nations and continents, all with an intent that God will glorify himself among his people wherever they meet.

"Local" concerns must equally capture our attention and petition. By *local* we mean the particular church which we belong to, the churches in our denomination and immediate neighboring community, and the church in our locale or region. Each region of the church has its own peculiar and unique issues, challenges, and concerns, and our intercession recognizes these specific concerns for our church community. We entreat the favor of the Lord on behalf of our local church assembly, and the assemblies in our city, locale, and region.

We therefore begin our intercession with special entreaties, supplications, and prayers offered on behalf of God's people for a dynamic spiritual *Awakening*. Let us pray for the Church in the world (and in different parts of the world) that believers would be refreshed by repeated and powerful outpourings and manifestations of the Holy Spirit's presence among his people. Let us pray that God will associate these outpourings with signs and wonders which direct attention to his glory and reign, and that the spiritual character of the churches would be renewed to obey the Great Commandment with full energy. Let us pray that the churches globally and locally will love God with all their hearts, and their neighbors as themselves. Let us pray for reconciliation, unity, and restored relationships among believers all over the earth, and ask God to create a new spirit of unity and agreement around the advancement of God's Kingdom in our churches.

In this regard, let us pray for a revolutionary rediscovery of the lordship of Jesus Christ in our churches, with refreshing manifestations of humility, confession, brokenness, and love among members, all for the glory of God. Let us pray these and like-minded prayers on behalf of God's people, as fervently and intelligently as possible, praying specific prayers of petitions to God for the revival and renewal of his people globally, and specifically in the cities of America.

With an open heart full of faith, then, let us pray for the churches in the inner cities of America. Let us pray for their protection from the violence and corruption all around them. Let us pray for boldness and frankness as they give witness to the risen Christ in their works of justice, love, and evangelism. Let us pray for a new sense of joy and power in the Holy Spirit, a greater revelation from the Word of God, a new experience of the cleansing power of the blood of Christ, and an enriched walk with God. Let us pray for a spirit of tranquility and peace, the binding of the enemy, in order that the Gospel can go forth.

Also, let us pray for a new spirit of praise, worship, and rejoicing in the urban churches, and for new creativity, delight, and pleasure in the presence of God. Let us pray for a new level of openness and unity among the believers, and a deeper, richer love and awe of God in the churches. Let us pray for new levels of reverence and fear among God's people, and new aggressive movements of worship, prayer, and celebration in the communities.

Let us not stop here. Let us pray that God will break the stranglehold of the enemy on the minds and hearts of those who dwell in America's inner cities (2 Cor. 4.4). Let us pray that the Holy Spirit will thwart the devil's programs of deception and despair, and that new doors will be opened for the display and proclamation of the Word of God at all levels. Pray that the Church will boldly give witness in word and deed to the reign of God in Jesus Christ, that individual believers, young, middle-aged, and senior, will demonstrate in their lives new levels of the Lord's love and power among their families, friends, and relationship networks.

Pray for new levels of interest, curiosity, and awareness of spiritual things among all who live in the city, but especially new levels of reality and power among believers in the inner city. Pray that the devil will not be able to stop the openings of God to Christ in all levels of the communities, societies, and neighborhoods. Pray for an outpouring of God upon the city, that entire cities of America can be awakened to their need for God in Jesus Christ!

For the Advancement of the Kingdom

As we humble ourselves in prayer for a dynamic spiritual *Awakening* among the people of God, we must equally petition God to move on behalf of the lost, those people and regions which have not yet come to know the mercy of God in the

Let God Arise! (continued)

person of the Lord Jesus Christ. Every time we gather in concerts of prayer, we ought to cry out to God to move in the inner cities, in order that there might be a sustained and aggressive *Advancement of the Kingdom* within them. One of the central features of the entire ***Let God Arise!*** movement is to see God move in this twofold sense: awakening the urban communities to his glory and power in a renewed and revitalized Church, and seeing his reign advance among those who live in the city and yet who have neither heard nor responded to God's love in Christ.

Let us therefore pray during our *Advancement* portion of the concert for the breakthrough of spiritual power over the enemy, both globally around the world, in specific contexts which we know about, and locally, in the specific areas in our locale and region. Let us pray that the Holy Spirit will pour his power upon God's servants, teams, organizations, and churches which are winning souls, making disciples, and planting churches around the world. In places that do not allow for Christian witness, let us pray that God will move on the hearts of government and religious officials, permitting believers to enter their societies and communities to speak freely of the Gospel of the Kingdom.

Pray too that the Holy Spirit will give extraordinary revelations of God and Christ to the lost, that he would give them dreams and visions, as he did in the case of the Macedonians (cf. Acts 16.9ff.). These manifestations could lay a spiritual foundation for the presentation of the Word of God concerning Christ in difficult and recalcitrant fields. Pray that revitalized churches, denominations, and mission agencies will form new strategic alliances which will lead to vital evangelistic thrusts and movements among the hardest, most difficult, and most unreached pioneer fields overseas and here at home.

Furthermore, pray that the awakening of the Church both globally and locally will lead to wholesale effective efforts to mobilize members of the Church for a new advance in mission. Let us pray that God will stir individuals, pastors, Christian workers, and ordinary believers from every congregation to pray for their unsaved family and friends, to be trained to share their faith effectively, and to commit to redouble their giving and contribution to fulfilling the Great Commission. Pray that many singles and couples will volunteer to do mission, not merely on a short term basis, but for some as a total life calling. Pray that some who respond will be sent by the Lord of the harvest to the harvest fields of America's untouched inner city communities.

Moreover, let us pray fervently that inner city churches will combine their efforts, funds, initiatives, and projects to make their own unique and powerful contribution to global and local mission. Pray that God would move on the hearts of those in charge of many mission agencies, that they will no longer ignore the rich resources of the urban churches, but will make it feasible for urban disciples to be deployed to evangelize, disciple, and plant churches, especially among the dozens and dozens of communities where no evangelical presence exists.

Above all, let us cry out to God day and night for a new level of rigor and discipline among his people. Pray for a tough minded but tender hearted faith to embrace the small congregations and store fronts in the city. Let us pray for them, that God will provide them with a kingdom warfare consciousness, the rigorous kind of mentality that will allow urban disciples to adopt the necessary mindset to endure hardness and suffer in spiritual warfare for their communities. Let us pray for new levels of boldness and power, for new aggressive outreaches, for more dedicated and prevailing prayer movements among urban churches, and new networks of leadership and support that will link urban disciples of good will to mobilize their resources for maximum impact on the city.

Intercede passionately to God to provide the resources for urban churches to initiate new outreaches of compassion, justice, and peace on behalf of the homeless, oppressed, fatherless, the mentally challenged, those plagued with HIV and other communicable diseases, for the elderly, those sick and in prison and neglected. Pray for an outpouring of love from the Church that amazes and creates new hunger for Jesus in the lost, a kind of love that serves as a foundation to express and authenticate the Gospel of Christ. Pray that God will use the efforts of justice and righteousness as a gateway for hundreds of thousands to be converted to the Lord.

Do not neglect to pray for your own particular locality, and its need to see the signs of the Kingdom manifested within it in word and deed. Pray for your church, your pastor, your community, civic and city leaders, your neighbors, principals, law officers, and all others in leadership in your midst. Pray for the release of new levels of boldness and clarity in preaching, and more authentic signs of the Kingdom in your community so God can reveal to the lost there the majesty and wonder of the Lord Jesus. Pray for yourself and family for a new availability to see the Kingdom advanced at your work, your school, your neighborhood, your family, in your life. God will answer us if we only will ask him in faith and authentic surrender to his will (Matt. 6.6; John 15.16).

Let God Arise! (continued)

In America's Inner Cities

The entire *Let God Arise!* idea began with a deep conviction that the American inner city cannot be won without the direct intervention and provision of the Lord. The hardness of this field makes plain and clear the truth of the psalmist's argument in Psalms 127.1 (ESV), "Unless the Lord builds the house, those who build it labor in vain. Unless the Lord watches over the city, the watchman stays awake in vain." This movement believes that all efforts at winning the unreached millions in America's inner cities will be futile unless God visits the city. We further hold that this visitation will only occur if godly men and women lay hold of God in intercession on the city's behalf. Only a breakthrough of God's power will transform our cities.

While the city is arguably the greatest single creation of humankind in civilization, it has nothing to glory of, in and of itself. The modern megapolis represents the bastion of injustice, ungodliness, and immorality. Truly, it is not possible to think of America without its greatest and most influential cities–New York, Washington D.C., Los Angeles, Philadelphia, Chicago, Houston, Miami, San Francisco, Boston, Portland, Atlanta, Denver, St. Louis, Dallas, Seattle, San Antonio, and on and on and on. These great centers represent the highest in culture, education, art, medicine, law, jurisprudence, government, politics, business, commerce, industry, entertainment, and power. Yet they also represent some of the most desperate places on earth; our cities bulge with teeming millions whose lives are filled with empty pleasures, great injustices, and horrible experiences.

Undoubtedly, the levels of darkness, poverty, and discouragement in America's inner cities are at an all-time high. Tragically, many evangelical congregations and Christian denominations have abandoned the city, escaping to calmer winds in the suburbs, taking along with them their Bible Colleges, seminaries, Christian publishing houses, and para-church organizations. Believers have left the cities in record numbers, and abandoned those who do not know Christ to their own devices and oppression.

Content to reduce Christianity to their own kind of parochial religion, many evangelicals have narrowed the scope of our Cosmic Drama; they have whittled down the majestic call of saving faith in Christ to nuclear family ethics, strong patriotic fervor and political conservatism. With no sense of a stained or disturbed conscience, many Christians have turned their backs to the cries of the dying in the city. For a Church called to be like our Master, this is totally unacceptable!

Affirmation and Acknowledgment

The final two dimensions of a *Let God Arise!* prayer concert, *Affirmation* and *Acknowledgment* respectively, allow for the giving of testimonies and final prayers which affirm God's truth about himself and his intention to win the city.

While we affirm the cruel oppression and persistent evil of the city, we likewise affirm the hope of the city's salvation, as in the case with Nineveh of the book of Jonah, Assyria's dark capital of violence, which God pardoned. In his forgiveness of their transgression and his relenting of judgment of that dark city, we see God's deep love for lost and rebellious humankind, and his willingness to relent from judgment of even the most wicked city if its inhabitants merely humble themselves before him. If God would deliver the thousands-filled Nineveh of biblical time, surely we can affirm that the same God can deliver the tens of millions-filled New York, or the dozens of millons-filled Mexico City! The analogy is biblical and persuasive; God Almighty responds to the cries of the broken, the contrite, and the penitent (Ps. 34.18).

During the *Affirmation* session, we affirm to God in prayer and to each other in testimony what the Lord has spoken to us during our time of seeking and entreating the Lord. We affirm the eternal love of a God who sent his only Son for our redemption (John 3.16), and we remind one another of God's historical action to respond when his people, called by his name, humble themselves, pray, seek his face, and repent from their wicked way of self-preoccupation, self-indulgence, and self-reliance (2 Chron. 7.14). God works in response to his people crying out to him in their affliction, brokenness, and neediness before him (Deut. 26.5-10).

We leave our session of *Affirmation* with a finale of prayers where we *Acknowledge* the veracity (truthfulness) and sovereignty of God. We covenant together to wait on the Lord, to look for his coming, to him who alone can strengthen our hearts (Ps. 27.14). Though we may grow weary in our praying, we are assured that we will prevail with God, for we are praying according to his will and to his heart (Isa. 40.28-31). We will not doubt or give up or lose heart (James 1.5; Gal. 6.9). If we start to intercede, we may be tempted to falter but, like the widow who pestered the judge until he responded on her behalf, we remind each other that we must beg God for action until he responds (Luke 18.1-8).

Our hearts are fixed, and we are determined, like the patriarch Jacob, to wrestle with God, to implore him, to lay hold of him and not let him go until he blesses us

Let God Arise! (continued)

(Gen. 32.24-32). Like Jehoshaphat, we have no strength against the rulers of this present darkness and spiritual forces gathered to destroy America's inner cities, nor do we know what to do, but our eyes are on the Lord (2 Chron. 20.12).

We are convinced that one day God will give the cities of this world to his Son (including America's inner cities!), which are merely one significant part of the inheritance the Father has been pleased to give to the Risen Lord (Ps. 2.8). Knowing that our Lord Jesus must reign until all of his enemies are placed under his feet (1 Cor. 15.24-28), we will neither doubt his intentions nor be impatient in the timing of his answers. God will respond to us, in his own time and in his own way. As we leave our gathering to scatter again in our particular circles of influence and relationship, we acknowledge our dependence on him whether our prayer session has been a half-hour, an entire morning, or full days and weeks of fasting and prayer, we know that the promise of the Lord is sure:

> Isa. 55.6-11 (ESV) - "Seek the Lord while he may be found; call upon him while he is near; [7] let the wicked forsake his way, and the unrighteous man his thoughts; let him return to the Lord, that he may have compassion on him, and to our God, for he will abundantly pardon. [8] For my thoughts are not your thoughts, neither are your ways my ways, declares the Lord. [9] For as the heavens are higher than the earth, so are my ways higher than your ways and my thoughts than your thoughts. [10] "For as the rain and the snow come down from heaven and do not return there but water the earth, making it bring forth and sprout, giving seed to the sower and bread to the eater, [11] so shall my word be that goes out from my mouth; it shall not return to me empty, but it shall accomplish that which I purpose, and shall succeed in the thing for which I sent it."

Truly, the Word of the Lord cannot return back to him either fruitless or empty. The purposes of our God, this great God, shall stand (Isa.40.8)!

Conclusion:
Respond in Humility to the
Sober Call to Prevailing Prayer for the Inner City

Dear friend, let me ask you a question: What do you take to be the critical need of the hour for the inner cities of America?

In my mind, it is not merely the infusion of more business and money, nor simply a new influx of better politicians, better urban crime-stopping initiatives, family planning seminars, nor food programs. The *critical* need for the city is for the Lord to make his presence known within it. The decisive factor that will lead to a transformation of America's inner cities is God's visitation, repeated outpourings of the Holy Spirit in the midst of his people in the city. Such visitations of the presence and power of God would revolutionize these communities; God's visitation would create such a variety of healing, compassion, and justice that no one, not even the most politically liberal-minded hopeful or stubborn atheist could explain it. Psalm 68 is a testament to what can occur when the Lord comes down, rather, arises and scatters his enemies, and leaves in his wake the blessings of his great heart love for humankind:

[1] God shall arise, his enemies shall be scattered; and those who hate him shall flee before him!

[2] As smoke is driven away, so you shall drive them away; as wax melts before fire, so the wicked shall perish before God!

[3] But the righteous shall be glad; they shall exult before God; they shall be jubilant with joy!

[4] Sing to God, sing praises to his name; lift up a song to him who rides through the deserts; his name is the LORD; exult before him!

[5] Father of the fatherless and protector of widows is God in his holy habitation.

[6] God settles the solitary in a home; he leads out the prisoners to prosperity, but the rebellious dwell in a parched land.

Let God Arise! (continued)

[7] O God, when you went out before your people, when you marched through the wilderness, Selah

[8] the earth quaked, the heavens poured down rain, before God, the One of Sinai, before God, the God of Israel.

[9] Rain in abundance, O God, you shed abroad; you restored your inheritance as it languished;

[10] your flock found a dwelling in it; in your goodness, O God, you provided for the needy.

~ Psalm 68.1-10 (ESV)

Let God Arise! in the midst of his people!

Let God Arise! in the midst of the urban squalor and decay!

Let God Arise! in the seats of power and influence!

Let God Arise! in the neighborhoods plagued by violence and fear!

Let God Arise! in the sanctuaries and congregations intimidated and under siege!

Let God Arise! with an outpouring of his Holy Spirit that will result in the spiritual awakening and dramatic advance of the Kingdom among the poorest of the poor in America's inner cities.

We issue to you the *call* to prevailing prayer: will you not join us in crying out to God day and night on behalf of the city and its inhabitants, from New York to Los Angeles, and all those who need to hear of God's saving love in Christ?

We issue to you the *sober* call to prevailing prayer: do you catch the sense of how significant your contribution can be if you only devote yourself to unbroken, unwavering, faith-filled entreaty to God on behalf of one of the greatest and most difficult mission fields in the world?

We issue to you the sober call to *prevailing prayer*: will you allow God, the Holy Spirit to train you to become a warrior in the spiritual realm, laying hold of God in intercession on behalf of a Church that is slumbering and needs to be awakened, and a world that is dying and needs to hear of God's life-giving and in-breaking reign won for us through Jesus Christ and his death on the cross?

Only God Can Renew His People. Only God Can Save the City.

Let us meet in holy agreement, whether two or three (Matt. 18.20) or an entire gallery of petitioners (2 Chron. 20) to seek the Lord and entreat the favor of the Lord on behalf of the city. Let us do so in our individual prayer closets, our cell groups and small group studies, in our congregations and church services, in our prayer meetings and convocations, in our concerts of prayer–in vigils, retreats, homes, schools–wherever the Lord lays on our hearts to petition him for a visitation for the cities, and for our city.

Let us commit to laying hold of God until he visits us. If we do, the cities of America (and perhaps, of the entire world) will never be the same.

APPENDIX 48

Editorial

Ralph D. Winter

This article was taken from Mission Frontiers: The Bulletin of the US Center for World Mission, Vol. 27, No. 5; September-October 2005; ISSN 0889-9436.

Ralph D. Winter is the Editor of Mission Frontiers and the General Director of the Frontier Mission Fellowship.

Dear Reader,

This time you must learn a new phrase: Insider Movements.

This idea as a mission strategy was so shockingly new in Paul's day that almost no one (either then or now) gets the point. That's why we are devoting this entire issue to "Insider Movements." That's why the 2005 annual meeting of the International Society for Frontier Missiology is devoted to the same subject. (See *www.ijfm.org/isfm*.)

First of all, be warned: many mission donors and prayer warriors, and even some missionaries, heartily disagree with the idea.

One outstanding missionary found that even his mission board director could not agree. He was finally asked to find another mission agency to work under. Why? His director was a fine former pastor who had never lived among a totally strange people. After a couple of years of increasingly serious correspondence between the director and the missionary family, the relationship had to come to an end.

Okay, so this is serious business. Why is *Insider Movements* such a troubling concept?

Well, everywhere Paul went "Judaizers" followed him and tried to destroy the Insider Movement he had established.

Some of those Judaizers were earnest followers of Christ who simply could not imagine how a Greek – still a Greek in dress, language and culture – could become a believer in Jesus Christ without casting off a huge amount of his Greek culture, get circumcised, follow the "kosher" dietary rules and the "new moons and Sabbaths", etc.

The flagrant language of Paul's letter to the Galatians is one result. The very serious text of his letter to the Romans is another. Years ago the scales fell off my eyes when I read that "Israel, who pursued a law of righteousness, has not attained it ... Why not? Because they pursued it not by faith but as if it were by works" (Rom. 9:32 NIV).

Paul was not saying the Jewish religious culture was defective or that the Greek culture was superior. He was emphasizing that heart faith is the key element in any culture—that *forms* were not the key thing but the *faith*. Greeks who yielded in heart faith to the Gospel did not need to become Jews culturally and follow Jewish forms.

Paul said, in effect, "I am very, very proud of a Gospel that is the power of God to save people who obey God in faith, no matter whether they follow Jewish or Greek customs" (Rom. 1:16).

But the real trick is not simply for people of faith in every culture to stay and stagnate in their own cultural cul-de-sac, but both to retain their own culture and at the same time recognize the validity of versions of the faith within other cultures and the universality of the Body of Christ.

Different sources of European Christianity flowed over into the United States, producing some 200 different "flavors" of Christianity—some born here (Mormons, Jehovah's Witnesses), some quite biblical, some not so biblical, some very strange.

The same thing happens on the mission field: a lot of different movements emerge. The ideal is for the Gospel to become effectively expressed within the language and culture of a people and not just be a transplant from the missionary's culture.

H. Richard Niebhur's famous book, *Social Sources of Denominationalism*, is known for pointing out that different denominations did not just have doctrinal differences (often very minor) but usually reflected, at least for a time, social differences that were the real difference. Note, however, the Christian faith was in many cases an "Insider Movement" and was expressed within different social streams, taking on characteristics of those different streams.

But, back to missions. The Jewish/Greek thing is far more and far "worse" than the differences between Methodists who pray that their trespasses be forgiven and Presbyterians who pray that their debts be forgiven!

No, in Paul's day circumcision was undoubtedly a major barrier to adult Greek men becoming culturally Jewish followers of Christ. Another sensitive point was the question of eating meat that had been offered to idols, and so on.

Ralph D. Winter Editorial (continued)

Later in history, the Jewish/Greek tension was paralleled by a Latin/German tension. This time, we see a profound difference in attitudes toward clerical marriage vs. celibacy and the use of Latin in church services.

For centuries Latin was *the language* of Europe, enabling ministers, attorneys, medical doctors, and public officials to read the books of their trade in a single language. That lasted a long time! For centuries a unifying reading language did a lot of good. But the Bible did not come into its own until it was translated into the heart languages of Europe.

The deep rumbling that modernized Europe was the unleashed Bible.

It is an exciting and maybe disturbing thing—the idea that biblical faith can be clothed in any language and culture. Witness the awesome reality in the so-called mission lands today. Whether Africa, India or China, it may well be that the largest number of genuine believers in Jesus Christ do not show up in what we usually call Christian churches!

Can you believe it? They may still consider themselves Muslims or Hindus (in a cultural sense).

Alas, today Christianity itself is identified with the cultural vehicle of the civilization of the West. People in mission lands who do not wish to be "westernized" feel they need to stay clear of the Christian Church, which in their own country is often a church highly Western in its culture, theology, interpretation of the Bible, etc.

For example, in Japan there are "churches" that are so Western that in the last forty years they have not grown by a single member. Many astute observers have concluded that there is not yet "a Japanese form of Christianity." When one emerges, it may not want to associate with the Western Christian tradition except in a fraternal way.

In India we now know that there are actually millions of Hindus who have chosen to follow Christ, reading the Bible daily and worshipping at the household level, but not often frequenting the West-related Christian churches of that land.

In some places thousands of people who consider themselves Muslims are nevertheless heart-and-soul followers of Jesus Christ who carry the New Testament with them into the mosques.

In Africa there are more than 50 million believers (of a sort) within a vast sphere called "the African Initiated Churches." The people in the more formally "Christian church" may not regard these others as Christians at all. Indeed, some of them are a whole lot further from pure biblical faith than Mormons. But, if they revere and study the Bible, we need to let the Bible do its work. These groups range from the wildly heretical to the seriously biblical within over ten thousand "denominations" which are not related to any overt Christian body.

Thus, not all "insider" movements are ideal. Our own Christianity is not very successfully [*sic*] "inside" our culture, since many "Christians" are Christian in name only. Even mission "church planting" activities may or may not be "insider" at all, and even if they are they may not be ideal.

Around the world some of these movements do not baptize. In other cases they do. I have been asked, "Are you promoting the idea of non-baptized believers?" No, in reporting the existence of these millions of people, we are reporting on the incredible power of the Bible. We are not promoting all the ideas they reflect or the practices they follow. The Bible is like an underground fire burning out of control! In one sense we can be very happy.

APPENDIX 49
When "Christian" Does Not Translate

Frank Decker

This article was taken from Mission Frontiers: The Bulletin of the US Center for World Mission,
Vol. 27, No. 5; September-October 2005; ISSN 0889-9436.
Copyright 2005 by the U.S. Center for World Mission. Used by permission. All Rights Reserved.

"I grew up as a Muslim, and when I gave my life to Jesus I became a Christian. Then I felt the Lord saying, 'Go back to your family and tell them what the Lord has done for you.'" Such was the beginning of the testimony of a sweet sister in Christ named Salima. As she stood before the microphone at a conference held recently in Asia, I thought about how her story would have been applauded by my Christian friends back home.

But then she said something that would have probably shocked most American Christians. She told us that in order to share Christ with her family, she now identifies herself as a Muslim rather than a Christian. "But," she added, "I could never go back to Islam without Jesus whom I love as my Lord."

Like this woman, countless people, primarily in Asia, who live in Muslim, Buddhist, and Hindu contexts are saying *yes* to Jesus, but *no* to Christianity. As Westerners, we assume that the word "Christian" *ipso facto* refers to someone who has given his or her life to Jesus, and a "non-Christian" is an unbeliever. However, in the words of one Asian attendee, "The word 'Christian' means something different here in the East."

Consider the story of Chai, a Buddhist from Thailand. "Thailand has not become a Christian country, because in the eyes of the Thai, to become a Christian means you can no longer be Thai. That's because in Thailand 'Christian' equals 'foreigner.'" So when Chai gave his life to Jesus, he began referring to himself as a "Child of God" and a "new Buddhist." He then related a subsequent incident in which he had a conversation with a Buddhist monk on a train. "After I listened to his story, I told him that he was missing one thing in life. He asked me what that was and I told him it was Jesus."

Chai continued to tell us the story in which the monk not only gave his life to Christ, but also invited Chai to come to his Buddhist temple to share about Jesus. Then Chai said, "At the beginning of our conversation the monk asked me, 'Are you a Christian?' and I said *no*. I explained that Christianity and Jesus are two

A former missionary in Ghana, Frank Decker currently serves as Vice President for Field Operations for the Mission Society for United Methodists.

different things. Salvation is in Jesus, not in Christianity. If I had said I was a 'Christian,' the conversation would have ended at that point." But it didn't end. And the monk now walks with Jesus.

Indeed, an American missionary that has been working in Asia for about two decades said, "For the first five or seven years of our ministry in [a Muslim country] we were frustrated because we were trying to get people to change their religion." He went on to say how in evangelical circles we talk a lot about how it is not our religion that saves us; it is *Jesus*. "If we really believe that, why do we insist that people change their religion?"

Asif is a brother in Christ with whom I have spent time in his village in a country that is 90 percent Muslim. Traditional Christian organizations in that country have only had a significant impact on the other ten percent that has never been Muslim. Make no mistake – Asif is sold out to Jesus, as are the other members of this Muslim Background Believers (MBB) movement. I will never forget seeing the tears stream down Asif's face as he told me how he and his brother, also a believer in Jesus, were beaten in an attack that his brother did not survive. These are Muslims who walk with Jesus and openly share with their Muslim friends about the Lord, who in Arabic is referred to as "Isa al-Masih" (Jesus the Messiah).

These "insider movements" are not intended to *hide* a believer's spiritual identity, but rather to enable those within the movement to *go deeper* into the cultural community – be it Islamic, Hindu, or Buddhist – and be witnesses for Jesus within the context of that culture. In some countries, such movements are just getting started. In other places, estimates of adherents are in the hundreds of thousands.

As the Body of Christ, we should be very careful that the things we uphold as sacred are not post-biblical accoutrements, but are indeed transcendent. If we are not open to "new wineskins," we may unwittingly find ourselves attached to traditions, as were the Pharisees in the day of Jesus.

The names in this story have been changed. This article is excerpted by permission from the May/June 2005 issue of Good News Magazine, a renewal ministry within the United Methodist Church (www.goodnewsmag.org).

APPENDIX 50

Pursuing Faith, Not Religion
The Liberating Quest for Contextualization
Charles Kraft

This article was taken from Mission Frontiers: The Bulletin of the US Center for World Mission,
Vol. 27, No. 5; September-October 2005; ISSN 0889-9436.

The following is excerpted from chapters 5 and 6 of **Appropriate Christianity** *(William Carey Library Publishers, 2005).*

It is not widely understood either outside of or even inside of Christianity that our faith is intended to be different from the religions in its relationship to the culture of the people who practice it. Whereas religions such as Islam, Buddhism and Hinduism require a sizeable chunk of the culture in which they were developed, Christianity rightly understood does not. Jesus came to bring life (Jn. 10:10), not a religion. It is people who have reduced our faith to a religion and exported it as if it is simply a competitor with the religions. And so, those receiving our message tend to interpret Christianity as if it was simply another religion—a culturally-encapsulated religion—rather than a faith that can be expressed in terms of any culture.

But Christianity correctly understood is commitment- and meaning-based, not form-based. A commitment to Jesus Christ and the meanings associated with that commitment can, therefore, be practiced in a wide variety of cultural forms. This is what contextualization is all about. And this is an important feature of Christianity that is often misunderstood by advocates as well as potential receptors.

Still another part of the reputation of Christianity worldwide is that it is more a matter of thinking than of practicality. For many, our faith has little to do with the issues of real life such as how to gain protection from evil spirits, how to gain and keep physical health and how to maintain good family relationships. Instead, Christianity is often seen as a breaker-up of families. And when the issue is a need for spiritual power and protection, even Christians need to keep on good terms with a shaman, priest or medicine man/woman since, in spite of biblical promises, Christian pastors can only recommend secular approaches to healing and protection.

A Christianity that is appropriate both to the Bible and to the receiving culture will confront these misperceptions and, hopefully, get them changed.

Dr. Charles H. Kraft has served as a missionary in Nigeria, taught African languages and linguistics at Michigan State University and UCLA for ten years, and taught Anthropology and Intercultural Communication in the School of Intercultural Studies, Fuller Seminary for the past 35 years. He travels widely, has pioneered in the field of Contextualization, and is widely used in a ministry of inner healing. He is the author or editor of many books, including Appropriate Christianity (William Carey Library Publishers, 2005).

Traditions Die Hard

Any discussion of this topic needs to take into account the fact that the situations most cross-cultural workers are working in nowadays are seldom pioneer situations. Thus, we who teach contextualization are dealing primarily with those whose major concern will have to be on how to bring about change in already existing situations rather than on how to plant culturally appropriate churches.

Typically, then, those who learn what contextualization is all about find themselves working with churches that are quite committed to their Western approach to Christianity. This has become their tradition and they are not open to changing it.

The leaders of many such churches may never have seen culturally appropriate Christianity and probably lack the ability to imagine it. And if they can imagine such an approach, they are unlikely to want to risk what they are familiar with in hopes of gaining greater cultural appropriateness. For many, the risk of losing their position may be very real since their colleagues, committed to preserving the "sacred" tradition, may turn against them and oust them from their parishes.

We need to learn, then, not only the principles of cultural appropriateness, but the principles of effective communication. And this needs to be coupled with patience and prayer plus a readiness to make the right kind of suggestions if asked to.

Fear of Syncretism

A major hindrance to many, especially those who have received theological instruction, is the fear that they might open the door to an aberrant form of Christianity. They see Latin American "christo-paganism" and shy away from what is called Christian but is not really. Fearing that if they deviate from the Western Christianity that they have received they are in danger of people carrying things too far, they fall back on the familiar and do nothing to change it, no matter how much misunderstanding there might be in the community of unbelievers concerning the real meanings of Christianity.

There are, however, at least two roads to syncretism: an approach that is too nativistic and an approach that is too dominated by foreignness. With respect to the latter, it is easy to miss the fact that Western Christianity is quite syncretistic when it is very intellectualized, organized according to foreign patterns, weak on the Holy Spirit and spiritual power, strong on Western forms of communication (e.g.,

Pursuing Faith, Not Religion (continued)

preaching) and Western worship patterns and imposed on non-Western peoples as if it were scriptural. It is often easier to conclude that a form of Christian expression is syncretistic when it looks too much like the receiving culture than when it looks "normal," that is, Western.

But Western patterns are often farther from the Bible than non-Western patterns. And the amount of miscommunication of what the gospel really is can be great when people get the impression that ours is a religion rather than a faith and that, therefore, foreign forms are a requirement. To give that impression is surely syncretistic and heretical. I call this "communicational heresy."

But, what about the concept of syncretism? Is this something that can be avoided or is it a factor of human limitations and sinfulness? I vote for the latter and suggest that there is no way to avoid it. Wherever there are imperfect understandings made by imperfect people, there will be syncretism. That syncretism exists in all churches is not the problem. Helping people to move from where they are to more ideal expressions of Christian faith is what we need to address.

As long as we fear something that is inevitable, however, we are in bondage. I remember the words of one field missionary who was studying with us, "Until I stopped worrying about syncretism, I could not properly think about contextualization." Our advice to national leaders (and to missionaries), then, is to stop fearing syncretism. Deal with it in its various forms as a starting point, whether it has come from the receiving society or from the source society and help people to move toward more ideal expressions of their faith ....

Domestication and "Cultural Christianity"

[Down] through the centuries, those who have come to Christ have tended to "domesticate" their Christianity. Just as the early Jewish Christians who disagreed with Paul required Gentiles to accept Christ in a Jewish cultural package, so Romans and Germans and Americans have pressured those who convert to Christ to also convert to the culture of those who bring the message.

Thus, our faith has come to be known as primarily a cultural thing, a religion wrapped in the cultural forms of the group in power. And from about the fourth century on it has been seen largely as a European cultural thing—captured by our European ancestors and domesticated in cultures very different from that in which the faith was originally planted. Converts to Christianity, then, are seen as those who have abandoned their own cultural religion and chosen to adopt the religion and, usually, many of the forms of European culture. Often such converts are regarded as traitors to their own people and their ways.

If ours is simply a "form religion," ... it can be *adapted but not contextualized*, it can be in *competition with other forms of religion* but not flow through those forms because by definition it seeks to replace those forms. But biblical Christianity is not simply a set of cultural forms. Cultural Christianity, however, is. And we get tangled up in our discussions because it is often not clear whether we are speaking of essential, biblical Christianity or of the traditional religion of Western societies that is also called Christianity. In one of my books (1979a) I have attempted to make this distinction by spelling biblical Christianity with a capital C and cultural christianity with a small c....

I would ... call religion a form thing, the expression through cultural forms of deep-level (worldview) assumptions and meanings. Religious forms are culture-specific and, if the religion has been borrowed from another cultural context, it requires certain of the forms of that other culture to be borrowed. Islam, for example, requires certain forms of prayer, a specific pilgrimage, an untranslatable Arabic book, even clothing styles. Likewise Judaism, Hinduism, Buddhism and cultural christianity. These are religions.

Essential biblical Christianity, however, requires none of the original cultural forms. That's how it can be "captured" by the West and be considered Western even though its origin is not Western. *Essential Christianity is an allegiance, a relationship, from which flow a series of meanings that are intended to be expressed through the cultural forms of any culture.* These forms are intended, then, to be chosen for their appropriateness to convey proper biblical meanings in the receptors' contexts.

I believe Christianity is intended to be "a faith," not a set of cultural forms and therefore different in essence from the religions. Religions, because they are cultural things, can be *adapted* to new cultures. Adaptation is an external thing resulting in smaller or larger changes in the forms of the religion. Christianity, however, can be *contextualized*, a process in which appropriate meanings may be carried by quite different forms in various cultures. Unfortunately, due to the interference of cultural christianity, we have not seen all the variety that is possible . . . .

APPENDIX 51

Contextualization Among Muslims, Hindus, and Buddhists:
A Focus on "Insider Movements"
John and Anna Travis

This article was taken from Mission Frontiers: The Bulletin of the US Center for World Mission,
Vol. 27, No. 5; September-October 2005; ISSN 0889-9436.

The following is excerpted by permission of the authors. A larger version of this article is found in chapter 23 of **Appropriate Christianity** *(William Carey Library Publishers, 2005).*

Much has been written over the past 25 years on the application of contextualization in ministry among Muslims. In 1998 I (John) wrote an article for the *Evangelical Missions Quarterly* in which I presented a model for comparing six different types of *ekklesia* or congregations (which I refer to as "Christ-centered communities") found in the Muslim world today (Travis 1998). These six types of Christ-centered communities are differentiated in terms of three factors: language, cultural forms, and religious identity. This model, referred to as the C1-C6 spectrum (or continuum), has generated much discussion, especially around the issue of fellowships of "Muslim followers of Jesus" (the C5 position on the scale).

Parshall (1998), an advocate of contextualization, feels that C5 crosses the line and falls into dangerous syncretism. In subsequent writings many of Parshall's concerns have been addressed (see Massey 2000, Gilliland 1998, Winter 1999, Travis 1998 and 2000). *Yet in spite of concerns that some may have on this issue, the fact remains that in a number of countries today, there are groups of Muslims who have genuinely come to faith in Jesus Christ, yet have remained legally and socio-religiously within the local Muslim community. . . .*

We will not be contending that C5 is the best or only thing God is doing in the Muslim world today; indeed God is bringing Muslims to Himself in a great diversity of ways, some of which we may only understand in eternity. What we will argue, however, is that one way God is moving at this point in salvation history, is by sovereignly drawing Muslims to Himself, revolutionizing them spiritually, yet calling them to remain as salt and light in the religious community of their birth. . . .

In recent years we have had the privilege of meeting a number of C5 Muslims, and although our religious backgrounds and forms of worship are quite different, we have experienced sweet fellowship in Isa the Messiah. There is no question in our

John and Anna Travis, along with their two children, have lived in a tight-knit Asian Muslim neighborhood for nearly 20 years. They are involved in contextualized sharing of the good news, Bible translation and the ministry of prayer for inner healing. They have also helped train field workers in a number of Asian, Middle Eastern and North African countries. Both are pursuing graduate degrees, with John a Ph.D. candidate.

minds that these C5 Muslims are born-again members of the Kingdom of God, called to live out the Gospel inside the religious borders of their birth. As we have continued to see the limits of C4 in our context, and as our burden for lost Muslims only grows heavier, we have become convinced that a C5 expression of faith could actually be viable for our precious Muslim neighbors and probably large blocs of the Muslim world. We ourselves, being "Christian-background-believers," maintain a C4 lifestyle, but we believe God has called us to help "birth a C5 movement" in our context . . . .

We have attended many Muslim funerals. We grieve every time we see another Muslim friend buried, having passed into eternity without salvation in Christ. As we have seen the resistance toward changing religions and the huge gap between the Muslim and Christian communities, we feel that fighting the religion-changing battle is the wrong battle. We have little hope in our lifetime to believe for a major enough cultural, political and religious change to occur in our context such that Muslims would become open to entering Christianity on a wide scale.

But we do have great hope, as great as the promises of God, to believe that an "insider movement" could get off the ground – that vast numbers could discover that salvation in Isa the Messiah is waiting for every Muslim who will believe. We sense the desire of Jesus Himself to take the "yeast" of His Gospel to the inner chambers of Muslim communities, calling men, women and children to walk with Him as Lord and Savior, remaining vital members of their families and Muslim communities.

Theoretical and Theological Issues Regarding C5 Movements

. . . Our intent is not to prove if C5 *can* happen, as case studies already indicate that it *is* happening. Rather, we hope to help build a framework from which to understand this phenomenon and to answer some of the questions which have arisen such as: From a biblical perspective, can a person be truly saved and continue to be a Muslim? Doesn't a follower of Christ need to identify himself as a Christian and officially join the Christian faith? Can a Muslim follower of Christ retain all Muslim practices, in particular praying in the mosque toward Mecca and continuing to repeat the Muslim creed? This section will be framed around ten premises [elaborated in the full version of this article].

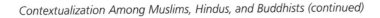

Contextualization Among Muslims, Hindus, and Buddhists (continued)

- *Premise 1*: For Muslims, culture, politics and religion are nearly inseparable, making changing religions a total break with society.

- *Premise 2*: Salvation is by grace alone through relationship / allegiance to Jesus Christ. Changing religions is not a prerequisite for nor a guarantee of salvation.

- *Premise 3*: Jesus' primary concern was the establishment of the Kingdom of God, not the founding of a new religion.

- *Premise 4*: The very term "Christian" is often misleading – not all called Christian are in Christ and not all in Christ are called Christian.

- *Premise 5*: Often gaps exist between what people actually believe and what their religion or group officially teaches.

- *Premise 6*: Some Islamic beliefs and practices are in keeping with the Word of God; some are not.

- *Premise 7*: Salvation involves a process. Often the exact point of transfer from the kingdom of darkness to the Kingdom of light is not known.

- *Premise 8*: A follower of Christ needs to be set free by Jesus from spiritual bondages in order to thrive in his/her life with Him.

- *Premise 9*: Due to the lack of Church structure and organization, C5 movements must have an exceptionally high reliance on the Spirit and the Word as their primary source of instruction.

- *Premise 10* : A contextual theology can only properly be developed through a dynamic interaction of actual ministry experience, the specific leading of the Spirit and the study of the Word of God.

A Look Beyond the Islamic Milieu

. . . An amazing book has just been republished by William Carey Library – *Churchless Christianity* (Hoefer 2001). The author, while formerly teaching at a seminary in India, began hearing stories of Hindus who in fact were worshipping and following Jesus in the privacy of their own homes. Knowing that there are many Hindus who have high regard for Jesus as a teacher, he set out to determine if

"The Church Emerges from the Inside"
A missionary couple working in Asia report, "In 1990 we were sent out into the field as church planters. But over the last year we have observed that when the gospel is sown on fertile soil within already established social groupings – like a circle of close neighbor friends, or the multi-generations an extended household – the church emerges from the inside. It is not so much that we are planting a church but that we are planting the gospel, and as the gospel seed grows, the church or churches form to the shape of existing networks."

indeed they had accepted Him as Lord and Savior or only as an enlightened guru. His quest became the basis of a doctoral dissertation in which he interviewed 80 such Hindu and Muslim families in the area of Madras, India.

Hoefer found that that a large number of these families, which have never been baptized or joined churches, indeed have a true relationship with Christ and pray and study His Word fervently. Hoefer says that most want baptism, but have never seen a baptism which is not one in the same with becoming an official member of a particular church. His conclusion after a very extensive process of interviews and statistical analysis is that in Madras there are 200,000 Hindus and Muslims who worship Jesus – an amount equal to the total number of Christians in that city!

It is instructive to note that 200 years ago, William Carey referred to Hindu followers of Jesus as "Christian Hindoos." Apparently this was due to the strong linkage in the minds of the Indians (and presumably William Carey) between being Hindu and being Indian (etymologically the word India comes from Hindia, the land of the Hindus). Rather than Hinduism being close to monotheistic faiths, it is just the opposite: adherents can worship any number of gods and goddesses. It appears that this openness allows room to exclusively worship the God of the Bible as the one true God (note the words of Joshua in Joshua 24:14-15).

In the early 1900s, Indian evangelist Sadhu Sundar Singh ran into hidden groups of Jesus followers among Hindus. As he preached the Gospel in Benares, his listeners told him of a Hindu holy man who had been preaching the same message. Singh spent the night at the man's home and heard his claim that his Hindu order had been founded long ago by the apostle Thomas, and now had up to 40,000 members. Singh later observed their services (including worship, prayer, baptism and communion) which were held in places which looked exactly like Hindu shrines and temples, minus the idols. "When Sundar tried to persuade them that they should openly declare themselves as Christians, they assured him that they were doing a more effective work as secret disciples, accepted as ordinary sadhus, but drawing men's minds toward the true faith in readiness for the day when open discipleship became possible" (Davey 1950:80) [*sic*].

Recently, we met a man doing outreach among Buddhists, among whom there is an extremely high fusion of culture and religion. To my surprise he had taken the C1-C6 continuum and adapted it to a Buddhist context. Though it appears impossible for the Gospel to thrive inside Buddhism, might there not be millions of Buddhists who are nominal believers and who are only Buddhist due to birth and

Contextualization Among Muslims, Hindus, and Buddhists (continued)

nationality? As Kraft has stated (1996:212-213), once this principle of true spiritual allegiance versus formal religion is grasped, "we begin to discover exciting possibilities for working within, say, Jewish or Islamic or Hindu or Buddhist or animistic cultures to reach people who will be culturally Jewish or Muslim or Hindu or animist to the end of their days but Christian in their faith allegiance". (Note: in his book Kraft defines Christian with a capital "C" as follower of Christ verses *christian* with a small "c" referring to the religious institution).

What is all of this leading to? Is there not blatant idolatry in traditional Hinduism? Yes, but not among those Hindu followers of Christ described by Hoefer and Davey. Is there not a denial by most Muslims that Jesus died on the cross? Yes, but not by those Muslims we have known who have put their faith in Christ. Is it not true that Jews teach the Messiah is yet to come? Yes, but thousands of Jews go to Messianic synagogues and believe, as did thousands of Jews in the first century, that Yeshua is indeed the long awaited Son of David.

We are tentatively coming to the conviction that God is doing a new thing to reach these remaining nations (*ta ethne*) dominated by mega-faiths. If Bosch had it right that faith in Christ wasn't meant to be a religion, could it be that we are witnessing some of the first fruits of vast movements where Jesus is causing the Gospel to break out of "Christianity"? Where those who know Jesus remain as a sweet fragrance inside the religion of their birth, and eventually the number of born-again adherents grows so large that a reform movement from inside that religion is birthed?

The process may be theologically messy, but we see no alternative. If we view both culture and religion as a person's own skin, we can look beyond it to the millions of human hearts longing for God yet longing to remain in community with their own people. This is in no way universalism (the belief that in the end all will be saved). Rather, this is a call to take much more seriously Christ's final words to go into all the world – Hindu, Buddhist, Muslim, Christian – and make disciples of all nations.

References

Bosch, David J. 1991 *Transforming Mission*. Maryknoll, NY: Orbis Books.

Davey, Cyril J. 1980 *Sadhu Sundar Singh*. Kent, UK: STL Books.

Contextualization Among Muslims, Hindus, and Buddhists (continued)

Gilliland, Dean S. 1998 "Context is Critical in Islampur Case." *Evangelical Missions Quarterly* 34(4): 415-417.

Hoefer, Herbert E. 2001 *Churchless Christianity*. Pasadena, CA: William Carey Library.

Kraft, Charles H. 1996 *Anthropology for Christian Witness*. Maryknoll, NY: Orbis Books.

Massey, Joshua. 2000 "God's Amazing Diversity in Drawing Muslims to Christ." *International Journal of Frontier Missions* 17 (1): 5-14.

Parshall, Phil. 1998 "Danger! New Directions in Contextualization." *Evangelical Missions Quarterly*. 43(4): 404-406, 409-410.

Travis, John. 1998 "Must all Muslims Leave Islam to Follow Jesus?" *Evangelical Missions Quarterly* 34(4): 411-415.

------. 2000 "Messianic Muslim Followers of Isa: A Closer Look at C5 Believers and Congregations." *International Journal of Frontier Missions* 17 (1): 53-59.

Winter, Ralph. 1999 "Going Far Enough? Taking Some Tips from the Historical Record." In *Perspectives on the World Christian Movement*. Ralph Winter and Steven Hawthorne, eds. Pp. 666-617. Pasadena, CA: William Carey Library.

APPENDIX 52

A People Reborn
Foundational Insights on People Movements
Donald McGavran

This article was taken from Mission Frontiers: The Bulletin of the US Center for World Mission,
Vol. 27, No. 5; September-October 2005; ISSN 0889-9436.
Copyright 2005 by the U.S. Center for World Mission. Used by permission. All Rights Reserved.

Editor's note: What follows are excerpts from the late Donald McGavran's foreword to the English edition of Christian Keysser's classic book, A People Reborn (William Carey Library, 1980). McGavran's pen portraits and autobiographical notes reveal the extent to which, consciously or not, today's proponents of either insider movements or church-planting movements are building on foundations laid by pioneers such as Keysser, McGavran, and others in the first half of the 20th century. Note, in the final paragraph, McGavran's prescient observations about mission in the 21st century.

[Christian Keysser] was born in Bavaria in 1877, went to Kaiser Wilhelm Land (East New Guinea) in 1899, and remained in or near Sattelberg as a missionary till 1921, when he returned to Germany.... A literal translation of [Keysser's book] is *A New Guinean Congregation*. A truer, better title is: *A People Reborn: Caring Communities, Their Birth and Development*. . . .

People Movements to Christ

. . . Around 1900 Keysser found himself evangelizing the Kate (pronounced Kawtai or kotte) tribe in the mountains near the sea.... Keysser's genius recognized that Christianization ought to preserve this people consciousness, and transform it into Tribal Christianity or Folk Christianity. . . .

In 1935, largely through [Waskom] Pickett's writings and lectures, I woke to a discipling of ethnic units. I accompanied him while he studied missions in Mid-India and contributed several chapters to his *Christian Missions in Mid-India*, 1938. I, too, saw that the goal was not one-by-one conversion out of the castes and tribes, but rather the conversion of social units which remained part of the caste or tribe, and continued living in their ancestral homes. For the next two decades I worked at encouraging a Satnami people movement to develop – and failed. In 1955, my *Bridges of God* called castewise or tribal movements to Christian Faith "people movements".... What Keysser, Pickett and [Bruno] Gutmann had described in New Guinea, India and Tanganyika – *Bridges of God* – indebted only to Pickett, described in universal terms.

The discovery of all of us was that group decisions, which preserved the corporate life of the society and enabled men and women to become Christians without social dislocation, was the route by which most humans have moved to Christian Faith from non-Christian Faith, and was a good route. For all four of us, the discovery was difficult because missionaries came out of the most dedicated parts of the Western Church. They had learned that real Christians are those who individually and at great cost believe in Jesus Christ, love Him, obey His word, and venture out alone across the seven seas to do His bidding. They believed that "one-by-one-against-the-tide" was the right, the best, and often the only way for men and women to become Christians. . . .

Keysser's discovery in 1903 should be seen against his common erroneous conviction. He broke through that mindset to see that for a people to come to Christ "with social structure intact" was the best possible way. He, of course, went on immediately to describe the way in which such a people movement should be nurtured, guarded against formalism, fed on the Word, and made strong through constant exercise of its Christian options. This is his great contribution. His book is essential reading for any who wish to understand a) that discipling ethnic units is a splendid way for multitudes to become Christian, and b) how discipling and perfecting can be done so they result in genuine Christians in a truly Christian Congregation – a true Homogeneous Unit Church.

The Objective Thinker

. . . The people movement really began to roll. The outlying clans and villages clamored to become Christian, precisely because they saw that the Christians had become *greatly changed for the better*. This is the fundamental reason why people movements occur. Human beings are highly intelligent. After all, man is homo sapiens. When he sees that the new order, the Church, is actually different from and *superior* to the old order, then homo sapiens in corporate decisions moves to Christian Faith. A chain reaction runs through the tribal fabric. Congregations multiply. In general, it may be said that the higher the standard of Christianity

A People Reborn (continued)

achieved by the first groups to become Christian, the more influential is their example. Keysser, the objective thinker, saw this. . . .

Forming a True Congregation

[Another reason] why missiologists will profit from this book is Keysser's determined emphasis on the privilege and duty of the missionary *to form a Christian congregation out of various villages and clans*. By this he does not mean taking individuals, as separate pebbles, and forming them into a new organization called the church. Rather, he means taking the social organism, which the clan or village had been from time immemorial, and by exposing it to God's will and God's Word, and by leading it to act in a Christian fashion *transforming it into a Christian tribe*. This is not done simply by baptizing it. Hearing the Gospel, seeing the Gospel, receiving ample instruction, some of it in dramatic form, being baptized with clanal approval, and then for years led by the missionary and the Word, thinking through what in specific circumstances Christ requires the village, clan or tribe (the Christian Congregation) to do – all these steps are required to transform non-Christian social units into a Christian congregation. . . .

Dr. Keysser's adverse judgments concerning the churches in Germany must be seen as part of his convictions concerning the True Church. Throughout this volume he criticizes congregations in Germany for not being true communities, i.e. true *congregations*. . . . When in 1922 Keysser went back to Germany, he experienced culture shock in reverse. He found "churches" which as churches exercised little if any pastoral care of their members. . . . The congregations were not real communities. . . .

Today, when the establishment of caring communities in western churches has become one of the main purposes of contemporary Christianity, Keysser's comments about the German Church are particularly pertinent. They can be affirmed about the Church in most developed nations. When society becomes fragmented, individualism rages out of control and loneliness afflicts millions. The Church must provide loving, caring, powerful *communities*. Life is richest when lived in such. In the ancient world New Testament churches were such communities. Churches can again become such in New Guinea and New York, in Tokyo and Berlin, and in short, in every land. *True Churches are functioning communities.*

A People Reborn (continued)

. . . Professor Keysser has given the world of mission many insights which will be of great use in the coming century. In his day, animistic tribes were turning to Christ by people movements and forming genuine communities (congregations) in the Christian fold. In the twenty-first century, we shall see great segments of developing *and developed* nations turn to Christian Faith without social dislocation. They will remain real communities in becoming real congregations. Modern missiology is indebted to Christian Keysser.

APPENDIX 53

Missions in the 21st Century
Working with Social Entrepreneurs?
Rebecca Lewis

This article was taken from Mission Frontiers: The Bulletin of the US Center for World Mission,
Vol. 27, No. 5; September-October 2005; ISSN 0889-9436.

The challenge is this: how to catalyze an "insider movement" to Christ in a society closed to traditional mission work? For this to happen, the gospel needs to spread through pre-existing social networks, which become the "church." People should not be drawn out of their families or communities into new social structures in order to become believers. God seems to be opening a new avenue of opportunity into closed societies through working with community agents of change – entrepreneurs working for social reform.

Historically, the most successful model for achieving lasting social change has been neither government nor business but the voluntary society (also known as the "citizen sector" or "civil society"). The idea of citizens banding together to reform society took a great step forward during the Evangelical Awakening, initiated by John Wesley in the 18th century. Out of this revival, and the Second Great Awakening in the early 19th century, came hundreds of voluntary, cross-denominational associations or "societies." Founded by visionary social entrepreneurs, each society attacked a certain issue, everything from abolishing slavery to creating special "Sunday schools" to teach reading to children who worked all week. Why not harness this successful model as a vehicle for advancing God's purposes among today's least-reached people groups?

Today the door is wide open in most countries to people who would catalyze grass-roots initiatives to address social problems. During the 1990s the number of international non-profit organizations jumped from 6000 to 26,000, a growth rate of over 400%. Likewise, hundreds of thousands of national NGOs (non-government organizations) have been formed in non-Western countries. Why the sudden growth? First, since the fall of the Soviet Union, many governments have been releasing control of the economy and nurturing the private sector. Second, social entrepreneurs and the civil society sector are now widely recognized for their success in solving formerly intractable problems.

Rebecca Lewis spent eight years in Morocco on a church planting team and currently creates curricula to help young people see how they can live their lives for God's purposes.

Missions in the 21st Century: Working with Social Entrepreneurs? (continued)

Third, governments are increasingly embarrassed if they try to block non-profit initiatives, because a global value for "empathy" has been established by the rapidly-spreading evangelical movement and the incorporation of Christian values in secular education worldwide. Fourth, there is a new openness to change in general. As people in remote places have become exposed to the rest of the world through mass media, they are reconsidering their behavior patterns and traditional beliefs. People everywhere are putting their hope in education and valuing progress as never before. As a result, local communities, as well as national governments, are getting behind citizen organizations seeking to implement solutions to systemic problems.

If the goal is to produce insider movements to Christ, why work with social entrepreneurs? Christian workers can build extensive relationships with leaders and families within a community by assisting social entrepreneurs (whether they are believers or not) with their vision to attack a problem. These types of broad relational networks – proactively bringing change to the community – form an excellent basis for the spread of the gospel in a way that leads to insider movements. Through helping the civil sector, workers have a role that is understandable and beneficial both in the eyes of the local people and the government. Also, like Jesus, they can announce the Kingdom in the context of bringing healing to the community.

To those who would like to learn more about finding and assisting social entrepreneurs, I recommend David Bornstein's fascinating book, *How to Change the World: Social Entrepreneurs and the Power of New Ideas* (Oxford University Press, 2003).

APPENDIX 54

Documenting Your Work
A Guide to Help You Give Credit Where Credit Is Due
The Urban Ministry Institute

Plagiarism is using another person's ideas as if they belonged to you without giving them proper credit. In academic work it is just as wrong to steal a person's ideas as it is to steal a person's property. These ideas may come from the author of a book, an article you have read, or from a fellow student. The way to avoid plagiarism is to carefully use "notes" (textnotes, footnotes, endnotes, etc.) and a "Works Cited" section to help people who read your work know when an idea is one you thought of, and when you are borrowing an idea from another person.

Avoiding Plagiarism

A citation reference is required in a paper whenever you use ideas or information that came from another person's work.

Using Citation References

All citation references involve two parts:

- Notes in the body of your paper placed next to each quotation which came from an outside source.

- A "Works Cited" page at the end of your paper or project which gives information about the sources you have used

There are three basic kinds of notes: parenthetical notes, footnotes, and endnotes. At The Urban Ministry Institute, we recommend that students use parenthetical notes. These notes give the author's last name(s), the date the book was published, and the page number(s) on which you found the information. Example:

Using Notes in Your Paper

> In trying to understand the meaning of Genesis 14.1-24, it is important to recognize that in biblical stories "the place where dialogue is first introduced will be an important moment in revealing the character of the speaker . . ." (Kaiser and Silva 1994, 73). This is certainly true of the character of Melchizedek who speaks words of blessing. This identification of Melchizedek as a positive spiritual influence is reinforced by the fact that he is the King of Salem, since Salem means "safe, at peace" (Wiseman 1996, 1045).

Creating a Works Cited Page

A "Works Cited" page should be placed at the end of your paper. This page:

- lists every source you quoted in your paper

- is in alphabetical order by author's last name

- includes the date of publication and information about the publisher

The following formatting rules should be followed:

1. Title

The title "Works Cited" should be used and centered on the first line of the page following the top margin.

2. Content

Each reference should list:

- the author's full name (last name first)

- the date of publication

- the title and any special information (Revised edition, 2nd edition, reprint) taken from the cover or title page should be noted

- the city where the publisher is headquartered followed by a colon and the name of the publisher

3. Basic form

- Each piece of information should be separated by a period.

- The second line of a reference (and all following lines) should be indented.

- Book titles should be underlined (or italicized).

- Article titles should be placed in quotes.

Example:

Fee, Gordon D. 1991. *Gospel and Spirit: Issues in New Testament Hermeneutics.* Peabody, MA: Hendrickson Publishers.

Documenting Your Work (continued)

4. Special Forms

A book with multiple authors:

> Kaiser, Walter C., and Moisés Silva. 1994. *An Introduction to Biblical Hermeneutics: The Search for Meaning.* Grand Rapids: Zondervan Publishing House.

An edited book:

> Greenway, Roger S., ed. 1992. *Discipling the City: A Comprehensive Approach to Urban Mission.* 2nd ed. Grand Rapids: Baker Book House.

A book that is part of a series:

> Morris, Leon. 1971. *The Gospel According to John.* Grand Rapids: Wm. B. Eerdmans Publishing Co. The New International Commentary on the New Testament. Gen. ed. F. F. Bruce.

An article in a reference book:

> Wiseman, D. J. "Salem." 1982. In *New Bible Dictionary.* Leicester, England - Downers Grove, IL: InterVarsity Press. Eds. I. H. Marshall and others.

(An example of a "Works Cited" page is located on the next page.)

For Further Research

Standard guides to documenting academic work in the areas of philosophy, religion, theology, and ethics include:

> Atchert, Walter S., and Joseph Gibaldi. 1985. *The MLA Style Manual.* New York: Modern Language Association.

> *The Chicago Manual of Style.* 1993. 14th ed. Chicago: The University of Chicago Press.

> Turabian, Kate L. 1987. *A Manual for Writers of Term Papers, Theses, and Dissertations.* 5th edition. Bonnie Bertwistle Honigsblum, ed. Chicago: The University of Chicago Press.

Documenting Your Work (continued)

Works Cited

Fee, Gordon D. 1991. *Gospel and Spirit: Issues in New Testament Hermeneutics.* Peabody, MA: Hendrickson Publishers.

Greenway, Roger S., ed. 1992. *Discipling the City: A Comprehensive Approach to Urban Mission.* 2nd ed. Grand Rapids: Baker Book House.

Kaiser, Walter C., and Moisés Silva. 1994. *An Introduction to Biblical Hermeneutics: The Search for Meaning.* Grand Rapids: Zondervan Publishing House.

Morris, Leon. 1971. *The Gospel According to John.* Grand Rapids: Wm. B. Eerdmans Publishing Co. *The New International Commentary on the New Testament.* Gen. ed. F. F. Bruce.

Wiseman, D. J. "Salem." 1982. In *New Bible Dictionary.* Leicester, England-Downers Grove, IL: InterVarsity Press. Eds. I. H. Marshall and others.

57056139R00236

Made in the USA
Middletown, DE
26 July 2019